The Nation-State and Violence

The Nation-State and Violence

Volume Two of A Contemporary Critique
of Historical Materialism

Anthony Giddens

University of California Press
Berkeley and Los Angeles

First published in the United States by the University of California Press, 1985.

Library of Congress Cataloging in Publication Data

(Revised for vol. 2)

Giddens, Anthony.
  A contemporary critique of historical materialism.

  Includes bibliographical references and indexes.
  Contents: v. 1. Power, property, and the state —
v. 2. The nation-state and violence.
  1. Historical materialism.   I. Title.
D16.9.G47   335.4'119   81—43382
ISBN 0-520-04535-1 (v. 1)
ISBN 0-520-04490-8 (pbk. : v. 1)

Typeset by Pioneer, East Sussex
Printed and Bound in Great Britain by
T.J. Press (Padstow) Ltd, Padstow, Cornwall

Contents

Introduction

This book is the second volume of three, all concerned with the relevance of historical materialism to today's world. The trilogy is not intended, however, as another contribution to the endless critical dissection of Marx's writings. Rather, it is an attempt to explore the contours of a post-Marxist analysis of contemporary society and politics. Marx's writings are of signal importance for understanding one of the most pervasive influences moulding the modern world. This influence is of course capitalism, regarded as a mode of economic enterprise that has a dynamic tendency to expansion far greater than any prior type of productive order. But capitalism is not the only force which has shaped modernity, and there are in any case cogent reasons to be dissatisfied with some of the main perspectives of Marx's portrayal of capitalist development.

Marx's discussion of the past origins and future fate of capitalism is part of an overall historical scheme the explanatory power of which is limited. The insights he provides about the nature of capitalist enterprise have to be prised free from the general framework of historical materialism, and integrated with a different approach to previous history and to the analysis of modern institutions. Treating modern societies as the culmination of a process of progressive expansion of the forces of production fails to disclose how *different* they are from all forms of traditional order. Modern 'societies' are nation-states, existing within a nation-state system. Traditional states — or what I call 'class-divided societies' — contrast very substantially with these, both in their internal characteristics and in their external relations with one another. Social scientists are accustomed to thinking of 'societies' as administrative unities with clearly defined boundaries. Class-divided societies were not like this, and if modern ones are, it is not because of anything intrinsic to social association in general, but a result of distinctive forms of social integration associated with the nation-state.

Historical materialism connects the emergence of both traditional and modern states with the development of material production (or what I call 'allocative resources'). But equally significant, and very often the main means whereby such material wealth is generated, is the collection and storage of information, used to co-ordinate subject populations. Information storage is central to the role of 'authoritative resources' in the structuring of social systems spanning larger ranges of space and time than tribal cultures. Surveillance — control of information and the superintendence of the activities of some groups by others — is in turn the key to the expansion of such resources.

In this book I also place a good deal of emphasis upon the role of military power in the organization of traditional and modern states. Who controls the means of violence, how complete such control is and to what ends it is deployed are plainly matters of significance in all societies with 'armed forces'. Surveillance and control of the means of violence are, however, phenomena that largely escape the purview of the most influential schools of social theory, including Marxism, both in the nineteenth century and today. They have to be studied in relation to the main preoccupations of Marxism — capitalism and class conflict — but they stand alongside them as independent influences upon the development of modernity.

There is a fourth 'institutional cluster' relevant to modernity the impact and consequences of which is largely obscured in Marxist thought. This is industrialism. One of the main debates in social theory has been between those who regard capitalism as the 'maker' of the modern world, and those who accord this perhaps dubious honour to industrialism. Thus to the Marxist interpretation of the spread of capitalism and its transcendence by socialism, there stands opposed the 'theory of industrial society', according to which both capitalism and socialism are minor variations on a major theme, the fashioning of modern social life by industrial production. This opposition is in large part a mistaken one because, although industrialism developed under the stimulus of capitalism, in various respects the two are distinct in their nature and their social consequences.

The twentieth-century world is a bloody and frightening one. I think it fair to say that Marx anticipated fierce class struggles and dramatic processes of revolutionary change — in which he was not wrong — but not the appalling military violence that has in fact characterized the present century. None of the major figures now commonly accepted as the main founders of modern social theory, including Max Weber, foresaw quite how savage and destructive would be some of the forces unleashed in current times. Weber lived to know of the carnage of the First World War, but could hardly have seen how rapidly it would be succeeded by a second war and by totalitarianism. No one could have foreseen the coming of the thermonuclear age, even if the trends that eventually led to it were well under way in the nineteenth century. These trends are to do with the development of the means of waging industrialized war. The merging of industry, technology and the means of waging war has been one of the most momentous features of processes of industrialization as a whole. But its importance has never been adequately analysed within the major traditions of social theory.

Having made such an analysis, as I attempt to do in the bulk of this study, where does it leave us in respect of the critical aspirations of which Marxism has been the main bearer? At a minimum, one must conclude: at a vast distance from the future anticipated by Marx, with few obviously available paths of moving towards it. Certainly 'the dialectical movement of history' will do nothing for us, in the sense of guaranteeing the transcendence of the problems which, as members of a global human community, we face today. We live in a world riven between extraordinary opportunity and wholesale disaster, and only the most foolishly optimistic would suppose that the former will necessarily triumph over the latter.

In order to provide systematic form to a text that spills out over large tracts of world history, I shall summarize the main claims of this study in the shape of number of basic observations. I imagine that most readers will regard some of these as contentious, but I trust that they will also find others illuminating. Of course, their meaning will only become fully clear during the course of reading the book, and they should be referred back to.

I   Traditional states (class-divided societies) are essentially segmental in character. The administrative reach of the political centre is low, such that the members of the political apparatus do not 'govern' in the modern sense. Traditional states have frontiers, not borders.

II   In the absolutist state we discover a break-away from traditional state forms, presaging the subsequent development of the nation-state. The concept of sovereignty, linked to the notion of impersonal administrative power, together with a series of related political ideas, become in some part constitutive of the modern state from absolutism onwards.

III   The development of nation-states presumes the dissolution of the city/countryside relations basic to traditional states and involves the emergence of administrative orders of high intensity (associated with borders).

IV   Nation-states are inherently polyarchic, in a sense of that term specified below. Their polyarchic character derives from their administrative concentration (achieved via the expansion of surveillance) and from the altered nature of the dialectic of control which this produces.

V   Nation-states only exist in systemic relations with other nation-states. The internal administrative coordination of nation-states from their beginnings depends upon reflexively monitored conditions of an international nature. 'International relations' is coeval with the origins of nation-states.

VI   Compared with traditional states, nation-states are for the most part internally pacified, such that monopoly of the means of violence is normally only indirectly the resource whereby those who rule sustain their 'government'. Military governments in modern states are quite different from traditional modes of rule in this respect. This is the valid element in the contrast between military and capitalist industrial societies drawn in nineteenth-century social theory.

VII   The spread of capitalism is of fundamental importance to the consolidation of a novel world system from the sixteenth century onwards. Both capitalism and industrialism have decisively influenced the rise of nation-states, but the nation-state system cannot be reductively explained in terms of their existence. The modern world has been shaped through the intersection of capitalism, industrialism and the nation-state system.

VIII The industrialization of war is a key process accompanying the rise of the nation-state and shaping the configuration of the nation-state system. It has led to the creation of a world military order that substantially cross-cuts the divisions between 'First', 'Second' and 'Third' worlds.

IX The development, in the twentieth century, of an ever-increasing abundance of global connections stretching across the borders of states should not be regarded as intrinsically diminishing their sovereignty. On the contrary, it is in substantial part the chief condition of the world-wide extension of the nation-state system in current times.

X There are four 'institutional clusterings' associated with modernity: heightened surveillance, capitalistic enterprise, industrial production and the consolidation of centralized control of the means of violence. None is wholly reducible to any of the others. A concern with the consequences of each moves critical theory away from its concentration upon the transcendence of capitalism by socialism as the sole objective of future social transformations.

Some comments should perhaps be registered about the nature and scope of these arguments. The main emphasis of this book is upon providing an interpretation of the development of the nation-state in its original, i.e. 'Western', habitat. Prior to the concluding three chapters, whenever I speak of 'the nation-state', the reader should understand 'Western nation-state' and, most often, 'European nation-state'. In those final chapters I try to trace out how and why this political form has become generalized across the globe; but I make no claim to offering an exhaustive analysis of variations among states in today's world.

1
State, Society and Modern History

Power and Domination

In this opening section I outline some general notions connected with the concept of power, which will help construct basic underlying themes of the book as a whole. 'Power', along with 'agency' and 'structure', is an elementary concept in social science.[1] To be a human being is to be an agent — although not all agents are human beings — and to be an agent is to have power. 'Power' in this highly generalized sense means 'transformative capacity', the capability to intervene in a given set of events so as in some way to alter them. The logical connection between agency and power is of the first importance for social theory, but the 'universal' sense of power thus implied needs considerable conceptual refinement if it is to be put to work in the interests of substantive social research.

Such conceptual refinement needs to be of two principal sorts. On the one hand, power must be related to the resources that agents employ in the course of their activities in order to accomplish whatever they do. Resources implicated in the reproduction of social systems that have some degree of continuity — and thus 'existence' — across space and time form aspects of the structural properties of those social systems. Two types of resource can be distinguished — the allocative and the authoritative. By the first of these I refer to dominion over material facilities, including material goods and the natural forces that may be harnessed in their production. The second concerns the means of dominion over the activities of human beings themselves.[2] Both sources of power depend in large degree upon the management of time-space relations.

In the sociological and anthropological literature, both Marxist and non-Marxist, primacy has often been given to allocative resources in the constitution of society and in the explication of social change. Such a view is given full and direct expression, of course, in historical materialism, if that term be taken to refer to the interpretation of history that Marx outlines in the 'Preface' to *A Contribution to the Critique of Political Economy*.[3] 'History' there is understood in terms of the expansion of the forces of production, underlying both the institutional organization of different types of society and their processes of change. But it is by no means only in historical materialism that this sort of emphasis appears. It is characteristic of virtually all those theories that can be classified under the rubrics of 'cultural' or 'social evolutionism'. Such theories attempt to understand social change in terms of the differential adaptation of forms of society to their 'environment'. I have criticized this view extensively elsewhere, and there is no point in recapitulating that critique here.[4] Suffice it to say that, according to the standpoint informing this book, no account of history that gives to allocative resources some sort of determining role in either social organization or social change can be defended.

To say this does not mean moving to the other extreme — placing the whole weight of the emphasis upon authoritative resources. If there are no prime movers in human history (even in the last instance) the problem for social analysis becomes that of examining a variety of relations between allocative and authoritative resources in the constitution of social systems and in the dynamics of social change.[5]

Resources do not in any sense 'automatically' enter into the reproduction of social systems, but operate only in so far as they are drawn upon by contextually located actors in the conduct of their day-to-day lives. All social systems, in other words, can be studied as incorporating or expressing modes of *domination* and it is this concept more than any other that provides the focal point for the investigation of power. Social systems that have some regularized existence across time-space are always 'power systems', or exhibit forms of domination, in the sense that they are comprised of relations of autonomy and dependence between actors or collectivities of actors.[6] As has been exhaustively discussed in controversies over the nature of power, forms of domination thus portrayed cannot be reduced to acts or decisions taken, or policies forged, by individual agents. Power as the capability to effectively decide about courses of events, even where others might contest such decisions, is undeniably important. But 'decisions', and 'contested policies', represent only one aspect of domination. The term 'non-decision-making' is an unhappy one to refer to the other aspect of power, but it has become quite firmly established in some sectors of political science. What matters is not just that certain decisions are not made, but that they are not even considered. Non-decision-making, in other words, is not accurately seen just as the obverse of decision-making, but as influencing the circumstances in which certain courses of action are open to 'choice' in any way at all. Power may be at its most alarming, and quite often its most horrifying, when applied as a sanction of force. But it is typically at its most intense and durable when running silently through the repetition of institutionalized practices.[7] As I use it, therefore, 'domination' is not a concept that carries an intrinsically negative connotation.[8]

All social systems of any duration involve an 'institutional mediation of power'.[9] That is to say, domination is expressed in and through the institutions that represent the most deeply embedded continuities of social life. But in the context of any collectivity, association or organization,[10] domination is expressed as modes of *control*, whereby some agents seek to achieve and maintain the compliance of others. I shall refer to relatively stable forms of control as types of *rule*. Forms of rule are (more or less) stable relations of autonomy and dependence in social systems and are sustained by the routine practices that those in superordinate positions employ to influence the activities of others. As such they are to be analytically separated from the institutional mediation of power.[11] Thus, for example, a given type of bureaucratic organization may generate a high level of power in the sense of transformative capacity. This is true, for example, of the modern, large industrial corporation, as judged in terms of both the allocative and authoritative resources it commands. However, the capability of any individual, or group of individuals, to control what goes on in the organization is not a direct extension of the 'amount' of power generated. An individual may be in a 'powerful' position in the sense that he or she has the capability to deploy a range of resources. But how far these can be used to secure specific outcomes depends upon securing whatever compliance is necessary from others.[12] The frequently stated experience of those in positions of 'high power' that what they can accomplish is hedged with very defined limits is not wholly disingenuous.

We should distinguish the 'scope' of rule from its 'intensity'.[13] The former refers to how far actors in superordinate positions are able to control large areas of the activities of those subject to their rule. The scope of control of a managerial executive over those in lower echelons of the labour force may be quite extensive, although usually confined to whatever goes on in the sphere of 'work' only. By the intensity of control I refer to the sanctions that can be invoked to secure compliance, the most extreme being the command over the means of violence, of life and death. A variety of possible relations exist between the scope and intensity of control — a matter of great significance for the themes of this book. Thus, many traditional rulers have possessed 'complete' power over their subjects, in the sense that those subjects are supposed to obey their every command 'under pain of death'. But such power by no means yields a wide scope of actual mastery over the conduct of the subject population. Ruling groups in traditional states, as I shall argue in some detail later, lack the means of regularly influencing the day-to-day lives of their subject populations. One of the major characteristics of the modern state, by contrast, is a vast expansion of the capability of state administrators to influence even the most intimate features of daily activity.

All types of rule, then, rest upon the institutional mediation of power, but channel this through the use of definite strategies of control. Strategies of control naturally always depend in substantial degree upon the form of domination within which they are invoked. In a modern industrial setting, for instance, strategies used by managers to achieve compliance from workers operate within a framework in which the direct threat of violence or the use of force cannot be brought to bear. Much of what 'management' means in modern industry derives from this fact. Nonetheless, the resources that managers are able to draw upon to sustain control over the work-force can be focused and applied in a range of different ways. All strategies of control employed by superordinate individuals or groups call forth counter-strategies on the part of subordinates. This phenomenon represents what I call the *dialectic of control* in social systems, something that connects back directly to the theme of human agency with which I opened this discussion. To be an agent is to be able to make a difference to the world, and to be able to make a difference is to have power (where power means transformative capacity). No matter how great the scope or intensity of control superordinates possess, since their power presumes the active compliance of others, those others can bring to bear strategies of their own, and apply specific types of sanctions. 'Self-consciousness', Hegel says, 'attains its satisfaction only in another self-consciousness',[14] speaking of the master-slave dialectic. Hegel makes of this a teleological philosophy of history but, stripped of such grandiose pretensions, what is at issue is the capability even of the most dependent, weak and the most oppressed to have the ability to carve out spheres of autonomy of their own.

All forms of rule have their 'openings' that can be utilized by those in subordinate positions to influence the activities of those who hold power over them. One consequence of this is that technologies of power — in other words, formalized procedures of rule — rarely if ever work with the 'fixity' which on the face of things they might seem to possess. The more a social system is one in which the control exercised by superordinates depends upon a considerable scope of power over subordinates, the more shifting and potentially volatile its organization is likely to be. The literature on prisons or asylums, for example, is replete with descriptions of the 'effort-bargains' which those who administer such organizations are forced to conclude with inmates in order to make their rule effective.

All social reproduction and, therefore, all systems of power, are grounded in the 'predictability' of day-to-day routines. The predictable — that is to say, regularized — character of day-to-day activity is not something that just 'happens', it is in substantial part 'made to happen' by actors in the diverse settings of social life. Of course, actors do not do this 'consciously' in the ordinary sense of the term, although they do often discursively reflect upon the nature of the activities in which they engage. Many of the characteristics of social life that actors 'make happen' are accomplished via non-discursive 'practical consciousness'.[15] That is to say, actors routinely monitor reflexively what they do in the light of their complex knowledge of social conventions, sustaining or reproducing those conventions in the process. Since agents in all societies are 'social theorists', whose discursively articulated accounts are in some part constitutive of the social forms they reproduce in their conduct, it is never the case that they blindly enact and re-enact the routines of daily life. Even in the most traditional of cultures 'tradition' is reflexively appropriated and in some sense 'discursively understood'.

In traditional societies, however, especially in small oral cultures, 'tradition' is not known as such, because there is nothing that escapes its influence and, therefore, nothing with which to contrast it. 'History' is not understood as the use of the past to mobilize change in the future, but as the repetitiveness of 'reversible time'.[16] A significant alteration in the conditions of human social existence comes about with the invention of 'history'. From then on the circumstances of social reproduction are themselves reflexively monitored in an effort to influence the form institutions assume. I take this to be the main feature that separates *organizations* from other types of collectivity. The term 'organization' will crop up a great deal in this study. An organization is a collectivity in which knowledge about the conditions of system reproduction is reflexively used to influence, shape or modify that system reproduction. All forms of state administrative bodies are organizations in this sense, for reasons I shall document at some length in what follows. In modern nation-states, however, the reflexive monitoring of system reproduction is much more highly accentuated than in any pre-existing form of state and, in addition, 'organization' characterizes many other aspects of social life.

I have earlier linked domination with the mastery of time-space. Elaborating the implications of this means giving some conceptual attention to the timing and spacing of human social activities.[17] It is particularly important to emphasize the association between power and *locales*, which will also be one of the leading themes of the book. I use 'locale' in deliberate preference to the notion of 'place' as ordinarily employed by geographers, because 'place' is often only a vaguely formulated notion and because it does not usually mean the co-ordination of time as well as space. Locales refer to the settings of interaction, including the physical aspects of setting — their 'architecture' — within which systemic aspects of interaction and social relations are concentrated. The proximate aspects of settings are chronically employed by social actors in the constitution of interaction, a matter of quite fundamental significance to its 'meaningful' qualities.[18] But settings also are everywhere involved in the reproduction of institutionalized activities across wide spans of time and space. Thus, a dwelling is a locale displaying specific architectural features: these are socially relevant in so far as they are bound up with the distribution and the character of behaviour in time-space. A dwelling which has several rooms is 'regionalized', not just in the sense that there are various distinct 'places' which it thereby contains, but in the sense that the rooms are habitually used for different types of pursuit, distributed differentially in the routines of day-to-day life. I do not mean by 'locale', however, just settings of a fairly confined nature. Locales include internally regionalized settings of very wide time-space extension, from cities to nation-states and beyond.

The importance of locales to the theory of power can be spelled out as follows. Certain types of locale form 'power containers' — circumscribed arenas for the generation of administrative power. A locale is a power container in so far as it permits a concentration of allocative and authoritative resources. In what I shall call class-divided societies, castles, manorial estates — but above all cities — are containers for the generation of power. In the modern world, the administrative settings of organizations — business firms, schools, universities, hospitals, prisons, etc. — are centres for the concentration of resources. But the modern state, as nation-state, becomes in many respects the pre-eminent form of power container, as a territorially bounded (although internally highly regionalized) administrative unity.

It is possible to give some general indication of how power is generated by the 'containment' of resources, although naturally there are many specific differences between settings within different types of society. Power containers generate power, as has been mentioned, first and foremost through the concentration of allocative and administrative resources. The generation of allocative resources is, of course, influenced directly by forms of available technology in any society, but the level of their concentration depends primarily upon factors creating authoritative resources. These are of the following kinds.

1   The possibilities of surveillance that settings of various kinds allow. 'Surveillance' refers to two related sorts of phenomena. One is the accumulation of 'coded information', which can be used to administer the activities of individuals about whom it is gathered. It is not just the collection of information, but its storage that is important here. Human memory is a storage device, but the storage of information is enhanced vastly by various other kinds of marks or traces that can be used as modes of recording. If writing is in all cultures the main phenomenon involved, in modern states electronic storage — tapes, records, discs, etc. — considerably expands the range of available storage mechanisms. All modes of information storage are simultaneously forms of communication, cutting across the face-to-face communication that is exhaustive of human interaction in oral cultures. The 'externalized' character of information traces inevitably severs communication from its intrinsic connection with the body and the face. But electronic communication for the first time in history separates 'immediate' communication from presence, thereby initiating developments in modern culture that I shall later argue are basic to the emergence and consolidation of the nation-state.

The other sense of surveillance is that of the direct supervision of the activities of some individuals by others in positions of authority over them. The concentration of activities within clearly bounded settings greatly enlarges the degree to which those activities can be 'watched over', and thus controlled, by superordinates. In most types of non-modern society, the possibilities of surveillance in this second sense (as in the first) are relatively limited. There are many examples of large aggregates of people being brought together in the construction of public projects, for example, the building of temples, monuments or roads. But these groupings usually only exist for a limited duration and are relatively marginal to the activities and involvements of the majority of the population. Within fairly confined areas, such as small rural communities, certain kinds of surveillance procedures can be sustained in class-divided societies and these can be linked to larger networks with varying degrees of success. Examples can be found in the role of local priests in medieval

Catholicism, or in the use of informers by the traditional Chinese state. But only in cities could direct and regular surveillance be maintained by the central agencies of the state, and then with a low degree of success compared with modern organizations. In modern organizations, either large segments of the daily lives of social actors (as in factories or offices), or substantial periods of their lives in a more 'total' setting (as in prisons, or asylums) can be subject to more-or-less continuous surveillance.

The two senses of surveillance belong quite closely together, since the collection of information about social activities can, and very often is, directly integrated with styles of supervision — something which again tends to be maximized in modern types of organization.

2   The possibilities of assembling, within definite settings, large numbers of individuals who do not spend most of their daily activity involved in direct material production. The formation of organizations, and of any substantial level of disciplinary power, depends upon the existence of specialized administrative officials of some kind. In orthodox versions of historical materialism, the early emergence of such administrative specialism is 'explained' in terms of the prior development of surplus production. But the way this explanation is often presented makes it neither plausible nor even a valid empirical description. It is hardly an explanation at all, even in the most general sense of that term, because surplus production has to be co-ordinated in some way if it is to become a resource for the generation of administrative power. However, it is also empirically wanting. If 'surplus production' means anything specific, the term must refer to material production which develops beyond what, for a given population of producers, are traditional or pre-established needs. Thus defined, surplus production is not even the necessary condition for the formation of specialized administrative apparatuses. Such organizations have very often come into being in circumstances of acute deprivation for many of the subjects of their rule — the appropriation of the 'surplus' perhaps being at the origin of that deprivation.[19]

As Max Weber emphasizes, the regularized 'containing' of assemblages of individuals within the settings of organizations can only be extensively achieved in a society given various other conditions in addition to the expansion of 'surplus production'. Some of these conditions are peculiar to the modern West. They include, particularly, the disappearance of 'prebendal' forms of renumeration and the associated development of a full-blown money economy. The purely 'vocational' official is one with a salaried income, whose sources of renumeration have become wholly cut off from the use of the official position to gather material resources put to private use.

3   The facilitating of the scope and intensity of sanctions, above all the development of military power. There are two locales of overwhelming significance here, or so I shall argue — the city in class-divided societies and, in modern societies, the nation-state. The relation between military power and sanctions of law is always important. Organizations of all types develop legal rules of some sort. All forms of law, in turn, involve sanctions administered in one way or another via officials. Such administration is backed, in a direct or a more indirect manner, by the threat of the use of violence.[20] It will be part of my main thesis later in this book, however, that in many modern organizations — in contra-distinction to what was the case in class-divided societies — the sanction of the use of violence is quite indirect and attenuated. Moreover, military power on the whole tends to become rather clearly distinct from policing power, the one turned 'externally', the other pointed 'internally'.

The first formation of permanent armed forces injects something substantially new into world history. But in all class-divided societies, no matter how strong the military forces commanded by the state, there are significant sources of armed opposition that escape the control of the central apparatus. The prominence of local war-lords, the existence of marauding nomadic groups, and all kinds of pirates and brigands, express the segmental character that class-divided societies display.

4   The creation of certain conditions that influence the formation of ideology. The system integration of class-divided societies does not depend in a significant way upon the overall acceptance of particular symbolic orders by the majority of the population within those societies. What matters is the hegemony achieved through such acceptance on the part of the members of dominant groups or classes. Concentration of activities within city *milieux* plays an important part here in more than one way. Through the expansion of surveillance, especially for example as pressed into the service of some kind of formal education, even if this is

confined to a small stratum of the literate, the influence of ideology can be considerably sharpened. But probably also the sheer physical lay-out of many traditional cities has ideological effects. In such urban forms, the city is frequently dominated architecturally by state and religious edifices, giving a visual representation of power that no doubt makes an impress upon the minds of those who move in the vicinity of them.[21]

The Concept of the State: Preliminary Remarks

'State' has two senses in ordinary language, but the ambiguity is not a particularly worrying one for social theory. 'The state' sometimes means an apparatus of government or power, sometimes the overall social system subject to that government or power. The two usages are not confusing in most contexts, but where they are a terminological distinction has to be observed between them. Thus I shall speak of 'the state apparatus' when I mean the administrative organs of government and 'society' or 'culture' when I mean the encompassing social system. Both 'society' and 'culture' have their own ambiguities. So far as the former is concerned, a word of caution is required. 'Society' has often been understood by sociologists, implicitly or otherwise, as a clearly bounded system with an obvious and easily identifiable set of distinguishing traits. But while this is true of modern nation-states, it is very often not the case with other types of societies, whether these are 'states' or small localized groups.[22]

All forms of state apparatus consist of a plurality of organizations in the sense in which I have outlined that term above, but for many purposes it is also worth treating that apparatus as a single organization. This is indeed the first characteristic I wish to single out as definitive of the state in general. *All states involve the reflexive monitoring of aspects of the reproduction of the social systems subject to their rule.* We should be careful to distinguish this from the view of the state set out by writers such as Durkheim. Durkheim takes as the main feature of the state its role as an organ of communication with the rest of society. 'The state', he says, is 'the organ of social thought'. This does not imply, he goes on to add, 'that all social thought springs from the state'. One source is to be found in 'the sentiments, ideals, beliefs that the society has worked out collectively and with time'; the other lies in the 'thought processes' of the state. 'There is something spontaneous, automatic, something unconsidered, about day-to-day social life', Durkheim writes. But 'deliberation and reflection, on the other hand, are features of all that goes on in the organ of government . . . There all is organised and, above all, organised increasingly to prevent changes being made without due consideration.'[23] Most of this, I think, is correct. But Durkheim goes on to suppose that the state thereby inevitably represents the interests of those it rules, save in certain exceptional and 'pathological' circumstances. He treats modern democratic state forms too much as a simple extension of state power in general and he also underestimates how far the state apparatus can become a source of power independent of the rest of 'society'.

Durkheim refuses to regard as characteristic of states just those phenomena that, for Weber, distinguish the state from other organizations. The definition of 'state' that Weber offers involves three main elements: (i) the existence of a regularized administrative staff able (ii) to sustain the claim to the legitimate monopoly of control of the means of violence and (iii) to uphold that monopoly within a given territorial area. While Weber's definition highlights characteristics (violence and territoriality) that Durkheim was surely wrong not to regard as characteristic of states in general, we cannot be wholly satisfied with it.[24] Weber defines the state in terms worked out first of all with reference to the modern state, generalizing them backwards as it were. 'The concept of the state', he says bluntly, 'has only in modern times reached its full development', so 'it is best to define it in terms appropriate to the modern type of state, but at the same time, in terms which abstract from the values of the present day, since these are particularly subject to change'.[25] The trouble with this procedure is that it tends to minimize differences between traditional and modern states in respect of the very features he singles out. For, as I shall try to indicate later, only in modern nation-states can the state apparatus generally — not, of course, universally — lay *successful* claim to the monopoly of the means of violence, and only in such states does the administrative scope of the state apparatus correspond directly with territorial boundaries about which that claim is made. The appropriation of the right to monopolize the means of violence and the association of this with some kind of conception of territoriality are characteristics of states in general. But we have to be careful to accentuate 'claim' in the first part and to recognize that the territorial element may be quite ill-defined as regards the second.

Weber not only defines the state in terms of control of the means of violence, but does the same for the 'political', which is a far wider category. A 'political' organization, according to Weber, cannot be specified in terms of the ends to which it is devoted. There cannot be a satisfactory 'substantive' definition of the political, because political organizations, including states, have been concerned with all sorts of different activities. 'All the way from provision for subsistence to the patronage of art, there is no conceivable end which *some* political association has not at some time pursued.'[26] The only feature which all political groups have in common is the means they employ, namely the use of force. But, as Weber himself points out, the use of force, or of the threat of its use, as a sanction is not confined to organizations that would usually be thought of as 'political'. Force 'has been used freely by kinship groups, household groups, consociations and, in the Middle Ages, under certain circumstances by all those entitled to bear arms'.[27]

I shall define the 'political' in the following way. All human interaction, as I have argued at some length in other sources, involves the communication of meaning, the operation of power (the use of resources) and normative modes of sanctioning (including the use of physical violence or the threat of its use).[28] In the production/reproduction of interaction, agents draw upon corresponding structural elements of social systems: signification (meaning), domination (power) and legitimation (sanctions). As implicated in the reproduction of social systems, these provide a way of categorizing institutions that can be represented as follows:

S − D − L	Symbolic orders/modes of discourse
D(auth) − S − L	Political institutions
D(alloc) − S − L	Economic institutions
L − D − S	Law/modes of sanction

The 'political' is not defined here in a substantive way. Nor does it inevitably concern the use of force. The 'political' aspect of organizations concerns their capability of marshalling authoritative resources or what I shall call *administrative power*.

All organizations have political features. But only in the case of states do these involve the consolidation of military power in association with control of the means of violence within a range of territories. A state can be defined as a political organization whose rule is territorially ordered and which is able to mobilize the means of violence to sustain that rule. Such a definition is close to that of Weber, but does not accentuate a claimed monopoly of the means of violence or the factor of legitimacy.

It should be noted that several of the major concepts associated with political theory, as developed from the sixteenth century onwards — and frequently generalized to all states — do not appear in the foregoing discussion. In particular, I make no mention of sovereignty or of the significance of popular representation. My reasons for excluding these are bound up in an intrinsic way with the main themes of the book. These concepts do not originate merely as a new descriptive language of rule, which can be generalized back to pre-existing state forms. Like the very notion of 'government', they signal the emergence of a novel political formation. More than this, I shall argue, they become key elements of what the modern state is — they help constitute its very distinctiveness as compared with traditional states.

All states — as state apparatuses — can be differentiated from the wider societies of which they are part. What is 'outside' the scope of the state has, since the Enlightenment, been understood in varying senses as 'civil society'. I shall have more to say about this later, but for the time being it is important to enter some early qualifications about the use of the notion. Let me concentrate here on the concept as it can be traced in the relation between Hegel and Marx. For Hegel, the state is the final development in the emergence of a series of 'ethical communities' in the course of social evolution, the others being the family and civil society. Hegel's views on these matters are by no means wholly consistent, but the main thread of what he has to say is that the state actualizes and furthers forms of 'the universal' which are lacking in society, particularly the *bürgerliche Gesellschaft* of modern times. The latter is largely composed of atomistic, self-seeking individuals. Civil society cannot exist without the state, and in virtue of its nature cannot achieve 'universal freedom'. The modern state embodies reason, not by absorbing civil society but by guarding certain of the universal qualities upon which it is predicated. The state is 'the Universal that has expressed its actual rationality', representing 'the identity of the general and the particular will'. It is 'the embodiment of concrete freedom, in which the individual's particular interests have their complete development, and receive adequate recognition of their rights'.[29]

In 'reversing Hegel', Marx argues that the state rests upon civil society, which it does not transcend but whose class composition it reflects, and he extends the concept of civil society to include not just the 'economic', but everything lying outside the immediate sphere of the state apparatus itself. The consequence, however, is a fatal flaw both in the resulting interpretation of the state/civil society relation and in the presumption that the state can be superseded in socialism. 'Civil society' now becomes something distinct from the state in its origin and nature, to which the state owes its own existence and form. This view sacrifices an important part of Hegel's insight into *bürgerliche Gesellschaft*, whatever else may be dubious about his conception of the state as the 'realization of the universal'. For Hegel sees that 'civil society', as *bürgerliche Gesellschaft,* is in substantial part created *by* the (modern) state or, put more accurately, that the two come into existence in conjunction with one another.

The importance of this is not just that Hegel accentuates the independent power of the political, as against Marx's tendency to economic reductionism. The point is that, with the formation of the modern state, 'civil society' is no longer that which co-existed with previous state forms. In class-divided societies there are large spheres of society which retain their independent character in spite of the rise of the state apparatus. That is essentially what I mean by saying that the political centre lacks the capacity to regularly shape the day-to-day lives of those who are its citizens. It is also why, in class-divided societies, 'city' and 'countryside', while in some ways interdependent, have a contrasting and distinctive character as compared with one another. The 'countryside' is not exactly the same as 'civil society' but, nonetheless, much of what that concept refers to is located there, in the spheres of agrarian production and local community life. With the rise of the modern state, and its culmination in the nation-state, 'civil society' in this sense simply disappears. What is 'outside' the scope of the administrative reach of the state apparatus cannot be understood as institutions which remain unabsorbed by the state.

Because of the difficulties to which the notion of civil society gives rise, I shall not employ it in the remainder of the book. I shall want to emphasize the significance of the elimination of the 'countryside' with the rise of modern urbanism, which I shall connect directly to the nature of the nation-state.

State, Nation-State and Military Power in Social Theory

At this point we have to shift conceptual gears somewhat, and consider briefly what appear to be perplexing problems in the sociology of knowledge, applied to sociology itself. By common agreement, 'society' is the object of study of sociology — more specifically, that form of society associated with the modern era. Understood as a bounded unity, 'society' here refers to the nation-state. But very little attention has been given in social theory to examining the nature of such a phenomenon. Why should this be?

There is a further oddity about the sociological enterprise as it is usually practised today. Opening any textbook of sociology, the reader will find there discussions of most modern institutions — the family, class, deviance, etc. But it is very unlikely that he or she will discover any discussion of military institutions, or of the impact of military violence and war upon modern society. Much of the same is true of more rarified treatises on social theory, which concentrate upon capitalism, industrialism and so on.[30] Yet who, living in the twentieth century, could for a moment deny the massive impact which military power, preparation for war, and war itself, have had upon the social world?

To explain what on the face of things seem extraordinary lapses in sociological thought, we have to look back to the influence of nineteenth-century social thought upon theoretical thinking in the social sciences. I think it true to say that we live today in circumstances for which the traditional sources of social theory have left us quite unprepared, especially those forms of social theory associated broadly with liberalism and with socialism. We live in a world dominated by the nation-state form, in which a fragile equality in weaponry possessed by the two most powerful nation-states is the main brake upon global violence within the context of a novel international order. The world is quite different from that which most nineteenth-century thinkers anticipated; and the styles of thought that dominate the social sciences today tend to be heavily indebted to their nineteenth-century origins.

Let us consider again Durkheim and Marx to illustrate both how and why this has come to be so. Durkheim was in a general way affiliated to liberalism, and Marx's writings are at the core of the most flourishing forms of socialist theory. Yet neither thinker gives any detailed attention to the nation-state as a generic phenomenon and neither, in a systematic way, connects the nature of the modern state either with control of the means of violence or with territoriality. Durkheim's theory of social evolution, from which his account of the state is derived, in general allocates little importance to military power, in traditional or in modern societies. This was not true of all authors of the same period, as the writings of Herbert Spencer demonstrate. In respect of the interpretation of non-modern societies, Spencer was more representative, perhaps, of nineteenth-century liberalism than was Durkheim. Spencer attributes the origins and nature of agrarian states largely to warfare. But whereas pre-industrial societies are pre-eminently warlike, industrial society, according to Spencer, is inherently pacific, depending upon peaceful co-operation rather than antagonism between human collectivities. With the expansion of industrial activities, 'in place of a uniform belief imperatively enforced, there come multiform beliefs voluntarily accepted . . . military conformity coercively maintained gives place to a varied nonconformity maintained by a willing union.'[31]

Durkheim may not have emphasized the importance of military power and war in non-modern cultures, but his analysis of the development of 'organic solidarity', in spite of the specific criticisms he offers of Spencer, has a similar orientation to Spencer's interpretation of industrialism. Organic solidarity refers to the interdependence in which individuals increasingly find themselves as a result of the expansion of the division of labour stimulated by the progress of modern industry. The modern state is a direct expression of this trend, because the co-ordination of complex economic ties demands a 'social intelligence' of a centralized type. In the biological analogy Durkheim sometimes favours, the complex but unified entity which is a modern society needs a differentiated 'brain' to oversee its co-ordination and further development. Durkheim is critical of concepts of the state associated with socialism — including that of Marx — which he saw as treating modern political organization as wholly concerned with economic transactions.[32] For Durkheim, the state cannot be *aufgehoben* and is of particular significance as a moral organization. But far from leading him to analyse the state as a nation-state, and as bound up with military power and territoriality, the effect is to distance him almost entirely from these concerns. The spread of organic solidarity, with its accompanying moralization of the 'cult of the individual', is inevitably international, because the ties of interdependence involved depend solely upon the spread of modern industry. 'War', Durkheim asserts, 'except for some passing setbacks [!] . . . has become more and more intermittent and less common'.[33] The traits of particular nations will not necessarily disappear in the grand sweep of social evolution, but will become elements of a peaceful order of humanity. 'The national will merges with the human ideal'; each state will have as its aim 'not to expand, or to lengthen its borders, but to set its own house in order and to make the widest appeal to its members for a moral life on an ever higher level'. By this means 'all discrepancy between national and human morals would be excluded'.[34]

Marx and Engels — especially Engels — did give some mind to military power and war. Engels wrote to Marx in 1858, 'I am now reading, among other things, Clausewitz's *On War*.'[35] Those other things included the work of Jomini and von Bülow; Engels continued to maintain his interest in such matters throughout his life, writing articles on military topics under Marx's name in the *New York Daily Tribune* and a number of other surveys of 'military science'. Marx also read Clausewitz and sporadically dipped into other sources suggested by Engels, but apart from one or two minor pieces wrote nothing on the nature of war.[36] The notion of 'the nation' crops up often in Marx's writings, but rarely if ever in the context of his major theoretical discussions of modern capitalism. Sometimes he means by it a state, but characteristically he uses it to refer to the cultural attributes of national communities. The *Communist Manifesto* rejects the idea that socialists have the objective of abolishing 'nationalities', arguing that these are legitimate expressions of cultural identity. But the same document does envisage the dissolution of all significant divisive influences among humankind, as socialism comes to further processes already begun by the spread of capitalism. Through promoting the existence of a 'world market', the bourgeoisie give 'a cosmopolitan character to production and consumption in every country'. Marx and Engels continue: 'All old-established national industries have been destroyed or are daily being destroyed . . . national one-sidedness and narrow-mindedness become more and more impossible.'[37]

Alert though Marx might have been to the significance of military power, like Engels his concern with it was above all in respect of revolutionary and counter-revolutionary violence. Warfare between nations would become increasingly less consequential than the struggle between classes. There seems no way to dispute the conclusion that Marx unaffectedly believed that what workers shared in common would eventually triumph over what divided them nationally. To hold that 'workers have no country' was obviously an expression of hope as much as a factual observation but, as a projection of immanent trends, it was perfectly in line with the main impetus of Marx's theory of capitalist development. For Marx, the modern world is far more riven with conflict than for Durkheim, because of the deeply founded class divisions that demand nothing short of revolutionary change for their resolution. Nonetheless, Marx's anticipated future commonwealth of nations in essence resembles that which Durkheim foresaw. As a student of Marx's writings on the nation and nationhood has commented:

> An enlightened patriotism which recognised the bearing of international progress upon national welfare seemed to Marx compatible and even fairly synonymous with sound international-ism. The true patriot must further the advance of other nations if only to assure the progress of his own; the true internationalist must strive for the advance of particular countries as the sound basis of world progress . . . [Marx] was an internationalist, not only in the sense of advocating a system of cooperative world relations, but in the more specific sense of conceiving that system as the resultant or function of the friendly interaction of large nations which were organised harmoniously from within.[38]

This absence in liberal sociology and in Marx's writings — the lack of a systematic interpretation of the rise of the territorially bounded nation-state and its association with military power — can be traced to the legacy of Saint-Simon in political theory and to the influence of classical political economy. There is more than a hint in Marx, and an open embrace of the idea by Engels, of the Saint-Simonian doctrine that, in the emergent society to which social evolution is leading, the administration of human beings by others will give way to the administration of human beings over things. Durkheim was less preoccupied with this theme of Saint-Simon than by the notion, also in some part drawn from Saint-Simon, that the state in an industrialized order will have a moral role to play in relation to the societal community. That is to say, in contrast to Marx, he was more influenced by Saint-Simon's later writings than by his earlier ones. But in neither case does there result an understanding of the state in an industrialized society as inherently associated with control of the means of violence, in which the administrative order relates to defined territorial boundaries. The industrial state, in short, is not a nation-state, and the industrial order — whether intrinsically marked by class struggle or not — is portrayed as progressively overcoming the militaristic tendencies of pre-existing types of society. Both liberal and Marxist conceptions of the state are heavily influenced by their respective critiques of political economy. Whatever their differences, which are of course in some respects very profound, both schools of thought conceive of industrialism as essentially a pacific force, inevitably going beyond national communities, unifying the globe through interdependent economic exchange. Marx may have been a more radical critic of the 'de-humanizing' effects of the division of labour than was Durkheim but, for both, modern economic life stimulates interdependence and therefore — once class division has disappeared — social unity on a global scale.

Now it might seem plain that, if these traditions of thought are deficient in the manner indicated, the answer is to turn to 'right-liberal' or conservative thinkers, who have tended to be more preoccupied with the state as a warlike entity. Thus Otto Hintze, a member of the so-called 'Prussian school' of historians, shares a good deal in common, in some of his emphases at any rate, with Max Weber. Hintze stresses the general association between the existence of states and the consolidation of military power, and sees such power both as involved with the development of capitalism/industrialism and as shaping their future course of development. He is strongly critical of Marxist assumptions: 'It is one-sided, exaggerated and therefore false to consider class conflict the only driving force in history. Conflict between nations has been far more important.'[39] Hintze criticizes Schumpeter for trying to show, in quasi-Marxist vein, that capitalism and 'the nation' are antithetical. 'The rise and development of capitalism', according to Hintze, 'remain unintelligible without insight into how they were conditioned by the course of national formation.'[40] In many respects, he goes on to claim, the expansion of capitalism and the increasing power of the nation-state march in tandem.

This is a view which, in a particular guise, I shall also later be concerned to defend and to further elucidate. But in spite of the importance which, put alongside liberal and Marxist traditions, the views of Hintze, Weber, and others holding comparable positions have, I do not think one can simply turn to them, abandoning the others, in analysing the nature of the modern nation-state in relation to military power. Thus in Weber, who attempted in a certain sense to merge those two incompatibles, Marx and Nietzsche, we do not find a satisfactory treatment either of the nation-state or of its relation to the development of capitalism and industrialism. As has been mentioned, this is partly because Weber defines the state in such a way as to make it difficult to distinguish some of the specific characteristics of the nation-state. It is also, however, because Weber, like most theorists inclined towards the political right on these matters, tends to see violence and war as an inescapable part of the human condition. The 'Nietzschean element' is most strongly represented in Weber precisely in the conjunction between his overall concept of the state and his philosophical stance about the irrationality of 'ultimate values'. Beyond 'ultimate values' there lies only force, the clash of mutually irreconcilable cultures, defended and protected by states that necessarily operate in a 'house of power'.[41] I do not believe this view to be philosophically defensible,[42] and it deflects attention from the ways in which the relations between nation-states in the modern world differ from those of earlier states. If the liberal and Marxist standpoints are notably deficient in certain respects, they do nonetheless draw our attention to the fact that capitalist-industrialism injects a whole set of novel dynamics into social change.

The above discussion concentrates upon the forerunners of modern sociology and we might ask the question, Have not each of the three general traditions of thought made considerable progress since then? Naturally they have done so in many respects, but I think it undemanding to demonstrate that their failings still remain. Marxist thought in the twentieth century has certainly not ignored the phenomena of war, force and violence. How could it be otherwise in a period which might not have seen the realization of Marx's projections for the revolutionary trans-formation of the industrialized countries, but has been otherwise the true 'century of revolutions'? Virtually everyone sympathetic to Marxism in current times accepts that Marx failed to develop anything more than the rudiments of a theory of the modern state. The result over the last two decades or so has been a spate of Marxist writing designed to help rectify this omission, some of which is very instructive indeed.[43] But virtually all of it is preoccupied either with the role of the state in economic life, or with the state as the focus of 'internal' oppression.[44] Where it is analysed theoretically at all, the nation-state still tends to appear in these discussions as reducible to economic relations of one kind or another. An example of the fatuous consequences to which this can lead is the division of the 'world system' into 'core', 'semi-periphery' and 'periphery', where the second of these categories includes the state socialist societies of Eastern Europe. The Soviet Union may be less developed than the Western countries economically, but in terms of its deployment of military power it is absurd to include it in the 'semi-periphery'.

Liberal authors have written extensively about the nation-state, although often in relation only to the 'state-building' efforts of the Third World. Unlike the majority of Marxists, some such writers have devoted considerable effort to grasping the nature of the nation-state. Examples are the works of T. H. Marshall and Reinhard Bendix. Each has written on the nation-state, and on nationalism, but in their thinking these occupy a strictly subord-inate place to what Marshall terms 'citizenship' or 'citizenship rights'.[45] Bendix's recent and most major work is, as he says, con-cerned with 'power and the mandate to rule', and with 'the use of force as an attribute of authority'.[46] But its overwhelming emphasis is upon how arbitrary power is overturned by the rise of government through popular delegation. 'Authority in the name of the people' has come to replace 'the authority of Kings'.[47] No one, surely, would wish to deny the importance of such a phenomenon. Bendix has, moreover, played a leading part in attacking evolutionary theories of social change, stressing the diversity of routes which different states have taken towards modernization. However, like others in this tradition of thought, he has fought shy of attempting to analyse how industrial organization has become bracketed to military power, and how each of these in turn is connected with the character of the modern nation-state. The state appears as 'political community' within which citizenship rights may be realized, not as the bearer of military power within a world of other nation-states. Bendix frequently cites Hintze as well as Max Weber. But some of their distinctive emphases, particularly the 'Nietzschean strain' in Weber, barely appear in Bendix's work at all.

Nietzsche has, however, become influential again in present-day social thought, particularly in the works of those critical of liberal and Marxist perspectives. Thus the 'new philosophers' in France, who started out on the left, in abandoning Marx have moved to Nietzsche.[48] In turning their backs on Marxism, and discovering the absence in Marx not only of an elaborated account of the state, but of a generic theory of power (as distinct from class power), the new philosophers have made the state and power the fundamental components of social life.

> We must break with the metaphysics of property, foundation and infrastructure . . . For the problem does not lie there; it is infinitely more radical: power does not appropriate the world, it continually *engenders* it in all its dimensions. It does not *expropriate* men and their homes, it *places them under house arrest*, deepens and fortifies the corners where they take part. Far from malignantly tearing the thread of their social fabric, power is what weaves the cloth of every reality . . . If the reality of capital, as we know, provokes despair, it is useless to place our dreams and hopes in another reality.[49]

This style of thought, with its rhetorical flourishes, sacrifices most of the insights it has achieved by a monolithic emphasis upon the ubiquity of power. Power is everywhere, so its particular manifestations are uninteresting. All states are pyramids of power; there is no point in differentiating between them in terms of their specific qualities or characteristics. In such writing, the nature of the state is approached only obliquely, never directly, and far from helping to identify the characteristics of nation-states, this approach hopelessly befuddles them.

I do not mean to imply by the preceding observations that no one has written interestingly about the nation-state in recent times, or that these comments are in any way exhaustive in relation to the forms of social thought to which they refer. There are today several bodies of literature relevant to the problems with which this book is concerned; my point is that these tend to be disconnected from the main trends of thinking in social theory. There is, and there has long been, a massive general literature on war and militarism. The difficulty with most works written in this framework is that they tend to generalize across all epochs. The contention tends to be that war has always existed, and corresponds either to some innate aggressive tendencies of humankind, or to inescapable clashes of interest between different human groups. Thus the military aspects of nation-states are merely one version of traits characteristic in some way of all societies, or at least of all states. On the other hand, there is a burgeoning literature to do with the threat of nuclear war, and with the chances the population of this planet may or may not have of surviving the next few decades. In contrast to the broader discussions of war, which are often all-embracing in character, most of this work operates within a very narrow time-span, being concerned with very immediate and urgent problems. Essential though it is, such literature necessarily tends to be tactical: it is concerned with what steps could conceivably be taken to arrest what seems to be a plunge towards disaster.

There is also an extensive literature of international relations, and it is here that much of the material germane to analysing the nation-state is to be found. However, the very notion of a distinctive field of international relations, separated somehow from what goes on inside nations or 'societies', is in some part symptomatic of the limitations in social thought I have described. For if 'capitalist development', or 'industrial development' are seen as the pre-eminent sources of social change, they are then regarded as the substantive core of sociological concern; the relations between states, seen as a more contingent matter, can be left to specialists who need have no particular ties with social theory.[50] This unfortunate and indefensible division also rests to some degree upon the proclivity of social theorists — in contrast to theorists of international relations — to adopt evolutionary or endogenous models of social development. If it is supposed that the most important influences upon social change derive from factors inside 'societies', and if it is held in addition that these factors are primarily economic, then is it hardly surprising that sociologists are content to hive off the study of the political relations between states to a separate field of investigation. Although there must be divisions of labour and specialism within the social sciences, there can be no justification for the theoretical aberrations which this particular disciplinary partitioning tends to perpetuate.

A Discontinuist Interpretation of Modern History

Evolutionary theories claim that, as a result of some discernable mechanisms of change, there are trends of development in history which culminate in the emergence of modern, i.e. Western, societies — these standing at the top of a hierarchy of types of society.[51] Such theories presume some dominant continuities over human history as a whole, whatever differences are recognized between types of society. In most forms of evolutionism, these continuities are portrayed as part of a generalized process of social differentiation, from the simple to the more complex. Marx's view shares something in common with other evolutionary theories in so far as social change is held to involve the progressive growth of the forces of production. It is a discontinuist account of history in the sense that social development is held to occur via successive episodes of revolutionary transformation. This is not the perspective I wish to endorse in proposing a 'discontinuist interpretation of modern history', by which I refer to a set of changes confined to relatively recent times. Such a conception is indeed found in Marx, but it is never fully articulated, and is kept secondary to the evolutionary view.[52]

According to this perspective, the emergence of modern capitalism does not represent the high point (thus far) of a progressive scheme of social development, but rather the coming of a type of society radically distinct from all prior forms of social order. It is exactly this I mean by a discontinuist interpretation of modern history. Marx's writings are not irrelevant to understanding it; however given limitations noted earlier, plus his primary adherence to an evolutionary conception, the contribution which can be drawn from him is inevitably only partial.

Let me distinguish several different pictures of human 'history', recognizing again what complicated issues are concealed behind the unassuming exterior of that apparently innocuous term. One is the version of evolutionism that regards history — here understood essentially as social change — as mainly governed by incremental processes of development. In this view, there are no fundamental discontinuities in social change. All phases of development that look like 'revolutions' of one kind or another turn out to involve less turbulent, underlying processes of change. This is the position taken by Durkheim; it has also been held by many others from Comte through to the present day. Another view sees history as being driven by processes of struggle, in which substantial disjunctures occur between different developmental stages. Historical materialism is one conception of this sort, but social Darwinism can also be put in this category. Here history is also understood as social change and has, as it were, a curving upward form, but punctuated by phases of rapid transmutation. The view I want to defend is quite different from either of these others. The equation of history with social change must be resisted, as both logically mistaken and empirically wanting. If history is temporality — the temporal constitution of social events — it is clearly false to identify it with change. Moreover, human history does not look like what Gellner has called a 'world growth story'.[53] For most of the extremely long period during which human beings lived in small hunting and gathering societies, history was stasis rather than change. If there are certain overall developmental patterns over that period, they are slight compared to the continuity in societal forms. The advent of class-divided societies — agrarian states or 'civilizations' — marks a distinctive break with what went before. These are, as Lévi-Strauss says, 'hot cultures', marked by a dynamism unknown previously. With them history both takes on a written form and comes more plausibly to mean social change.

But the pace of change in class-divided societies, particularly

economic or technological change, is very slow when contrasted
to the modern industrialized societies. That is why Marx is not
wholly misguided in speaking of the 'stagnant' nature of the
Asiatic states of traditional India and China. His mistake was to
suppose that the West, prior to the origins of capitalism, was any
more dynamic, or 'progressive' than other class-divided societies
have been. It is only with the arrival of capitalism, more
particularly industrial capitalism, that the pace of social change
becomes really dramatic. Over a period of, at most, no more than
three hundred years, the rapidity, drama and reach of change
have been incomparably greater than any previous historical
transitions. The social order — increasingly a genuinely global
system but not an intrinsically pacific one — initiated by the
advent of modernity is not just an accentuation of previous trends
of development. In a number of specifiable and quite fundamental
respects, it is something new.

In speaking of a discontinuist conception of modern history,
therefore, I do not wish to deny the importance of transitions or
ruptures in previous eras. I do, however, want to claim that,
originating in the West but becoming more and more global in
their impact, there has occurred a series of changes of
extraordinary magnitude when compared with any other phases
of human history. What separates those living in the modern
world from all previous types of society, and all previous epochs
of history, is more profound than the continuities which connect
them to the longer spans of the past. This does not mean that we
cannot draw upon the study of pre-existing types of society to try
better to understand the nature of the world in which we now
live. But it does imply that the contrasts which can be made will
often prove more illuminating than the continuities that may be
discerned. It is *the* task of 'sociology', as I would formulate the
role of that discipline at any rate, to seek to analyse the nature of
that novel world which, in the late twentieth century, we now find
ourselves.

In the preceding volume of this work I have discussed at some
length the nature and origins of the discontinuities that separate
us from the past and I shall not repeat that analysis here.[54] These
discontinuities stretch from changes in the intimate textures of
day-to-day life to transformations of a truly world-wide kind. In a
period of three hundred years, an insignificant slither of human

history as a whole, the face of the earth has been wiped clean. That is to say, traditional societies of all types have become more or less completely dissolved. To date these changes as originating somewhere in the sixteenth or seventeenth centuries — although developing in a maximal way only later — might seem imprecise. But we should see these against the background of the whole sweep of human history and in relation to major processes of transition of other sorts. We are able to fix them much more exactly, for example, than most episodes involving the origins of agrarian states, even though their consequences have in my view been more profound.

The formation of the nation-state, and the associated nation-state system, is an expression of the dislocations of modern history. It is one such expression among others and in focusing primarily on it I do not pretend to provide a comprehensive treatment of modernity. But attempting to understand the development of the nation-state as a specific institutional form inevitably means embarking upon a broad spectrum of tasks. Among other things it is necessary to look into the nature of capitalism, its relation to industrialism, and the connections that have existed between both and the origins of the nation-state in the West. As a prior consideration, however, we have to make clear the distinctive features of modern states by contrasting them to earlier forms of state organization.

2
The Traditional State: Domination and Military Power

City and Countryside in Traditional States

Of the various ways of classifying traditional states,[1] or class-divided societies, that offered by Eisenstadt is as useful as any. He distinguishes between city-states; feudal systems; patrimonial empires; nomad or conquest empires; and 'centralised historical bureaucratic empires'.[2] All such classifications are somewhat insecure, since there are various possible overlaps between these categories. Thus, the differentiation between patrimonial and bureaucratic empires is not a hard and fast one, and it would be difficult to find a historical case that did not in some part fit into both. China, in some ways the type-case of a bureaucratic empire, has for large periods of its history been commonly regarded as a variant of patrimonialism. For my purposes here, however, it will be sufficient to concentrate on the smallest and largest types — the city-state and the large agrarian empire. It might seem as though the existence of a category of 'nomad empires' is a major source of difficulty for the view that the city is the main power container involved in class-divided societies. However, examination of the character of such empires tends to substantiate the thesis rather than place it in question. Nomad societies have managed to conquer large swathes of land in the sense of subduing the people living on them. But wherever they have sought directly to administer a population in a regularized fashion, rather than merely pillaging its resources, the resultant system has tended towards the patrimonial or bureaucratic types, with fixed settlements playing as important a role as anywhere else. The most significant possible exception is, in fact, Egypt of the Old Kingdom. Although the archaeological evidence on the matter has to be regarded as inconclusive, some have claimed that the city was never developed in more than a relatively rudimentary way there.[3]

Sjoberg is the main advocate of the view that the city in class-divided societies has something of a universal form, architecturally as well as in its social characteristics. As he puts it, 'Our principal hypothesis is that in their structure, or form, preindustrial cities — whether in mediaeval Europe, traditional China, India, or elsewhere — resemble one another closely and in turn differ markedly from modern industrial-urban centres.'[4] I have no dispute with the concluding part of the assertion (I want to strongly emphasize the distinctiveness of modern urbanism), although there is some reason to be cautious about the major proposition. According to Sjoberg, the non-modern city almost always displays certain particular traits. It is walled, and the walls are very often part of a more general set of defence installations. The central area, containing government and religious buildings, usually dominates the skyline visually; it also characteristically contains the main market, located on an open square. The central part also tends to house the residences of the elite, with those in the poorer groups living furthest from the main area.[5] Sjoberg rejects the idea that concentration of commercial activities has normally been the main factor involved in the emergence or growth of traditional cities. This is partly in conscious contra-distinction to Weber, who on the whole gives strong emphasis to the commercial importance of cities. A city, Weber says, 'is always a market centre'.[6] Now the importance of the traditional city as a generator of allocative resources cannot be denied. This is not just because of the marketing and manufacturing enterprises it helps sustain. If there is any validity to Jacobs's claim that urban areas have been the main foci of technological innovation, even in respect of strictly agrarian production, the city has an even more significant role in this respect than is ordinarily thought. But Sjoberg is surely right to stress that the main influence underlying the development of cities is the administrative resources they generate. In his words, 'we must, if we are to explain the growth, spread and decline of cities, comment upon the city as a mechanism by which a society's rulers can consolidate and maintain their power.'[7]

Although Sjoberg is justified in pointing to overall similarities that distinguish traditional cities from modern urbanism, there is no doubt he exaggerates their uniformity. They definitely tend to resemble one another more than they do the modern urban conglomeration, but Sjoberg's characterization is too generalized. Moreover, cities in class-divided societies usually exist in networks with other power-containers or generators of power. As Jacobs argues, quite substantial settlements have probably normally been found even among hunters and gatherers, and have co-existed with cities in larger societies. Such 'villages' may be larger than the settlements that would be categorized as cities in Sjoberg's formulation, forming marketing centres for the trade of agrarian or craft products.

Non-modern cities have not always been walled, as I have previously mentioned. This was sometimes the case, for example, in the early phase of existence of the traditional Chinese state, although during the whole of the Chou period cities had walls.[8] The city is not the oldest type of fortress nor, of course, the only type. Fortified villages have been common in many parts of the world. According to Weber (although this is disputable) the palisaded village was not generally the forerunner of the walled town. Rather, the latter developed more often from the seigneurial castle — a fortress housing a lord, his warriors and retinue.[9] Where bureaucratic empires have declined, giving rise to some sort of quasi-feudal system, castles, whether or not linked to manorial estates, often remain as significant centres of power while cities lose their grandeur.

> Castle construction and castle-seated princes were diffused universally. The early Egyptian sources knew the castle and castle commanders, and we can be almost certain that these castles housed just as many petty princelings. In Mesopotamia the development of the later territorial Kingdoms was preceded, to judge by the oldest documents, by a castle-seated princedom such as existed in western India in the time of the Vedas and such is as probable for Persia at the time of the oldest [Zoroastrian] Gathas. In northern India, on the Ganges, the castle apparently was universally dominant during the period of disintegration.[10]

Sjoberg argues that in non-modern societies, including European feudalism, the dominant classes are always urban. Again there is something in this claim that is correct. In general it is true that wherever states have maintained a sufficient degree of cohesion to be worth calling 'states' at all, it is the city rather than the rural area that has been the pre-eminent locale in which the members of the dominant class are to be found. But there is no point in stretching the claim too far because, after all, there has been a considerable range of variation in the composition and distribution of upper classes in traditional societies. Sjoberg is too anxious to stress the independent, self-sufficient character of the city as an administrative centre in agrarian states. This is not the position I advocate here, which is more complex, and does not depend upon over-straining the sorts of generalizations that can be made about non-modern cities. The city is the main power-container generating authoritative resources in class-divided societies, but it does not follow from this that each city is itself a defined and coherent administrative centre. There is never more than a small minority of the population living in cities in non-modern societies. The modes of domination found within them always depend upon the relations between cities and the countryside, not only upon the internal composition of cities themselves. Cities that have a high degree of administrative concentration and military autonomy tend for the most part only to be found in city-states, whose centres they are. The 'city communes' of post-feudal Europe are in many ways distinctive, and certainly should not be used as a yard-stick against which to assess the administrative capabilities offered by cities in general. Chinese cities are actually much more typical in this respect. In traditional China, villages were in some part 'self-administered', but cities were not, or at least were not to the same degree.[11]

The small proportion living in cities in class-divided societies is indicative of the low level of administrative power which the traditional state was able to achieve over its subjects. Ever since the term 'oriental despotism' was coined by Western observers looking East, there has been a strong tendency to assume that bureaucratic empires are highly centralized societies. But this presumption is fundamentally mistaken if such societies are compared with modern states. Consider, for example, the Incas. Some have seen the Inca empire as a prime example of a despotic state (occasionally, even an early form of a state socialist society). Baudin has linked an analysis of Inca society to a critique of modern socialism in a way somewhat akin to Wittfogel.[12] But this type of view is misleading indeed, not only because it rests upon a factually erroneous description of the Inca state, but because of the implication that modern states merely accentuate features of traditional ones. As Moore and others have shown, the scope of imperial power was very much less in Peru than has frequently been suggested, the society being largely segmental and localized in character. As in other class-divided societies, most trade consisted of local marketing; there was no more a strong economic interdependence between the areas covered by the state administration than there was political integration.[13]

Similar conclusions have to be drawn in the case of the Aztecs, the Maurya, Gupta and Mogul imperial states in India, and ancient Egypt. The latter of these is worthy of comment since, like the Inca state, it has often been seen as a particularly solidly concentrated social formation. Weber in fact draws direct comparisons between Egypt and the rationalizing tendencies of modern capitalism, likely to be exacerbated by socialism. A 'shell of bondage' is being fabricated 'which men will perhaps be forced to inhabit some day', and in which they will be 'as powerless as the fellahs of ancient Egypt'.[14] Egypt is like 'a single tremendous *oikos* ruled patrimonially by the pharaoh',[15] Weber says. As early as the Old Kingdom, 'the entire people was pressed into a hierarchy of clientage', this being 'propelled by the overriding importance of systematic centralised river-regulation and of construction projects during the long season in which the absence of agricultural work permitted drafting on an unprecedented scale'.[16] But such a view does not accord with the findings of more recent archaeological work on ancient Egypt. Bureaucratic centralization was much less developed than Weber implies and the projects of irrigation control he mentions were both sporadic and far removed from the experience of the majority of the population. The effective power of the pharaohs, even when at its height, was probably less than that sometimes wielded by imperial rulers elsewhere.[17]

Similar points can be made about city-states, at the other end of the scale in terms of their size from bureaucratic empires. City-state organization precludes the existence, within the relevant territorial areas, of centralized political authority of a broad kind. It might be thought that the city-state, being small and confined, can achieve a more comparable degree of concentration of authoritative resources to the modern nation-state. However such is not the case. City-states have, indeed, characteristically been small, rarely covering more than several hundred square miles. Where they have expanded to include neighbouring states or peoples, the expansion has either been transitory or the state has developed towards the patrimonial/bureaucratic types. Small though it is, the city-state typically only develops a low level of direct administrative control over its subjects. A recent comparative study of city-states has indicated that there are certain general characteristics which they display.[18] City-states, like larger agrarian states, sustain marked distinctions between their urban centres and rural areas, with the large majority of the population living and working in the second rather than the first. The city environments are small. Thus, for example, Sumerian Erech measured less than two square miles; the centre of Athens was less than one square mile. Tiny though they may be in terms of the standards of modern urban life, such centres form the locus of state institutions. As the authors of the study put it: 'Although the central space was narrowly confined, it was from that core that the life of the city-state was directed. In modern terms, this centre would be known as the capital city inasmuch as the machinery of government was concentrated within the walls separating city from countryside. In all five cultures [studied], walls were a normal feature serving to define the centre of the city-state.'[19]

The small size of the administrative organizations of the city-state, together with the restricted nature of its military power, ensures that the level of control over most of its population is normally no greater than that of the large-scale bureaucratic empire. One specific feature of city-states, however, is that they tend to be found only where there are other city-states in relatively close proximity. They make up a type of loosely formed state system, differing both from those involving larger states, and from the modern nation-state system. Although the city-states within a local system may share more or less the same culture and the same language, the endeavour to maintain separate political and economic identity takes precedence over influences that might tend towards the combination of all within a single overarching state. More or less chronic inter-state warfare is more common than prolonged efforts to secure unity. When they are absorbed into larger imperial states city-states seem often to sustain a considerable degree of autonomy within the larger society, preserving some of their forms of government.[20]

Surveillance and Administrative Power

Although there are exceptions to the generalization that the rise of non-modern states has everywhere been accompanied by the development of writing (most notably, the Incas), the association is much too strong to be simply happenstance.[21] To understand the nature of the connection, the comments I made previously about the nature of writing need to be expanded. Although it seems a very long way from questions of the philosophy of language to the analysis of power in traditional civilizations, consideration of the former can in fact contribute a good deal to the elucidation of the latter. Many linguists have regarded writing as no more than an extension of speech, the transcription of utterances to transcriptions on stone, paper or other material substances that can be marked.[22] But neither the first origins of writing in ancient civilizations nor a philosophical characterization of language bears out such a view. Writing did not originate as an isomorphic representation of speech, but as a mode of administrative notation, used to keep records or tallies. Rather than being treated, on a more abstract plane, as a material representation of speech, writing must be recognized as having its own distinctive characteristics. Some philosophers, dissatisfied with the usual view that the basic form of language is oral communication, have made the case that it is actually writing rather than speech which discloses the primary characteristics of language.[23] But it is more plausible to see speech and writing as two related, but specifiably independent, modes of language-use. We can draw profitably upon the work of Ricoeur to illuminate this.[24] While recognizing the importance of structuralist thought to showing how language cannot consist only of syntagmatically ordered utterances, Ricoeur pursues the critique of Saussure developed by Benveniste and others.[25] Benveniste distinguishes between a 'semiotics of the sign' and a 'semantics of the sentence'. The one cannot be reduced to the other, although they are necessarily connected. While the study of signs is a legitimate form of enquiry, it cannot in and of itself cope with the semantics of the sentence, because a sentence consists of more than an arrangement of signs. Sentences have a predicative character, which not only gives them meaning, but furnishes them with the capacity of reference. Sentences are the basic units of discourse, the means whereby 'language transcends itself, taking hold of the world, of the self and of others and expressing this hold in language'.[26]

Now discourse can be spoken or written and, as writing, it makes up a text. Texts are totalities, not just combinations of sentences, any more than sentences are combinations of signs. Whereas spoken discourse by its very nature is evanescent, its duration being limited to the circumstances of its production, texts assume a fixity that endures across time and space. In speech what an actor means to say, and the meaning of what is said, are ordinarily one and the same — speakers employ all sorts of 'methodological devices' to ensure that this is so.[27] But, as Ricoeur says, the text escapes 'the finite horizon lived by its author' and 'what the text says now matters more than what the author meant to say.'[28] The author of a text may intend it for a particular audience, and intend to convey certain meanings through it. But in principle the text can reach audiences quite removed from its author, and can be read in ways which he or she might never have imagined. Texts also become separated from the moorings that 'ostensive reference' provides for spoken discourse. The communication of meaning in situated action depends in a basic way upon shared awareness of elements of the context of that action.[29] This is lacking in the case of texts, and is substantially responsible for the hermeneutic issues which their existence immediately brings into being. At the same time as it is no longer saturated by ostensive reference, however, a text opens up new referential possibilities denied to oral communication. Since they do not depend for their interpretation upon the situation in which they are produced, texts open up new horizons or 'project new ways of being'.[30]

Writing does not begin as texts, even if all written documents necessarily have a 'textual aspect' to them. That is to say, the earliest examples of writing do not consist of sentences, even in some very rudimentary sense of 'sentence'. Mesopotamian picture-writing, as it first developed, was employed almost wholly to make inventories of various sorts.[31] In other words, it was made up of discrete signs, not of semantic units. It is probably the case that Sumerian characters originally were not marks on clay at all, but actual objects used for counting and classifying. Although the Incas did not develop a system of writing, and probably did not have a recorded calendar, they did possess a counting measure capable of quite sophisticated calculating and tallying procedures, using knotted cords (*quipus*) as a mnemonic device. There is some general similarity between the Inca artifacts and those found in Sumer, although the actual form is different. At Uruk clay labels were discovered with holes through them through which strings were drawn so that they could be used for counting and recording. Objects were also tagged according to whom they belonged. It seems that these various objects later were represented in pictorial form, becoming the basis of Sumerian writing.[32]

Lists, as Goody puts it, antedate texts in the development of writing, and administrative lists precede lexical ones.[33] If writing originated in the perceived need for facilitating the storage and distribution of allocative and authoritative resources, it also made for other possibilities that its inventors may not in any way have anticipated. 'Lexical lists' — word lists used for study and practice — existed in Mesopotamia as early as the third millenium BC, and some five hundred years later more specialized 'text lists' are found which, according to one commentator, represent the first steps towards the creation of an encyclopaedia. That is to say, writing became connected to the categorizing and discovery of knowledge in a systematic fashion.[34] How quickly the script employed became a conventional and phonetic system of writing is disputed, but some have claimed that this was a relatively early development. Whatever is the truth of the matter, written materials that are discernibly 'texts' in Ricoeur's sense do not begin to proliferate until the time at which Sumerian was no longer a spoken language, but a 'classical' or 'dead' one. Goody provides a classification of tablets excavated at Ugarit, written mostly in a local Semitic language in script that has an alphabetic form. Out of a total of 508 documents, the categories are as shown in table 1.[35]

Table 1

Categories	Number of tablets
1 Literary texts	33
2 Religious or ritual texts	31
3 Epistles	80
4 Tribute	5
5 Hippic texts	2
6 Administrative, statistical, business documents:	
I Quotas (conscription, taxation, obligations, rations, supplies, pay, etc.)	127
II Inventories, miscellaneous lists and receipts	28
III Guild and occupational lists	52
IV Household statistics and census records	6
V Lists of personal and/or geographical names	59
VI Registration and grants of land	16
VII Purchases and statements of cost or value	5
VIII Loans, guarantees and human pledges	7
7 Tags, labels or indications of ownership	18
8 Other	31

The predominance of organizational materials is very considerable, and although it is always possible that this is the result of selective survival, the ratio accords well with similar finds elsewhere. Few, if any, of these documents are likely to derive from the work of literate scribes representing spoken performances and many probably have no oral equivalents at all.

The implications of writing for the surveillance activities of non-modern states are several. Writing provides a means of coding information, which can be used to expand the range of administrative control exercised by a state apparatus over both objects and persons. As a mnemonic device, even the simplest form of the marking of signs makes possible the regular ordering of events and activities which could not be organized otherwise. Storage of information allows both for the standardizing of a certain range of happenings and, at the same time, allows them to be more effectively co-ordinated. A list is a formula that tallies objects or persons and can order them relative to one another. This is perhaps the most elementary sense in which writing, even in its simplest guise, enhances time-space distanciation, that is, makes possible the stretching of social relations across broader spans of time and space than can be accomplished in oral cultures. Surveillance associated with listing is, however, necessarily rudimentary in terms of the power it can generate, at least when unaccompanied by other types mentioned below. All of these are largely dependent upon the development of conventional script, and the emergence of 'texts' in the full sense of the term.

Written texts, once they have combined signs so as to create a semantic content, no longer just sort events, objects or people, but make descriptions of them possible. Moreover, with the 'autonomy of the text' that Ricoeur analyses so well, such descriptions can endure across the generations. Given the importance of tradition in class-divided societies, texts tend to become 'classical', demanding and receiving continued interpretation by literate specialists, often priests. But the existence of 'classical texts' is also directly involved in the invention of 'history' of which I have spoken earlier. In so far as texts describe 'what went on' plus 'what should go on' in a range of social situations, the 'history' that is written can form a consolidated part of the apparatus of power. What were once a series of customary forms of conduct, informally sanctioned in the daily practices of local communities, become in some part appropriated and administered by the state apparatus. Knowledge of 'history' becomes an interpretative device whereby separate 'authorities' can define what used to be controlled by localized custom. 'Authority' has a double sense which accurately expresses this, because it is possible to be both an authority on a given sphere of knowledge, and to have authority over others. In the manner described here, the two coincide.

Writing that has a semantic content can be used in a direct way to describe and monitor the activities of potentially recalcitrant sectors of a population. The keeping of detailed 'official statistics', plus 'case histories' and other quite exhaustive forms of documentation on the day-to-day lives of individuals is specifically characteristic of modern states and organizations. But more diffuse versions are found in all types of traditional state. 'History' is again involved here — as the term 'case-history' indicates — for information of this type forms files or archives in which 'the present' can be scrutinized in the light of the 'documented past'. Among the Sumerians, for example, records were collected in the form of chronicles of yearly events and activities reported to the gods (and to the state). According to Wiseman, the Babylonian scribes made records of 'the dates of all public events, accessions, deaths, mutinies, famines and plagues, major international events, wars, battles, religious ceremonies, royal decrees and other pertinent facts'.[36]

Writing can be used to formulate codes of conduct, easily the most important aspect of this being the existence of written principles of law. The Sumerian system of law is again a good example. It seems to have been the result of a gradual development out of customary practices, and was formalized into a comprehensive code towards the latter part of the third millenium. It became the basis of the code of Hammurabi, and in turn was in substance taken over by all the Semites — Babylonians, Assyrians, Chaldeans and Hebrews. It was primarily a system of criminal law, based on the *lex talionis*. As in the case of all legal codes in traditional states, it was not linked exclusively to administrative organs of law enforcement — a phenomenon once more exclusive to modern states. The administration of justice was semi-private. It was up to the injured party, or to that party's relatives, to bring the wrongdoer to the judicial authority, and normally also to be responsible for ensuring that the decision of the court was implemented.[37] In cases held directly to affect state security, or to seriously impugn the honour of the gods, direct punitive action was usually taken by state officials or guards without recourse to any public judicial procedure.

I have made the point earlier that surveillance, as the collation and integration of information put to administrative purposes, is closely related to surveillance as direct supervision. It is appropriate at this juncture to further elucidate how this is so, and to relate this analysis to the nature of administrative power. The use of regularized information about social activities and about events in nature, as has been explained, is fundamental to the existence of organizations. Where organizations (in this case, the state) order and co-ordinate human activities, they do so by displacing aspects or spheres of conduct formerly resulting from local community practices. In all societies, traditional and modern, administrative power is the core of domination generated by authoritative resources, although it is not the only such resource that exists (there is in addition power deriving from control of sanctions and from ideology). By administrative power I do not mean primarily, as Foucault does in speaking of 'disciplinary power', that which is founded upon the 'moral education' of those subject to it.[38] Rather, I mean something else which brooks quite large in Foucault's analyses, *control over the timing and spacing of human activities*. Administrative power is based upon the regulation and co-ordination of human conduct through the manipulation of the settings in which it takes place. Surveillance as the coding of information is an essential element of such power, because the mnemonic and distributional advantages it allows over purely oral culture are immense. But administrative power can only become established if the coding of information is actually applied in a direct way to the supervision of human activities, so as to detach them in some part from their involvement with tradition and with local community life. In class-divided societies, opportunities for connecting the two forms of surveillance are distinctly limited, compared with modern states. Surveillance in the sense of supervision is only possible in restricted settings, due to their segmental character; and even then it rarely involves the precise co-ordination of timing and spacing that is found in modern organizations.

In some agrarian states, irrigation schemes have been a significant feature of production, and in *Oriental Despotism* Wittfogel associates many of the organizational accomplishments of traditional states with the administration of such schemes.[39] Without again going over what is by now much-trampled ground, it is clear enough that Wittfogel wildly exaggerates the amount of administrative centralization involved in the building or the day-to-day working of irrigation projects. Leach, Eberhard and others have offered contrary views which are much more persuasive than that adopted by Wittfogel. Leach indicates that, while there were irrigation works of considerable size and overall complexity in Sinhala, these did not form a unified system and they were neither constructed to a general administrative plan nor co-ordinated in their regular use. The works were built up gradually, without the large-scale mobilization of labour-power, over a period of some one and a half millenia.[40] Eberhard shows that the irrigation systems in China were similarly quite decentralized; in their working they were regulated not by state officials but by elders appointed by the local communities.[41]

I have mentioned in the opening chapter that public construction projects, found in some degree in all traditional states, are inevitably marginal to the main arenas of production. Although the scale of some of these buildings is extraordinary, given the rudimentary technology available, the methods used to construct them were only in the crudest sense instances of administrative power. The pyramids of the Egyptian Old Kingdom provide an example. A massive amount of human labour-power was expended in their construction. Herodotus estimated that 100,000 individuals were employed for twenty years to build the single pyramid of Khufu at Gizeh, which is by any standards a massive edifice. It is made of some two million limestone blocks, fitted together with considerable precision. But does the preciseness of its engineering express an organizational co-ordination of labour of equal complexity? The answer is almost certainly not. Most of the labour used in building the pyramids was derived from massed groups of workers, subjected to appalling conditions of forced work, engaged in quarries or in the transportation of the stones. The synchronizing of production was achieved largely through coercion, save in the case of the skilled workers putting the finished blocks in place.[42]

The main instances in which anything resembling modern administrative power organized on a regular basis is to be found in traditional states are in military and religious settings and slave-labouring in mines and on plantations. Slave plantations and mines have certainly often involved direct and continuous supervision concerned with the co-ordination of production. But again, for the most part, such circumstances are clearly distinguishable from the integration of time, space and authority characteristic of modern administrative power. It is only in the other cases mentioned, in the army and in aspects of religious organization, that we find anything closely resembling modern administrative power and, even there, relatively infrequently. I shall have more to say about the military in a subsequent section of this chapter. So far as administrative power in religious organizations goes, it might be pointed out that this has often been most developed when those organizations have been clearly demarcated from involvement in the rule of the state, as in monasteries of various sorts.[43]

The expansion of surveillance in its two primary senses is, without doubt, of key importance to the formation and sustained existence of all types, of non-modern state. However, the concentrated focusing of surveillance as 'governmental' power is largely, if not completely, a phenomenon of the modern state. As such, it is inherently involved in the capability of the state to co-ordinate its administrative scope in a precise fashion with the bounds of a clearly delimited territory. All states have a territorial aspect to them but, prior to the advent of the nation-state, it is unusual for the administrative power of the state apparatus to coincide with defined territorial boundaries. In the era dominated by the nation-state, however, this has become virtually universal.

Territoriality, State, Society

Geographical authors have devoted a great deal of attention to discussing the boundaries of states, although such analyses have not become well known in the literatures of anthropology or of sociology. Ratzel, acknowledged as one of the founders of modern geography, elaborated a theory of boundaries which, in common with much of the sociological literature of the time, saw states as akin to biological organisms.[44] According to him, states are surrounded by 'border margins', consisting of three zones. Two are the peripheral areas of adjoining states, and the other is an 'autonomous zone' merging the social and political characteristics of the two states. Ratzel's work has many interesting features. He argues that the margins of the territory of a state have to be regarded as just as important elements of the state as are its more central regions, the borders being an expression and measure of state power.[45] Boundaries are dynamic aspects of a state, with all vigorous states seeking to expand their spatial spread, and declining ones contracting to physically easily defensible land-contours.

Besides having a markedly deterministic flavour, Ratzel's ideas are, however, unsatisfactory as a generalized theory. In distin-guishing the territoriality of traditional states from nation-states, it is essential to see that the 'frontiers' of the former are significantly different from the 'borders' that exist between the latter. In political geography the term 'frontier' is used in two senses. It means either a specific type of division between two or more states, or a division between settled and uninhabited areas of a single state.[46] The second of these can be usefully further subdivided. 'Primary settlement frontiers' are those involved where a state is expanding outwards into territory previously either having virtually no inhabitants, or populated by tribal communities. 'Secondary settlement frontiers' are those within the territory of a state only sparsely inhabited for one reason or another — usually because of the infertile nature of the land or because of the general inhospitality of the terrain. In all cases, 'frontier' refers to an area on the peripheral regions of a state (not necessarily adjoining another state) in which the political authority of the centre is diffuse or thinly spread.[47] A 'border', on the other hand, is a known and geographically drawn line separating and joining two or more states. While there may be, and often are, 'mixed' social and political traits displayed by groups living in border areas, those groups are distinguishably subject to the administrative dominion of one state or the other. Borders, in my view, are only found with the emergence of nation-states.

The physical environment has manifestly been important in influencing where the frontiers of traditional states have lain and where the borders of nation-states have been drawn. Deserts, seas, mountain chains, swamp or marshland, rivers and forests have all formed frontiers in traditional states. Such natural boundaries have often been primary settlement frontiers. However, 'wildernesses' have frequently been inhabited by warlike groups who have, on occasion, swept outwards to take over areas administered by pre-existing states. States which have either overrun natural boundaries, or have not in the first place been enclosed by such boundaries, have sometimes set up artificial partitions of some sort. The Kafa Kingdom of Ethiopia was surrounded by fabricated barriers in those areas where there were no natural frontiers. While the Kafa frontier to the north was formed by a river, the rest of the territory was encircled by broad, deep ditches, defended by wooden palisades. The only points of entry were through gates, which were fortified with high ramparts and with several lines of entrenchment.[48] Such artificial divides are relatively rare, because they are expensive to install and difficult to maintain; and this manner of construction is only a feasible mode of defence in small societies. In larger imperial systems, the two most renowned examples of artificial boundary-making are, of course, the walls built by the Romans, and the Great Wall of China. Thanks mainly to the work of Lattimore, we know a good deal about the latter, and there are a variety of sources of information about the former.[49] The walls built by the Romans seem to have been put up wholly for defensive purposes — some of the 'barbarians' took the hint and built their own earth-works at a remove from the Roman constructions.[50] The Romans tended to treat their walls as primary settlement frontiers, establishing farmers in the adjoining areas, *agri limitanei*. But although self-sufficient, their main task was to provide a preliminary line of defence and communication. The Great Wall was apparently built to keep out foraging nomads, but had the additional role of helping to limit the mobility of various peripheral groups inside.

It would be a mistake to suppose, even where the boundaries of traditional states are physically clearly marked by such installations (something which is in any case rare), that these are something akin to borders in the modern sense. In non-modern states, walled boundaries remain frontiers, well outside the regularized control of the central authorities; the larger the state, the more this is the case. In neither Rome nor China did the walls correspond to the limits of 'national sovereignty' in the sense in which that term is applied today. Rather, they formed the outer extension of an 'in-depth' defensive system. Modern state borders may coincide with natural defensive boundaries, but while this may be important to the fortunes of a state in war, it is irrelevant to the character of borders. Borders are nothing other than lines drawn to demarcate states' sovereignty. As such, it is irrelevant to their nature what types of terrain (or sea) they pass over. As demarcations of sovereignty, they have to be agreed upon by each of the states whose borders they are. In a few traditional states, such as the Kafa and their neighbours, there have been some mutual agreements about where boundaries lie; but these have been unusual rather than the norm, have applied in small states rather than large ones, and have nothing of the precision with which borders are drawn today.

Traditional states, especially the larger ones, contained many secondary settlement frontiers. If these were normally in areas offering physical limitations to stable habitation, there are numerous known instances where settlements were deliberately installed in order to alter the socio-political make-up of a particular *milieu*. In conquest empires it was generally the case that indigenous populations would be left to carry on their pre-existing patterns of conduct — even their established administrative system being left largely untouched — so long as they paid their taxes or delivered the necessary tribute. But quite often the newly arrived conquerors made systematic attempts to displace some segments of the population and settle the areas with others.[51]

City-states have everywhere been both territorially and culturally the most internally homogeneous of class-divided societies — simply a result of their very limited size. Larger societies have almost always been internally strongly differentiated regionally, the regional differentiations being cultural ones as well. The cultural heterogenity of regional communities exists in addition to the cultural distance at which dominant classes stand from the mass of the population.[52] Writing of the Ottoman Empire, Gibb and Bowen comment upon 'the paradox' of

> a government, generally apathetic, unprogressive, and careless of the welfare of its subjects, and often arbitrary and violent in its dealings with them, and a society upon whose institutions and activities such a government had little or no effect. The explanation is to be found in the very lack of a complex, all-embracing political organisation . . . We may visualise Moslem society as composed of two co-existing groups, the relations between which were for the most part formal and superficial. One group formed the governing class of soldiers and officials, the other the governed class of merchants, artisans and cultivators. Each was organised internally on independent lines, and neither group interfered with the organisation of the other in normal circumstances.[53]

Let me summarize the discussion up to this point. Traditional states depend upon the generating of authoritative and allocative resources, made possible by the intersecting relations between city and countryside. The development of surveillance capabilities is the basis of the administrative power created by states as organizations. Traditional states are, however, fundamentally segmental in character, with only limited sustained administrative authority of the state apparatus. The fact that such states have frontiers, including secondary settlement frontiers, rather than boundaries is indicative of their relatively weak level of system integration. It is essential to emphasize how different, as 'social systems', traditional states are from modern ones. Because of their internal heterogeneity, a case can be made for regarding larger traditional states as 'composed of numerous societies'.[54] However, I think it reasonable to continue to use the term 'society' in a generic way, with the proviso that the administratively unified modern state be understood as highly exceptional, not the type-case against which others should be measured.

Military Power in Traditional States

Whether or not most non-modern states have their origins in war,[55] no one can doubt that warfare has been a leading preoccupation of dominant classes everywhere. This, of course, was the very foundation of the contrasts between 'military' and 'industrial' societies fastened upon by nineteenth-century social thinkers. Some have questioned whether warfare is found at all in some, or even most, tribal cultures. It has been said (by Marvin Harris) that 'any anthropologist can recite the names of a handful of "primitive" peoples who are reported never to wage war.'[56] However, it is not clear if a single one of these examples can be regarded as reliably authenticated. Some seem to refer to cases of refugees who, precisely as a result of warlike conflict with their neighbours, have been driven into remote areas or become demoralized by coming off the worse in the encounters. 'Primitive war' is undeniably different in certain main respects from the wars conducted by more organized political communities. Sometimes, although by no means universally, it is more ritualized and restrained than warfare in other contexts.[57] But the bulk of both the archaeological and anthropological evidence leads to the conclusion that war, i.e. armed combat between groups in which physical violence is used by or on behalf of one community against another, is prominent in all types of human society.[58] 'Primitive war' tends to involve little specialization, however, apart from a gender division of labour. All able-bodied and younger men (very occasionally, women) are warriors, their weaponry often being exactly the same as that used for the hunting of game. In class-divided societies, by contrast, there is always a distinct 'military' agency — although supplemented in various ways for the actual engagement of war — and a development both of administrative power and weaponry.

In accounts of social change linked to, or influenced by, historical materialism, it is often suggested that technological innovations bring about the transformation of societies through their direct effects on production. A more accurate emphasis would be upon the application of technological development to weaponry. As McNeill points out, in a certain sense the 'industrialization of war' is as old as civilization: the development of bronze metallurgy made possible the weapons and the armour that is as characteristic of class-divided societies as are writing or organized religion.[59] However, as he then also goes on to stress, the parallel with modern industrialization is only a limited one. There was no permanent co-ordination of the means of waging war with technological development, as there is in the modern world. There was no 'weapons production industry'. Arms and armour were usually constructed only slowly, with elaborate attention to detail. Once made, they lasted for lengthy periods of time, and armourers always remained few compared to warriors — the latter, in non-nomadic communities, generally also being only a tiny minority of the population.

Warfare is such a prevalent feature of traditional states of all types that it is easy to assume that all such societies display equivalent militaristic traits. Certainly there are many examples of the more or less continuous waging of war over very long periods. During the whole time of existence of the Roman Empire, the Temple of Janus, opened only during war, is reputed to have been closed just for two very short intervals of under a year each. V. Gordon Childe, speaking of the early civilizations of the Near East, remarks that 'quite certainly Oriental monarchies were created by war, maintained by continual war, and eventually destroyed by war.'[60] In the city-state study quoted earlier, it is written that 'interstate warfare between city-states was so normal that it can be defined as a natural attribute.'[61] Discussing India, Weber observes that it 'remained inconceivable to secular and religious Hindu literature' that a monarch 'should ever fail to consider the subjugation of his neighbours by force or fraud.'[62] However it is not easy to define what 'a condition of war' is, since manifestly it is not possible to engage in direct armed combat continuously, even when 'open hostilities' exist between states. Moreover, there is no paucity of examples of relatively peaceful periods in the history of non-modern states, although it is true that these were usually characteristic of states removed for one reason or another from neighbours of a threatening kind. Thus ancient Egypt was not engaged in major wars during extended phases of its history, although under the reign of Thut-mose the Third there began a period of intense military expansionism.[63]

While it is true that very many class-divided societies have been pervaded by militaristic values, at least among their ruling groups, there are wide differences in this respect, and it would not do to underplay them. The Assyrians are towards one extreme. Some of the main aspects of administrative power found in the military for some three millenia afterwards were first established in the Assyrian armies. Assyria had a large standing army, with clear and ordered divisions of authority and promotion. It has been said of Assyria that 'the state was a great military machine', in which 'the army commanders were at once the richest and most powerful class in the country,' and that 'the military establishment itself represented the last word in preparedness.'[64] The Assyrians also pioneered a range of new and intimidating military equipment, including iron long swords, heavy bows and lances, wheeled fortresses and siege devices. However, the Assyrian empire at its peak lasted no more than a century, and when it fell its collapse was sudden and complete.[65] Almost certainly no such a devotedly militaristic society could achieve the long-term stability found in some of the other 'world civilizations'.

In some cases, most particularly China at certain periods of its history, states have moved away considerably from militarism. During the T'ang period, China was relatively secure from serious threat of external attack, and civilian control prospered. The emperor retained ultimate military control in principle but there was, nonetheless, a clear differentiation between the military and civil authority. The army was small, certainly relative to the overall size of the society, and military virtues were accorded rather low status. There are few comparable examples of non-modern states, indeed, where the military were looked upon with such condescension by others in the ruling circles. They ranked bottom in the five categories into which the social order was categorized, along with bandits, thieves and beggars. The scholar-gentry group was at the top, followed by farmers, artisans and merchants. Military leaders were not usually given political office, and troops and their commanders were rotated in order to diminish their solidarity.[66]

China is one of the very limited number of large traditional states where the role of the army was as much concerned with internal policing as it was with repelling invaders or expanding the terrain of the state. But in China, as elsewhere, the claim to monopoly of control of the means of violence on the part of the state apparatus was never more than partially successful. Only in city-states could this be said to be the case and these, as has been mentioned, could not manage to enlarge the territorial scope of their power without losing the characteristics that defined them. In all larger class-divided societies, the success of the state in claiming monopoly of the means of violence was limited by two factors: the manner in which the military was organized, and the relative slowness of transport and communication.[67] The difficulties of maintaining large standing armies over lengthy periods were more or less intractable for the rulers of traditional states. All non-modern states have assembled an inner core of trained, regular soldiery, but were forced to supplement this in numerous different ways to put down rebellions and conduct foreign wars. Levies, the raising of slave armies, the gathering of bonded serfs and, especially, the recruitment of mercenaries have been some of the means used to such ends. In most of these cases, including mercenary armies, payment was in kind rather than in the form of monetary compensation and was usually provided through booty gained during the course of whatever conflict was being fought out. Soldiers (the term means literally 'hired man') recruited in these various ways normally were self-equipped, and were loyal to their own leaders rather than to the ruler who conscripted them. Given that centralized military power played a large role in the system integration of traditional states, the rulers of such states were chronically caught in a dilemma. Building up the armed forces meant gathering together recruits and preparing them for military duties. Since it was impossible in most circumstances for such recruits to be welded into a 'bureaucratic army',[68] the military preparation of such soldiery could easily rebound upon those who had instigated it, by creating potentially independent, rival sources of power within the state. On the other hand, without the capability of swelling whatever regular soldiery might exist, the state might either succumb to external attack, or face the internal decay of its rule.

In larger traditional states, therefore, it is almost always the case that significant elements of actual or potential military power exist outside the control of the central state apparatus. Such states typically show a fluctuating tension between centralized control of the means of violence and decentralized military power wielded by local warlords or various sorts of insurrectionary leaders. But there are also other ways in which monopoly of the means of violence eludes the state. Armed tribal groups, bands of nomadic warriors, robbers, brigands and pirates often flourish in areas remote from the purview of urban administration and, not infrequently, even in its immediate vicinity.[69] In so far as these groups are effectively controlled at all, this has to be done locally, since the time needed for transport and communication precludes the deployment of centralized forces, save when threatened by major challenges to state power. The more localized armed forces are encouraged in order to control brigandage, however, the more the centrifugal tendency towards quasi-independent military fiefdoms may be further promoted.

It is misleading to describe the forms of rule typically found in non-modern states as 'government', if 'government' means a concern of the state with the regularized administration of the overall territory claimed as its own. *Traditional states did not 'govern' in this sense.** Their 'polities' were mainly limited to the governance of conflicts within the dominant classes, and within the main urban centres. As John Kautsky says, 'politics' exist 'principally not between classes but within classes. The aristocracy (and those attached to it in the towns, like servants and low-level

---

* Some specific comments should be made here about the city-states of Classical Greece. In most evolutionary interpretations of modernity, the Greek city-states are portrayed as being 'early stages' in the development of modern government, since notions of republicanism, democracy and citizenship appeared first of all there. But this type of viewpoint is very misleading. The 'Classical inheritance' was undeniably highly important in the subsequent emergence of modernity, as filtered through the influence of Rome and as appropriated in post-Renaissance thought. However no other cases exist among the many documented histories of traditional states in which such ideas are developed in a comparable fashion. Greece is specifically untypical of traditional states, not a 'stage' in the progressive creation of modernity. Classical republicanism, Greek or Roman, was not an early anticipation of the 'impersonal sovereign power' found in the theory and practice of the modern state established in sixteenth- and seventeenth-century Europe.

bureaucrats) and each village and to some extent also town organisations like guilds are separate communities or societies and hence constitute separate political arenas.' Military force, or the threat of its use, was normally a highly important basis of the traditional state because the state lacked the means to 'directly administrate' the regions subject to its dominion.

If it is a considerable oversimplification, it is not too far from the truth to say that in larger non-modern states the main overall link connecting the state with the mass of its subjects, i.e. the peasantry, was its requirement for taxation. 'To rule in aristocratic empires is, above all, to tax.'[70] Many taxation systems in traditional states seem to have developed in a fairly immediate way from the taking of booty. Thus, for example, while the Mongols remained nomadic warriors, they supported themselves from the wholesale plunder of the areas through which they passed. When they became the rulers of a territorially fixed empire, they regularized and legalized the practices previously carried out in more haphazard fashion. No doubt they provided certain economic services which helped some sectors of the peasantry — improving the yield of farm-land, for example, by providing fertilizers, through irrigation improvements and building up long-distance trade. But the capability to back up taxation demands through the use of force remained the single most essential element of state power.[71] Of course, levels of taxation have varied widely between different states, regions and periods; prebendal officials in local areas were often more extortionate than those in the higher reaches of the state apparatus. The case of imperial Rome seems fairly representative in this respect. In the core areas in Italy, taxes were relatively low, and largely indirect, but in the Empire they were crushing, in large part because of the inability of the central state apparatus to control the activities of military administrators far from Rome. 'From the beginning', according to one authority, 'the purpose and utility of empire making had been financial, to acquire lands to plunder and then to tax.'[72]

I have mentioned previously that in the ancient Near-Eastern civilizations codified laws were only rarely sanctioned directly by the central state apparatus. This is, in fact, very generally true of class-divided societies as a whole, including most city-states as well as larger imperial formations. Laws may in principle refer to all subjects of the state — with the exception of the ruler, and sometimes his retinue[73] — but their enforcement depends upon agencies that the law-makers rarely directly command. Thus it was aptly remarked of Tsarist Russia that 'There are thousands of laws . . . but there is no law.'[74] China of the T'ang period has often been taken as the model case of a traditional society in which a legal order instituted on the higher levels was able successfully to regulate the conduct of the mass of the population. But this is a double misconception. In contrast to the Roman Empire, which was notable for having a clearly codified system of formal law, the Confucian scriptures were interpreted to indicate that the authority of the state should rest upon moral rather than legal precepts.[75] The emperor was held to supply an example that all others should follow. State officials, as a result of their classical education, were supposed to intuitively recognize the ethical principles they should pursue in dealing with infractions that came to their notice; they were not expected to adhere to formal categories, but to find the best solutions from case to case.[76] But also the precepts of the central authorities had little direct influence upon social relations in local communities.

In class-divided societies, 'deviance' exists and can be controlled by the state in a significant way only among its own personnel and those in regular administrative contact with them. It is not really relevant what the rest of the population do in their day-to-day lives, so long as they do not rebel and are compliant in respect of the payment of taxes (whether taxes be levelled in money, in kind, or as *corvée* labour). The persistence of custom and tradition in village communities, even if strongly divergent from the beliefs and practices of those in ruling circles, usually solidifies state power rather than tending in any way to undermine it. In China, as elsewhere, the villages and smaller towns were effectively self-governing — a point Marx makes in his celebrated discussion of the 'oriental communes',[77] but which Weber elaborates at much greater length in his studies of China. Although in some respects the findings of more recent Sinology do not accord with Weber's interpretation of traditional China, this is not one of them. Whereas, Weber points out, the city was the seat of the mandarin, and not a self-governing entity, the village was the reverse in each of these respects. Village disputes were settled either by the clan groups or by the local temple, with the people actively avoiding the state courts and the state rarely intervening. The temple 'took care of the roads, canals, defence, safety', whereas the state 'ignored the village as a unit, purely fiscal interests repeatedly coming to the fore'.[78]

This should not be taken to imply that day-to-day life for the populace of traditional states was characteristically one of *gemeinschaftlich* security. On the contrary, although this has no doubt varied widely, daily life was very often a much more tenuous, and potentially violent, affair in non-modern states than it is for most of the population in the Western countries today. The peasant subjects of traditional states have frequently lived in conditions of grinding poverty, whatever 'surplus' they produce being appropriated by tax-gathering officials; they have suffered famines, chronic disease and plagues. They have also been open to attack by bandits and armed marauders; and the level of casual violence in day-to-day life seems to have been high. Thus what Le Goff and Sutherland have described for pre-modern France probably applies very widely to the rural communities in class-divided societies. In most of rural France there was chronic gang violence and feuds of various sorts. The state authorities did not particularly concern themselves with attempting to restrain such activities. The authors' conclusion fits closely with evidence from elsewhere. So long as these happenings did not hamper 'the collection of taxes and general order, the state preferred not to interfere'. The old regime, they continue, 'governed largely by not governing; it allowed rural communities to settle the bulk of their own affairs'.[79]

3
The Traditional State: Bureaucracy, Class, Ideology

Bureaucracy and Class Domination

By definition, a 'state' presumes an administrative apparatus, a hierarchy of officials who specialize in administrative tasks (including the arts of war). Patrimonial administration is found where a monarch heads what is essentially a greatly expanded 'household'. The prince surrounds himself with a 'myriad of cupbearers, fauners, spittoon bearers, hairdressers and manicurists, doormen, cooks, miscellaneous entertainers, and many flunkies who perhaps do little but stand around decoratively'.[1] The description is a florid one, and while it conveys the flavour of the sumptuous courts that rulers have often enough relished, it does not indicate the range of less visible and more sober administrative labours linked to the household domain. While all officials are nominally dependent upon the personal whims of the ruler, they often manage to carve out distinct spheres of influence of their own. The inner court is often in practice fairly separate — both in terms of its recruitment and its style of life — from the officials whose work is the necessary basis of its perpetuation. The Ming emperor who dissolved the office of prime minister found himself deluged with documentation; in the course of a week, 1,160 papers concerned with 3,291 different issues were proffered for his personal attention.[2]

Patrimonial office differs from bureaucratic office, among other ways, in so far as there is no differentiation between what is 'vocational' and what is 'private'. Political power is regarded as the personal disposition of the ruler, and anyone who participates in that power does so as a personal right rather than as the 'incumbent of an office'. Centralized bureaucratic empires always retain strongly patrimonial elements and in various quite fundamental respects it is an error to treat modern organizations as extending traits already found in such 'bureaucracies'. What Weber labels generically the 'benefice' exists in different forms in all non-modern organizations (although it does not entirely disappear in modern societies). A benefice is a 'right to office'. Weber distinguishes three types.[3] The first is a benefice in kind, involving an allowance of goods or products from the ruler. A second is the fee benefice, whereby certain payments are made to an official for the enactment of a specific range of tasks. This is not similar to the salary a modern office-holder receives; it is a 'living' which, once having been assigned to a particular individual, can often be inherited by that person's descendants. Finally, and easily of greatest importance, are landed benefices, in which areas of land, including the right to exploit their resources, are made the basis of the official's livelihood. Landed benefices, in other words, normally carry with them prebendal rights. The procurement of landed benefices can have the effect of giving officials a good deal of autonomy from the ruler, because they can become a means of tying the locally administered population directly to those officials rather than to the more remote overlord.

The pre-eminence of the landed benefice and accompanying prebendal prerogatives in the state administration of class-divided societies is important because they are directly relevant to the nature of class domination in those societies. Some have seen the state administrative apparatus, at least in centralized bureaucratic empires, as itself a class. Thus Wittfogel asserts that we must question established concepts of class, which 'emerged in a society [i.e. modern capitalism] that was decisively shaped by conditions of property . . . in fact in modern societies as well as traditional ones state power is the main determinant of class structure.' Certainly in centralized bureaucratic empires, according to Wittfogel, those who run the apparatus of the state are a ruling class, the remainder of the population being subject to their despotic dominance.[4] A somewhat contrary view, advanced by other writers, holds that the concept of 'class' has no effective application at all prior to the modern world. Class formation, according to this standpoint, depends upon the emergence of capital and labour markets in a full-blown fashion.[5] In between, as it were, is the orthodox Marxist conception, in which class domination in feudalism is traced to control of the means of production, while other non-modern states share the characteristics of the 'Asiatic mode of production', suspended at an early stage of evolution and never becoming a class-based social order.

None of these views is acceptable, and in exploring why this is the case, I shall prepare the way for later discussion in this book by offering a categorization of the differences between 'class-divided society', on the one hand and the 'class society' of modern capitalism, on the other. The prebendal form of the allocation of offices in traditional states characteristically ties state administration to the privileges of aristocracy or gentry. That is to say, there are few if any examples of non-modern states in which membership of a distinct 'dominant class' is not locked in to the administrative apparatus of state power. In China, unusually, there were written examinations, which applicants for official positions had to undergo. However, preparation for the examinations required many years of study and was, therefore, only open to the few, even among the literate. Those who gained entry were subject to periodic reappraisal by the higher echelons, and in practice patrimonial favour was vital in securing prebendal assets of any consequence.[6] The administrative apparatus was run by wealthier members of the land-owning class in probably a more restrictive and closed fashion than in most other forms of traditional state. However, to say that in class-divided societies the state apparatus was for the most part staffed at its top levels by the members of land-owning classes is not to identify state power and class formation. Class formation is not determined by state power, as Wittfogel claims. But neither is the power of the state an expression of class domination, as Marxist theory would have it. The privileges of aristocratic/gentry classes depend upon their control of landed estates; the prebendal form of such control links their class position (in differing ways in varying types) with patrimonial features of the state.

These points can be expanded and clarified by means of table 2, which differentiates two types of class system.

In class-divided societies it makes sense to talk of the existence of a 'dominant' or 'ruling' class, but this term has to be hedged with qualifications. The dominant class has a great deal of influence over the apparatus of state, which it staffs. The state in

Table 2

Class-divided society (of all types)	Capitalist society (i.e. the modern Western state)
Ruling class	Governing class
Lack of class conflict	Endemic class conflict
Severance of 'political' and 'economic' life	Separation of 'political' and 'economic' spheres
Low alienability of property	Property freely alienable as capital
Absence of labour markets	Labour markets govern occupational allocation
Sanction: control of the means of violence	Sanction: economic necessity of employment

turn, particularly in the figure of its ruler, has wide-ranging, often 'despotic' power over the fate of the populace. But the state cannot 'govern' an array of activities in the day-to-day life of its subjects in the same fashion as modern states can and do. In capitalist societies, by contrast, the dominant class (the owners of large capital, in whatever form that be held) has access to 'government'. But such access, for reasons to be analysed later, is more indirect than that ordinarily employed by the land-owning aristocracy or gentry in class-divided societies, who rule in a direct way. As I employ it here, therefore, 'governing class' is understood in a rather heterodox fashion.

I use 'class-divided' to characterize traditional states since, although there are massive divisions of wealth and privilege between the dominant class and the majority of the population, class conflict is not a major axis of group formation and not a source of the major transformative influences shaping social change. To say this may seem questionable at first sight, for even many of the most trenchant critics of historical materialism have accepted that there is some validity to Marx's dictum that 'the history of all hitherto existing society is the history of class struggles.'[7] But, rather than the prevalence of class conflict — that is, active class struggle — in class-divided societies, it is its relative absence that is striking. In a certain sense Marx acknowledged this in his characterization of the 'Asiatic mode of production' as a non-class society. But, rather than drawing the conclusion that lack of class conflict is a generic feature of societies other than modern capitalism, he tended to treat the East as a discrepant case, concentrating his attention on the 'main line' of development in Europe from the Graeco-Roman World to feudalism.[8]

It is not difficult to explain why class conflict is relatively rare in class-divided societies (feudalism is no different in this respect). The agrarian communities that form the basis of the production system are in substantial degree autonomous in their day-to-day operation, not only from the state but from each other. Cities sometimes provide arenas for class struggles but these are either between segments of the ruling class or between the rulers and the urban poor. The sheer physical, social and cultural distance between dominant and subordinate classes ensures that they rarely meet in open, collective struggle of any sort. Except in very unusual circumstances, peasant labour is not conducted under the direct surveillance of members of the dominant class. Peasants cannot threaten to 'withdraw their labour', not just because they lack the organizational means to do so, but because they could not then survive, since they produce their own means of subsistence. In the twentieth century, peasant movements have been in the vanguard of social revolutions, thereby disposing of the idea that peasants are always and everywhere 'conservative'. But we certainly cannot generalize back from modern revolutions to peasant rebellions in class-divided societies. Eric Wolf remarks that 'the historical record is replete with peasant rebellions.'[9] We should recognize, however, that their similarity to modern revolutionary movements is remote. It must certainly also be remembered that 'the historical record' covers many centuries and most of the globe, in respect of the existence of class-divided societies; that it is easy to find historical instances does not necessarily mean anything more than that they sporadically occur.

Most studies of peasant rebellions cover periods since the early phase of consolidation of commercial capitalism in the West and elsewhere. Substantive research into the nature and origins of earlier peasant uprisings is relatively difficult to find.[10] One such analysis, however, is that by Eberhard, who has produced a comprehensive inventory of rebellions occurring in Northern China under one of the Wei dynasties.[11] He does, in fact, find that there were a considerable number of peasant uprisings in the area

— some 120 between 397 and 547 AD. As Eberhard says, this helps confute the idea of traditional China as a peaceful and unified state. The oppressive character of the fiscal demands which the state required of the peasantry probably more often made for a smouldering resentment rather than the resigned acceptance of providence that supposedly is the natural condition of the peasant. But the rebellions documented by Eberhard were nearly all transitory, localized uprisings. They had little or no impact on the pre-existing order of things, and seem to have been mainly a sub-category of the general patterns of local violence found in many contexts in non-modern states. Those that did develop in a more chronic way merged with the banditry generally prevalent in the more outlying areas of China, sometimes in this guise eventually producing armies embarking upon quite major conquests.[12] However, where this happened the gang leaders became warlords, adopting the same modes of conduct as the local officialdom they managed to displace.

The main divergence between such phenomena and those characteristic of modern capitalism is not to be found in the distinction between non-modern 'rebellions' and modernizing 'revolutions', important enough though that is. It lies in the 'structural significance' of class conflict in capitalism, lacking in class-divided society. Put briefly, class conflicts in modern capitalism tend to cluster at two 'sites', or types of locale. One is the work-place. In capitalist societies, unlike in traditional states, the work-force is generally subject to direct surveillance, by employers or 'management'. The imposition of discipline in the place of work, in conjunction with the asymmetrical rights which capital-ownership confers, make for chronic struggles in the work-place. 'Industrial conflict' is thus a prime and more-or-less chronic feature of capitalist enterprise. Since, however, control of capital is the underlying basis of authority wielded in the place of work, there is a relation between work-place struggles and broader patterns of political conflict. Class division, in short, is a significant vehicle of political organization in a society in which the 'political sphere' is universalized, not the restricted prerogative of the dominant class that it is in traditional states.[13]

This is an appropriate point at which to move on to consider the question of the connections of the 'political' and the 'economic'. In Marxist thought, and some other types of class theory, it is common to speak of the 'separation of the political and the economic' as one of the chief distinguishing features of capitalism, contrasted to other types of society. This is an issue which goes back to the problem of 'civil society'. With the advent of capitalism, the state supposedly becomes distinct from civil society, although in Marxist thought civil society remains its true progenitor. Now there is something awry here, and this is one of the reasons why I do not use the concept of civil society in this book. For, in class-divided societies, economic activity is normally much more clearly separated from the political arena than is the case in the modern social order. That is to say, even in centralized bureaucratic empires the state 'intervenes' only in a remote way in economic life, the bulk of the peasantry carrying on their labour independently of whatever happens in the political centre.[14] With the development of modern capitalism, and its attendant political form, the nation-state, the political and economic become more closely meshed than ever before.

How should we seek to resolve this issue, which superficially looks to be something of a paradox? The answer depends upon specifying what form the 'political' and the 'economic' take in the two types of society, and how these differentiations relate to the structural principles upon which those types of society are based.[15] In non-modern societies, as Polanyi emphasizes, there is no clear sphere of the 'economy'.[16] In other words, economic activity is not distinct from other forms of conduct and social relation in which producers are involved. The peasant does not recognize a separate sphere of 'work', distinct from what he or she does in the remainder of the day or week; and on the larger scale there is not a demarcated set of 'economic mechanisms' separated from the state. There may be quite developed forms of commercial and trading transactions carried on by independent merchants, but the state is directly involved in the main overall economic tie — the collection of taxes. To this we should add that the scope of the 'political' is concurrently limited. The 'polity' in traditional states is limited to the active participation of the few, whose policies and internal conflicts mainly determine the distribution of authoritative resources. With the arrival of modern capitalism, a definite sphere of the 'economic' — as 'the economy' — comes into being. Traditional states, of course, had economies in the sense that their existence depended upon the generation and distribution of allocative resources. But the modern 'economy' is a (relatively) distinct sphere of activities from other institutional sectors in capitalist societies. 'Distinct' in this context has to be understood as 'insulated' from political life, not as cut off from it. 'Politics', on the other hand, has a broader definition in modern societies (that is, in nation-states), encompassing the mass of the population.

Marx makes the emergence of private property, as the basis of class formation, an essential element of his account of history. However, there are major problems with this idea, upon some of which, in his less evolutionary moments, Marx himself casts a good deal of light.[17] He presumes that in small, tribal communities there is no private property in the means of production, all property being owned communally. Private property is supposed to be an evolutionary development (depending upon the existence of surplus production) out of the original human condition of collective ownership. A plausible conclusion to draw from the anthropology of his time, it is not a conception that has been substantiated by the findings of subsequent anthropological research. This indicates that there is no particular overall relationship between level of 'primitiveness' and the existence of private property; various kinds of private ownership of land are found in settled agricultural communities, as well as commonly held property.

When subject to scrutiny, each of the terms in 'private property' discloses complexities. In modern societies, 'private' property usually means that the owner freely has the right to alienate that property — to sell it to whoever he or she wishes. But in preceding types of society matters often tend to be both more ambiguous in some respects and to place strong limits on alienability on the other. Property implies 'ownership'; and ownership presumes the existence of a legal system through which ownership rights are defined. In societies without writing, what 'law' is remains only vaguely formulated and normally rests substantially upon possession. In most class-divided societies, legal rights of ownership are not defined with anything like the precision they are in modern societies. Roman law is a significant exception in this respect, and one which undoubtedly had a major influence over the emergence of capitalism in Western Europe at a later date. Private landed estates have existed in all non-modern societies, but 'private' here refers more to prebendal rights rather than to ownership rights in the modern sense. Where the landowner has something akin to 'legal rights' over property, these are usually rights to exploit its produce and the workers associated with it. Many different concrete forms of land-tenure are found. Large landowners may own their property in perpetuity, but with virtually no recourse to independent processes of law if the monarch or rival should usurp it. Sometimes the aristocracy or gentry own their lands on lease from the state, contingent upon satisfactory performance of military service. In other systems, peasants own their plots of land, but are still required to give over some of their produce either to the local lord, the state, or both.[18] Ownership rarely implies free alienability, either on behalf of peasants or of large landlords. So far as the peasants are concerned, land can often not be disposed of without the permission of the local community council or elders, or of the representatives of the clan. In the case of the large landowners, the right to disposal of property is normally confined by the obligations involved in holding prebends, as well as by constraints over inheritance.

It is not devoid of all sense to say that, in both class-divided society and in capitalism, class is centred upon property relations, that is to say, in its broadest outlines, ownership versus non-ownership of the means of production. But to issues concerning what 'ownership' is, we have also to add problems to do with what 'property' is (property in the means of production). To say that class division depends upon property relations gives a strong flavour of generality to class systems. However, as Marx in some contexts strongly emphasizes,[19] what 'property' is in non-modern societies is almost entirely different from what is in capitalism. In non-modern states, property means, above all, land. For the producer, this entails a life led close to the rhythms of nature and for the dominant class intrinsic ties with certain landed domains, however much the main tenor of their life may in fact be urban. 'Capital' is property, but of a quite different order to traditional landed property: its pre-eminence within the newly emergent 'economy' implies a whole set of institutional transformations, compared with those characteristics of class-divided society. Capital is essentially property that is freely alienable and, thus, can change hands in a manner governed wholly by its exchange-value. Land as capital is no different from any other commodity, and can be exchanged against any other commodity including, crucially, labour-power.

In both its 'private' and its 'property' aspect, 'private property' as capital thus differs from the private ownership of land in non-modern states. That is why those who have held that 'class' only comes into being with the development of modern capitalism have some plausibility in their view. What a 'free peasant' does in terms of style of life and labour is more or less the same as what a bonded or taxed peasant does,[20] even in societies with large-scale irrigation schemes. But in capitalism, class intrudes into the very heart of the labour process and also connects with some of the main lineaments of the broader society, contributing in a major way to their form. As capital, private property is part of a set of connected economic mechanisms tied to specific modes of social organization and social transformation. The fact that the mass of the population is 'propertyless', that its members have to sell their labour-power to employers to earn a living — a phenomenon unknown on such a scale in any preceding type of society in history — is an essential feature of the class divisions in modern societies. Moreover, the class relations that nestle at the core of modern capitalist production in turn are closely connected (although the nature of these connections must be explored, not merely assumed) with the main traits of the Western nation-state. It is here, I shall argue, that we can in some part trace how it has come about that the continuities of the past have been so radically and irrevocably ruptured in the modern era.

The alienability of labour-power in capitalism is the pre-condition for the existence of a mass 'labour market'. In class-divided societies, regardless of whether in some sense they own the land from which they produce, peasants are 'fixed' to the land they till by a multiplicity of ties. They may 'need' the dominant class to protect them from external threat from the warriors of other states or to provide economic services of valid coinage, irrigation, roads, etc. in so far as their productive activities are not purely local in scope. But they are, nonetheless, in a very different position from propertyless wage-workers, who 'need' employers if they are to make a livelihood at all. The relatively high degree of productive autonomy of the peasant entails that the main sanction which the dominant class must invoke in case of non-compliance is the direct use of force. There is not chronic class confrontation here, but the sporadic pattern of peasant risings followed by military repression previously described. In capitalism something very unusual has come into being, compared with prior history. The dominant class no longer directly controls the means of violence. As Saint-Simon and many other nineteenth-century thinkers remarked, the 'industrialists' are not a military class. In place of the means to force a potentially reluctant peasantry to pay whatever is demanded of them, employers have as their main sanction that 'dull economic necessity' of which Marx speaks. But how does this happen? Why is it that a dominant class has foregone direct control of the means of violence? On this issue Marx is silent. In this respect, however, for reasons already examined, he is no different from other leading thinkers in the social sciences.

Ideology and the Non-Modern State

'The ideas of the ruling class', Marx writes in a celebrated passage, 'are in every epoch the ruling ideas', and he continues: 'The class which has the means of material production at its disposal, has control at the same time over the means of mental production, so that thereby, generally speaking the ideas of those who lack the means of mental production are subject to it.'[21] If we ignore the wider relation of this statement to Marx's historical materialism (and the complexities and inconsistencies in his various discussions of ideology),[22] it serves as a useful starting point for ideological analysis. Disentangling its implications, however, means a significant move away from views which have characteristically been derived from it since Marx, and no doubt from Marx's own position also.

In non-modern states, ideology is characterized by certain quite distinctive features compared with tribal cultures, on the one hand, and modern societies, on the other. The rationalization of religion, to the study of which Weber made such a remarkable contribution, is one such feature. The development of theodicy is closely bound up with the emergence of writing and with the formation of sacerdotal groups; and all class-divided societies have been associated with the existence of some kind of 'professionally' organized religion. The ideological implications, however, are complex and it is ludicrous to suppose, as those making use of the above comments by Marx sometimes have done, that religious belief is no more than the non-material aspect of class domination.

While there are instances of 'warrior-priest' and 'administrator-priest' ruling classes, in most cases state officials and military leaders are distinct groups from the priests, with whose views there may be major differences and tensions. There has been no shortage of religions that have glorified war and which, in so doing, have helped to knit a state cult tightly to the military pursuits of a dominant class. Among the most gory of examples are the Aztecs, whose sacrificial practices demanded a never-ending stream of victims, propelling them to sustain constant wars of imperial expansion. It is said that, in circumstances where there was no major war, the Aztec monarchs agreed with their neighbours to stage mass combats in order to procure captives who could be sacrificed to the gods.[23] At the other extreme, however, there are cases like that of the Maurya prince, Ashoka, who was influenced by Buddhism to abandon war, initiating a major schism within the ruling circles.[24] As Weber points out, the majority of traditional dominant classes have been oriented to military or to other secular values, not to religious ones. 'Aristocratic irreligion', in Weber's term, has been more common than 'warring for the faith'.[25] The modes of behaviour of the warrior have little affinity with the notions of humility, sin and salvation characteristic of Christianity, for example, any more than with the self-negating ideals of the major religions of the East. It is where a belief in an exclusive, universal god is combined with the notion of the moral degeneracy of unbelievers — Weber concentrates particularly upon Islam — that religious enthusiasm can be put directly to work in the cause of territorial aggrandizement.

Rationalized religion is everywhere a 'double-edged' pheno-menon, expressing the polyvalency of the written texts that are its scriptural sources. While some interpretations of a given set of texts may favour the established order, others may contest or threaten it. Priestly groups often maintain a monopoly of interpretation by guarding access to holy texts, by regulating acquisition of the skills of literacy necessary to decipher them, or by strict processes of educational training amongst themselves.

But the construction of a 'cosmically ordered' world always carries its dangers for any ruling class that depends upon religious sources of legitimation. The cosmic order of interpreted religion may inhibit or forbid action that would be in the interests of the domninant class, foster sectional division among ruling groups, or actively stimulate oppositional movements.

It is a mistake to associate even strongly rationalized religion too closely with ethical practices that act to 'standardize' day-to-day behaviour. Even among the most devout of believers custom and tradition, on the one hand, and the secular demands of daily life, on the other, constantly cut across whatever ethical connotations may be associated with religious belief. Christianity is untypical in its emphasis upon moral danger (sin) and moral salvation, and in the detail with which what counts as desirable behaviour and what is turpitude are described. Many religions are little concerned with, or have no impact upon, either the routine activities of day-to-day life or the grand projects of political leadership. The monarch may be a god, but rather than being at the apex of a religious pantheon, he/she may be subordinate to other, supposedly more powerful or influential, deities. Even where a god or gods are malleable to human wishes, through sacrifice or propitiation of some kind, their influence may be small compared with the overriding sway of an impersonal divine force impervious to human persuasion. Sometimes, no doubt, belief in such a force encourages a resignation that might perhaps facilitate acquiescence in the *status quo*. Thus it may be that the divine influence is represented as 'fate', an 'ethically neutral predestination of the fundamental aspects of every man's destiny'.[26] On the other hand, according to context, it may prove to be compatible with just those activities that ethically elaborated types of religious code can inhibit. Thus, according to Weber at least, the very lack of ethical rationalism associated with 'fate' can prove very congenial to the outlook of a warlike aristocracy. While not prone to belief in a beneficent 'providence', a conception of 'destiny' may prove attractive to those whose position is founded upon the practice of warfare.

Rationalized religion tends to be confined in its appeal to the upper echelons of society, differentiated from the rituals and the beliefs of the mass of the population. The fact that class-divided societies are not cultural unities is once more very relevant here.

Those in the local village communities may speak a different language, have entirely different religious beliefs, and follow quite distinct customs from the members of the dominant class. Chinese officialdom made probably the most consistent and dedicated attempt to convey a state-sanctioned religion to the population as a whole. In the Han period, a policy of systematic ethical education was introduced, and Confucian themes were deliberately incorporated into widely disseminated stories and plays.[27] Under the Manchus, a body of lecturers was set up who would tour round peasant communities, inculcating doctrines of general morality.[28] However none of this was notably successful except among some strata of the state officialdom themselves and certain groups in the urban areas. Moreover, there were lateral divisions of religious affiliation over long periods as well as horizontal ones. Buddhism was introduced into China as early as the first century AD, although it was only considerably later that it made much headway. It was violently opposed by some of the emperors, but later achieved a wide following. Taoism also made great strides, having its own ecclesiastical hierarchy which was officially recognized in the eighth century, and thereafter sporadically achieved some imperial support. It was largely to counter the popularity of Buddhism and Taoism that in the Han and T'ang periods the policies of sponsored Confucian education were actively fostered. But many individuals in the higher circles were Buddhists as well as Confucianists, and sometimes simultaneously professed beliefs in other religious views as well, the exclusivist nature of Near-Eastern religion not having taken hold in the further Orient.

Religion resists attempts to reduce it to a wholly social content. Marx saw religion as an alienated expression of this-worldly strivings and of material suffering; Durkheim as the expression of collective values, the sacred being the manifestation of the respect in which these values are held. No religions consist only of beliefs; all embody social practices and, therefore, are social institutions. But it does not follow from this that religious beliefs, of any sort, can be analysed as transmuted expressions of social imperatives. To acknowledge that religious beliefs have an 'authenticity' that eludes such a reduction is again to emphasize that religion is not simply ideology — a cloak for asymmetrical domination — but stands in complex relation to the distribution of power.

None of the above remarks compromise the validity of the propositions that all class-divided societies have possessed forms of 'state religion'; that such state religions have been in variable degree actively fostered by monarchs or groupings within the ruling class as props to their power; and that religious elements permeate culture at all levels prior to the emergence of modern capitalism. But these things having been said, we have to add qualifying statements of considerable importance. We should not suppose that religion, even 'state religion' is a wholly conservative force; rather, religion is a framework of thought and social organization through which many aspects of life in traditional states may be filtered, including innovative forces and schismatic ones. It is also very generally an error to suppose, even within the most cohesive of non-modern states, that the rationalized religions followed by those in the dominant class have much purchase over the day-to-day lives of the majority of their subject populations.

This brings us back to the field of application of the passage quoted from Marx. The dominant class has control over 'the means of mental production'. If we reject the idea that, in class-divided societies, the ruling class is able to create a consensus of belief and value 'internalized' by those subject to its rule, what meaning can be attributed to such a phrase? One phenomenon of importance is that the dominant class is able to sustain a 'discursive arena' of political thought and discussion from which most of the subject population is excluded. The influence of writing is significant here, although it is by no means the only factor involved. The urban settings in which the members of the dominant class typically move, certainly those most closely involved with the administration of the state apparatus, provide for the possibility of a 'cultural cosmopolitanism' which is specific to small segments of the overall population. A framework of discourse, a series of environments in which politics is discursively organized, and administrative information co-ordinated, are basic to what 'politics' is in class-divided societies.

The exclusion of most of the population from participation in the discursive sphere of politics makes it extremely difficult — in some respects effectively impossible — for them to articulate a conceptual 'field of opposition'. All cultures, whether they are overall societies or segments of larger states, depend upon repetition and re-enactment for the reproduction of discursively articulated beliefs. Tradition and custom have the weight they do, not primarily because of the normative compulsion of 'the old ways', but because there is not the 'opening out of the future' and the 'seizure of the past' which the organized mobilization of information facilitates. Those in oral cultures manifestly have not lacked 'the means of mental production'. As Lévi-Strauss among others has made clear, the elaborate cognitive classifications developed in oral cultures are both rich in detail and internally coherent in form. Even the most 'primitive' of societies are not without their theorists (and their sceptics). But the lack of a discursive sphere for the articulation of generalized policies and their integration with the systematic collation of information is of fatal significance for those excluded from the political centre in class-divided societies.

It is in the light of the preceding two points that we can best understand why the system integration of class-divided societies does not depend in any essential way upon an 'overall ideological consensus'. What matters is the ideological hegemony of the ruler and the higher circles of the state apparatus over the remainder of the dominant class and administrative officialdom. The main axis of the dialectic of control in traditional states does not necessarily, or even usually, involve strong cultural homogeneity between rulers and ruled. As in all power relationships, there is reciprocity and autonomy on the part of both the ruling groups and those subordinate to that rule. But the reciprocity is primarily a politico-economic one, that is to say one mediated by the demands of the dominant class for revenue and of the peasantry for economic and governmental services, with the position of the dominant class being bolstered by command of the means of violence. The peasant producers preserve a high degree of autonomy over their own community life, over the basic conditions of their labour, and over their traditional modes of behaviour generally. The main spheres in which ideological controls are important are the inner court, the higher circles of the patrimonial apparatus and the military leadership. In many monarchical systems the inner court has been far more than just the place where the personal needs of the ruler are catered for; it has been a political unit, the centre of both policy-making and intrigue. As a definite locale, it is open to surveillance by the monarch and the very surreptitious nature of the alliances formed therein bear witness to the 'visible' ideological control ordinarily sustained within it. Those closest to the ruler in the inner court are often chosen from groups outside the membership of the ruling class, for example eunuchs, slaves or foreigners. While their nominal authority may be non-existent, their real power has frequently been very substantial indeed.[29]

Those in the inner court on many occasions, although certainly not universally, may traverse the lines of authority running from the monarch to both the administrative apparatus and to the army. The problem of sustaining monarchical control over each of these was a perennial, and in some degree intractable, one in all non-modern states. The larger the state, the more this was the case, because the behaviour of subordinates could be influenced with much success only when they were within regular and easy access. The strategy of divide and rule has naturally been very common in societies where the possibility of challenges by the provincial military to the power of the central state tend to be chronic. Thus Diocletian sub-divided the provinces of the Roman empire in a careful and complicated fashion. Each governor was only permitted a short period in any particular area, and they were separated from the organization of military command. Sometimes their children were held in Rome as hostages; in order to distance them from the governed, they were not allowed to administer regions from which they came, to purchase property or to marry there.[30] Such a procedure, however, was very difficult to employ in respect of the armed forces, for obvious reasons — a divided leadership was not likely to prosper on the battleground. Very often the monarch sought to maintain the position of supreme commander of the military. But unless that ruler was actually a war-lord or battle leader this did not amount to very much in terms of effective power, and the threat of deposition by the military tended to be an ever-present one for the monarchical authority. China seems more or less unique in this respect, since the military leadership was rarely a threat to internal imperial power. However, in the Chinese state apparatus there were extraordinarily pervasive networks of spies and informers, whose task it was to ensure that officials maintained appropriate codes of conduct and belief. In the T'ang period, for example, officials were required to attend regular re-education sessions, to keep them in the proper ways. They were not permitted to live in their home provinces, and given only short-term appointments in an effort to keep them loyal to the higher levels of command. But they were also required to report on one another, keeping special notes of any tendencies among their fellow officials towards slack conduct or querulous behaviour. The Censorate was effectively an investigatory police, charged with uncovering any potential sources of dissidence.[31]

The divergence between factors influencing the ideological hegemony of the ruler over the state officialdom on the one hand, and those affecting the power of the dominant class over the remainder of the population, on the other, underlies the phenomena mentioned by Marx in his observations about the 'Asiatic mode of production'. While there may be only relatively slow change in the overall institutions of class-divided societies, and in the ways of life of the peasant communities they incorporate, there is characteristically a rapid turnover of power among elites within the dominant class. The main social institutions, as Marx puts it, remain 'untouched by the storm-clouds of the political sky'.[32] However, the storm-clouds loom more or less permanently for the members of the ruling elites themselves. Patrimonial power is inherently unstable for the individuals involved, resting as it does upon personal affiliation and kinship relations. Murder, loss of favour, punishment for incompetence or corruption, all these make for a volatile distribution of authority within the higher echelons of the state apparatus and the military. While some rulers of traditional states retained their position for many years, this was usually achieved only through the constant juggling of those just below them in the hierarchy. A case can be made for the claim that monarchical figures have, in fact, only successfully maintained their rule for lengthy periods where there has been a good deal of instability directly below them, inhibiting coalitions in the court or household that might mount an effective challenge. Studies of dynasties indicate that periods of stable individual rule are usually quite short, and broken by forcible overthrow. Seventeen of the thirty-seven Ottoman sultans were deposed by force of arms;[33] the duration of the average reign of Umayyad caliphs (in the seventh and eighth centuries) was six years, while that of Seljuk sultans (in the eleventh and twelfth centuries) was eleven years.[34]

State Systems

Virtually all distinguishable 'societies' have existed in the context of wider inter-societal systems, in relation to which their own internal characteristics have in some part to be understood. The existence of frontiers rather than boundaries is one way in which the external aspects of class-divided societies differs from the modern system of nation-states, but it is plainly not the only difference. The nation-state system in the twentieth century has become a global one, in which only the greater part of the oceans and of the polar wastes are free from the claims of national sovereignty. Moreover, these claims are more or less universally agreed to be valid by the governments of states in the world political order. The 'world systems' of previous eras were of course much more fragmentary; and each major empire or 'world civilization' has taken itself to be the geo-political and cultural centre of whatever wider theatres of affairs were known to its rulers. Mencius's aphorism that 'In the sky there is only one sun and above the people there is only one emperor,'[35] could apply to the outlook fostered by all large empires.

Four general types of non-modern inter-societal systems can be distinguished, although each can overlap or co-exist with the others. First, there are localized systems of tribal cultures, whether hunter-gatherers or settled agriculturalists. Class-divided societies have only existed for a small segment of the history of human beings. For the vast proportion of human history — which is sometimes, not without reason, called 'pre-history' — systems of tribal societies have been the sole type. They have continued to exist in areas of the world that have not seen the rise of states, unbeknownst to the state powers that might dominate elsewhere. Second, there are city-state systems. While there are examples of isolated city-states, these are virtually all port cities, turned 'outwards' to the seafaring trade upon which their prosperity was built. City states have normally existed in systems of such states — as noted earlier, distinguished by chronic warfare and mutual hostility more often than by peaceful cooperation. Third, there are systems of feudal states. Although there has been much debate about how far the concept of feudalism has precise application outside medieval Europe, fairly close parallels to the system of European feudal states can be found elsewhere. The fourth type is the system dominated by the large imperial formation, with either smaller states or areas inhabited by tribal cultures around its peripheries. All of these are evidently very different from the modern nation-state system, with which, however, they have for a short period co-existed. For much longer phases, they have co-existed with one another and have displaced one another in time and space in the course of social change.

Since something like the fourth millenium, imperial systems have easily dominated the others in terms of their grandeur and scale. Some, most notably China, have retained identifiable similarity of institutional form over long eras, however much their territorial domains might have waxed and waned over that time. Other geographical areas, most notably the Near East and the Mediterranean basin, have been dominated by imperial states even though their central locations have shifted with the rise and decline of particular kingdoms. All traditional empires have derived from the expansion of an originally more confined state, or from the conquest and appropriation of an existing imperial domain by outsiders; there are no known cases where large empires have been built exclusively upon the co-operative agreement of pre-existing states in some kind of federation. That is to say, empires have been constructed primarily through the deployment of military power; and their existence thereafter, for reasons already discussed, has depended primarily upon their continued maintenance of military strength. In the modern nation-state system, each state is a defined political entity, embedded in international economic exchange transactions, upon which it depends for its continued existence. In traditional empires, this relation is in a certain sense reversed. There is normally a certain amount of long-distance trading, which may stretch well beyond the territorial boundaries of the imperial formation. But imperial expansion tends to incorporate all significant economic needs within the domain of the empire itself, relations with groups on the perimeter tending to be unstable. Once established, most imperial states find limits to the degree to which military power can be extended and have sought to pacify adjoining states or tribal societies by means other than the sword. After the early periods of dynastic expansion, the Chinese emperors were never able to achieve much more than nominal administrative influence over Tibet, Indonesia or Korea, and made no attempt to subdue Japan. They conducted innumerable treaties with surrounding nomadic societies, giving honorific and material rewards to those who were co-operative with their wishes. Of course, just as many punitive expeditions were also sent against, and wars fought with, threatening outsiders. In somewhat similar vein, soon after the end of the Republic the Romans relied increasingly upon policies of buying off the barbarians around their frontiers where their attempts at military advance fell short or were repulsed.

Imperial formations that maintain an existence over any length of time do not adjoin other domains of equivalent power, as nation-states may do today. Whatever states abut their frontiers are lesser states, and are generally lumped together by the ruling groups with all other barbarians. Empires, in other words, have had a universalizing quality within their own territories. The Romans, for example, recognized no type of international rights or law, treating their own institutions as in principle generalizable across the rest of the known world. This seems characteristic of all non-modern imperial systems, and is a large part of the reason why the peaceful establishing of boundaries by treaty was inherently unstable. The frontiers of the Ottoman empire, for example, were regarded by the state officialdom as marking the edge of the 'land of war', and for long periods were substantially depopulated, not because of the characteristics of their physical geography but because of the almost endless skirmishes that ranged across the terrain.[36] China provides perhaps the most defined example. According to orthodox teaching, which remained the state philosophy for many centuries, China had no needs depending upon goods or services that had to be fetched from beyond its boundaries. Trade outside the empire was ordinarily carried on in conjunction with demands for tribute.[37]

The relations between city-states were naturally different from any such pattern. City-states seem rarely to have been economically autonomous, and normally established regular long-distance trading relationships with groups outside their immediate vicinity. Merchants have usually held a higher status than in empires, to whose existence they have been much more marginal. The Sumerian states dispatched traders far into Central Asia to seek ores and other vital goods.[38] The demand for external sources of supply increased the more a city-state was successful in extending its territory at the expense of its neighbours. In Sumer, as in Greece, protracted warfare had the consequence of substantially reducing the amount of available cultivable land. Chronic military struggle required the continual conscription of soldiery, draining away workers from the land; and much of the produce of the soil that was tilled was taken to supply the armed forces. The consequences for Sumer were particularly dramatic, since irrigation was necessary for effective farming and the outcome of leaving considerable tracts of farmland uncultivated was their reversion to semi-desert. The ultimate fate of the Sumerian city-states is typical of the end-result of this volatile type of state-system. That is to say, they were absorbed into a larger imperial order established not by the expansion of one of their number but an outside power. Following their conquest by the Akkadian invaders, they became provinces of Sargon's empire, paying taxes and tribute to the imperial regime.[39]

4
The Absolutist State and the Nation-State

In the preceding discussion of traditional states I have made virtually no mention of feudal society. Nor shall I attempt to provide a systematic account of feudal orders in what follows. Such a tactic sounds at first sight quite odd. For how can we understand the specific characteristics of modern states without examining the contexts of European feudalism out of which they arose? However, it is precisely because the modern state has often been understood only against the background of its origins in a disintegrating medieval order that its distinctive qualities are often underplayed.[1] European feudalism has certain characteristics that separate it both from other feudal systems and from other types of class-divided society.[2] Some of these elements were of vital importance in the processes leading to the formation of the modern state. But concentrating upon these tends to lead to a 'progressivist' interpretation of history, epitomized by historical materialism, in which the dynamism of the modern West is traced to a sequence linking the Classical world, feudalism and modern societies.[3] I do not wish to deny that there are unique features in the long-term development of Europe to which we have to look to explain the genesis of modernity. But my main concern is to demonstrate that modern states can be contrasted in a generic way to traditional ones. Thus I do not seek to provide an interpretation of how absolutist states developed out of feudalism; I shall not be concerned to date the emergence of absolutism in an exact way, or to analyse the differences between particular states in respect of the traits typical of absolutist rule. My purposes are more typological and comparative. In indicating just how different modern states are from all forms of traditional state, I endeavour to highlight some key elements of the discontinuities of modernity referred to earlier.

Rather than beginning with a characterization of the absolutist state as a specific form, I shall first of all consider aspects of the European state system. For the system of states that was consolidated in the sixteenth and seventeenth centuries was not just an environment in which each individual state was formed; it was inherently involved in that process of formation.

The System of Absolutist States

Prior to the development of absolutism, Europe was, of course, already a state system — a diversity of frequently warring states. With its arrival the state system was greatly transformed and, indeed, for the first time something quite clearly recognizable as 'Europe' in the modern sense came into being. It is conventional to hold that the fall of Constantinople in 1453 was the beginning of Ottoman pressure upon European independence. However, quite apart from the fact that the Turks had been making substantial inroads into the continent for a long while previously, 'Europe' then more accurately meant 'Christendom'. The Holy Roman Empire and the Papacy gave Christendom its identity, although the former was not an imperial formation in the sense discussed earlier. Valéry's well-known observation that Europe 'is only a peninsula of Asia' has some accuracy if applied to the European feudal states, which appear more as at the periphery of the major world cultures than as a civilization in their own right. As Barraclough has pointed out to good effect, the traditional idea that the unity of medieval European civilization 'was compounded of the Latin language, the classical inheritance, and the Christian religion'[4] is something of a myth. The Roman Empire had its centre on the Mediterranean, taking in substantial parts of Asia and Africa, but not including all of the British Isles, Scandinavia or Germany. Medieval Latin was only an established and durable cultural element in certain areas of the continent and neither the Papacy nor the Holy Roman Empire were ever genuinely universal in their appeal. The Byzantine Empire was the main centre of consolidated power, located towards the edge of what later came to be 'Europe'.[5]

Absolutism changed all this. It did not lead, of course, to a newly united Europe. Quite the contrary; the European continent became riven anew by the divisions between states and by the scars of battle. But Europe, nonetheless, became a political order with discernible and clear linkages to the nation-state system that was to come later. In the system of feudal states, the principalities dotted across the continent were, for the most part, small. The connections between them, whether formed peacefully or through war, were mainly between segments of a ruling class which, in common with class-divided societies as a whole, was remote from the culture and activities of the rest of the population. Under absolutism, the state began to have more of a 'pyramidal' character, even if the large majority of its subjects continued to live their lives much as before. The internal consolidation of the state served more clearly to accentuate its territorial form and it is during the period of absolutism that Europe became altered in respect of states' boundaries. In feudal Europe, boundaries were frontiers, chronically disputed and nebulously administered. 'Diplomacy' existed, but it was of the traditional type. In other words, it consisted mostly of attempts to buy off other groups by the offering of goods and rewards, or to exact tribute that would be recognition of dependency. Standing diplomacy has some antecedents in the feudal era but, for the most part, it is a development novel to the sixteenth century and thereafter. It is the best single expression of the fact that a new type of state system had come into being, as dominated by war as were traditional states, but depending also upon the recognition of each state of the spheres of legitimate autonomy of others.

French diplomacy was the leader, as the French state was the most powerful in the Western sector of the continent; but the institution of permanent diplomatic activities became rapidly established throughout Europe. If Louis XIV was the prototypical absolutist monarch, his administration was also the most notably advanced in respect of diplomatic training and of diplomatic manoeuvring. The Comte d'Avaux, by reason of his despatches, produced something like a standard account of the practice of the new diplomatic ordering of the European states. The French secretaries of state possessed a complex set of sources of information about the position and fortunes of other states, contained in regular reports and memoranda.[6] The specific importance of this is that it marks the extension of surveillance activities into the international sphere, thereby helping to constitute what subsequently came to be called 'international relations' as a phenomenon. Nothing precisely analogous seems to have previously existed in the whole long history of traditional states, and it is an essential element of the watershed that divides the modern nation-state system from the prior types. Even in seventeenth-century France, diplomacy was still only organized in a fairly rudimentary way. At the end of his reign, Louis XIV continued to consign some important missions to generals and clerics. Resident diplomats had little in the way of training for the task, the more prestigious errands being almost solely the prerogative of high-ranking noblemen. Only by the eighteenth century did most countries have large corps of diplomatic staff, at home and abroad, working permanently upon foreign affairs.

A major innovation of the period of absolutism was the establishing of congresses.[7] There were international gatherings in the Middle Ages, especially among ecclesiastics, and some of the etiquette that grew up in them survived into later times. But the congresses were essentially different, and have aptly been described as 'one of the great landmarks of the [seventeenth] century'.[8] Prior to that century, the representatives of several states had sometimes met in one place; but the congress of Westphalia, at the conclusion of the Thirty Years' War, was in various ways radically different. It was something close to a general European congress, concerned with settling the relations between the diversity of European states. The meetings occurred in two cities, Münster and Osnabrück, and involved the representatives of every European state save those of the less central regions of England, Poland and Denmark. By the time of the death of Louis XIV, nine other congresses had been held, although none so grand and all-embracing as that of Westphalia. The plethora of treaties that emerged established a distribution of territorial state authority throughout Europe in each successive congress, subsequent wars and conflicts bringing further meetings in their train. From the seventeenth century onwards, the history of Europe has been decisively influenced by such meetings, almost always following periods of protracted war, up to and including Yalta.

The concept of the 'balance of power' among European states has become such a familiar and hackneyed one that it is difficult to recapture either how new it was in the seventeenth century, or how important it thenceforth became in the state system of absolutism and in the nation-state system. The treaties of Utrecht established its first solid foundation; afterwards it became an acknowledged principle by states both in order to wage war and to sue for peace. It was a theory of achievable equilibrium fully as consequential for the development of modern societies as that of the 'hidden hand' in the sphere of economic relations. Its significance does not depend mainly upon the idea of a balance of forces to be actively striven for by the leaders of states. More important is the explicit acknowledgement of the legitimacy of other states, none of which has the right to universalize its own elements of administration or law at the expense of others. It is a formula for organization, in the sense in which I defined that term in the opening chapter. But it is simultaneously a formula for 'anarchy', for each state, in gaining acceptance of its own sovereignty, acknowledges the separate sovereign spheres of others. As Sorel observed, '*Il se forme ainsi entre les grands États une sorte de société en participation: ils entendent conserver ce qu'ils possèdent, gagner en proportion de leurs mises, et interdire à chacun des associés de faire la loi aux autres.*'[9] If the phrase '*une sorte de société en participation*' is too strong, it does help capture the paradoxical character of an increasingly integrated state system which nevertheless gives strong and explicit recognition to the distinct legitimacy of all states thereby linked together.

The states of Europe tended to fall into two categories: those that were able to exploit the new doctrine and, by means of diplomacy and war, to expand; and those that, as a result, lost large tracts of territory or were shattered altogether. The risk of war was compounded rather than lessened, because diplomatic manoeuvring could lead to the outbreak of armed conflict where none was intended; and, having begun, the impact of consolidated alliances could lead to a much more widespread military confrontation than might otherwise have been the case.[10] The likelihood of the 'accidental' outbreak of war on a large scale was furthered by the relative paucity of systematic information that states were able to gather both internally and about one another. The resources of an enemy or ally might be grossly miscalculated, as well as the capability of the particular state to wage a lengthy war. As late as the middle of the eighteenth century Lord Chesterfield observed in a letter to his son: 'There is one part of political knowledge which is only to be had by inquiry and conversation: that is, the present state of every power in Europe with regard to the three important points of strength, revenue and commerce.'[11] The collaborative efforts of the European states, in the Eastern sections of the continent, did bear fruit in one highly consequential way, in procuring the defeat of the last great threat of an external imperial formation of a traditional type — the Ottoman Empire. The repulsion of the Turks at the gates of Vienna in the late seventeenth century was an event perhaps as important to the later ascendancy of the West as — if Edward Meyer and Weber are right — the Greek victory at the Marathon was a millenium and a half earlier. With the progressive retreat of the Turks the 'Eastern question' began to be posed in something like a recognizably modern form.

Following the emergence of the main rudiments of a reflexively monitored state system in the era of absolutism, new borders began to be established between states, although many frontiers remained. It must be emphasized that it is not sheerly in respect of the substitution of borders for frontiers that the modern state differs from traditional ones. The nature of the territoriality of the state becomes transformed in the light of the quite distinctive theories of state sovereignty that coincide with the rise of the absolutist state. The conception of the 'sovereign state' has so often been discussed as a purely internal affair that it is worth stressing that it necessarily has external implications for the state in the context of others. The state is to have exclusive authority within its own domain, all other rights being conferred by the sovereign and revocable by him. By its very nature, this formula draws a clear-cut distinction between the authority of different states, and gives a new significance to the territorial demarcations between them.

The relations between feudal states were largely oriented to the acquisition of territory, as the dynastic addition to an amorphously defined cluster of provinces. The territories of medieval rulers were not necessarily continuous, but often scattered and divided. While a monarch might pursue the ambition of consolidating all his lands in a single territory, it made no great odds if this was not achieved. Moreover, of course, within the monarchically claimed territories of feudal states there were large areas in which the king's writ either was not recognized at all, or effectively counted for nothing. The centralization of political power associated with absolutism was not a simple process of the expansion of effective control over areas already nominally subject to the authority of the ruler. It demanded substantial alteration in the external and internal frontiers of states. A king might own a segment of territory lying deep within lands claimed by another. The furthering of sovereign rights could, therefore, intrinsically involve major clashes and, at a minimum, peacefully conducted realignments of territory between states. An example of the ambiguities involved is given by the differing historical interpretations that have been made of the shift in the position of the principality of Sedan in the mid-seventeenth century.[12] Sedan is often regarded as a distinct realm. But others have seen it as a boundary province of the larger state of France, in which the monarch was not able to sustain more than minimal authority. The hesitations of historians are not particularly surprising, reflecting in some part those current at the time. The dukes of Bouillon held direct lordship over the area, but owed some of their possessions to the bishops of Liège, who in turn were princes owing allegiance to the French crown. The ducal family relinquished Sedan in exchange for certain other areas in France. On occasion, this has been regarded by historical writers as the annexing of previously foreign territory, by others as the consolidation of royal power over French lands.

In the process of the realignment of states' boundaries, previously existing frontiers were not only altered, but significantly altered towards becoming borders in the sense given previously. It was a process that did not culminate until well into the nineteenth century, particularly in the less settled parts of the continent. In the seventeenth century, many frontiers remained as they traditionally had been: diffusely specified, and bearing no direct relation to the political or the economic activity of the states concerned. In the Dutch republic, for example, there were a whole variety of oddities and inconsistencies, as judged in terms of the new conceptions of sovereignty rather than the old practices. Several portions of Dutch territory were completely cut off from the main segment of the state. Spanish fiefs, on the other hand, existed within that segment. The bishops of Liège held joint dominion over some Dutch territory. It was primarily the wars and resultant congresses of the seventeenth and eighteenth centuries that rationalized frontiers into borders, although many boundaries were left untouched by these happenings. In the seventeenth century, for the first time, the practice of giving boundary populations an 'option' to belong to one state or another came into being. Thus, when various cities in the Spanish Netherlands were appropriated by France in a treaty of 1640, those living in them were given the choice of remaining and becoming 'French', or moving back over the newly drawn line to stay Spanish or German as they had been previously. The progression from frontiers to borders as mutually agreed lines on a map does not, however, appear until the eighteenth century: the first boundary literally drawn as a line seemingly being constructed only in the year 1718, as part of a treaty made in respect of Flanders in that year.[13]

Other innovations that became of major importance in shaping the reflexively monitored system of nation-states that was to come only make their first entry in the closing stages of the 'age of absolutism'. One is the doctrine of natural frontiers. In traditional states leaders had certainly often tried to secure dominion over areas that offered natural protection against the encroachment of other states. But, as elaborated from the late eighteenth century onwards, the idea that a state ought, as far as possible, to have natural frontiers was closely tied to the greatly expanded coherence of the state as an administrative unity. It was not just protection in certain contested bordering areas, but an emphasis upon the integral character of statehood that lay behind the new doctrine. The 'natural' boundaries involved were not parameters that somehow organically link a state to the habitat but were, rather, an expression of a highly developed conception of state sovereignty. 'Natural frontiers' also eventually came to be seen as defined in terms of the linguistic or cultural homogeneity of the subject populations within states. But this is a later phenomenon still, and something more or less completely specific to the emergence of the European nation-state.

Of course, the formation of a reflexively monitored state system in Europe was not the only external set of changes of basic importance in absolutism. This development was also coeval with the expansion of the power of certain of the European states by sea. What became 'Europe' was tiny compared to the imperial states further east, and was smaller even than the Roman Empire had been. It seems remarkable, even virtually impossible, that a mosaic of separate states should increasingly have been able to subdue, or to bring under their sway, massive areas in the rest of the world. It has to be emphasized that it was, indeed, quite extraordinary — there is nothing comparable in the past history of states stretching over several millenia. However, the point I have sought to make in the preceding few paragraphs is that Europe by the seventeenth century no longer was just a mosaic of states. The consolidated independent sovereignty of each individual state (or rather those states that were able to survive the wars and the territorial reallocations which took place over several centuries) was at the same time part of a process of overall inter-state integration.

The mastery of the seas which the Europeans achieved, however, cannot be explained as an immediate outcome of this, but depended upon a number of quite contingent elements. The days of long-distance sea travel, and what from the point of view of the Europeans was the 'discovery' of the world, pre-date the technological developments which made European naval fire-power irresistible. In the thirteenth century there was a certain amount of long-distance trade with China in silks, spices and a few other goods. China was, in fact, better known to Europeans than India, since some travellers had crossed the Asian mainland in pursuit of commerce, whereas Arab merchants controlled trade from Indian ports via the Middle East to Europe. The disintegration of the Tartar Khan Empire altered that situation, as the Ming regime in China started to insulate that state increasingly from outsiders. Europe became more cut off from the rest of the world than it had been before, since the intrusion of the Ottoman Turks dislocated other trade routes. It was partly for these reasons that adventurers ('explorers', as the specialized purveyors of geographical knowledge, only come at a much later date) began following new routes that 'opened up' the rest of the world to Europe. The making of ever-bolder voyages across the world was no doubt in a general way stimulated by the impact of the Renaissance, but does not seem to have been very directly influenced by it. The recovery of Ptolemy's *Geography*, first made available in a printed edition in 1475, had considerable general intellectual influence. But Columbus had apparently not read it, and was much more indebted to *Imago Mundi*, a work written by the late-medieval scholar, Cardinal d'Ailly.[14]

Absolutism, in fact, coincided with a period in which most of the great voyages of discovery had been accomplished and the main geographical forms of the continents of the world, known. In one sense, of course, the significance of this can hardly be underplayed. Whatever their magnificence, or their territorial scope, the great empires of past times had never achieved a genuine knowledge of the globe as a whole. However cosmopolitan they might have been, their knowledge was always basically 'local knowledge'.[15] For the first time in history human beings lived in a world of which, whatever the ethnocentrism of European thought, they had 'universal knowledge'. If this is a discontinuity with prior ages, so also is the spread of European military armed and commercial strength by sea. All large-scale empires had some sort of long-distance trade, and there were many smaller states whose prosperity was built very largely on a mixture of commerce and sea-power. But no major 'world civilization' had previously been established mainly by sea-power as, with the development of sea-borne trading operations on a grand scale, and of colonialism, that of the West came to be.[16] The development of absolutism was no doubt facilitated in some degree by the wealth brought into Europe by the influx of precious metals. But again there was little direct connection, and it would be foolish to try to press all of this into some sort of functionalist frame. There was a lull in the process of geographical discovery and of trading expansion for something like a period of a century from about 1650. The settlement of Westphalia in some considerable part led the European countries to concentrate their energies on their own continent. Commercial policies were restrictive rather than expansionary and colonization, with the exception of Latin America, still largely a matter of the stationing of outposts in other areas of the world. The expansion of commercial and then industrial capitalism on a global scale would not have been possible without the initiation of Western 'universalism'; but it derived fundamentally from other sources.[17] The main linking phenomenon was to be the superiority of European naval power, which permitted the carrying of commercial capitalism on a large scale to many parts of the globe.

The Absolutist State as an Organization

In terms of the development of a novel type of reflexively monitored state system, then, absolutism began to prise open the discontinuities that separate the modern world from prior epochs. Absolutism still retained large elements of the feudal order that preceded it, and was more different from the nation-state system that was its heir than it is from feudalism. If I cannot agree with Anderson's assessment that 'In diplomacy . . . the index of feudal dominance in the Absolutist State is evident,' there can be no quarrel with his observation that the absolutist states were 'hybrid compositions', 'whose surface "modernity" again and again betrays a subterranean archaism'.[18] What is important in judging the novelty of the absolutist state is not just to measure it against feudalism, as generations of historians have done, but to contrast it to other forms of traditional state in general. The absolutist state is still, in my terms, a traditional state. That is to say, in some of its main characteristics it remains a class-divided society. But in other respects it has features barely found at all elsewhere.

These are not easily distinguished if one supposes, as some have done, that absolutism is a sort of Oriental Despotism writ small. Not only does such an analysis repeat the error of holding that centralized bureaucratic empires were much more cohesive than actually was the case, it fails to give sufficient weight to certain distinctive aspects of the rule (and the claims to legitimacy) of the European monarchs. These largely centre upon both the notion and the actuality of sovereignty.[19] Rulers in traditional states were always in a certain sense 'sovereigns': they were acknowledged (at least by those lower in the state apparatus) to be the supreme authority in the political order. Like the absolutist monarchs, they claimed legitimacy by reference to sacred symbols; the notion of 'divine right' to rule in its core meaning is hardly a European innovation, whatever its specific form might indicate. But traditional rulers elsewhere had not, as it were, incorporated the state within their own person; they sat at the pinnacle of it. The religious symbolism of 'divine right' should actually be seen as a traditional accoutrement to something very new — *the development of 'government' in the modern sense, the figure of the ruler being a personalized expression of a secularized administrative entity.*

The progressive shaping of the concept of 'sovereignty' in the hands of political thinkers from the fifteenth to the end of the seventeenth century is instructive in this regard. 'Sovereign' suggests an etymological connection with the idea of an individual ruler but such is not its main origin, which helps explain why it was easily transferred into an impersonal form of 'sovereignty'. Prior to Bodin, the term 'sovereign' had been applied as an adjective in an imprecise way to any individual of rank. In the fifteenth and sixteenth centuries in England, even a relatively minor personage such as a mitred abbot was officially referred to as a sovereign but only because he stood at the head of an ecclesiastical organization. The word was more usually employed to refer to characteristics of organizations themselves — three sovereign courts of law were recognized in France, for example.[20] In asserting (with some reservations) that there can be only one sovereign, Bodin was not simply asserting the transcendent authority of the individual monarch, he was describing and advocating a co-ordinated system of administrative rule.[21] It can justifiably be claimed, I think, that neither the fact of a non-monarchical regime, nor the various theories of republicanism and libertarianism associated with the English Revolution could have come about without the prior establishing of a 'discourse of sovereignty'.[22] As connected to political theory of the time, the concept of absolutism was open to elaboration because it juxtaposed the assertion of the supreme authority of an individual to a more generalized interpretation of state power, in which there was in fact no necessary role for kings or monarchs at all. Once the idea of sovereignty had effectively been turned into a principle of government, the way was open for it to become connected to that of 'citizenship' — no longer applied within the confined reach of the urban commune but having as its reference the political 'community' of the state as a whole. However much a connection might be stressed between the divine right of kings and absolute sovereignty, it remained vulnerable, a focus of ideological concentration but also a sparking point of struggle.

The political theory of absolute state power operated at some distance from reality, momentous as were the administrative changes which the most developed states displayed and, obviously, absolutism was not all of a piece either regionally or temporally. Nonetheless, certain general characteristics can readily be distinguished. Three main elements are involved, each connected with the others: (i) the centralization and expansion of administrative power; (ii) the development of new mechanisms of law; and (iii) alterations in modes of fiscal management.

Courtly life in the absolutist state, especially in the most magnificent example — that of Louis XIV — resembled that observed in numerous imperial societies. In Louis' case, however, it was stripped of the patrimonialism characteristic both of feudal rulership and of the majority of other monarchical states. The inner court was not composed of the higher sectors of his household, but of favoured nobles and attendants. It was certainly a 'political' realm — always rife with intrigue and gossip — but it was not part of the mechanism of administration. This helped make possible the creation of bureaucratic administration in principle, and in some part in practice, directly responsible to the ruler. The ministers appointed by Louis XIV were often of the nobility but not always so. They sometimes reported personally to him but more usually through councils of government, connected directly to the executive organs of administration, the posts which were not prebendal for the most part, but occupied by salaried, vocational officials.[23] Colbert's policies were actively and deliberately oriented towards the consolidation of bureaucracy in this manner — in the system of *intendants*, for example. Beginning with an attempt to rationalize taxation, and to centralize the collection of revenue, Colbert helped to build a hierarchical system of administration, co-ordinating central and local officialdom to a much greater degree than had previously been the case. The *intendants* were originally sent out to conduct surveys about the effectiveness of the deployment of fiscal resources, reporting back with a view to reform. Instead, they stayed on in the provinces, sending back regular reports, and effectively becoming resident administrators directly responsible to the crown.[24]

The co-ordination and centralization of state power, in France and throughout Europe, brought the monarchy into confrontation with corporatist organizations, including the cities, diets and parliaments, where such existed. French towns, many of which had enjoyed some considerable independence from the central political apparatus were, by an edict of 1692, brought under the regulation of mayors appointed by the crown. The authority of the *Parlement* of Paris was reshaped and curtailed. In 1673 its right of making representation about contemplated legislation was limited to the period after an edict was registered. Nonetheless, the crown had regularly to consult with the provincial Estates in the *Pays d'États*, as well as with the Assembly of Clergy. Moreover, since in many instances new official positions had been created alongside the pre-existing ones, without fully replacing them, the result was a complex web of intersecting relations of authority, distributed laterally as well as hierarchically.[25] Something similar happened elsewhere, although with great variations from state to state. Thus the Estates of Bohemia, Brandenburg and Russia were quite ruthlessly repressed. Charles XI of Sweden prevented the Riksdag from meeting other than sporadically after 1680; before the end of the reign of Felipe IV the Cortès of Castile were emasculated. Since such organizations were for the most part composed of nobility, gentry or their representatives, these processes have sometimes been understood to indicate that the absolutist state was founded upon an alliance between the crown and the commercial capitalist bourgeoisie. This was, in fact, Marx's view. According to him, in a characteristic observation on the matter, 'The centralised State power, with its ubiquitous organs of standing army, police, bureaucracy, clergy and judicature — organs wrought after the plan of a systematic and hierarchic division of labour — originates from the days of absolute monarchy, seeing nascent middle-class society as a mighty weapon in its struggles against feudalism.'[26]

There is no doubt that in France, and in variable degree elsewhere, some of the urban corporations co-operated with the ascendant state apparatus of absolutism in ways in which the Estates did not. A certain amount of the administrative autonomy of the cities was ceded, in exchange for the consolidation of broader frameworks of law that facilitated the expansion of commercial and manufacturing interests. There were several reasons for this. In some part, the parties concerned discerned the advantages that would accrue to them from the development of such frameworks. Also, some increasingly powerful elements were no longer greatly concerned to defend the established forms of corporative autonomy, in which the craft guilds represented a barrier to the use of free wage-labour as a means of expanding production. However, as important as anything was the fact that for the first time the city had become no longer a significant defensive form in war — breakthroughs in military technology rendered its role in this respect largely obsolete. The growing obsolescence of the city, in its traditional form, in political, economic and military terms, is one of the most fundamental transitions initiated — although certainly not completed — as part of the emergence of the absolutist state.

Marx's interpretation is today largely discredited, as even historians strongly sympathetic to Marxism acknowledge. Thus Anderson accepts that the absolutist state 'was never an arbiter between the aristocracy and the bourgeoisie, still less an instrument of the nascent bourgeoisie against the aristocracy.'[27] Rather, it is most accurately seen as expressing the perpetuation of the class domination of a traditional, land-owning minority, which became substantially transformed largely as an unintended consequence of attempts to cope with threats internally and externally. The external processes involved in the development of a novel state system are in my opinion much more important than many historians have been given to suppose. Internally, the most significant factors were probably, as Anderson suggests, attempts on the part of ruling authorities to cope with changes leading to the partial dissolution of the autonomy of localized peasant communities. The outcome was a 'displacement of authority upwards', considerably strengthening the centralized apparatus of royal power. Almost certainly the presence of the partially autonomous urban communes was of major importance (together with other distinctively 'European' or 'Western' influences) in preventing the post-feudal state from crushing the peasantry in time-honoured fashion. A quite distinctive political order was thereby created.

The effects of absolutism in strengthening the bureaucratic rule of a territorially bordered state should not be exaggerated. Marx's statement notwithstanding, it is only with the emergence of the nation-state that a centralized administrative apparatus of state power becomes 'ubiquitous'. If it can justifiably be regarded as the highest development of the absolutist state, France under Louis XIV was still fairly remote from the nation-state form. It was in some respects possibly the most homogeneous country in

Europe. Most of the inhabitants spoke the same language, although the differences between the dialects used in various provinces were extreme by later standards. But in some key ways the scope of the state apparatus remained quite limited. Even the monarch was not simply the King of France; in the South he was referred to, and called himself, the Comte de Provence, while in Dauphiné he was the Dauphin de Viennois. If the self-enclosed character of the local peasant community had been substantially undermined, the regions retained a great deal of administrative control over their own affairs. Both in respect of legal and of fiscal administration there were large regional variations and overlapping criteria of application. Voltaire observed that 'what is just or right in Champagne should not be deemed unjust or wrong in Normandy.'[28] But such remained the case to the end of Louis XIV's reign. While Roman law predominated in southern courts, in other provincial areas customary law still prevailed. Moreover, sometimes a single community could be subject to multiple types of legal system. For instance, in the Beauvaisis there were some villages within which customary law varied according to several differentiations.[29] In spite of the accomplishments of Colbert and other ministers in regularizing the tax system, methods of tax-collection remained capricious. The primary form of direct taxation, the *taille*, was collected by officials responsible to the central state. Other taxes were farmed, and the *Pays d'États* had their own procedures of tax-gathering. Moreover, there were two kinds of *taille*, one levied chiefly on land, and applied mainly in the south, the other a form of personal taxation. Many categories of persons were exempt from the *taille*, as were most of the large cities. Throughout the reign of Louis XIV, some cities maintained tariffs against trade with large parts of France, while conducting free trade with other states outside.

It is against this background that the development of legal and fiscal systems under absolutism should be assessed. That they mark an extremely important step in the consolidation of the state apparatus is not open to doubt. But they were as transitional as the other aspects of the absolutist state that have been mentioned. The promulgation of abstract codes of law, which apply to the whole population of a state, is again closely connected with the notion of sovereignty. If absolutism were seen only as the concentration of authority in the hands of the monarch, the development of law could be pictured as the subordination of the overall political order to the will of a despot. But if the absolutist state is considered in terms of the co-ordination of 'sovereign administration', the expansion of codified law appears in quite another light. It is then part and parcel of a generalized apparatus of power. Rather than being the plaything of the monarch, it signposts an avenue to a legal system to which the latter is either formally irrelevant, or should be deemed subject to the same legal principles as all other members of the society.

Several aspects of the development of law can be distinguished in conjunction with the rise of the absolutist state. One is the increasing promulgation of statutes designed to apply in an impersonal fashion to the whole of the population, with no exclusions for rank. Thus Louis XIV set up a range of codes of procedure of such a kind, covering both criminal and civil law. The importance of such an occurrence, to which there are parallels in the other major European states, is by no means limited just to the formulation of a general corpus of law, significant though that certainly is. It lies also in the concept that the monarch could create and enforce new law. In feudalism, the Estates claimed legal prerogatives of a traditional character which they also had the right to sanction, with the use of force if necessary. The territorial ruler had similar rights but was supposed to enter into a compact with the Estates in any modifications of legal procedure. In the absolutist state, bodies and organizations outside the central administrative apparatus become at most 'a privileged audience whose individual components might be graciously exempted from the unpleasant effects (especially fiscal ones) of the new rules'.[30]

A second factor of major importance concerns changes in the content of law, most particularly in respect of private property. The recovery of Roman law played a significant part in moulding these changes, although its role can be exaggerated, especially if the characterization of its origin is taken seriously. Some features of late- and post-medieval 'Roman' law are not found in Antiquity at all, and others were substantially modified, such as the notions of *dominium* and *possessio*. According to Weber, the 'authentic' institutions of Roman law were barely more abstract than those of Germanic law.[31] The process of 'rediscovery' of Roman law, therefore, also reformulated it.[32] In its reconstituted form, Roman law provided the means of separating private property from the 'public' domain in a way not open to the feudal order. This was more salient than any specific elements of such law actually employed to define private property, since in the cities corpuses of commercial law had been worked out that owed little to the Roman heritage. The differentiation of *jus* and *lex*, however, rendered the formalizing efforts of absolutist administrations highly consequential for subsequent political and economic development. The latter gave a ready foundation for the attempts of rulers to clear away medieval licenses in favour of their own law-making capacity. But the former, at the same time and in some degree as part of the self-same process of law-making, helped engineer new possibilities of 'private ownership' of both land and goods outside the scope of state power. The claim that the effect of changes in the nature of law was simultaneously to shore up the overall dominance of the traditional feudal class, and help confirm the growing strength of commercial and manufacturing capital, is not a paradoxical one.

A third set of changes in the mechanisms of law concerns criminal law and the modes of sanction appropriated by the state apparatus. A great deal of attention has been paid by historians to the development of the general properties of law under absolutism, but much less has been written about changes affecting criminal law specifically. In the period of absolutism there occur the beginnings of incarceration and the extension of sanctioning agencies controlled by the state, replacing the forms of local community sanction that had previously been preponderant. There are close connections between the first two types of juridical transformation mentioned and this third one. The conception that a unitary sovereign authority should replace feudal corporatism — and that this is the condition of eliminating civil strife — found in variant guise in Bodin and in Hobbes, incorporates a stress upon 'order' or social discipline. Thus, according to Bodin for instance, the 'end of the state' is to produce a 'well-ordered life'.[33] The juxtaposition of 'order' and 'anarchy' (as also existing, in different form, in the state system) is intrinsic to the conception of sovereignty. It points the way not just to acknowledging the need for generalized social discipline, but to the emergence of an idea of 'deviance'. Although, as with most of the traits of absolutism, there were wide variations between different countries, it is in the sixteenth and seventeenth centuries that carceral organizations tend first to become fairly widespread. The reorganization of the *hôpital général* of Paris in 1657 is symptomatic of the trends of the time. This was made up of a number of older buildings grouped into one, but in other cities new purpose-built edifices were constructed — at Lyon, for example, such a construction was undertaken as early as 1612. A statute of 1676 required every French city over a certain size to establish an *hôpital général* to be modelled upon the Parisian example.[34]

Similar developments had begun previously in England — undoubtedly connected with a rather earlier administrative rationalization of state authority there — with the building of houses of correction dating from an edict of 1575. These did not become extensive and they were, thereafter, largely superseded by the establishment of work-houses in a later period. However, England could boast what has been regarded as probably the first example of 'modern imprisonment' in Europe — widely copied in other countries — Bridewell, set up in 1556. Bridewell may have been the model for the Rasp Huis in Amsterdam, although some have disputed this.[35] A type of disciplinary punishment had, in fact, existed prior to the establishment of Bridewell and similar reformatories in the rest of Europe. This was the penitential confinement of the monasteries. Some of the major monastic groups had long since developed rules for the corrective punishment of offenders by the confinement and isolation of the offender. The monasteries were not the proximate source of early houses of correction, but there is a line of connection running right from them to the prison system of the late eighteenth and nineteenth centuries — a phenomenon of the nation-state rather than the absolutist state. Of course, the spread of carceral organizations was not limited to the sphere of criminality as such, but forms a much broader drift of social change associated with absolutism, later maximized in the nation-state. The sick, the mad, and those in certain other categories came to be segregated from the remainder of the 'normal' (sane/law-abiding/healthy of body) population. What Dorner, following Foucault, terms the 'epoch of the administrative sequestration of unreason' (1650— 1800) can plausibly be described as one in which 'the church could no longer, and bourgeois-capitalist society could not yet, encompass the various forms of the irrational, especially the poor and the deranged.'[36]

If some of these elements are quite peculiar to the absolutist state, the need for fiscal management is not. That is to say, like all states, the absolutist state depended upon the collection of taxes on a large scale. Becoming engaged in the prosecution of extended military confrontations entailed a massive drain on the resources of the major states. It has been calculated that in the late sixteenth century over three-quarters of the revenue of the Spanish state was being expended for military purposes. According to Clark, during the entire seventeenth century there were only seven calendar years during which there was no major war between the European states. In one of these years large armies were, in fact, mobilized for battle, there was an exchange of artillery, and a full-scale war was avoided only by a hair's breadth. War 'became an industry of the state'.[37] Of course, states had always carried on wars. But at a time at which the conducting of war became more expensive and complex, with technological change in weaponry and changes in the recruitment and training of the military, the management of relevant fiscal resources took on a different dimension. The early expansion of capitalism was certainly given a major impetus (how far, and in exactly which ways, remains controversial) by the demand for huge sums of money to finance military agencies. One of the main series of events that influenced the subsequent pattern of the European state system was the bankruptcy of Spain, culminating in the late seventeenth century, when that country to all intents and purposes could not muster an army to place in the field. France was on the point of bankruptcy by the turn of the seventeenth century, but the reforms in modes of fiscal administration (following also the so-called 'general crisis')[38] already referred to in relation to Colbert, set the standard which the rest of Europe followed.[39]

As with most aspects of the absolutist state, the centralizing and bureaucratizing influences which the rationalization of finance promoted were relatively rudimentary. The system of tax-farming preserved a prebendal element right at the heart of the administrative system. There were so many exemptions in direct taxation deriving from rank and region that no country possessed anything like the graduated systems of taxation that came later. The information about earnings upon which such systems depend could not be gathered effectively even by the most advanced of states. It is usually accepted that Prussia under Frederick the Great was the most bureaucratized of European states. But the size and scope of its administrative reach was small compared to even the least bureaucratized of state apparatuses in nation-states. In Prussia at the time there was one civil servant for every 450 inhabitants; in Germany in 1925 there was one for every 46 of the population. It is reasonable to hold, as one observer comments, that the absolutist state created 'a government whose decisions were really carried out (that is, an effective government)'. But it is also fair to say, as the same author does, that even eighteenth-century Europe 'was still in the thrall' of institutions 'which had been brought to life during the Middle Ages'.[40]

The absolutist state, then, is a distinctive political order in several key respects, compared with the generality of traditional states. The development of the European states begins to diverge from the pre-established pattern of the rise and fall of empires. This involves, above all, the formation of a new type of reflexively monitored state system, associated substantively and conceptually with the development of sovereignty. The conception of sovereignty, tied simultaneously to the position of the absolutist ruler and to the formation of a heightened bureaucratic centralism, is one of the most important elements binding the 'internal' development of the state with the 'external' solidifying of the state system.

Military Power from the Absolutist to the Nation-State

A myriad of battles and wars, growing in size and destructiveness, shaped the territorial alignment of both absolutist states and the emergent nation-states in Europe. The fact that there were 'continuous states' should not blind us to the dazzling panorama of changes that occurred across the centuries. As Tilly points out,

> the enormous majority of the political units which were around to bid for autonomy and strength in 1500 disappeared in the next few centuries, smashed or absorbed by other states-in-the-making. The substantial majority of the units which got so far as to acquire a recognisable existence as states during those centuries still disappeared. And of the handful which survived or emerged into

the nineteenth century as autonomous states, only a few operated effectively — regardless of what criterion of effectiveness we employ.[41]

Several geo-political patterns are observable in the transition from absolutism to the early phase of development of the nation-state in the nineteenth century.[42] One is the rise and decline of Spanish influence. To speak of the role of 'Spain' in Europe, America and elsewhere in the fifteenth and sixteenth centuries is obviously not to refer to the nation-state that later emerged with that appellation. Spanish power was 'international' in the traditional sense of feudal Europe. Charles V, also the head of the Holy Roman Empire, ruled over various Spanish Kingdoms, Naples and Sicily, the Duchy of Milan, Habsburg territories in and near to Germany and the colonial lands across the Atlantic. There was little connection between them other than their formal allegiance to the Spanish crown. But it is not far-fetched to suppose that, given certain differences in the leadership of the state, Spain might have become the centre of a newly forged empire of the traditional kind.

By the beginning of the seventeenth century, this possibility had receded rapidly; the dwindling of Spanish mastery left a permanent imprint upon the rest of Europe and eventually the world. If the English had been defeated at sea at the time of the Armada, it is difficult to see that what was to become Britain would have turned into a leading commercial or industrial power. The decline of Spain hastened the fragmentation of Germany, a phenomenon whose significance it would also be hard to underestimate. The failure of the Spanish monarchy to take advantage of a power vacuum in Western Europe, brought about by a temporary decline of France, allowed that country later not only to step back into the political arena, but to become the dominant European power. Absolutist France is the first example of a state that played a directive role in European politics without becoming a transnational entity of the old type, and thus genuinely ushered in the beginnings of the modern era.

It is not just the fighting of wars and the conducting of diplomacy that is at issue here; equally important were far-reaching changes in military technology and organization that partly preceded and partly accompanied the rise of absolutism.

Sobriety is needed on the part of the Western historian when these are compared with what already existed in China, but the difference they made to the course of European history was quite fundamental. China, by the eleventh century, possessed large armies and a variety of weaponry lacking in the West, adding to this in the thirteenth century the use of gunpowder to fire projectiles.[43] There seems to have been a good deal of technological innovation in warfare and military practice in China in the twelfth and thirteenth centuries. Although there were long periods when Chinese interest in sea-power was marginal, in the early fifteenth century China developed a fleet of huge proportions, easily capable of managing the sort of explorations and trading initiatives undertaken by the Europeans.[44] Moreover, commercial entrepreneurs built and organized their own fleets, trading throughout south Asia and east Africa. Again, it is easy to see a possible course that world history might have taken — Max Weber to the contrary — if the connections between technological development, the military and the spread of commercial capitalism in China had progressed further.[45] Confucian principles, disdainful of the military and, to a lesser degree, of the trader, no doubt acted in a diffuse way to inhibit such progression. But the single most important influence was a directly political decision. Just prior to the middle of the fifteenth century long-distance expeditions across the Indian ocean were prohibited by imperial edict, as was shortly afterwards the construction of the ships capable of making the necessary voyages. The successful intrusion of European military and trading missions in the East, in the early period of Western maritime expansion, was undoubtedly facilitated by this Chinese about-turn.

At the risk of a good deal of over-simplification, it could be said that there were three sets of military developments that decisively influenced (but were also influenced by) the rise of the absolutist state. One was a series of linked technological changes in armaments, which rendered certain traditional land-based ways of making war largely obsolete. The second was the emergence of greatly accentuated administrative power within the armed forces, both in respect of behaviour on the battlefield and military training in general. 'Discipline', in the modern usage of the term, originates in a military context and still preserves a special resonance there. The third was the development of European naval strength, which from somewhere in the sixteenth century onwards (partly again because of technological changes) proved irresistible in the rest of the world. Although there are prior examples of substantial trading-cum-military states, such as Phoenicia, Europe provides the only instances of far-flung empires based first and foremost on control of the oceans. However much traditional empires might have depended upon sea-borne communications, their expansion usually resulted from their control of large land-masses.

Medieval armies were normally made up of fluctuating bodies of men serving the territorial lord in exchange for land-tenure. They were armed with short swords and pikes. Since warfare tended to revolve around mounted knights, the use of infantry formations was largely precluded. The logistics of supply were against the preservation of anything much more than armed bands of retainers over lengthy periods of time. Armies of any size could usually only be supported for a few weeks, normally in the summer. The existence of fortified castles and later walled cities gave defenders large advantages over attackers.[46] During the Hundred Years' War, in the fourteenth century, some warrior bands were raised as mercenaries by individuals commissioned by the monarchs, and there were also 'free companies' of soldiers who sold their services in return for plunder and promises of land. Neither of these types of army had any kind of stable existence, however. Where the rewards were insufficient, the army either broke up or took to banditry; if success did come, the leaders would usually be taken on as the lord's retainers. The dominance of the knight on horseback in early feudal Europe was strongly influenced by a simple but highly effective technical device, the iron stirrup.[47] This made it possible for the lance held by the warrior to carry the weight on impact of horse and rider, rather than just that provided by the strength of the human arm. However the costs of producing and maintaining the armour and equipment were extraordinarily expensive by the standards of the feudal economy — ruinously so for anyone but the most wealthy. As Finer comments, it was something like expecting a modern soldier to provide a tank and crew, with full supporting services.[48]

The development of the English longbow and the pike, as used by the Swiss infantrymen (borrowing the idea from tactics used by the Romans in the later years of the Empire) were twin changes in military technology that helped to dissolve feudal modes of battle. The second was considerably more influential than the first, because mastery of the longbow needed a substantial period of learning and the English yeomanry did not hire themselves out for mercenary service in continental Europe. The Swiss pikemen were mainly composed of mercenaries, and their formation on the battlefield required disciplined co-ordination. The Swiss Confederation became a source from which soldiery were recruited from all over Europe; their tactics were adopted by most of the successful European armies until well into the fifteenth century. However, the pike was in turn gradually overtaken by weaponry that harnessed the explosive force of gunpowder, surely one of the most momentous technological changes in human history. The gun had some very profound consequences for the shaping of modern civilization because, in the shape of early artillery, it helped sharply reduce the significance of the castle and the city as containers of military power. A gun is an 'industrial' device in the sense which that term has when applied to the Industrial Revolution. That is to say, it is a mechanical artifact whose impetus depends upon the application of inanimate sources of material energy.[49]

The Spanish armies were the first to use guns in large measure among the infantry. Something like a sixth of their foot soldiers in the Italian Wars carried guns; the majority, however, remained pikemen. A variety of explosive weapons were tried but the two main ones early on were the ten-pound, four-foot arquebus and the fifteen-pound, six-foot musket. By the middle of the sixteenth century the two-man musket, fired from a forked rest, had become the leading weapon; it fired a two-ounce ball that could penetrate all existing forms of armour, and had a range of some three hundred yards.[50] A great deal of other equipment had to be carried to make the guns work, which they might in any case refuse to do in bad weather. However, their use promoted tight discipline, because something like a hundred separate movements had to be carried out in order to achieve any sort of rapid firing. The concentrated fire-power of ranks of men demanded even more stringent and routinized co-ordination.

Field artillery quickly became a significant factor in laying siege, and its very immobility helped shift the locales of battles away from concentration on castles and cities — the vanquishing of an army on open terrain would allow the artillery pieces subsequently to be brought into action against fixed fortifications if needed. New types of fortification that were invented to counter explosives had no particular connection with urban areas. The gun as well as gunpowder may well have originally been a Chinese invention but the European development of them, under the pressure of more or less continuous war, moved far ahead.[51] Gustavus Adolphus (who with Maurice of Nassau must rank as the greatest innovator among military leaders in the absolutist period) was responsible for two major contributions to military technology. He was among the first to carry on sustained winter campaigns, something which was made possible by the alterations he made in modes of military transportation and supply. But he also helped invent a new cartridge which, together with a lightened musket-barrel, made the field gun considerably more portable. Loading and reloading became sigificantly quicker, with the result that new battlefield formations could be achieved, heightening the offensive capabilities of the gun-carrying troops in relation to others. The subsequent invention of the flintlock and the bayonet decisively turned warfare in the modern direction. The former greatly augmented the rate of fire, while the second made the gun-carrying soldier simultaneously a pikeman. The days of the massed ranks of pikemen were then over.

The various technological developments in weaponry from the thirteenth to the late seventeenth centuries cannot be easily separated from organizational changes within the military, and changes in the relations between the armed forces and the state. Nonetheless, it is not difficult to show that they were consequential in their own right for the cluttered feudal order of kingdoms and principalities. The smaller, more traditionally organized states were either swallowed up by the new concentrations of military strength or simply became irrelevant to the main influences shaping the destiny of the European continent. The advances in military technology heavily favoured those states which could, by whatever means, not just mobilize mass armies, but train and deploy them in a regularized fashion.

It is generally agreed that the French companies 'of ordnance' (that is, of a standard strength), created during the Hundred Years' War, composed the first standing army owing its allegiance directly to a monarch. In 1445 the French King hired twenty such companies on an annual basis, and guaranteed payment to their members through the state. They were each made up of one hundred 'lances' and several officers, each lance including a man-at-arms, his squire, two archers, a valet and a page.[52] They were a mounted force, not infantry, and there is not a particularly direct line of connection between them and the standing armies that were to come later. However, with their formation a clear-cut division began to be established between land-owners who preoccupied themselves with their estates and those who opted for a more professional military career. In France, and some other countries, this converged with a gulf between recruitment to the military and the occupations of the mass of the peasantry. As the feudal *levée* dropped away, the Swiss instructors of the French infantry regiments took their recruits predominantly from the *'enfants perdus'* — the rural vagrants and rabble. By the latter part of the fifteenth century, the French and the Spanish armies were easily the dominant forces in Europe, and the French army in particular had in some respects taken on a recognizably modern form. That is to say, it was attached to a state authority (via the monarch), was armed with explosive weaponry — together with other weapons — and had a permanently organized core.

The ascent of France and decline of Spain as military powers can be dramatically charted by the changing size of their armies across a period of close to a century, as seen in table 3.[53]

Table 3

	Spanish army	French army
1630	300,000	150,000
1650	100,000	100,000
1670	70,000	120,000
1700	50,000	400,000

The simple increase in size of armies among the leading countries from the declining period of feudalism to the turn of the eighteenth century is one of the most striking features of European military history. The Battle of Hastings involved some 12,000 men, with about the same numbers on either side. Gustavus Adolphus mustered 30,000 men for his campaigns, and Wallenstein perhaps as many as 100,000 — nominally he was only a military contractor but in reality he was a quasi-imperial ruler in his own right. However, it was the growth of the French army, as table 3 indicates, that was the most impressive feature of European armed strength. Under Louis XIV, the French army surpassed in numbers that of the Roman Empire at its height — an index of the degree of administrative and fiscal power generated by the leading absolutist state, which was certainly not thereby easily able to have everything its own way. The conclusion of the Thirty Years' War, a major point of transition in the consolidation of a reflexively monitored state system, was also marked by a radical expansion in the size of standing armies in most of the major European states. It should be emphasized, however, that virtually everywhere these armies were mainly made up of mercenaries, usually supplied by the poorer countries to the more wealthy. Even by the end of the seventeenth century there were few barracks anywhere in Europe; troops were billeted on civilians.

Naval power is obviously not just an extension of the land-based armed forces. Access to sea-going routes differs widely between states according to their geographical position; naval history is inevitably one of a particular mode of transportation; and ships have to be run by those who devote their lives to that end. In any relatively permanent navy, ships that concentrate upon the specialized business of making war must be backed up by a range of vessels providing other services, plus land-based facilities. As Brodie puts it, a navy consisting only of battleships would be like a railway having nothing but locomotives.[54] In feudal times, the main concentration of 'European' sea-power was around the Mediterranean and the primary fighting vessel there — the galley — had not changed much for centuries. Of course, around the North Sea and Atlantic there were already sea-borne adventurers — the Norsemen; but in spite of their extraordinary exploits they were never much more than intrepid sailors, traders and marauding bandits, not making up a 'navy' in the usual sense. As a vehicle of war, the galley depended upon ramming and boarding, or was simply a transportation vehicle for soldiery who would enter combat on land. The invention of sailing ships that could survive in all weathers and, thus, were not confined to the Mediterranean basin, was one factor making galleys outdated. Much more important was the appropriation of guns for warfare at sea. Sailing ships could concentrate barrages of cannon much as arrangements of siege guns could on land. Not only galleys, but the generally much lighter monsoon-wind sailing ships of the East were no match for the heavily armed European vessels. The latter could also be sailed close to the wind, a technique unknown to Eastern sailors whose experience was confined to the monsoon seas.

The fact that the states with strong Mediterranean interests stuck to the widespread use of galleys until deep into the sixteenth century was one of the factors aiding the rise to prominence of the English, the Dutch and later the French as major naval powers. This, in turn, strongly influenced the decline not only of Spain but of a range of Mediterranean states that were, in the post-feudal period, of the first importance in the overall distribution of power in Europe. Like land-based armies, but persisting to a later date, the fleets of the maritime countries were largely composed of hirelings, not owned by the state. About 40 per cent of the Armada was composed of galleons owned by the Spanish crown, the rest being armed merchant vessels; and only about 16 per cent of the English fleet consisted of royal warships.[55] Regular navies date mainly from the latter part of the seventeenth century, by which time the merchant vessels had been forced out of the line by increases in both the fire-power and the manoeuvrability of warships. Nonetheless, the armed strength of the merchant vessels that roamed the world in search of trade and plunder was formidable; by the middle of the sixteenth century, and for a long period thereafter, 'European ships could count on crushing superiority in armed encounters with vessels of different design on every ocean of the earth.'[56]

If these various transformations of land-based and naval armed strength had merely accompanied the development of the absolutist state, or were simply results of that development, there would be no point in offering such an account of well-documented military history. But the changing nature of military power is far more important than that in explicating not only the nature of absolutism but also the character of the nation-state.

Various main features of European state development were shaped in a decisive way by the contingent outcomes of military confrontations and wars. Nothing shows more clearly how implausible it is to regard the emergence of modern societies as the result of some sort of evolutionary scheme that inexorably leads from the alluvial dirt of Sumer to the factory shop-floor of latter-day Europe. If Charlemagne or another ruler had managed to re-establish an imperial formation in Europe with the scope and the sway of the Roman Empire, the continent would no doubt have 'stagnated' in just the same way that it seemed to later Western observers the great empires of the East did. 'Capitalism' may have developed in another sector of the world altogether; but the most likely result would almost certainly have been that history would have followed an entirely different course. If the Mongols in the thirteenth century had chosen to build upon their victories on the borders of Europe, rather than being more concerned with the East, or if the Ottoman Empire had won comparable victories in the seventeenth century, 'Europe' would not have existed as a socio-political entity.

The European state system was not simply the 'political environment' in which the absolutist state and nation-state developed. It was the condition, and in substantial degree the very source, of that development. It was war, and preparations for war, that provided the most potent energizing stimulus for the concentration of administrative resources and fiscal reorganization that characterized the rise of absolutism. Technological changes affecting warfare were more important than changes in techniques of production. In general it is a mistake to contrast the supposed technological inertia of the Middle Ages with a vision of rapid technological change from the Renaissance onwards. Technological change was not foreign to medieval life,[57] and did not greatly accelerate in the post-feudal era, at least prior to the seventeenth century. It is often pointed out that the medieval guilds resisted technological change, but forgotten that the new state authority regarded such change with as little favour as the trade corporations had done.[58] The fairly rapid rate of technological development in the means of making war was first of all substantially separate from the main core of production, which it affected much more than the other way around.

The emergence of standing armies is a phenomenon of much greater sociological interest than is ordinarily recognized. A comparative standpoint can sometimes lead to a certain confusion here, for standing armies are not, as such, distinctive to Europe. In some form or another, all the larger types of class-divided society have maintained standing armies — it is feudalism that is unusual in that respect. Thus it might seem as though there is nothing particularly new in the European developments, which actually come more into line with what has existed elsewhere. But this is misleading. In other traditional states, the military was the main foundation of both the internal administrative power of the state apparatus and its external defence (or means of aggression) against foreign threat. Given the segmental character of class-divided societies, it is often difficult to separate the two in a meaningful way at all. But in the absolutist state, for the first time, there begins to come about a situation in which the army is not the main basis of the preservation of internal 'order'. This is a transition which culminates in the European nation-state and — so I shall argue — explains certain of its intrinsic structural characteristics. The other face of the developments in the means of waging war is the process of internal pacification previously referred to (and discussed more fully below). This was not brought about by the growth in the size of armies or by the elaboration of military technology. Rather, the existence of large standing armies and the progression of internal pacification are complementary expressions of the concentration of the administrative resources of the state. In both cases what is involved is a leap forward in the expansion of administrative power.

In this leap, the organization of the military played a prime role, influencing both the state apparatus and other organizations including, at a later date, business firms. For it was to a large extent in the military sphere, as Mumford in particular has reminded us,[59] that administrative power in its modern guise was pioneered. The innovations of Maurice of Nassau, the Prince of Orange, are both the most prominent example of this and at the same time exemplify more long-term trends in military organization. Maurice helped initiate two connected administrative changes later seen in all more bureaucratized organizations — the formation of a body of experts holding exclusive knowledge of certain essential administrative techniques, and the simultaneous creation of a 'de-skilled' population of ordinary soldiery. There is a very real sense in which, through Maurice's interventions, the techniques of Taylorism became well embedded in the sphere of the armed forces several hundred years before, in industrial production, they came to be known by such a label.[60] As van

Doorn remarks, comparing the two apparently quite contrasting figures, 'with both persons one is struck by the solid knowledge of the practice of their trade, their sharp analytical powers and a desire for experiment which was supported by a firm belief in the organisability and manipulability of human behaviour.'[61] As Taylor was to do, Maurice divided the technical aspects of the work of soldiery into specific, regular sequences of single activities. Thus, building upon what had already been accomplished by the Spanish commanders, he produced flow charts for the handling of the musket and the pike, each part of the sequence of acts involved being clearly specified. Soldiers were required to practise these until they could automatically follow the 'correct' procedures. Rather than being treated as 'craftsmen', skilled in the use of weaponry, recruits were regarded as having to be drilled to acquire the necessary familiarity with handling military equipment. The members of a unit were taught to respond simultaneously to command instructions, so as to co-ordinate the movements of each individual with the group as a whole.

Under the impact of these modes of administrative reshaping, profound changes occurred in the nature of the armed forces and in behaviour on the battlefield. Maurice set up the first military academy in Europe, whose teachings by one avenue or another became standard practice throughout the continent. The modern senses of 'uniform' and 'discipline' can be traced to their spread. The former of these terms was originally only an adjective but became a noun as the wearing of standardized clothes grew to be the norm in armies. So far as the ordinary soldier goes, uniforms date from the New Model Army in the English Civil War. Even in the eighteenth century some troops dressed more or less as they pleased; but for the most part in the course of the seventeenth century the wearing of uniforms became firmly established among all ranks of soldiery. 'Discipline' used to denote a property of someone who followed a set of teachings, but under the influence of military training came to be regarded not as the individual receiving instruction but the end-result of such instruction.[62] In the new mode of fighting wars, personal display and heroism became dramatically reduced in importance, demonstrating that the transition from display (spectacle) to anonymity which Foucault traces for punishment is not solely associated with incarceration.[63] The barracks came into being in close association with uniforms and regularized disciplinary training.

The administrative techniques of Maurice were partly derived from copying procedures used in the Roman legions, and were partly the result of adopting notions of training suggested in pedagogy. They reflect processes of administrative reform which by the end of the seventeenth century were penetrating many spheres of activity and have, as their *fons et origo*, the absolutist state. But there can be no doubt that the model of the army — as Cromwell made clear in a particularly bold example — was directly looked to by many of those seeking to expand the administrative resources at their disposal. The picture in concrete terms was, of course, a complicated one. The officer corps in most states retained a hostility to the bureaucratizing of the armed forces in so far as it affected their own life-styles; there was no professional officer corps prior to 1800. Officers were usually mercenaries or aristocrats; 'the former pursued profit, the latter honour and adventure.'[64]

The fact that the early development of the armed strength of the European states was organized in a 'capitalistic' fashion may be relevant to explaining the spread of entrepreneurial enterprise that subsequently became such a significant element of Western social institutions. The princely rulers of post-feudal Europe all became dependent on loans from bankers, who in conjunction with entrepreneurial mercenary commanders, were the makers and breakers of monarchs.[65] The role of the *condottieri* and the banking families was of key importance in the 'break away' from traditional patterns of military organization in the early formation of absolutist states. Later, as the carrying on of wars became even more formidably expensive, those states that had successfully negotiated the transition from feudalism intact assumed control of credit. We are so accustomed to seeing the rise of commercial, and then industrial, capitalism as due to the results of private initiative that it looks as if an initial phase of capitalist development ground to a halt with the consolidating of the absolutist state. But really the activities of Sully, Colbert and the others set certain patterns which persist to this day. The states assumed control of money, placed their apparatus of sanctions in the service of guaranteeing its value, and a national system of credits and debts was established. Although individual bankers and other entrepreneurs may have been pushed out of business, the further development of capitalist enterprise was in the long run decisively strengthened rather than weakened.

To examine this issue, in relation to the formation of the nation-state, some basic conceptual questions have to be raised. What exactly does 'capitalism' mean when used of the economic development of Europe from the fifteenth or sixteenth century onwards? How does capitalism *en gros* differ from 'industrial capitalism'? And what relation does each of these types have to the emergence of the nation-state? These are the problems which I shall make the focus of the next chapter. But first it is necessary to provide a conceptualization of the nation-state.

Nation-State, Nation, Nationalism

The terms 'nation-state', 'nation' and 'nationalism' are often, even characteristically, used in the literature of the social sciences and history as though they were synonymous. But I shall distinguish between them.[66] By 'nationalism' I mean a phenomenon that is primarily psychological — the affiliation of individuals to a set of symbols and beliefs emphasizing communality among the members of a political order. Although sentiments of nationalism often coincide with the actual distribution of populations within states, and while those who govern modern states usually seek to promote such sentiments wherever possible, there is by no means always a clear correspondence between them. By a 'nation' I refer to a collectivity existing within a clearly demarcated territory, which is subject to a unitary administration, reflexively monitored both by the internal state apparatus and those of other states. Both the nation and nationalism are distinctive properties of modern states and in the context of their original emergence as well as elsewhere there is more than a fortuitous connection between them. There can be no nationalism, in its modern form at least, without the formation of nations, although the reverse relation is a more problematic one.

In order to indicate that nationalism is a recent development we have to contrast it to pre-existing forms of group identity. Barth is probably right to say that sentiments of group identity at all times and in all places are exclusionary: how a group or community is thought of depends upon the traits attributed to others, to outsiders.[67] In many tribal cultures, the word denoting member of the community is identical to that used for 'human', outsiders not being accorded that dignity. The characteristic association of outsider with 'barbarian' has sometimes the same linguistic connotation. Occasionally, exclusionary terms seem to be the only ones in terms of which group identity is conceptualized. Thus the Germanic peoples referred to themselves as 'between Wend and Walsche', not having any other conceptual means of self-designation. The referent of 'Wend' altered from Finnic nomad herders situated to the north-east to incoming Slavic groups moving in further south; while 'Walsche' was transferred from the Celts to the Romans. The notion of 'tribe', of course, presumes some conceptions of a descent group, or association of such groups; and such conceptions, together with religious symbols, have everywhere been the main sources of group identity and exclusion. Genealogical myths seem to have been the most common means whereby actual descent and kin connections became solidified with group identity, and have been as much part of the history of ruling classes within class-divided societies as of overall cultures. The same is not true of language. Even in small tribal communities it is not generally the case that language is, or is felt to be, a significant index of identity and exclusion. Surrounding groups often speak the same language, or a variant of it. The ruling classes in class-divided societies have frequently been polyglot, this being an expression of the cultural mergings produced through conquest and partial assimilation.[68] The language of the Ottoman imperial court in the sixteenth century, for example, comprised large numbers of mixed Arabic, Persian and Turkish words and phrases, and most of the courtiers could speak these and other languages.[69]

In medieval feudalism, as in many class-divided societies with the exception of centralized bureaucratic empires, courts were usually peripatetic. The Holy Roman Empire did not have a fixed capital, the ruling administration regularly moving between various cities. The lack of a capital city in the traditional European states both contributed to, and expressed, the low degree of territorial integration. It helped strengthen communality of outlook and identity among the dominant classes but, by that very token, it inhibited an extension of them to those in the subject populations. Those states that relatively early on developed fixed capitals tended to be the ones associated with the most distinguishable nascent forms of nationalist sentiment, thus indicating that the means of propogating symbols from a national cultural centre was probably as important even early on as any more 'spontaneous' identity forged at the lower levels of society. Two of the primary examples, France and England, were 'continuous states' for several hundred years. That is to say, they were not conquered from the outside or subjected to alien dominion over their central regions. Because of the mutual claims of their dynasties, their territorial and cultural development were closely tied. Prior to the thirteenth century it would make most sense when referring to them to speak of the existence of two French kingdoms, one located in continental Europe and the other off its shores, since both were ruled by French-speaking monarchs whose retainers and higher administrators were also French-speaking. In Scotland at that period, four languages were spoken — French among the dominant class, Anglo-Saxon towards the south-east, Gaelic in the Highlands and the Western Isles, and Celtic in marginal areas towards the south-west.[70] Nevertheless, by the fifteenth century there were some definite stirrings of something like nationalist feeling, stimulated by the experience of constant struggles with the English. These sentiments have their origins, as Barrow observes, not in ethnic or linguistic communality, but in the state's mobilization of different classes and strata for the fight against a common enemy.[71]

Of course, such 'peripheral nationalisms' persist to this day in Europe, and the dynamics of their development are in some respects different from those of the more major states. In the latter, stable administration from early established capitals seems to have been crucial. 'English' dates from about the fourteenth century, and in some considerable degree spread outwards from usages first firmly established in London.[72] By the sixteenth century there can readily be traced a few core components of 'being English', associated also with 'speaking English'. Whether it could accurately be described as 'nationalism' is highly dubious; the nationalism that emerges in the nineteenth and twentieth centuries is 'British' rather than 'English', although complicated by both Scottish and Welsh nationalist feelings. France expanded in a relative stable way across the centuries from the Île de

France, and it surely not accidental that the most powerful and centralized absolutist state is also the one in which the lineages of modern nationalism can most easily be discerned. What became 'France' in the sixteenth and seventeenth centuries was nevertheless moulded from a collection of provinces that were earlier both culturally and linguistically distinct. The battle of Muret, in the first part of the thirteenth century, was one of those events which, trivial enough in itself, was fraught with consequences. It led to the dominance of the northern monarchs over Languedoc, which otherwise might have become a powerful state based around the central Mediterranean coast and the Rhône delta.[73] The spread of French was in some part the result of deliberate state policy — it became the sole official language by an edict of 1539. The *Académie Française*, founded by Richelieu, became a major influence on both the form and the successful diffusion of the French language through the whole territory of the state. However, most historians agree that nationalist sentiments in the seventeenth and early eighteenth centuries in France were both rudimentary and regionally specific. Most 'French' men and women thought of themselves as belonging either to one of the provinces or to one of the cities.

Common though it is to portray nationalism in 'continuous states' as emerging in an inevitable way from the doctrines of sovereignty which they took up, there is actually little intrinsic association between them. A link was only forged subsequently; Bodin and his fellow political thinkers were not 'nationalists'. The French revolution undeniably had an influence on the subsequent flowering of nationalism, within *'une nation une et indivisible'*. But it was mainly in the non-unified states and principalities of central and northern Europe that modern conceptions of nationalism have their origin — in Romanticism rather than constitutional rationalism.[74] Nationalism is essentially a phenomenon of the late eighteenth century and after. The question as to why this should be so is one I shall take up later.

A 'nation', as I use the term here, only exists when a state has a unified administrative reach over the territory over which its sovereignty is claimed. The development of a plurality of nations is basic to the centralization and administrative expansion of state domination internally, since the fixing of borders depends upon the reflexive ordering of a state system. We can follow

Jones in recognizing four aspects of the transformation of frontiers into borders.[75] These he calls allocation, delimitation, demarcation and administration.

The first refers to a collaborative political decision taken among states about the distribution of territory between them. Delimitation concerns the identification of specific border sites.[76] Demarcation in Jones's scheme — written as a guide for policymakers and not just an academic study — refers to how borders are actually marked on the physical environment. Many borders, even within the heart of Europe today, are not demarcated. That apparent modern equivalent of the walls built by traditional states, the Berlin Wall, is an anomaly because it symbolizes the failure of a modern state to exert the level of administrative control over its population which its governing authorities deem proper and necessary. The border between East and West Germany must be one of the most highly 'administered', in Jones's terms, in the world. That is to say, a high degree of direct surveillance is maintained along it. Traditional states sometimes constructed frontier posts, demanding payment, and occasionally documentation, of those who travelled through. But where these existed they were usually, in fact, at divisions between provinces rather than between states as such. The coupling of direct and indirect surveillance (customs officials and frontier guards, plus the central co-ordination of passport information) is one of the distinctive features of the nation-state.

A nation-state is, therefore, a bordered power-container — as I shall argue, the pre-eminent power-container of the modern era. How this has come about it will be one of the chief tasks of the following chapters to explain. But among other things it involves processes of urban transformation and the internal pacification of states. These are phenomena that go together with the creation of generalized 'deviance' as a category and with processes of sequestration. All traditional states have laid claim to the formalized monopoly over the means of violence within their territories. But it is only within nation-states that this claim characteristically becomes more or less successful. The progress of internal pacification is closely connected with such success — they are, as it were, different sides of the same process.

The objection may be raised that there are very many instances, even in current times, of states whose monopoly of the means of violence is chronically threatened from within by armed groups; that insurgent movements, often poorly armed and organized compared with state authorities, have sometimes challenged and overthrown those authorities; and that there are diffuse levels of violence in minor contexts of even the most politically quiescent societies (crimes of violence, domestic violence and so on). None of these, however, compromise the point at issue, which concerns a comparison between nation-states and traditional states. There are circumstances in which civil war, involving chronic confrontations between armed movements or coalitions of more or less equal strength, have been quite protracted. However, not only are such circumstances highly unusual, the very existence of 'civil war' presumes a norm of a monopolistic state authority. By contrast, conditions which in a modern state would be defined as examples of 'civil war', that is, divisive 'internal' armed struggles, have been typical of all class-divided societies for very long periods. Again, armed groups or movements today are almost always oriented to the assumption of state power, either by taking over an existing state's territory or by dividing up a territory and establishing a separate state. Such organizations do not and cannot 'opt out' from involvement in state power one way or another as frequently happened in traditional states. Finally, I have no wish to underplay the importance or extent of violence that takes place in small-scale contexts in modern societies. But I am principally concerned with the means of violence associated with the activities of organized armed forces, not with violence as a more blanket category of the doing of physical harm to others.

Collecting together the implications of the foregoing observations, we can arrive at the following concept of the nation-state, which holds for all variants and is not intrinsically bound to any particular characterization of nationalism. It is the same definition given in the volume to which this book is the successor. 'The nation-state, which exists in a complex of other nation-states, is a set of institutional forms of governance maintaining an administrative monopoly over a territory with demarcated boundaries (borders), its rule being sanctioned by law and direct control of the means of internal and external violence.'[77]

5

Capitalism, Industrialism and Social Transformation

What is Capitalism?

Among both sociologists and historians, the fortunes of the concept of 'capitalism' have waxed and waned in different periods over the past century or so. Historians characteristically have been suspicious of the notion, although often on grounds that apply to many generalizing concepts, that it is too diffuse to do justice to the subtleties of historical detail and particularity. Where they have not been close to Marxism, sociologists have often favoured other terms to refer to the changes associated with modernity, such as 'industrialism', or the more global concept of 'industrial society'. Marxists tend to use the word 'capitalism' with casual profligacy, regarding the development of capitalist production as the most fundamental phenomenon affecting the modern world, but not always being too careful to identify its traits in any sort of precise way. Behind the conceptual admixtures there are, however, a number of basic disagreements of substance. One concerns the primacy of the events or changes associated respectively with 'capitalism' and with 'industrialism'. For Marx, and for his self-professed followers, industrialism is in its essential respects a furthering of characteristics found in capitalism, which is both more general and which precedes it in time. According to the majority of non-Marxist social scientists, on the other hand, capitalism is but a transitory phase in the formation of modern 'industry' and 'industrial society'. The latter notions are thus more important for analysing the modern world, and of a more generic nature, than is the former.[1]

Clearly the points at issue here are in large degree empirical: How should we seek to characterize the major economic transformations that have occurred over the past two centuries? But they are also conceptual. For evidently neither the terms 'capitalism' nor 'industrialism' are always used in the same way by those on each side of this particular theoretical fence.

It will not be my purpose in what follows to provide a general survey of vagaries in usage of these terms in the literature of the social sciences. Rather, I shall take two 'classical' sources as a point of departure, contrasting Marx and Weber on the nature of 'capitalism'. Both tend to speak predominantly of 'capitalism' rather than 'industrialism'. But Weber's position is close to — and has frequently inspired — the views of those who see industrialism as the major influence shaping the institutional parameters of modern society. Inverting chronology, I shall first of all discuss Weber, then move to Marx. Although I shall in some respects support Marx's view rather than that of Weber, the standpoint developed will differ from both. In European history, the development of capitalism antedates that of industrialism, and by a considerable period of time. The former was also the necessary condition for the emergence of the latter. But capitalism and industrialism have their own distinctive features. They cannot be conceptually collapsed into one another and empirically they can exist in some substantial separation. This is also true, I shall argue later, of other quite elemental aspects of the development of European states in the nineteenth and early twentieth centuries.

According to Weber, capitalistic activities can be found at many times and places. There is nothing in capitalism as such that links it specifically to the West; modern (Western) capitalistic activity has certain definite characteristics that mark it out from earlier types. In Weber's writings capitalism is tied to an interpretation of 'economic action' as a type or aspect of social conduct. Human activity, in his terms, is 'economically oriented' according to whether or not it is concerned with the satisfaction of a material need. 'Economic action' refers to any form of economically oriented activity that is carried out peacefully. Not all economic action involves exchange, but exchange (which can take various different forms) is easily the most important means of securing desired utilities. 'Exchange' is any non-coerced agreement offering an existing or future utility against another or others given in return. In what Weber sometimes calls 'natural economies',[2] exchange barely occurs at all, or is made principally in kind. Natural economies are inimical to capitalism, although something approaching 'profit-making' may exist in them, since barter may be used to accumulate a range of goods by one or more of the involved parties. But calculation in kind is essentially concerned with the catering for known and relatively fixed wants. Capitalism, in all its forms, depends upon the existence of money. It is important to see what Weber is getting at here. One might think that money is necessary to capitalistic activity primarily because it provides a means for the assessment of 'profit'. But the importance of money is much more profound than this. For, as Weber portrays it, money is above all a means of the storage and transformation of resources — a means of the expansion, in my terminology, of time—space distanciation and thereby of power.[3]

Money is a standard of exchange-value which, by nature of its very standardization, removes economic exchange from the contextual limitations of barter. Barter requires that those who exchange goods, at some point in the trading process, physically meet to carry out the transaction. With the use of money, exchange is no longer (in principle) tied to any particular locale. There is an inherent connection between the 'calculability' that money promotes and its transcendence of the immediacy of context. The same is true of the accounting procedures money inevitably entails. 'Money', in a general sense, has existed in a diversity of societies, not only in those of the class-divided type. But monetary exchange of a fairly developed sort presupposes just those forms of listing and collating of resources that are at the origin of writing, so important to the generation of power in traditional states. Weber places much emphasis upon the invention of double-entry book-keeping in the formation of the specifically Western type of capitalism, and no doubt he is right to do so. But no less important is his stress upon the generic connection of money with accounting procedures and, therefore, with information storage.

As Marx does — although not of course with the same implications being drawn for economic theory — Weber emphasizes that economic transactions involving money have a 'use' as well as an exchange (calculative) aspect. Every capitalistic enterprise — as Weber applies that term — involves 'calculations in kind',[4] to do with the needs to which the commodities sold are to be put. These 'considerations of use' also extend to the instruments of production. Thus in a workshop producing yarn, the entrepreneur must give attention to wear and tear of the looms and so on. In barter systems there is no effective way of assessing 'investment', depreciation or waste in relation to the achieved outcome of production. But money provides the possibility of organizing and regularizing 'stocks' as well as 'products' across time-space. Monetary accounting is a particular version of the co-ordination of resources made possible by listing and cross-listing in general, which is why we should see a close analytical connection between the 'account' and the 'file' in the generation of power in organizations of all types. As Weber remarks, money accounting

> is the method of assuring the conditions of future productivity of the business which combines the greatest degree of certainty with the greatest flexibility in relation to changing circumstances; with any storing of real stocks of materials or any other mode of provision in kind such flexibility would be irrationally and severely impeded. It is difficult to see, without money accounting, how 'reserves' could be built up without being specified in detail.[5]

In analysing money, Weber is not always as careful as he should be to indicate how specific, in certain ways, are the properties of money in modern capitalism — something which is relevant to criticisms that can be made of his use of the concept of capitalism in general. Of course, there now exists a much greater variety of anthropological and archaeological studies of money in tribal and class-divided societies than was available in Weber's day. These allow us to fill in some of the gaps in Weber's discussion. The degree of 'universalisability' of money was low in virtually all cultures until modern times and features which have since become integrated were usually dissociated from one another. In some societies, money was a medium of exchange but not a standard of value. There are many cases in which money served as a standard of value but was not used for the other purposes with which it is associated today.[6] It is rare or unknown to find currency that does not retain a strong connection with forms of use-value. Prices often also maintained this connection, even in those class-divided societies in which quite highly standardized coin was in wide circulation. Thus a price might be expressed in terms of a number of livestock, even where that meant more or less the same quantified monetary value whenever it was used. Liquid reserves were normally very low compared with those involved in modern monetary systems, since the unit of value used for the long-term storage of assets was normally different from that employed for immediately convertible exchange. Deferred payments (of various possible sorts) are a major feature of the time—space distanciation of modern economic activity but were always restricted in traditional states. The means of deferred payment were often different from the standard in terms of which such payment was calculated, since the units of value may not have been in supply in the requisite quantities. For example, the code of Hammurabi permitted debtors to repay loans contracted in silver in the form of quantities of barley.[7]

Weber defines 'capitalistic' enterprise as any type of economic action undertaken in the anticipation of achieving profit through exchange.[8] In several guises, it has existed 'all over the world for thousands of years wherever the possibilities of exchange and money economy, and money financing, have been present'.[9] One major type is mercantile capitalism, deriving from a range of profit possibilities in trade. These include the simple selling of goods, whether manufactured or not, but also numerous devices of extending credit and speculation in different currencies. Weber separates these activities analytically from profit opportunities concerned with political or military organizations; and from an orientation to profit on the part of a political authority or state itself (e.g. tax farming). Modern capitalism differs from these pre-existing types in a range of ways. It involves the following.

1   'Rational capitalistic enterprises with fixed capital'.[10] Weber lays a great deal of stress upon this, and it is closely associated with his assessment of the significance of double-entry book-keeping. Prior to the modern era, mercantile capitalism and certain sorts of finance capitalism were the only forms of capitalistic economic enterprise that may be durable and regularly organized, apart from those controlled directly by the state. 'Fixed capital' implies not only the existence of a definite locale in which the enterprise is situated but also the control of stable amounts of production equipment and investment stocks. Of course, much

has been written about the concept of rationalization in Weber's work and this is not the place to attempt to recapitulate even the main outlines of that debate. In this context, however, Weber makes his meaning reasonably clear. 'Rational' refers to the use of means of production and investment which, given available allocative resources, are most effective in attaining a given end — the achievement of profitable economic activity.

2   The existence of a mass of free wage-labour. In prior types of capitalistic enterprise, especially those involving the organization of production for profit, rather than purely commercial or banking transactions, unfree labour has often been used. The economic disadvantages of organizing capitalistic production through slave labour are discussed by Weber at some length. According to him they are quite formidable and, hence, the widespread employment of slave labour is only possible where slaves can be maintained very cheaply, where there are opportunities for regular slave recruitment and the production in question is agricultural. The employment of workers for wages or salaries involves much less capital risk and investment. The sanction of dismissal, in Weber's view, is a more efficient basis of the disciplining of a work-force than are the punishments that can be inflicted upon slaves.[11] Of course, the functional advantages of free wage-labour over unfree labour do not in and of themselves explain the adoption of the former by capitalist entrepreneurs in the emergent phases of modern capitalism. Weber agrees with Marx that the condition of this was the large-scale expropriation of peasant workers from their means of production, a phenomenon that can by no means be wholly explained in terms of the perceived needs of expanding capitalistic enterprises.

3   The formation of clearly designated and co-ordinated tasks in the business organization. This theme obviously overlaps very substantially with Weber's more general treatment of bureaucracy. Capitalist firms share with other modern organizations the characteristics of administrative power, involving the hierarchical specification of offices and procedures governed by written codes of conduct. But they have a distinct disciplinary problem. That is to say, a large proportion of those subject to bureaucratic authority do not themselves directly participate in it. Workers are a 'horizontal' grouping — Weber occasionally says 'class' — subject to the collective authority of 'management'.

4   The connecting of individual capitalistic enterprises within a market economy. By the 'market' here Weber means both labour and product markets, in which labour-power as well as a vast range of goods have become commodities. A market economy presumes national and international markets, thereby again depending upon the existence of highly standardized money. In all class-divided societies there have been markets, which in some respects stretch well beyond the physical confines of specific market-places. But, as Weber says, these have always not only been limited in their extensiveness, but have been regulated by many factors other than the economic demands of price, investment and profit.

> The original modes of market regulation have been various, partly traditional and magical, partly dictated by kinship relations, by status privileges, by military needs, by welfare policies, and not least by the interests and requirements of the governing authorities of organisations. But in each of these cases the dominant interests have not been primarily concerned with maximising the opportunities of acquisition and economic provision of the participants in the market themselves; they have, indeed, often been in conflict with them.[12]

5   The provision for the wants of the whole of the population predominantly by means of capitalist production. This is in a sense nothing but a summary version of the preceding points but is, at the same time, evidently a quite elemental feature of modern capitalism. The capitalist enterprise is not just one type of production organization among others — as in all societies where capitalistic ventures have been found previously — but *the* form of production upon which everyone becomes dependent.

Weber makes it clear that he regards the origins of capitalism as lying well before those of industrialism, and that the latter comes about because of pressures introduced by the former. According to him, the main period of large-scale expansion of capitalism is in the sixteenth and seventeenth centuries. In the seventeenth century in particular there was 'a feverish pursuit of invention', dominated by the perceived imperative to cheapen production.[13] It is at this point, Weber argues, that technological innovation and the pursuit of profit in economic action tend to begin to come together. Although there is a history of invention dating back into the Middle Ages, only in war — as I have mentioned in chapter 4 — did these previously go along with one another.

It is hardly surprising that Weber treats industrialism as a more or less direct outcome of capitalism, since he has already accentuated the centrality of the 'rationality' of production to modern capitalistic enterprise as a whole. His discussion of industry is, nevertheless, a sophisticated one, linking factory and machine to their immediate organizational forerunners. Steam machinery derives from earlier mechanized forms of production and is not quite the radical innovation Victorians took it to be. However, the most essential characteristic of industrialism is not the use of power-driven machinery in the production process but the concentration of ownership of the work-place, means of production, source of power and raw material in the hands of the entrepreneur. Such a combination, Weber observes, was rarely met with prior to the eighteenth century.[14]

Marx's dating of the origins of modern capitalism differs little from that of Weber. 'The capitalistic era', Marx says, 'dates from the sixteenth century.'[15] Unlike Weber, however, he is reluctant to use the term 'capitalism' to apply to economic activity at other times and in non-European contexts and only does so rather infrequently. Capital pre-exists the development of modern capitalism but Marx denies that either mercantile activities or the pursuit of profit on the part of financiers are accurately identified as types of capitalism. Although variant interpretations of Marx are possible on this point, it can scarcely be denied that he gives little attention to the organizational features of capitalistic enterprise upon which Weber places so much weight. Marx's analysis concentrates above all on the commodity, giving particular attention to a theme that political economy supposedly had previously ignored — the fact that, for the majority of the working population, labour-power becomes a commodity. While Weber acknowledges the significance of this, and pays due obeisance to Marx for having analysed it with great insight, it does not play quite as pivotal a role for him as it does for Marx. According to Marx, the conjunction of capital and wage-labour both supplies the historical clue to unravelling the origins of capitalism and, at the same time, constitutes the axis of its class system. As Marx says,

> In themselves money and commodities are no more capital than are the means of production and of subsistence. They want transforming into capital. But this transformation itself can only take place under certain circumstances that centre in this namely, that two very different kinds of commodity-possessors must come face to face and into contact: on the one hand, the owners of money, means of production, means of subsistence, who are eager to increase the sum of values they process, by buying other people's labour-power; on the other hand, free labourers, the sellers of their own labour-power, and therefore the sellers of labour . . . With this polarisation of the market for commodities, the fundamental conditions of capitalist product are given.[16]

Marx's analysis therefore concentrates much less upon the conditions necessary for the stabilizing and expansion of product markets than upon the production processes linking the transformation of nature to the commodification of labour-power. It is a basic part of Marx's critique of political economy that, as he puts it, 'so-called primitive accumulation' finds its main impetus in the expropriation of the peasantry rather than in the specific achievements of entrepreneurs themselves. Major lacunae in Marxist analysis stem from this at the same time as do some of its major strengths. The sanctity of private property in orthodox political economy is explained in terms of the diligence of the 'frugal elite'.[17] By their careful husbandry, some groups of individuals accumulate wealth which they 'place at the disposal' of the indigent, offering them the means of their livelihood by putting them to work. For Marx, the situation is not like this at all. This 'insipid childishness' disguises not only a series of social changes in which 'conquest, enslavement, robbery, murder' play the greater part,[18] but occludes the class relations at the core of capitalism. It would be too easy and, in some respects, utterly misleading to say that, for Weber, capitalism is distinguished by its 'rational' nature, whereas for Marx capitalism is specifically 'irrational' because its success is chained to human servitude. Two different senses of 'rationality' are in play here, related to variant epistemological positions. Nonetheless, 'modern capitalism' for Weber is intrinsically tied to an expansion of the organizational features of the capitalist enterprise, which assume pride of place in his analysis over its class character. For Marx, however, the heightened power generated by capitalism is traced largely to the vastly augmented control it allows over the material world, in which the development of technology is combined in a novel way with human labour.

Marx's discussion of the commodity explains why he is reluctant to label pre-modern forms of economic activity 'capitalism', as Weber does, and why capitalism has to be regarded as a 'mode of production' but one that is very different from preceding types.[19] 'Capitalism' is nowhere defined by Marx in the formal way it is by Weber. But it is clear enough that for Marx 'capitalism' is not conceptualized as to do with the pursuit of profit through exchange relations, but as this conjoined to the exploitation of 'abstract labour power'. It is not only that the majority of the population are propertyless and have to sell their labour on a market to maintain a livelihood. What is essential is that labour power becomes 'detached' from other traits or characteristics of the worker and can thus be integrated with technology. The labour contract is the focal element in Marx's analysis here, demonstrating how distinct capitalism is from all previous systems of the exploitation of labour.[20] In capitalism, labour-power is a commodity in virtue of its abstract form. The fact that the worker has to sell his or her labour to an employer in order to gain a living is the main constraint through which the compliance of the labour-force is achieved. It replaces, Marx stresses, the various admixtures of bondage and the threat of the use of violence characteristic of traditional states. On the one hand, it connects with the upsurge in material transformation made possible by the conjunction of abstract labour and technology and, on the other with the 'bourgeois rights' to private property so central to capitalist enterprise (and to the modern state, as Marx conceives it). For, as Marx so forcefully points out, the rights of 'free and equal' political participation have as their other side the subordination of the worker to capital.

Given the manner in which Marx formulates his interpretation of capitalism, it is not surprising that his discussion of money carries certain different emphases from that of Weber. Rather than the significance of money accounting, and of the state in acting as a guarantor of standard value, Marx once again relates money to the nature of the commodity. There is an unbroken thread running from Marx's early strictures about money, that 'universal whore', that 'pander between men and nations',[21] to his analysis of the phenomenon in his mature economic writings. Money is the medium — or, rather, the material expression — of the commodification of labour-power which makes it 'translatable' into material goods in terms of numerically assessed equivalences. Labour-power can be evaluated as a cost in terms strictly comparable to material goods or products, in spite of the fact that these share nothing in common in terms of their substantive traits. Money, according to Marx, is 'the reflection, in a single commodity, of the value relations between all commodities'.[22] When a commodity is converted into money, the exchange confirms the specific value-form rather than providing its value; it makes manifest that the qualities of a service as good are not exhausted by what it can be 'used for'.

Marx's analysis of money, traced back through his general discussion of commodification, has considerable importance for characterizing how 'capitalism' should be understood, although his view cannot be accepted as it is. In refusing to apply the concept to pre-modern economic enterprise, Marx signals something very important. Put in the terms I have suggested previously, what this amounts to is that capitalism is involved in a central way in the discontinuity of modern history.[23] This issue is somewhat submerged in the otherwise characteristically acute interpretations that appear in Weber's writings, at least in some part because of his preoccupation with what distinguishes the long-term development of the West from the other 'world civilizations'. The strength of Marx's theory is that it provides the leverage for analysing that massively sharp wrench away from traditional modes of economic enterprise that occurs in Europe in the sixteenth and seventeenth centuries. It can confidently be asserted that Marx's view is the more sophisticated in this respect, in spite of the prominence that has been achieved by Weber's thesis of the association between Puritanism and the development of modern capitalism. This thesis may or may not be valid — the gap between proponents and antagonists yawns as widely as ever — but in any case it is more relevant to the question of explaining the first origins of capitalism than to interpreting how it is that it differs from pre-existing forms of economic activity. Weber's analysis of the 'rational' nature of modern capitalist enterprise is undeniably important, although I shall not choose to use that term in what follows. However, Marx's account of commodification directs our attention to a particularly significant nexus of relations.

How, then, should we best conceptualize what 'capitalism' is? I suggest that the following elements are involved. As I shall henceforth use the term, capitalism is a form of economic enterprise that has its origins only some four centuries ago in European history. That is to say, although there have been many forms of profit-making enterprise at other times and in other places, these are sufficiently different from what has occurred in modern history that it is more misleading than helpful to use the same term to refer to them all.

Capitalism involves the production of commodities. In this it is not distinctive, since the production of goods for purposes of profitable exchange has been carried on in many other contexts. But it has two distinct characteristics:

1 The process of commodification has not proceeded remotely as far in any prior type of society, for various reasons. Limitations on the alienability of property, especially in the most overwhelmingly important means of production — land — fundamentally blocks the expansion of commodified relationships. But so also do the 'modes of market regulation' of which Weber speaks, meaning that the sustained pursuit of profit rarely emerges untrammelled by other, divergent considerations.
2 The commodification of labour power is the essential accompaniment of the expansion of commodity production in general in capitalism. Marx is entirely right to insist upon the significance of this, as distinguishing modern economic enterprise from all other forms of economic order. For the first time in history, large segments (eventually the vast majority) of the working population do not directly produce the means of their own subsistence, but contract out their labour to others who, in the form of money wages, provide the wherewithall for them to survive.

This presupposes the intersection of two markets, labour and product markets. To speak of 'the market' in general, however, is not without sense, because of the close relation that necessarily exists between the two. While markets transcending the local level have existed in all class-divided societies, only in capitalism does the market become linked to the production of goods required for the day-to-day needs of a considerable proportion (subsequently again nearly a complete majority) of the population. Market relationships in capitalism presume the existence of a distinct 'economy', insulated from other institutional sectors.[24] The insulation of the economy is basic to the cycle of investment—profit—reinvestment characteristic of capitalist enterprise. 'Private property' plays an essential role here, in the sense that the accumulation process is influenced mainly be decisions taken by those owning 'privately held' capital. 'Privately held' here should be understood as contrasted to one main sense which the adjective 'public' can have, not as meaning resting in the hands of individual entrepreneurs. 'Private property' in this context means capital controlled by agencies — whether individuals, families or joint-stock corporations — rather than by the political apparatus of the state.

Capitalism involves the centrality of the 'financially accounting' organization, in which balance-sheets of investment and cost are used as the main index of whether the organization should expand or contract. The business firm shares much in common with other, non-capitalistic organizations in respect of its bureaucratic features — at least, such is the case with the larger economic organizations. But its continued existence depends upon sufficient profitability to provide renewed investment: its whole nature, as it were, is 'commodified'. Such is not the case with other organizations, including the state. Although all these organizations depend upon allocative resources, and their continued existence is tied in some sense to 'fiscal management', they are 'non-commidified' in the sense that the provision of their needed resources is not governed primarily by the operation of market forces.

All of this so far refers to capitalism as a form of economic activity. It does not satisfactorily elucidate how one should use the term 'capitalist society'. 'Capitalism' can be, and frequently is, used to designate a type of overall societal order, not only a distinctive series of economic relationships. I do, indeed, want to claim that capitalism is the first and only form of society in history of which it might be said with some plausibility that it both 'has' and 'is' a mode of production. I do not mean this, however, in the semi-technical sense in which Marx applies the term 'mode of production'. I mean that in capitalism, more than any other kind of social order, economic influences play a major dynamic role — if not unequivocally the dominant one in the way in which many social thinkers, close and distant from, Marxism have presumed. But what are the principal characteristics of the type of society that can be designated 'capitalist'? I shall give a preliminary answer here, but a fuller discussion of the question demands understanding phenomena to be discussed subsequently. For there has been no capitalist society which has not also been industrialized and which has not been a nation-state. I date the emergence of 'capitalist societies' at the same period (somewhere about or subsequent to the turn of the nineteenth century) at which nation-states come into being. Both have their roots several centuries earlier, and it is obvious enough that any temporal identification of their first formation must be only quite general.

A capitalist society has the following major characteristics.
1   'Capitalism', defined as a form of economic system in the manner indicated, is the primary basis of the production of goods and services upon which the population of that society as a whole depends. Because of the combination of the investment—profit—investment cycle and the mechanized co-ordination of human labour-power, capitalist societies are heavily influenced by what goes on in 'the economy', which has a very high degree of technological motility.
2   The existence of a distinct sphere of 'the economy' involves the insulation of the 'economic' and the 'political' from one another. Such insulation may take various concrete forms and mistakes that are often made in characterizing it must be avoided. As mentioned earlier (pp. 67—8), it is misleading to speak too readily of the 'separation' of economy and polity since, compared with class-divided societies, these are more closely connected than ever before. But the insulation of the economic and the political should also not be equated with competitiveness in labour and product markets.[25] Such a view has often been taken by those influenced by classical political economy, even where in other respects they have been critical of it. The classical economists tended to identify the sphere of the 'economic' with the competition of independent and autonomous capitalist firms,

in which any form of state intervention breaches the division between economy and polity. This not only greatly underestimates the ways in which the existence of an insulated 'economy' depends upon the state in the first place, it suggests a decline in the scope of the 'economic' with the increasing state intervention in productive activity. But what is usually termed the 'intervention' of the state may have the consequence of actually protecting the insulation of the economy — in fact, it may even be its necessary condition.

3   The insulation of polity and economy presumes institutions of private property in the means of production. Caution is again necessary here. I have indicated earlier that 'private' should not be equated solely with wealth that is at the disposal of the individual entrepreneur. However 'property' also has to be understood not just as a series of rights but as having a definite content associated with its nature as capital. It presumes, in other words, the processes of commodification noted above, which affect the 'propertyless' as much as the 'propertied'. In this sense wage-labour is, indeed, the other face of capital. It is for this reason that capitalism is a 'class society', in contrast to societies of the class-divided type. This does not imply, as Marx tends to argue, that class divisions and conflicts are the institutional dimension to which most (all?) other divisions and conflicts can be traced. It does mean that class conflict (in various guises) plays a more important dynamic role than in any previous type of society.

4   The nature of the state, as a mode of 'government', is strongly influenced by its institutional alignments with private property and with the insulated 'economy'. The autonomy of the state is conditioned, although never completely 'determined', by its reliance upon the accumulation of capital of which its control is to a large degree indirect.

5   That 'capitalist state' can be used as synonymous with 'capitalist society' demonstrates that the 'boundary maintaining' qualities of the nation-state are integral to its existence. On the face of things it would seem as though capitalism, as a form of economic activity, has no intrinsic relation to the nation-state. This indeed was the underlying assumption of many nineteenth-century thinkers, including Marx, and is relevant to the characteristic limitations of social theory remarked upon in

chapter 1. Capitalism promotes the development of long-distance economic activities that stretch well beyond the borders of states. That there are 'capitalist societies', as bounded entities then, is something that demands some considerable analysis rather than being merely be taken for granted.

Capitalism and Industrialism

In looking at the nature of industrialism, there are two questions to be tackled. One is the conceptual problem: how should 'industrialism' be understood? But we also have to consider the relation between capitalism and industrialism and ask in what sense, if any, one might be deemed the 'outcome' of the other.

It is of some interest and relevance to consider the etymology of the word 'industrialism' and associated terms to do with production. The term 'industry', which started to come into common coinage in English and French in the latter part of the eighteenth century, was originally associated primarily with diligent labour (thus indicating its close connection with administrative power, to be explored later). Adam Smith defines 'industry' in contrast to idleness, often using the first term to refer indifferently to both human labour and the means of production.[26] Ferguson links 'industry' with the learning of habits of 'responsible work activity', the endeavours of men to improve their arts, to extend their commerce, to secure their possessions, and to establish their rights'.[27] The term was not employed in such a way as to distinguish manufacture from either commerce or agriculture. Similarly, 'mechanical' was used to refer to a quality of an assemblage of work-tasks, not to machines as such; and 'manufacture' was not understood in the sense I have just employed it, but as referring to the 'productive arts' in general. Only some way into the nineteenth century did this group of terms start to assume the usages they have today.[28] Etymological consideration of such words helps emphasize that it would not be apposite to treat 'industrialism' as a strictly technological phenomenon. In the concept of 'industrial society', as applied by Saint-Simon, industrialism preserves these wider connotations. Saint-Simon's *industriels* are not defined in terms of their control over newly emerging industrial power but in terms of their propensity for disciplined work. In an industrial society, in contrast to feudalism, everyone — including those in the directive positions — is involved in productive labour.

Although I shall not use the term 'industrial society', I think it correct to hold that industrialism refers to more than mechanized technology alone. It also should be understood to embrace more than such technology plus factory production — this for two reasons. The 'factory', a locale in which direct productive activity is carried on through manual labour, is too narrow a notion to capture the organizational changes that occur with the advent of industrialism. Rather, it is better to speak of the 'industrial work-place' (which is also first of all a 'capitalistic work-place'): a locale in which vocationally organized labour is carried on separately from the home. But 'industrialism' should not be confined in its meaning to phenomena directly involved with the work-place, however that be described. Mechanization in modern economic life has helped produce economic transformations affecting the circulation of commodities. The development of mechanized transportation and modes of communication in particular is a major feature of industrialism.

I shall define 'industrialism' as presuming the following traits.

1   The use of inanimate sources of material power in either production or in processes affecting the circulation of commodities. What has come to be termed the 'Industrial Revolution' is usually associated above all with the harnessing of steam power to economic ends. But in the late eighteenth- and early nineteenth-century Britain, the water-mill was at least equally important in some of the main sectors of production that expanded most dramatically at that period. Moreover, the harnessing of electricity to production has proved to have as profound consequences as the more directly 'mechanical' sources of material power.

2   The mechanization of production and other economic process. What a 'machine' is cannot be defined as easily as might at first sight appear, but can be said to involve an artefact that accomplishes certain set tasks through the regularized application of inanimate power resources. All machines, no matter how automated they may be, have of course in some sense to be tended by human labour. Early processes of industrialization normally involved the direct integration of mechanization and human labour-power. The machine demanded corresponding human activities of a routine type to 'work' it. But there seems no

reason to build this into the definition of mechanization, which has also to include more automated processes in which the role of the worker is 'supervisory' and the mechanization of the labour-task in question more or less complete. Mechanization should not be associated intrinsically with the economic utilization of science. The first stages of the 'Industrial Revolution' were only quite marginally connected with scientific discoveries; the closer integration of science and technology is largely a more recent phenomenon.

3   Industrialism means the prevalence of manufacturing production, but we have to be careful about how 'manufacture' is to be understood. It is very frequently used to designate the production of non-agricultural goods but it should refer to the manner of production, rather than simply the creation of such goods. Manufacture should be regarded as connecting (1) and (2) in a regularized fashion, such that there are routinized processes creating a 'flow' of produced goods.

4   It is in this regularized component of production that we find a link with the existence of a centralized work-place in which productive activity is carried on. Industrialism cannot be a wholly 'technological' phenomenon because the three elements mentioned above presume an organization of human social relationships. I do not mean to imply some sort of technological reductionism here. The process of industrialization in its original form, in Britain, demonstrates various dislocations between elements that later came together as a more homogeneous productive order. Several of the more advanced sectors of production in respect of traits (1), (2) and (3) were organized largely through the putting-out system rather than in terms of the centralized work-place. Some of the early factories, by contrast, were established in sectors of production not distinguished by a particularly high level of mechanized manufacture.[29] But once these factors had come together, they formed something of a unitary 'productive package' that generated novel economic opportunities and was perceived as such within the framework of expanding capitalist enterprise.

The relation of capitalism to industrialism needs to be directly discussed, but first it is worth briefly asking why the concept of 'capitalist society' is acceptable while that of 'industrial society' is not. This issue, of course, raises questions of general importance, since the contrast between 'capitalist society' and 'industrial society' has tended to epitomize distinct theoretical traditions. If both Marx and Weber themselves favoured the former of the two terms, Weber's writings, as has already been mentioned, have often been drummed into service to support 'the theory of industrial society'.[30] But the concept of 'capitalist society' is defensible in a way in which that of 'industrial society' is not. Both notions have a similar format. That is to say, in each case it is held that a particular type of economic formation is so important for other institutions that it serves to designate the overall form of society linked to it. In both instances, a particular dynamic impetus is attributed to economic transformations — in the one case to capitalism, in the other to industrialism. And, in each, economic institutions are presumed to have a definite alignment with other institutions within a societal totality. Now in the case of capitalism, as I have defined it above, the source of the dynamic impetus is clear. Namely, capitalistic enterprise involves the pursuit of profit through the production of commodities for sale on a market; the perceived need to achieve profits sufficient to guarantee an adequate return on investment generates a chronic impetus towards economic transformation and expansion. But in the instance of industrialism considered alone, such a source of dynamism — one of the main features of the discontinuities of modernity — is lacking. Industrialism is a highly effective form of productive activity but it carries no inner dynamic of the sort associated with capitalist enterprise.

A further aspect of the contention that modern society both 'has and is a mode of production', in its two different versions, is that some kind of definite articulation between the 'economic' and other institutions must be established. Again, in the case of the conception of capitalist society this is clear, whereas in that of 'industrial society' it is not. As a type of production system dominant in a given society, capitalism is predicated upon an alignment of the 'economic' and the 'political', focused through private property and the commodification of wage-labour. However, industrialism is 'neutral' in respect of wider institutional alignments. That is to say, it is not at all obvious that industrialism carries any definite implications for the wider societal totality that would place it in a particular type *sui generis*. Of course, I do not want to pretend that these matters can be settled on the level of conceptual cogency alone. They depend also upon a definite empirical assessment of the trends of development of modern societies, which will emerge in the context of my later arguments.

For both Marx and Weber, in variant ways, industrialism is regarded largely as an extension of the basic features of pre-existing capitalist enterprise, as it developed in preceding centuries in Europe. In well-known sections of the first volume of *Capital*,[31] Marx discusses the progression of the workshop from a division of labour between skills to manufacture and 'machino-facture'. The intensification of production through the concentration of the labour force in factories, and the application of machinery to the labour process, are regarded as the culmination of capitalist development. Weber traces the emergence of mechanization and the factory in terms generally akin to those of Marx.[32] But the similarity of the historical description disguises their contrasting orientation, that derives from their contrasting appraisal of capitalism. In Weber's writings there is a generalized connection between bureaucracy, the capitalist enterprise and the machine. Capitalism, defined in terms of the rational organization of economic activity, is tied via the concept of rationalization to bureaucratic organization in general and to mechanization. Weber in fact frequently compares bureaucracy to a machine, each constructed in terms of 'technical' application of formalized knowledge.

I shall take a position here which is different from both of these authors, although at the same time drawing on elements of each. But my view also differs from those who suppose that 'capitalism' is a sub-type of industrialism. The problem with them all is that they fail to think through what is implied treating 'capitalism' or 'industrialism' as modes of economic organization, on the one hand, and as types of society, on the other. 'Capitalist society' is a 'society' only because it is also a nation-state, having delimited borders which mark off its sovereignty from that claimed by other nation-states. The characteristics of such a state form, I shall propose, depend (in its initial European development) upon conjunctions of capitalism, industrialism and certain administrative apparatuses of government. But none of these can be merely reduced to either of the others. They constitute three distinct *'organizational clusters'*, associated in a direct way with one another in their original European context, but which should be kept analytically distinct and which can have separate substantive consequences when instituted in other societal orders.

In the original European development, the close ties that existed between capitalism and industrialism can be explicated as follows, with many variations between different societies. The emerging hegemony of capitalist enterprise as a system of production introduced a novel source of dynamism within economic organization. Part and parcel of this process was the formation of the differentiated and insulated economy, which became a much more prominent source of generalized institutional transformation than had ever been the case in pre-existing types of society. The economy of capitalist societies, both internally and externally, is inherently unstable for reasons diagnosed by Marx. These concern the motility and economic expansionism associated with the investment—profit-reinvestment cycle. The stability of capitalist production, small- or large-scale, depends — and is known to depend — upon the generating of profit sufficient to provide for 'expanded reproduction'. There is a primary sense in which all 'economic reproduction' in capitalism is, of necessity, in Marx's terms 'expanded reproduction' because the economic order cannot remain more-or-less static as all traditional economic systems tend to. The drive to maintain profit, or to enhance profitability where this is consistent with the perceived investment needs of firms, is associated with an intrinsic propensity to technological innovation via mechanized manufacture. Technological adaptations can be used both to directly cheapen the immediate costs of production and offset investment costs in respect of the hiring of labour. This should not be seen, of course, as a smoothly flowing historical process. In its original phases of development in particular, it involved a stuttering and fractured series of changes, poorly understood by most of those who played the leading parts in initiating and furthering them.

The impetus towards economic expansion and the heightening of productivity thus described by no means exhausts what we might call the 'elective affinities' between capitalism and industrialism. Quite fundamental is the commodification of labour-power. Here we can trace one of the most basic discontinuities that separate modernity from pre existing forms of socio-economic order.[33] It is a phenomenon that directly connects the class system of capitalist society with industrialism as a form of production. Nonetheless, it does not follow from this that the transformation of that class system *ipso facto* implies a radical reordering of the nature of industrialism. Marx's writings, and those of most of his followers, are 'class reductionist'. In other words, they seek to explain too many of the characteristics of modern societies in terms of class domination and class struggle. I have emphasized that, in contrast to agrarian states, capitalist societies are 'class societies' — class conflict is 'structured into' them in a way quite distinct from the forms of class antagonism characteristic of traditional cultures. But we cannot infer from this that class structure is at the origin of all aspects of domination in modern societies.

Such an observation is hardly new, for it has been the stock observation of critics of Marx since the first time at which his ideas became generally known. Many such critics, especially those who have propounded one or other version of a theory of 'industrial society' have, however, simply substituted 'authority' for 'class' in their analyses of modern society.[34] Marx, it is argued, mistook one particular form of authority (class domination, focused through private property) for authority relations in general, essentially assimilating authority and property. Now it is my argument that Marxism is deficient in respect of its concept of power, which is traced first and foremost to control of allocative resources. But it will not do simply to substitute a notion of authority for that of class in analysing the institutions of modern societies. Control of allocative resources — as capital — assumes a peculiar importance in capitalist societies, in which the 'economy' has the dynamic impetus previously mentioned. But authority is not all of a piece. There are various possible types or categories of authoritative resources.

Let me trace through the relations between private property, the commodification of labour-power and industrialism at their 'point of origin' in the European societies. The commodification of labour-power is at the root of the class system of capitalist society in the sense formulated by Marx. In prior types of class domination, class exploitation took the form of the appropriation of 'surplus' production.[35] The dominant class largely apart from the productive activities of those from whom it drew its revenues — something inherent in the segmental character of class-divided societies, as discussed in previous chapters. In capitalism, however, the expropriation of the majority of the members of the population from direct control of their means of subsistence means that the resultant labour-force falls under the immediate sway of the entrepreneur or of 'management'. At the same time, the commodification of labour-power not only permits but demands its consolidation as 'abstract labour', malleable to the organizational directives of employers. The result is a significant nexus of connections to mechanized manufacture, making possible the 'design' of work processes in ways which integrate labour-power with the technological organization of production. This does not occur directly through the construction of machinery, but depends upon perceived opportunities for the calculative co-ordination of productive activity.[36]

A further basic point of connection between capitalism and industrialism is to be found in the expansion of administrative power in the work-place. This is closely bound up again with the commodification of labour-power, although once more we must be careful to avoid the supposition that it is therefore wholly reducible to class relations. Industrialism, as I have said, involves the emergence of the centralized work-place, within which manufacturing operations can be concentrated and co-ordinated. The possibilities of industrial production are thus very limited in class-divided societies, quite apart from the lack of existence of sophisticated machinery there, because of the difficulties facing the sustained application of surveillance in work settings. Several factors influence this. These include, first and foremost, the aforementioned segmental character of class-divided societies, entailing that production is for the most part carried on in locales physically and socially distant from the direct influence of the dominant class. However, where labour-forces of some size are gathered together, with the objective of carrying on concentrated and collaborative processes of production, the level of available surveillance measures is also slight compared to those which can be mustered in modern systems of production. As Weber claims, modes of organizing production that rely upon slavery, or upon some more-or-less nakedly coercive type of *corvée* labour, are probably intrinsically ineffective compared to the disciplinary possibilities opened up by the mass utilization of 'free' wage-labour. In addition the 'storage capacity' of organizations in respect of information is, however, low prior to the developments which Weber identifies — systematic accounting and filing.

The extension of surveillance operations within modern societies is neither confined to the capitalist work-place, nor does it have its sole origin there. However, given the dynamism which the insulated economic sphere injects into other institutional arenas, it is a reasonable supposition that the expansion and consolidation of surveillance in the work-place strongly influences what happens elsewhere. This can readily be demonstrated to be tied to the commodification of labour-power. The 'freeing' of peasants from their involvement with fixed plots of land in agrarian production, and their transmutation into 'wage-labour', is also a 'freeing' from their dispersal in separate, localized communities. As newly 'mobile', they are available to be concentrated in more centralized locales in which production is carried on via mechanized manufacture.

The considerations discussed in the preceding paragraphs make it possible to speak generically of 'industrial capitalism' as a type of productive order and as a form of society. It is a key part of my argument that it is only when the conjunction between capitalism and industrialism is well advanced that it becomes plausible to speak of the existence of 'capitalist societies'. When I henceforth use the notion 'capitalist society', therefore, I shall mean a society in which industrial capitalism is the main motor of production and one which displays the various institutional traits previously described. But it should perhaps be re-emphasized that this does not mean that industrialism is confined in its influence, or its potential influence, to capitalist societies alone.

It will be useful at this juncture to pursue the implications of such a claim a little further. In so doing I shall seek to introduce some themes that will underlie most of the remainder of this work. Four clusterings of institutions can be distinguished in the conjunctions between capitalism, industrialism and the nation-state in the European societies, as shown in figure 1. In Western capitalism they have been closely tied to one another, so much so that the reductive tendencies demonstrated by Marx, and by others from opposed positions, are readily understandable.

The nexus of institutions disclosed by Marx's analysis of the commodification of goods (epitomized by money capital) and the commodification of labour-power (abstract labour) constitutes the core of the class system in capitalist societies. Private property in capitalism, as has been indicated, unites rights of freedom of contract and the 'universal transformability' of capital, in goods or in the purchase of labour, which is so distinctive of the modern money economy. In the sense both of opposition of interest and of semi-chronic struggle, class conflict is an inherent element of capitalist production and therefore — in many varying degrees or guises — of capitalist society. There are a series of issues to be further elucidated here, but for the time being I shall postpone discussion of these.

Some words are necessary about why industrialism does not appear in figure 1. When capitalism is conjoined to industrialism, as it has been in the European societies, the outcome is the

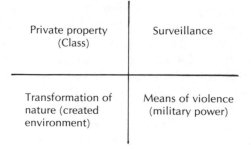

Figure 1

initiation of a massively important series of alterations in the relation between human beings and the natural world.[37] It is in these alterations that industrialism is embedded. In class-divided societies, production does not greatly transform nature, even where, for example, major schemes of irrigation exist. The city is the main power-container and is clearly differentiated from the countryside but both partake of the 'content' of the natural world, which human beings live both 'in' and 'with', in a condition of symbiosis. The advent of industrial capitalism alters all this. When connected to the pressures of generalized commodification, industrialism provides the means of radically altering the connections between social life and the material world. The main mediator of this process is urbanism and I repeat here the theorem introduced in the first volume of this work, that 'urban sociology' cannot merely be regarded as one branch of sociology among others, but has to be treated a major part of what sociology *is* as an endeavour to comprehend the modern world. Modern urbanism (both within Western societies and elsewhere) is not an extension of the traits of traditional cities, even where urban areas have grown up in and around the sites of such cities. It forms a 'created environment', which is the backdrop both to the organization of capitalist-industrial production and to the territoriality of the nation-state. As I have argued in the previous volume, the obsolescence of the city walls is both symbolic of, and substantially implicated in, the emergence of that new administrative space that is the nation-state.

For reasons already discussed, a very considerable development in modes of surveillance in the work-place is a primary feature of the emergence of industrial capitalism. But surveillance activities also expand the realm of the state itself, both within its borders and externally, as states begin to monitor the character of 'international relations'. As I have stressed, surveillance is a medium of power which, whatever its ties to the ownership of private property, does not derive directly from it. The same comment applies to control of the means of violence.

6
Capitalism and the State: From Absolutism to the Nation-State

In analysing the connections between the expansion of capitalism and the consolidation of the modern state, two successive phases of development need to be assessed. The first, dating from the sixteenth to the late eighteenth century, concerns absolutism and the early diffusion of capitalist enterprise. The subsequent phase is one linking the nation-state and industrial capitalism. The maturation of capitalism involves a commodification of land and products, on the one hand, and of labour-power, on the other. While these do not proceed wholly independently of each other, the former is intertwined mainly with the development of the absolutist state. The latter — or so I shall argue — depends for its large-scale extension upon the formation of the nation-state.

Commodification and State Development

The commodification of land and products — a vast expansion of the areas of economic activity penetrated by exchange-value — involves several elements associated with the solidifying of the absolutist state. The emergence of a guaranteed, centralized legal order permitting and protecting an expanding range of contractual rights and obligations is one; another is the development of a monetary system co-ordinated and sanctioned by state power; yet another is the formation of a centrally organized taxation system.[1]

What matters in respect of the development of a framework of law is, of course, both the substance of law and the possibilities of its enforcement by the centralized state apparatus. Economic exchange as such, as has been noted, can operate with a minimum of legally enforceable ties between the parties involved, and in preceding forms of society ordinarily has done so. An exchange of goods implies the transfer of the 'factual control' of objects from one party to another, where the assumption is that (whether in direct barter or separated in time-space) other objects will be also transferred from the second party to the first.[2] Such a relationship, when established in a durable way, involves trust in anticipated future transactions and returns. In so far as this is institutionally 'guaranteed', in traditional orders, it is often more in the context of ritual exchange than in sheerly commercial transactions. Trading companies have sometimes possessed various sanctions to back up payment of debts, including the use or threat of military violence. Civilizations in which commerce has been strongly accentuated, and where mercantile groups have been particularly powerful, have normally developed forms of both public and civil law relevant to trading operations. Trade has in these circumstances frequently been financed and directed by the state, in conjunction with other revenue-generating activities. But in few of these instances has law combined the 'calculative' and 'contractual' orientations, separate from direct state involvement with economic enterprise, such as came about in post-medieval Europe. Rome was one such instance, and the direct inheritance of certain of its codes, plus its more diffuse long-standing influence, was important largely for this reason.

As Weber stresses, the recovery and transmutation of Roman law in Europe promoted 'calculability' plus a range of forms of alienability under contractually regulated circumstances. The former of these traits is actually more important than the latter. Although he does not develop the point, it is clear that the large-scale extension of the calculability of law depends upon the development of the principled conception of sovereignty that absolutism promoted. While royal remissions might still intrude into otherwise 'rational' calculations of economic activity and exchange, at the same time traditional aristocratic prerogatives become stripped away. This should not be seen as a process of the uncovering of a 'cash nexus' centred in 'civil society', released from the constraints of pre-existing political supervision. Some who have held such a view have pointed to the fact that in Britain, the 'home of capitalism',[3] Roman law never took a hold.

Certainly it was in British political economy that such interpretations of the 'rise of civil society' came to be pre-eminent. But this conception does not adequately distinguish the form of law — its promotion of calculability — from distinct codes and procedures associated with it. In regard of the former of these, the influence of Roman law, as a generalized 'inheritance' and as a revitalized phenomenon from the sixteenth century onwards, was considerable everywhere, including areas that did not directly adopt its tenets. Most of the legal codes immediately involved in capitalist enterprise did not in any case derive primarily from Roman law (something also pointed out by Weber). Annuities, stock certificates and bills of exchange arose from a combination of Germanic, English, Italian and Arabic law. Legal provisions for the identity of companies have their origins in part in the medieval corporations and in part in urban law. Moreover, it is not the case that Britain was the 'home of capitalism' if this means the main centre of the spread of commercial and mercantile operations. Capitalism in this sense was first of all most strongly developed elsewhere. Britain became the first 'home of industrial capitalism', but as I have indicated previously this cannot be regarded only as extension of pre-established capitalist enterprise.

The importance of a body of law connected to sovereignty, then — so far as the internal organization of societies goes — is mainly that in specifying the 'political' sphere it at the same time defined a distinct arena of 'economic' transactions. Already containing such a differentiation, Roman law was an important source for consolidating the insulation of the political and the economic. The point is that the 'economic sphere' should not be seen as a residual one, merely left outside the constitutional form of the modern state, as an unincorporated 'civil society'. *Rather, it derives from the very same sources as the sphere of sovereignty so elemental to the nature of the modern state.*

In saying this I do not want to deny the significance of forms of civil law that were not originally primarily promoted by the state, and that universalize possibilities of exchange transactions. Here it is important to accentuate that, although broken up into numerous competing states, post-feudal Europe drew on a common cultural legacy, deriving not only from the remnants of secular Roman influence but from the impact of the Church as a pan-European organization. Some Germanic legal practices, later to have a major role in the development of civil law in Northern and Central Europe, were early on filtered through ecclesiastical sources and through economic transactions in which the Church was directly involved. The divergences between capitalistic activity, as intrinsically 'transnational' in character, and the consolidation of the absolutist state, as a territorially bounded formation, were in some respects much less pronounced than might appear. For a common series of legal prescriptions and mechanisms, in some degree already informing commercial transactions of various kinds, facilitated intra-continental economic connections. They even informed the circumstances in which European trading companies related to one another in other parts of the world, in so far as there were regularized economic ties between them.

The expansion of sovereignty was partly achieved through centralization of methods of law enforcement — a matter which applies to the achievement of generalized social discipline as well as to the means of backing up contracts. Weber tends to be rather dismissive of the importance of legal sanctions in relation to the extension of capitalist enterprise. The power of law over economic activity, he points out, weakened in some aspects with the expansion of capitalism, compared with what had sometimes been the case previously. The enforcement of controlled maximum prices, for example, became much more difficult than it was in some prior economic systems. Legal coercion in economic activity is limited in two chief respects. One is to do with the goods possessed by individuals subject to litigation — these may be too few, or of the wrong type, to make good whatever a given contractual obligation entails. Rather than being decreased by a general commodification of products, Weber suggests, this type of difficulty tends to become accentuated. Repayment of defaults in cash becomes, in principle, easier but this only applies to an isolated instance, or set of instances, of the breaking of contracts. Most economic units become so inter-dependent that there is no way in which legal sanctions could be brought to bear to influence the conduct of overall sectors of the market. The co-ordination of economic agencies has to be left to the negotiated activities of production, pricing and investment, carried on without direct reference to the possibility of coercive sanctions.[4] A second reason can be found in the relative strength of private economic interests compared to those favouring conformity to codes of law. Where economic opportunities exist, Weber says, the temptation to engage in them will tend to be irresistible, save where they flout strongly held moral imperatives originating in other spheres of life. Thus there will be little chance of making nominal forms of legal compulsion count, given that the promulgator of laws — the state — depends increasingly upon the fruits of capitalistic endeavours for its own continuation.

Whether or not these observations are correct, what they seem to neglect is the significance of a coercive framework of law in relation to property rights — this surely is of great importance to capitalist development. Where most property was in land, ownership rights were usually guaranteed by a mixture of custom and law, bolstered very often by the direct possession of the means of violence by those laying claim to such rights. But where property becomes capital, even landed property, ownership cannot be defended primarily as a 'sitting claim of possession'. A centralized set of legal codes, backed by effective means of coercion, would seem to be the necessary condition of the defence of 'private' rights where these are no longer the 'visible' accoutrements of land ownership. Private property, as Marx so consistently stressed, has as its other face the dispossession of masses of individuals from control of their means of production. The incorporation of such individuals as wage-workers within regularized conditions of industrial production belongs mainly to the second phase under discussion (the formation of the nation-state). But the 'freeing' of wage-labour was undeniably a major aspect of the early establishing of capitalist enterprise on the grand scale. Without the centralization of a coercive apparatus of law, it is doubtful either that this process could have been accomplished, or that the rights of private property as capital could have become firmly embedded.

The formation of a generalized 'money economy' is undoubtedly the *sine qua non* of widespread commodification. Marx makes this abundantly clear, both in respect of products and of wage-labour. But he does not provide a coherent discussion of the role of the state in the provision and guaranteeing of monetary units. Indeed, we may aptly remark with Perez-Diaz that this is not a direction in which Marx could feasibly have propelled his analysis very far, because it would have tended to undermine his view of the state as resting upon relations of class domination.[5] Money has always been used for two main purposes — those of payment and exchange — but in traditional states the former tended to predominate over the latter. Even in some large imperial systems, for example the Persian empire, coined money was used almost wholly for the making of payments, usually military ones. It was not necessarily either minted or its value underwritten by agencies of the state, and could co-exist with various other monetary forms. Money has, of course, also been used traditionally for hoarding and some have in fact suggested that this is usually the prime factor making for the use of precious metals as coinage. Prior to seventeenth century Europe, the amount of coinage in circulation tended to be limited by purely technological considerations. Medieval money was made and stamped by hand, and typically involved the labour of up to a dozen craft-workers using different skills. The costs of production were very high — up to a quarter of its value for smaller denominations — and the accuracy of coining was widely variable. Thus the usual practice was to assess coinage in terms of weight.

While Rome did have a standard coinage, more developed than that found in any other traditional state, in the Middle Ages there were numerous localized coinages. The Carolingian coinage system never became more than of marginal importance in most of Europe and was produced by an association of craft-workers, not by any political organization. The influx of precious metals into Europe in the sixteenth and seventeenth centuries without doubt played a key role in making possible the large-scale diffusion of money.[6] It has often been remarked how much this increased the available wealth in Europe, but probably more important was its conjunctural effect in promoting money as a medium of exchange rather than only of payment or hoarding. For this made possible a transition that combined increased state control over the provision of money with a burgeoning capitalist development in the 'civil' sector. It provided the springboard for the emergence of paper money (and subsequently, electronic money).

In analysing the phenomenon of money it is useful to distinguish between 'commodity money' — in modern times most notably gold and silver — and paper money.[7] Commodity money exists where the quantity of the money, assessed in physical units, corresponds to the amount of money on a designated quantitative scale of value. The quantity of commodity money is limited by the availability of the scarce materials used in its fabrication, although the bullion value of the coin may be considerably less than its exchange value in circulation. Commodity money may take the form of paper money. What matters is that it is tied to the existence of a fixed quantity of scarce material; the amount of money which can be generated is limited by the availability of that material. The convertibility of money into gold or silver is not *ipso facto* an indication of the existence of commodity money. The tying of currencies to the gold standard in the early part of the twentieth century, for example, does not reflect the prevalence of commodity money, since the exchange value of money no longer in any significant fashion depended upon a fixed quantum of scarce material resources. Money has become 'fiduciary'; that is, dependent upon confidence in the political and economic organizations in which it is produced and through which it is circulated.

In these terms we can readily grasp, in a general way at least, the relation between the development of the modern state and the expansion of a 'money economy'. The centralization of state power was the necessary condition of the formation of commodity money, in particular making it possible to detach money in circulation from its convertible bullion value. Only where the state is able to create a monopoly of the certification (not necessarily the direct production) of money, via legally accredited means, can a vast impetus towards the commodification of products be achieved. In the absolutist state this process was only incompletely developed, debasement of the coinage being one of the main tactics used to temporarily swell the state's revenues. While state backing is required for a substantial development of commodity money, the basis of generalized confidence in its value remains closely bound to the value of the scarce material that physically composes it. Commodity money — like the form of state which was its guarantor — is a sort of 'halfway house' between the most predominant traditional forms of money and fiduciary money. It is important to see that the development of commodity money is not just a matter of the internal organization of legal tender, but is bound up directly with the reflexive monitoring of the state system. Commodity money, backed by a mixture of the guarantee of an individual state and its bullion value, was the basis for the international exchange of goods in market relations of broad scale and depth. It allowed for a tremendous spread of capitalistic exchange outside the increasingly more consolidated boundaries of the state, but at the same time was in some considerable degree an outcome of that very consolidation.

The condition of the existence of fiduciary money is a fully articulated state apparatus, having administrative power over its own territory and a legal monopoly over internal 'order' that is more-or-less complete. Commodity money need not be legal tender and confidence can be sustained in it even through the vicissitudes in the material fortunes of particular states, although of course the tendency to revert to 'bullion value' in circumstances of crisis is an ever-present one. Fiduciary money operates in the absence of such fall-back possibilities, depending upon confidence in the productive capabilities of business organizations within the penumbra of the state, and upon the state's own guarantees of the value of its currency. It is right to say of fiduciary money that it is, 'at least in the first instance, national money in the sense that the limits of its general acceptability as the medium of circulation are determined by the domain of exercise of the political power on which the fiduciary money is based'.[8] But it is just as essential to emphasize that fiduciary money has from its first origins been international. This is so not just in the sense that it circulates beyond the borders of the states that issue their respective currencies. Fiduciary money has not been the creation merely of individual states but has been tied to an extension of the reflexively monitored state system, and the 'confidence' that keeps it afloat has never been confined to the citizenry of the state which is its legal guarantor. The development of fiduciary money — the condition of a global extension of commodified exchange of products — is part and parcel of the formation of a world-wide nation-state system. It should be emphasized again, perhaps, that this does not deny that there may be major conflicts or tensions between the perceived political imperatives of states and those of economic organizations.

The development of paper money should not be seen as only a 'step beyond' commodity money. Its origins lie in the capital accounting basic to the time-space distanciation of capitalist enterprise. Capital accounting, as I have emphasized, allows for the distancing of economic relations across time-space, facilitating the storage and co-ordination of information used to regularize such relations. In capital accounting, money (as tabulated or indexed costs, profits and losses) is already information, having no physical existence apart from marks upon paper or some other recording medium. The expansion of capitalism thus already presupposes the formation of aspects of money that presage the character it later assumes. Paper money, hence, should not necessarily be thought of as the only concrete form that fiduciary money displays. Fiduciary money maximizes traits inherent in the early development of money as information; thus 'electronic' money is a furthering of already established trends.

Deferred payment, particularly in the shape of credit, is one of the prime forms of time-space distanciation facilitated by the emergence of a money economy. Credit, or the borrowing of money against profits expected from future transactions, is a major point of connection between the state as guarantor of currency and as the propagator of taxation. Credit can of course be organized in a barter system, or in a system in which coinage is used mainly for payment and for hoarding. But credit possibilities are obviously limited both by difficulties in calculating what is owed and by the need to keep in close contact with the debtor in case of default, especially where the legal means of sanctioning debtors are ill-developed. Money allows for the deferment in time that is the essence of credit. But this cannot be seen as exemplified in a single transaction between creditor and debtor. The point is that, in modern economic orders, credit becomes structured into the circulation of commodities. While it would be something of an exaggeration to see the deferment of payment intrinsic to the exchange of commodities across extended spans of time-space as a form of credit, there is no clear dividing-line between this and credit proper. The expansion of credit transactions was linked in the period of absolutism to the general development of financial markets and independent financial organizations, gaining a major momentum through the provision of resources for war. Girding up for war, as indicated previously, also provided the main impulsion towards the assumption of novel acceleration to the formation of a money economy, because the new forms of taxation were directly monetary in character, and involved the state as both creditor and debtor to the rest of the society.

During the period of absolutism, taxation became 'fiscal' in the proper sense of that term, involving the economic organization of a recognized public domain of finance and expenditure. In many ways the development of the modern 'tax state' epitomizes the formation of impersonal sovereignty and the insulation of the political and the economic. The tax-collecting activities of traditional states always had a certain 'public' character, in so far as the administrative apparatus was involved with co-ordination of tasks relevant to the lives of various segments of the popualtion as a whole. But only with the development of the modern state does it come to be the case that the administrative purview of the state begins to relate to the entire population, integrating its activities with the course of their daily lives. Such a transmutation is accompanied by an expanding range of officialdom, carrying out tasks which are 'in the public domain' in the sense that they are no longer linked patrimonially to the ruler's household. Taxation in the modern state is a means of underwriting the state's expenses, since productive enterprise is largely carried on outside the scope of its direct control. But taxation also becomes closely bound up with the surveillance operations of the state. Tax policies come to be used both to monitor and to regulate the distribution and the activities of the population, and participate in the burgeoning of surveillance operations as a whole. Taxes, it has been said, 'are used as tools to increase population (tax burden on bachelors; tax reduction for children), to reduce laziness and to force people to work, to check certain human vices, to influence consumption patterns (particularly conspicuous consumption) and so forth. The education or social goals of such taxes characteristically prevail over the fiscal goals.'[9] The statement may be somewhat exaggerated in its emphasis and, in my view, applies more to the nation-state than to the transitional form of the absolutist state, but it nonetheless draws attention to one of the main characteristics of modern tax-systems.

Let me concentrate here on the primary theme, the connections between the state, money and taxation, on the one hand, and the commodification of products on the other. Although in some respects there was a reciprocal relation between each of them, the development of tax collecting and disbursement of taxes provided a major stimulus towards monetization, and fused the twin roles of guarantor of currency and fiscal manager within the sphere of the state. Prebendal taxation privileges were the main basis for the organizing of taxing in feudal Europe. Territorial princes, estates, towns and other corporate bodies enjoyed their own distinct prebendal advantages. In France and elsewhere it was supposed to be the case that the ruler lived exclusively off his own taxation prerogatives, with the Estates only making contributions under special and unusual circumstances. Both the concept and the reality of sovereignty developed in some part from the claim to the *dominium eminens*, increasingly channelled to meet whatever were designated by the monarch as 'public' needs. As in so many other respects, the seventeenth century was the critical period in the movement towards centralized fiscal policies. Those states that survived or expanded their boundaries were also the states in which the various aspects of taxation, including the specification, collection, administration and disbursement of taxes, were gathered firmly in the hands of the centralized regime.

This much is common-or-garden history of the time, but wherein lay the connections with a rapidly strengthening area of capitalist enterprise? The main factors involved were these. The solidifying, and monetarizing, of taxation in the control of the state apparatus were both expression and instrument of the erosion of the privileges and power of the land-owning aristocracy. They helped to open up the space for the intrusion of commerce and of capitalistic endeavours, at the same time as being facilitated by those endeavours. But they also expanded the areas of commodification of social life in ways in which entrepreneurial enterprise as such probably could not have done. In class-divided societies, tax schemes rested normally upon a mixture of moral suasion and force, often subjecting those involved to extreme material deprivation, but for the most part not reordering their day-to-day lives in a significant way. However the new taxation policies, integrated with fiscal management, cut across the types of relationship previously involved in fused politico-economic domination of the old kind. A system of regular direct taxation can only be sustained if those due to pay translate at least a certain proportion of their assets into monetary income. This does not imply that these individuals were necessarily drawn into commodity markets, but the scope of such markets undoubtedly received a major boost.

Finally, we should not underestimate the importance which state economic direction from the beginning had for the growth of generalized capitalist enterprise. Fiscal management, the influence of the state over money supply, production and consumption do not date only from the later period of the 'interventionist state' but were in substantial degree necessary conditions of the large-scale expansion of capitalist activity. In the early phases of capitalist development, these have to be seen largely as unintended consequences of policies initiated primarily for other reasons, most particularly the prosecution of war externally and the quelling of discord internally. Only later did they become undertaken deliberately in order to create favourable conditions for the expansion of capitalist production and even then, of course, only in a halting way and against the resistance of landed interests in most countries. The writer who in fact first used the term 'tax state', Rudolf Goldscheid, regarded warfare as the 'moving motor of the whole development of public finance', and certainly one cannot deny this during the period of the absolutist state.[10]

Central to the emergence of industrial capitalism is the commodification of wage-labour. This cannot be interpreted as simply the working out of some sort of endogenous 'logic' of capitalist development but has to be independently explained. The commodification of products, especially as involved with the commercialization of agrarian production, provided one of the causal conditions leading to the 'freeing' of a mass wage-labour force from the residual bonds of feudalism. But the commodification of wage-labour — in the shape of an industrial work-force — depended upon a range of circumstances other than those directly involved in the expansion of economic enterprise itself. It will be part of my concern in chapter 7 to analyse these. They are factors directly bound up with the nation-state and its involvement with other states.

My main thesis runs as follows. In industrial capitalism there develops a novel type of class system, one in which class struggle is rife but also in which the dominant class — those who own or control large capital assets — do not have or require direct access to the means of violence to sustain their rule.[11] Unlike previous systems of class domination, production involves close and continuous relations between the major class groupings. This presumes a 'doubling-up' of surveillance, modes of surveillance becoming a key feature of economic organizations and of the state itself. The process of what — for want of a better phrase — can be called the internal pacification of states is an inherent part of the expanding administrative co-ordination which marks the transition from the absolutist state to the nation-state. It is this internal pacification, which coincided historically with a pro-longed period of absence of major wars between the European powers, that is the backdrop against which those in the 'classic traditions' of liberalism and socialism developed their views of the intrinsically pacific nature of industrial capitalism.

Certain elements of Marx's characterization of industrial capitalism must be sustained here.[12] It is quite right to claim that the advent of industrial capitalism signals a new type of productive order, in which the buying and selling of labour-power, quantified into temporal units, combines with rapid technological change to inject an extraordinary dynamism into production processes. But (a) Marx's account is a class-reductionist one, in respects already indicated and to be more fully elaborated upon below; (b) Marx does not analyse in anything like an adequate way the authoritative resources mustered to stabilize industrial capitalism nationally and internationally; and (c) he does not ask what happens to the means of violence 'extruded' from the labour contact. This third phenomenon is admittedly characterized here in a rather crude way, and will have to be developed more precisely. However, my theme will be that the correlate of the internally pacified state — class relationships that rest upon a mixture of 'dull economic compulsion' and supervisory techniques of labour management — is the professionalized standing army. The process of internal pacification, I shall argue, is only possible because of the heightened administrative unity that distinguishes the nation-state from previous state forms. On the other hand, this very administrative unity depends upon the 'infrastructural' transformations brought into play by the development of industrial capitalism, which help finally to dissolve the segmental character of class-divided societies.

Capitalism and World System Theory

From an early date the development of capitalism in Europe was linked to the political and economic penetration of what became 'the West' into many other areas of the world. The diffusion of European power, as I have already noted, did not occur in the time-honoured fashion of traditional imperial states, by direct military expension into adjacent areas — with the exception of the recovery of some of the Mediterranean regions occupied by the Ottomans. It occurred mainly via sea-going commercial and military endeavours, connecting Europe to a global system of production and commercial relationships, fuelled by capitalistic economic mechanisms. Of course, colonialism in its various forms is also a highly important associated phenomenon, both in respect of areas in which an existing indigenous population was made subject to European rule and in areas in which European settlers became predominant.

I have frequently criticized elsewhere those standpoints in social science that have adopted endogenous models of social change.[13] Such models tend to treat 'societies' (nominally societies in general but usually meaning, in fact, nation-states) as isolated entities, whose patterns of change can be understood primarily in terms of internal processes. One of the main attractions of what has come to be called 'world system studies', associated especially with the work of Wallerstein, is that these specifically oppose any such view. As a generalized critique of endogenous models of change, 'world system theory' therefore shares a good deal in common with the approach adopted in this book and the volume preceding it. Since Wallerstein's main preoccupation is with the impact of post-sixteenth-century Europe upon the rest of the world, there are important substantive points of relevance to my concerns here.

World system studies are concerned with the *longue durée* of institutional transformation, giving particular emphasis to the discontinuities between modern history and what went before. What Wallerstein calls 'world economies' have, according to him, existed previously, but they were very different from what has come into being over the past four centuries or so.[14] States, particularly large imperial ones, have in earlier times been at the centre of long-distance networks of commerce and manufacture, in which there was some degree of regional interdependence in a division of labour stretched across substantial sectors of the globe. The world economy ushered in by the development of capitalism, however, is the first genuine 'world system' in that it eventually comes to be a fully global phenomenon.

World system theory is offered in conscious contrast to two alternative views which have sought to analyse social change outside Europe since the development of European global hegemony. One, associated mainly with a liberal political stance, is modernization theory; the other, linked primarily with certain versions of Marxism, is dependency theory. The first school of thought usually has proposed endogenous interpretations of change. It focuses upon what has often ingenuously been called 'nation-building', in parts of the world other than where nation-states were established relatively early on. Against this type of viewpoint, Wallerstein stresses that 'We do not live in a modernising world but in a capitalist world.' The so-called 'modernizing societies' today are not countries that have not yet caught up with the processes of development witnessed in the West. They have been, and are, shaped by their involvement in global economic relationships stemming from the world-wide reach of capitalism. According to Wallerstein:

> once capitalism was consolidated as a system and there was no turnback, the internal logic of its functioning, the search for maximum profit, forced it continuously to expand — extensively to cover the globe, and intensively via the constant (if not steady) accumulation of capital, the pressure to mechanise work in order to make possible still further expansion of production, the tendency to facilitate and optimise rapid response to the permutations of the world market by the proletarianisation of labour and the commercialisation of land. That is what modernisation is about, if one wants to use such a contentless word.[15]

In advancing this position, Wallerstein is critical of those authors who have looked to the notion of dependency to demonstrate how the West has managed to develop such a prime economic role in the global economic order. According at least to the cruder versions of dependency theory, the prosperity of the capitalist countries is purchased at the expense of the impoverishment of large areas of the remainder of the world. Not only this, but there is held to be a single main set of processes underlying the uneven development of the advanced and the dependent countries. Wallerstein's views share something in common with these ideas — certainly more than with the proponents of the modernization standpoint — but are also clearly distinguishable from them. The thesis of most of the dependency theorists is that, precisely because of their dependent economic situation, the factors influencing the course of development of peripheral states are different from those pertaining within the advanced capitalist core. In Wallerstein's eyes this is mistaken, because both advanced and 'dependent' states are parts of a single capitalist economy, world-wide in scope. Peripheral states are certainly seriously disadvantaged in the world economy but their paths of development are to be explained in terms of dynamics of that economy as an overall phenomenon. The main phenomena involved are the existence of world-wide capitalist markets and a division of labour in production for those markets.

The capitalist world economy has its origins in the sixteenth century or, rather, Braudel's 'long sixteenth century' running from about 1450 to 1640. In identifying its main features, Wallerstein lays particular stress upon the divergence of state and economic institutions. Previous 'world economies' were politically administered by imperial formations. But the capitalist world economy is integrated economically, not politically, having multiple political centres. The core of the system was early on located in north-west and central Europe, with the Mediterranean becoming progessively transformed into its semi-periphery. The notions of core, semi-periphery and periphery all have to do with location in the single economic system composed by the new world economy. In the core areas are found a range of emerging manufacturing industries and relatively advanced forms of agrarian production. Their development adversely affected the semi-peripheral regions, which became 'retarded' and were forced into relatively stagnant economic patterns. Towards the conclusion of the long sixteenth century the power of the states in those areas also showed a marked decline. Thus Spain lost its pre-eminent position and the formerly prosperous city-states of Northern Italy suffered a diminution in their influence. The periphery of the early capitalist core, in Eastern Europe and

Latin America, became dominated by cash-crop production on large estates. These various regions thus became locked into an interdependent division of labour. Their relative standing within the nascent world economy was reflected in their varying political fortunes. The core states were those in which absolutism was most strongly developed, with centralized bureaucratic administrative orders and large standing armies. The periphery, on the other hand, was characterized by 'the *absence* of the strong state'. In the eastern marches of Europe there emerged sprinklings of principalities, while in Latin America 'there was no indigenous state authority at all.'[16] In the semi-periphery, as befits its name, things were somewhere in between.

The divergent experience of states in the three sectors can be traced out by comparing the divergent fortunes of Poland (periphery), Venice (semi-periphery) and England (capitalist core). At the opening of the fifteenth century, Wallerstein says, the social characteristics of Poland were not very different from those of the other two societies. Trade and commerce were fairly vigorous, with commercialized agriculture developing in a progressive fashion. The Polish nobility however managed to enact legislation binding the peasantry to their estates — the so-called 'second feudalism' of Eastern Europe. The products of coerced, cash-crop labour were sold directly to markets in the Low Countries and elsewhere, helping to stultify the consolidation of a capitalistic class of entrepreneurs. Financing this trade enmeshed the ruling groups in very large debts to external creditors, from which it proved difficult for them to extricate themselves. By the early years of the seventeenth century, Poland had devolved into an early version of a 'neocolonial state'[17] linked to a large-scale economy, the main centres of which were elsewhere in Europe.

In Venice conditions were first of all very different. It was itself the core state of a regional economic system and an imperial power with various possessions in the Mediterranean area; it also had far-flung commercial ties across other parts of Europe. The reasons for the decline of Venice are complex, Wallerstein accepts; but as the Baltic and Atlantic became the main arenas of sea-power and trade, Venice was geographically marginalized and a range of factors eroded its erstwhile commercial success, channelling money into the countryside. Venice became 'deindustrialized' without the total elimination of its commercial and banking activities.

In England, the process was something of a reverse one, as what was initially a relatively rather poor relation of its more glittering Continental neighbours became launched on a path towards economic pre-eminence. The enclosure movements had the effect of completing the break-up of feudal relations that had begun some considerable while before. There existed a reasonably strong state apparatus in England that was able to block efforts of the aristocracy to return to more traditional styles of agrarian production. A diverse system of manufacture for markets, plus an expansion of trade, placed the country in a particularly suitable position to exploit opportunities offered by the expanding capitalist world economy. A key part of Wallerstein's approach depends upon the idea that phenomena of basic importance to capitalism — including its class system — cannot be interpreted in 'internalist' terms but have to be understood in the context of the world economy as a whole. When 'capitalism' is seen to refer to the world capitalist economy, we see that it does not involve a single axis of class domination, but two. One is that of wage-labour and capital. But this dimension has from the early origins of capitalism been interwoven with the spatial hierarchy in the 'international' division of labour, setting off core from periphery.

From the sixteenth century onwards the capitalist world economy has stretched beyond the European continent to the Americas and eventually to virtually all parts of the globe. As against those who have supposed that it only in the twentieth century that capitalism has in any real sense become a global phenomenon, Wallerstein insists that its world-wide reach was established very early on. 'Capitalism', as he puts it bluntly, 'was from the beginning an affair of the world economy and not of nation states . . . capital has never allowed its aspirations to be determined by national boundaries in a capitalist world economy, and the creation of "national" barriers — generally, mercantilism — has historically been a defensive mechanism of capitalists located in states which are one level below the high point of strength in the system.'[18] It is because capitalism is, in a quite essential sense, an economic rather than a political order that it has been able to penetrate into far-flung areas of the world which — even if simply because of their distance from the core states —

would have been impossible to bring under political sway. The spread of the capitalist world economy, following the 'long sixteenth century', continues the tri-partite sectoral interdependence established in its beginnings. But, of course, the specific geographical locations alter and certain new patterns of core—periphery exploitation are introduced. A growing need for raw materials was the principal factor underlying the colonization or enforced incorporation of new regions within the world economy. These materials were mostly produced through the setting up of what Wallerstein loosely calls 'plantation systems' — forms of production based upon the use of large areas of land and involving coerced labour rather than legally 'free' wage-labour as in the core countries.

With the further development of the world system, the more directly coercive aspects of cash-crop labour became lessened. Serfdom, slavery, peonage were abolished. Wallerstein proposes various reasons for this. The gradual incorporation of zones previously outside the world capitalist economy — those, for instance, from which slaves were derived — elevated the cost of systems of forced labour and generally made them less practicable. The political expense of maintaining control over plantation systems rose, since 'the process of maintaining relative social peace in the core areas required the elaboration of various ideological schemes of "freedom", which had the inconvenience that the concept spread to realms for which it was not intended.'[19] Finally, Wallerstein says, converging here with the argument of Weber, the increasing adoption of employment policies approximating to 'free wage-labour' in the Western sense was prompted by the fact that they prove in the end to be more economic than coerced labour. Those who pay the workers' wages are not directly responsible for providing the reproduction of their families.

The importance of Wallerstein's contributions is considerable. In providing a critique of endogenous conceptions of social change, he also develops what has proved to be an empirically fruitful interpretation of the nature and dynamics of capitalist enterprise. It is an interpretation that strongly emphasizes the regionalization of political and economic systems and which, thereby, lays stress upon spatial features of social organization and change. By pointing to the differences that separate the capitalist world economy from imperial formations, Wallerstein helps demonstrate the discontinuities between modern world history and what went before. Nonetheless, there are a range of criticisms that should be made about his views, which serve quite sharply to distinguish the position I wish to advance from them.[20] It is important to make these differences of standpoint clear since, although Wallerstein is critical of a number of well-established viewpoints which I also want to attack, his formulations do not offer a framework within which the main problems with which this book is concerned can be satisfactorily addressed.

Wallerstein's conception of 'capitalism' is suspect, something which tends to have consequences for various other aspects of his discussion of the dynamics of the capitalist world economy. He persistently identifies capitalism with sale of products in a market for profit, a definition which oddly is closer to that of Weber than it is to that of Marx, in spite of Wallerstein's claimed affiliation to a Marxist standpoint. In emphasizing markets, Wallerstein's view obscures the significance of the commodification of labour power as distinctive of capitalist production and, therewith, some of the most consequential dynamics of capitalist class structure. To some extent this is because he stresses too much the external involvement of states in the developing world system.[21] But there is a more subtle and telling way of putting the same point. One cannot interpret what the meaning of 'internal' compared to 'external' influences *is* without an analysis of the consolidation of the modern state as a political form. For Wallerstein the existence of separate states seems to be largely a historical residue of the fact that capitalism came into being within a pre-formed state system. While he is quite right to point to the significance of this — that is the contrast between the history of Europe following the demise of the Roman Empire and the history of the other 'world civilizations' — the formation of the modern state, including the nation-state, is left unexplicated.

Wallerstein's arguments involve an uncomfortable amalgam of functionalism and economic reductionism. In these respects they are certainly closer to commonly held presumptions of Marxism. The functionalism involved in Wallerstein's writings is evident and quite pervasive, but perhaps one example of it will serve to make the point. The existence of semi-peripheral regions is explained by reference to the 'needs' of the world system. It is an order based upon unequal distribution of reward, and as such, he says, 'must constantly worry' about the possible dissention of those who are most ill-favoured within it.[22] Disruptive consequences could come about if the high-income sector were directly confronted by low-income, deprived ones. Such confrontation is avoided by the spatial separation of one from the other provided by the development of the semi-peripheral regions. This sort of observation would be defensible if it were offered simply as an interpretation of the results of the formation of semi-peripheral areas, but becomes illegitimately teleological when posed in the manner suggested by Wallerstein. More damaging, however, than its functionalist connotations is the marked tendency of Wallerstein's standpoint to downplay the impact of specifically political and military factors upon processes of social change in the modern world. States appear as territorial subdivisions within gross economic sectors of the world economy, not as organizations able to mobilize forms of power other than economic power and with interests other than economic interests. The multiplicity of states within the world economy is interpreted in two main ways (each of which continues in a functionalist vein). One is that the absence of a single political authority prevents any general control of the world system and thus the potential curbing of the world-wide scope of capitalist enterprise. The other is that separate states can often provide the means for the core elements of capitalism to preserve their advantages at the expense of those in the disfavoured sectors of the world economy. The core states are able to defend their privileged position within the system of 'unequal exchange'.

Concentration upon economic relationships within world markets also infects Wallerstein's tri-partite classification of states. The concepts of 'core', 'semi-periphery' and 'periphery' are obviously in any case fairly crude, as are their rough counterparts in other writing of 'First', 'Second' and 'Third' worlds. Political and military strength are not straightforwardly an expression of economic development, even if closely related to it. This leads to definite oddities in Wallerstein's mode of classifying societies. A good example is his placing of the Soviet Union within the world system. It is no doubt the case that the USSR operates within a world economy dominated by capitalistic mechanisms. Wallerstein appears to hedge his bets somewhat about the USSR, but still treats it as at most on the margins of the 'core'. As I have remarked earlier in the book, even if this were a feasible view economically speaking, it is plainly fatuous in politico-military terms when the Soviet Union is one of the two 'super-powers' that dominate the modern world system. This means acknowledging that the world system is not only formed by transnational economic connections and interdependencies, but also by the global system of nation-states, neither of which can be exhaustively reduced to the other.

These observations have to be extended to include democratization and modernity more generally. Wallerstein's comments about the unintended consequences of the exportation of ideas of 'freedom' and 'democracy' are surely too gratuitous to be acceptable. Virtually all states in the world today lay claim to being democratic. This is clearly not something that can merely be understood as the result of some sort of unexplicated ideological accompaniment of the spread of capitalism. The impact of political ideas and motives cannot be explained away as matters of economic expediency. I shall argue below that the factors involved in the extension of 'democracy' — leaving aside for the moment how that term might best be conceptualized — are closely bound up with the nature of the nation-state. A tendency to see them as of rather marginal importance is closely connected with the failure to acknowledge the independent significance of political and military power in shaping 'international relations'.

Most of Wallerstein's criticisms of 'modernization theory' are well-taken and apt. But it is not altogether possible to avoid use of concepts of modernity, or equivalent terms. The discontinuities associated with the ascendant position of Europe are not limited to economic transactions, but range much more broadly. In chapter 7 I shall further develop the thesis that four partly separable clusters of institutions have been generated by the convergent development of capitalism, as an economic order, and the nation state, as a political form. It is through these that the generalized impact of modernity can be understood and its implications for both current and potential future modes of social organization traced out.

In what sense, then, is it worth talking of the emergence of a 'world system' from the sixteenth century onwards and what is the specific nature of its connections with the expansion of capitalism? I shall have more to say on these issues later and my comments here will be limited and general. The early development of capitalism was indeed predicated upon an insulation of the political and the economic not only internal but external to the territorially bounded state. The external relations involved are broadly speaking those pointed to by Wallerstein, connecting a multiplicity of states within an economic order which none of them wholly control, although over which some have much more influence than others. This economic order is one largely constituted of market relationships, and thus is not a simulacrum of the organization of capitalism within states in respect of class divisions. It is, nonetheless, one in which strongly defined imbalances are created and perpetuated. The global reach of the economic relations stimulated by — although not even as economic relations wholly reducible to — the spread of capitalism can accurately be called a 'system', and a single system, as long as certain reservations about that notion are borne in mind.[23] A system should not be regarded, in this connotation at least, as a unified and coherent whole. Rather, the term refers to certain relations of interdependence, which may be diffuse and fractured, and may involve imbalances of power. The concepts of core, semi-periphery and periphery should only be used with considerable caution to describe the regionalization of the world system. They are general, indicative notions rather than ones that have any precision and, in any concrete analyses more precise designations are called for. The 'world capitalist economy' refers only to one particular aspect of the world system, not to it in its entirety. Of equal importance is the state system, especially in the later period at which it becomes a globally encompassing nation-state system. More abstractly put, this means giving due weight to the effects of political and military power in the shaping of the international order. *The very term 'international' only has full meaning with the emergence of nation-states which, because of their strictly demarcated character, give a very particular shape to 'internal' versus 'external' relations.*

Dropping the functionalist elements in Wallerstein's views, we must emphasize that the origins of interdependence in the capitalist world economy are diverse. That is to say, it is not necessary to hold — and neither is it in fact empirically plausible to claim — that all the influences affecting interdependence in a trans-state division of labour have emanated from the activities and engagements of the 'core' countries. There is no *prima facie* reason to suppose that the forms of interdependence which have been most prominent at particular phases in the development of the world system have been those that have most favoured the position of the economically advanced societies. Social change is a multiform affair and, although certain master trends can be isolated, it is of the first importance to resist the temptation to squeeze everything within them.

7
Administrative Power, Internal Pacification

The nation-state, let me repeat, is the sociologist's 'society'. The nonchalant use of the term 'society' in the literature of sociology belies the complexity of the changes creating that bounded and unitary whole that is its usual referent. I say this not in order to prohibit use of the concept in the social sciences but to point to a range of problems it ordinarily conceals. Unlike traditional states, the nation-state is a power-container whose administrative purview corresponds exactly to its territorial delimitation. How is this administrative power generated? This will be the topic that will occupy my attention in the first part of this chapter. But it leads on to further issues. For the creation of such administrative capabilities is immediately related to the combined influences of industrialism and urbanism. And it is important in turn to analyse how these connect to key aspects of the nation-state as a capitalist society, which means elucidating the nature of class structure in relation both to sovereignty and democracy. A word of warning to the reader: in this chapter I shall assume greater familiarity with ideas introduced in the first volume of this work than I have done hitherto since, although they are essential to the arguments deployed, there is not room enough to provide a full justification of them.

Administrative Power I:
Communication and Information Storage

Several factors concerned with the extension of communication are deeply involved with the consolidation of the administrative unity of the nation-state. They include: the mechanization of transportation; the severance of communication from transportation by the invention of electronic media; and the expansion of the 'documentary' activities of the state, involving an upsurge in the collection and collation of information devoted to administrative purposes. However, the second and third of these have increasingly merged in the twentieth century as electronic modes of the storage of information have become more and more sophisticated. Moreover, electricity becomes increasingly involved in the means of mechanical propulsion. All three are tied together in terms of the scheme of concepts that inform this book. Each represents a mode of biting into time and space, providing the means of radically increasing the scope of time-space distanciation beyond that available in class-divided societies.

The simplest, and most effective way of analysing the direct impact of innovations in transportation is via the notion of time-space convergence.[1] Somewhere about the middle of the eighteenth century, was initiated a series of innovations in modes of transportation, paring down the time taken to make journeys from one point to another. In all traditional states there were road systems of some kind, often of a fairly complex sort, as in the Roman Empire. Small bands of individuals could move quite rapidly over long distances, particularly if there were staging-posts where fresh horses could be obtained. The Vikings were able to make very fast — as well as on occasion very long — voyages, which compare favourably with anything achieved later, until the advent of mechanically powered vessels. However, the main impetus underlying such forms of (relatively) swift transportation was very often military, commercial long haulage being slow and usually confined to rivers or seas. Until the eighteenth century, Europe was no different from anywhere else in these respects. Roads were generally extremely poor, except for a few highways between major cities and ports. In Britain, a 'turnpike boom' began about the middle of the eighteenth century, prior to which 'the roads throughout the Kingdom were extremely bad and almost impassable, so that it was very difficult to convey from place to place either bulky or heavy articles. Wheel carriages could be little used, and pack horses were the general means of conveyance.'[2]

Not until around the turn of the nineteenth century was there a cohesively organized network of turnpikes, providing for reasonably cheap commercial transportation, in which respect they were in any case undercut for bulk transport by the rapidly developing canal system. The stage-coach system was the first modern rapid-transit form of transportation operating regularly and over a wide spatial pattern. It was also the first to be organized in terms of a time-table, even if those in use well into the nineteenth century were very haphazard and poorly co-ordinated by the standards of subsequent rapid-transit systems. A timetable is one of the most significant of modern organizational devices, presuming and stimulating a regulation of social life by quantified time in a manner quite unknown to prior types of society. Timetables are not just means of using temporal differences in order to identify and specify regularized events — the arrival and departure of coaches, trains, buses or planes. *A time-table is a time-space ordering device, which is at the heart of modern organizations.*[3] All organizations, up to and including the world system today, operate by means of time-tables, through which the sequencing of activities in time-space is choreographed. Organizations have always involved some sort of time-table — the invention of the calendar, for example, was a characteristic feature of traditional states. But only within regularized time-space settings, organized via 'clock time', can time-tables assume a more precise form. The monastery may have been the earliest example of such a setting,[4] but the commodified time inherent in capitalist production undoubtedly was its most decisive propagator. Time-space convergence provides, then, a dramatic index of the phenomenon of which it is by now barely possible to speak without relapsing into cliché — the shrinking world. But lying behind time-space convergence there is the more diffuse, but profoundly important, phenomenon of the increasingly precise co-ordination of the time-space sequencing of social life.

It is somewhat specious to focus mainly upon the mechanization of transportation in interpreting the dissolution of the segmental character of class-divided societies. The effects of such mechanization would have been much more limited were it not for its conjunction with the invention of electronic communication. Without the telegraph, and subsequent electronic communication modes, rapid-transit transportation would be confined to a few journeys per day for a small minority and a tiny proportion of manufactured goods. Mass transportation demands precisely timed and 'spaced' movement, which in turn presumes the capability of communicating 'ahead of time' what is planned. Only given these can an overall traffic system be reflexively monitored and thus comprehensively 'organized'. Thus, rather than the steam train, it is Bradshaw's directory, co-ordinated by telegraphic communication, that epitomizes modern transportation. Contemporaries understandably enough were awed by the railway, 'a plexus of red, a veritable system of blood circulation, complicated, dividing, and reuniting, branching, splitting, extending, throwing out feelers, offshoots, taproots, feeders.'[5] But the combination of the railway and the telegraph was what brought this complex into being, not the locomotive and its rails on their own.

Most historians and sociologists perhaps do not recognize the extended process that was involved in the spread of mechanized modes of transportation, a process that did not culminate until the introduction of world standard time in 1884. At the Prime Meridian Conference held in Washington during that year, following a series of acerbic political debates, Greenwich was adopted as the zero meridian. The globe was partitioned into twenty-four time zones, each one hour apart, and an exact beginning of the universal day was fixed.[6] In some states, railways and other transport time-tables were quite quickly brought into line with these delimitations, but in others more chaotic practices prevailed. How far one or the other was the case depended substantially upon the pre-existing system. As late as 1870 in the USA there were some eighty different railway times.[7] However, in 1883 representatives of the railroads met to establish a uniform time, referred to as 'the day of two noons', since in the eastern part of each region clocks were put back at midday.[8] When the Washington Conference was held, France — whose delegates were the most bitter opponents of the choice of Greenwich as the zero meridian — still had four different regional times, none of which was readily convertible to Greenwich time. Paris time, nine minutes and twenty-one seconds in front of Greenwich, was adopted as the time of the railways, and in 1891 this was made the statutory time for the whole of France. Curiosities remained. The trains were in fact scheduled to run five minutes behind their 'official' times, so as to give passengers opportunity to board in a leisured way. Nonetheless, it was the French who initiated the International Conference on Time, held in Paris in 1912; this was the congress that set up a uniform method of specifying accurate time signals and transmitting them around the world.[9]

The separation of communication from transportation which the telegraph established is as significant as any prior invention in human history. It reduces to a minimum what geographers call the 'friction of distance'. Separation in distance had always been not only separation in time, but had been directly correlated with the expenditure of costs and effort. More or less instantaneous communication may not eliminate either cost or effort, but it does break the coincidence of these with spatial segregation. Postal networks are, of course, a major supplement to the telegraph and its successor, the telephone. Figures 2 and 3 show the increasing time-space convergence between New York and San Francisco.

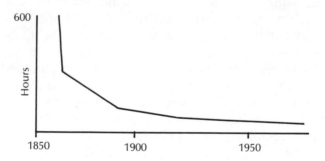

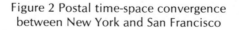

Figure 2 Postal time-space convergence
between New York and San Francisco

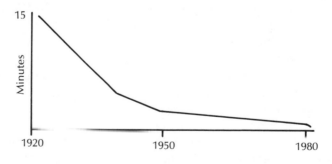

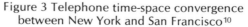

Figure 3 Telephone time-space convergence
between New York and San Francisco[10]

Postal services of a national and international type originated in the eighteenth century. But early postal communications were both slow and sporadic. Prior to the mid-nineteenth century, mail was rarely transported at more than ten miles an hour over lengthy distances.[11] The point already made about modern transportation systems in general — that co-ordination in time-space is as important as the mechanization of the actual channel of movement — applies to postal services as a transport communication device. But highly efficient postal systems certainly antedate their telephone counterparts. In the USA, a fully national telephone service has only existed since the laying of the first transcontinental cable in 1915. Even then trunk-calling was time-consuming compared with later on. In 1920, some quarter of an hour was needed to make such a call, involving the collaboration of as many as eight operators. As figure 3 indicates, by 1930 improvements in network connections cut down the average service time to two minutes; the introduction of automatic switching equipment reduced this to one minute in 1950. The coming of direct long distance dialling reduced this to as long as it takes to compose the number and for someone to answer the call.

In telephone communications there is almost complete time-space convergence both within states and internationally. There is small difference between placing a local call and one across thousands of miles.[12] Of course the telephone is only one among a range of electronic media that permit more or less instantaneous (or, if it is preferred, delayed) communication over indefinite distances. Television has developed as a 'one-way' medium of communication, but there is no intrinsic reason why it should remain so, since various forms of two-way link are in principle, and in some cases in practice, possible. Facsimile, video and computer transmission represent more novel forms of actual and potential communication, the likely impact of which social life is still largely unknown, but which will undoubtedly further extend processes of time-space convergence.

I mention these phenomena here not in order to attempt to bring the discussion of the nation-state through to the present day. My point is to emphasize the significance to the consolidation of the nation-state in the latter part of the nineteenth and early twentieth centuries of the separation of the communication of information from transportation. The initial leap forward in the administrative power generated by the nation-state was accomplished prior to the development of electronic communication. But modern societies have been 'electronic societies' longer than we ordinarily imagine and 'information societies' since their inception. There is a fundamental sense, as I have argued, in which *all* states have been 'information societies', since the generation of state power presumes reflexively monitored system reproduction, involving the regularized gathering, storage, and control of information applied to administrative ends. But in the nation-state, with its peculiarly high degree of administrative unity, this is brought to a much higher pitch than ever before.

In discussing traditional states, Innis makes a distinction between communication media which 'emphasise time' and those which 'emphasise space'.[13] The former are durable but heavy, and are the main textual materials of the earlier civilizations. Stone, clay and parchment belong in this category. They carry the marks of the written word over very lengthy passages of time but are not conducive to the generation of administrative power across wide spans of space. Papyrus and paper tend to be less long-lasting but are light, more easily transportable and also more easily reproducible. The Roman conquest of Egypt, according to Innis, was peculiarly important to the expansion of the Empire, not primarily because of the territory thus acquired, but because it allowed access to large supplies of papyrus which were then used widely to carry administrative documentation. Following the fall of Rome, the European states reverted to the use of the parchment codex, papyrus virtually disappearing after the eighth century. Paper was initially used mainly for commercial purposes, as credit documents and bills of exchange. Texts of any length, including scholarly texts, continued to be inscribed on parchment until the development of the printing press. The invention of printing was a phenomenon as important to the formation of the absolutist state as the other factors mentioned in chapter 6. It would be difficult to overestimate the generalized impact of printing in the shaping of modernity.[14] Printing is the first major step in the mechanization of communication and, in making documents and texts widely available, it initiated the process of drawing European culture away from mimetic imagery in material, intellectual and artistic domains.

So far as the state is concerned, the most important

consequence of the easy and cheap availability of printed materials was an enlargement of the sphere of the 'political'. The growth of a 'public sphere' of state administration is inseparable from textually mediated organization. The discursive arena thereby opened up is quite mistakenly described if it is regarded as one in which 'free speech' is in principle possible. It is not primarily speech which is at issue, however important debating chambers might become. Rather it is the 'intertextuality' of the exchange of opinions and observations via texts that are 'freely available' — in Ricoeur's terms, distanciated from their authors — that marks the decisive shift in the lurch towards a new form of state. I shall pursue this theme in a later section but for the moment I want to concentrate upon the implications for the enlargement of the administrative power of the state. What printing made possible, and what it was increasingly used for during the phase of the consolidation of absolutism, was a very profound furtherance of the surveillance operations of the state. It was essential to the codification of law upon which Weber rightly places so much stress. Laws had long been in some part written but in the preceding scribal culture their influence was necessarily limited and diffuse. Printed codes of law, within an increasingly literate culture, made for the increasing integration of 'interpreted' law within the practice of state administration and for a much more consistent and direct application of standardized juridical procedures to the activities of the mass of the population. But the sphere of the law is only one area in which such changes can be observed. Records, reports and routine data collection become part of the day-to-day operation of the state, although of course not limited to it.

As good a single index as any of the movement from the absolutist to the nation-state is the initiation of the systematic collection of 'official statistics'. In the period of absolutism, such data-gathering was particularly concentrated in two areas, at least as regards the internal affairs of states. One was that of finance and taxation, the other the keeping of population statistics — which tended, however, until the eighteenth century to be localized rather than centralized. The first bears witness to the significance of fiscal management, already alluded to. The second is to do with a phenomenon I shall discuss in the next section — a preoccupation of the centralizing state with maintaining internal 'order' in respect of rebellion, vagabondage and crime. The official statistics that all states began to keep from about the middle of the eighteenth century onwards maintain and extend these concerns. But they also range over many sectors of social life and, for the first time, are detailed, systematic and nearly complete. They include the centralized collation of materials registering births, marriages and deaths; statistics pertaining to residence, ethnic background and occupation; and what came to be called by Quételet and others 'moral statistics', relating to suicide, delinquency, divorce and so on.

There is a very important point to be made about official statistics. From the time of their first beginnings onwards students of society have regarded them as offering a fund of material that can be used to chart the characteristics of social organization and social change. The origins of empirical social research in the social sciences are closely bound up with the use of official statistics as an index of processes of social activity.[15] Durkheim's *Suicide* is only one among many nineteenth-century works to have relied upon the analysis of such statistics to substantiate its conclusions. Now it might well be accepted that, given certain reservations about the manner of their collection, official statistics are an invaluable source of data for social research. But they are not just 'about' an independently given universe of social objects and events, *they are in part constitutive of it*. The administrative power generated by the nation-state could not exist without the information base that is the means of its reflexive self-regulation. Other implications also derive from this. Social science, even its earliest formulations did not come fresh-faced and innocent to an ordered array of empirical data. The collection of official statistics is impossible without those involved having a systematic understanding of the subject-matter that is the concern of those statistics. Such an understanding is progressively monitored, in the modern state, by much the same methods as 'independent' social scientists use to analyse the data thus produced. From this it follows that the social sciences have themselves been persistently implicated in the phenomena they set out to analyse. The connections involved here are in some part empirical (because the collection of modern statistics normally involves learning processes used to 'systematize' and 'improve' them) but also conceptual or theoretical. The discourses of social science are recurrently absorbed into what it is that they are about, at the same time as they (logically) draw upon concepts and theories already employed by lay actors.[16]

Social science, in other words, has from its early origins in the modern period been a constitutive aspect of that vast expansion of the reflexive monitoring of social reproduction that is an integral feature of the state. In the period of absolutism, two forms of discourse were particularly relevant in this respect. One, which I have previously mentioned, was the discourse of early political theory, constitutively entangled in the formation of the modes of sovereignty that distinguish the absolutist state from traditional ones. The other, belonging to a slightly later phase, is the discourse of early economic theory, which helped to give the modern senses to 'economic', 'economy', 'industry' and a whole set of surrounding terms. However, these usages only became firmly established in the nineteenth century and it is economics, together with sociology and psychology, that have been most deeply involved with the rise of the administrative power of the nation-state. In saying this, I do not mean to claim that the social sciences cannot in some part stand outside that power and subject it to analysis and critique, as I consider myself to be doing in this text. But we should recognize that one of the features of the modern state — and of modern organizations in general — is the systematic study and utilization of materials relevant to their own reproduction.

Administrative Power II: Internal Pacification

Surveillance as the mobilizing of administrative power — through the storage and control of information — is the primary means of the concentration of authoritative resources involved in the formation of the nation-state. But it is accompanied by large-scale processes of internal transformation which have their origins in substantial part in the development of industrial capitalism and which essentially can be represented as producing internal pacification. The meaning of 'internal pacification' needs to be carefully understood and interpreted against the backdrop of the character of the internal administration of traditional states. It is a question which returns us to the theme of violence.

As I have previously pointed out, in traditional states the

concept of 'deviance' makes very little sense, except within the restricted locales of the ruling groups. The administrative scope of the state did not extend to encompass the practices of the local community, even within cities where these were spatially distant from the centres in which state power was most concentrated. Moreover, patterns of violence did not resemble those which have become familiar in the (Western) nation-state. In traditional states the relatively insecure hold of the political centre over the means of violence meant that there could be little possibility of 'policing' in the modern sense; that there were always potential sources of challenge, of a military kind, to the centre; and that bandits, marauders, pirates, urban and rural gangs of various sorts tended to be ever-present.

From the sixteenth century onwards within the European societies, fears were constantly expressed in ruling circles about 'popular disturbances'. But although many of these involved traditional modes of protest, they mark the beginnings of a new relationship between state and populace. Two partly independent but increasingly convergent trends of development appear to be involved. One was in most countries substantially the result of the early emergence of capitalistic economic activity, turning loose large numbers of dispossessed peasants, who became semi-unemployed cash-crop labourers or settled in towns and cities as a potentially querulous mass, only partially absorbed into the new social setting. The other was the establishing of remedial organizations in specific types of locale that separated off certain categories of individuals from the remainder of the population. This is the process, or set of processes, that Foucault calls 'sequestration'.[17] In seventeenth century England, it has been estimated, the 'army of poor and jobless' amounted to between 10 and 20 per cent of the adult population, with this figure rising in times of economic crisis to some 30 per cent. Acknowledgement of this as a 'social problem' of large proportions on the part of those in ruling circles was undoubtedly one of the main reasons for the creation of work-houses and the early 'hospitals'.[18]

Since the hospital was the prime model involved in the early phases of the mushrooming of carceral organizations, it is worth briefly commenting on its origins in relation to later developments. 'Hospitals', sometimes in forms to which the modern sense of the term could be applied — concentrating upon the care of the sick and infirm — have a long history outside Europe.[19] Thus hospitals in Byzantium were specialized agencies of this sort, although they were always closely associated with monasteries. For example, the monastery hospital established by John Commenos in 1112 had five separate wards caring for different types of illness, each ward having about a dozen beds in it. Every ward had two physicians, with full-time assistants and orderlies, together with administrators responsible for the organization as a whole; there was also an out-patient department. There were a few hospitals resembling this in Europe in the Middle Ages, such as that at the Abbey of St Gall, in Switzerland, built in the ninth century.[20] The Abbey building contained a hospital with a number of wards, tended by a chief physician and other doctors. But such organizations bear only a marginal relation to those constructed from the seventeenth century onwards. The religious influence and the monastic model remained strong but the new organizations were often established by the state, and their concern was more with crime and vagrancy than with the care of the sick.[21]

If carceral organizations have their origins in the period of absolutism, they only assumed the guise with which we are familiar today in the course of the transition to the nation-state. There is no need to accept the whole sweep of Foucault's arguments to acknowledge that 'disciplinary power' becomes associated with a range of organizations involving new modes of regularizing activities in time-space.[22] Prisons and mental asylums become differentiated from other organizations, like medical hospitals, in which individuals are not incarcerated against their will. 'Deprivation of freedom' becomes the main punitive mode, replacing those spectacular forms of punishment of which Foucault writes but which were, in fact, never more than the dramatic exceptions to more mundane forms of pre-existing sanctions.[23] The enforced deprivation of liberties is clearly in some part an expression of the centrality which 'democratic' or citizenship rights come to assume within the state. The debate — particularly as stimulated by Foucault's writings — over how far the trend towards confinement as a punitive sanction conforms to humane ideals,[24] is in some respects misguided. The point is not only that there occurred a transition from one type of punishment (violent, spectacular, open) to another (disciplinary, monotonous, hidden), but that a new nexus of coercive relations was established where few were located before. The creation of a perceived need for 'law and order' is the reverse side of the emergence of conceptions of 'deviance' recognized and categorized by the central authorities and by professional specialists. These are intrinsic to the expansion of the administrative reach of the state, penetrating day-to-day activities — and to the achievement of an effective monopoly of violence in the hands of the state authorities.

The major schismatic conflicts within the Western nation-state become class struggles and struggles associated with the rise of mass movements of various types. The 'criminal' is specifically no longer a rebel but a 'deviant', to be adjusted to the norms of acceptable behaviour as specified by the obligations of citizenship. In previous types of society, the regularized acquiescence of the mass of the population had not been sought or required by ruling classes, except according to fairly narrow criteria of material submission. The maintenance of 'order' — a term which does not have the same application in any case in those types of society — was a matter of a combination of local community control together with the possibility of armed intervention when necessary. But, in the nation-state, imprisonment plus policing largely replaces both these influences. 'Civil war', where it occurs, normally is henceforth clearly distinguishable from even quite substantial violent confrontations between the state authorities and fractious class groupings or other organized dissident groups.

'Disciplinary power' as described by Foucault depends perhaps primarily upon surveillance in the sense of information-keeping, especially in the form of personal records of life-histories held by the administrative authorities. But it also involves surveillance in the sense of direct supervision. In this sense, prisons and asylums share some of the generalized characteristics of modern organizations, including the capitalistic work-place, but a range of other organizations as well. All involve the concentration of activities either for a period of the day, or for a period in individuals' lives, within specially constructed locales. We may regard disciplinary power as a sub-type of administrative power in general. It is administrative power that derives from disciplinary procedures, from the use of regularized supervision, in order either to inculcate or to attempt to maintain certain traits of behaviour in those subject to it. Since, in previous eras, the monastery was one of the few locales in which large portions of people's lives could be concentrated, it is not surprising that some of the main features of disciplinary power originate there. Disciplinary power is built around the time-table just like other more spatially diffuse aspects of modern organizations. But in this case time-tables are used to organize the time-space sequencing of settings of action within physically restricted locales, in which the regularity of activities can be enforced by supervision of individuals who might not otherwise acquiesce. Supervision demands either continued observation (as, for example, in the case of a teacher confronting a classroom of pupils) or ready access to such observation when it is thought necessary (as in the instance of devices that can be used to keep a watch upon prisoners when they are in their cells). In the sense that disciplinary power involves observation, Foucault is right to take Bentham's panopticon as its epitome, regardless of how far it was actually used as a model by those who designed or operated prisons or other organizational locales.

But Foucault is mistaken in so far as he regards 'maximized' disciplinary power of this sort as expressing the general nature of administrative power within the modern state. Prisons, asylums and other locales in which individuals are kept entirely sequestered from the outside, as Goffman has made clear, have to be regarded as having special characteristics that separate them off rather distinctively from other modern organizations. In virtue of the fact that it is 'total' in its effects upon inmates, the former type of organization specifically disrupts the ordinary routines through which human agents live their lives.[25] Goffman's notion of 'total institution' may or may not have been consciously coined in awareness of its affinities to 'totalitarianism' but certainly the concentration camp is, in recent times, the most dramatic and frightful example of enforced sequestration. The use of techniques of surveillance in such enclosed and brutally time-tabled settings undeniably has set a malign stamp on the modern era. One can see from this regard why Foucault chooses to accentuate the implications of those forms of disciplinary power that were perhaps often first established for essentially humanitarian motives. But we still have to insist that it is the work-place or, more generally, the specialized locale within which administrative power is concentrated, that is prototypical of the Western nation-state. Characteristic of the work-place setting of the business firm or of the school, and most other modern organizations, is that the individual only spends part of the day within their walls; and that during that segment of the day the application of disciplinary power is more diffuse than in 'total institutions'. In all organizations, in virtue of the dialectic of control, there is some sort of 'effort bargain' that is explicitly or implicitly concluded by participants. But outside locales of forcible sequestration, this is one which both *de jure* and *de facto* acknowledges strict limits to the degree to which activities can be forcibly constrained to fit designated or desired patterns. There are certainly quite close architectural similarities between, for example, nineteenth-century prisons and factories in Britain and in other countries. As has been remarked, the thoughts of the early industrial entrepreneurs readily turned to looking for sources of docile, unfree labour in their attempts to create stable conditions of production within the enterprise. One historian observes that, 'There were few areas of the country [Britain] in which the modern industries, particularly textiles, if carried on in large buildings, were not associated with prisons, workhouses and orphanages.'[26] But as the same writer goes on to add, one of the most important characteristics of industrial capitalism is that wage-labour is 'free'. Hence the imposition of disciplinary power outside contexts of enforced sequestration tends to be blunted by the very real and consequential countervailing power which those subject to it can, and do, develop.

This suggests that there are two substantive features of the association of disciplinary power with the modern state that should be distinguished. On the one hand, there takes place a marked impetus towards the expansion of this form of power, made possible by the establishment of locales in which the regularized observation of activities can be carried on in order to seek to control them. This is important for the nature of the modern work-place and, thereby, is a major tie connecting industrial capitalism (as a mode of economic enterprise) to the nation-state (as an administratively co-ordinated unit). It is not, as such, part of the directive influence of the state apparatus, but a generalized phenomenon enhancing internal pacification through promoting the discipline of potentially recalcitrant groups at major points of tension, especially in the sphere of production. This is distinguishable from a growth in disciplinary power linked to, and expressive of, the sanctions that those in the state apparatus are able to wield in respect of 'deviance'. It is this second aspect that is most closely meshed with the development of surveillance as the policing of the routine activities of the mass of the population, by specialized agencies separate from the main body of the armed forces.

Internal pacification involves several related phenomena, all to do with the progressive diminution of violence in the internal affairs of nation-states. One element, given particular prominence by Foucault, is the disappearance of violent forms of punishment associated with the legal system. Perhaps the most striking single index of this is to be found in the history of capital punishment. In post-medieval times, capital punishment could be meted out for a range of transgressions, many of them seemingly quite trivial. On the other hand, the killing of another person could often be atoned for by payment of a fine and, in practice, was frequently sanctioned by the local community or by kin groups rather than by the state. Regarding murder as at the peak of the scale of crimes, whatever level in the social hierarchy the perpetrator might be, and separating murder unequivocally from the killing of alien populations in times of war, are attitudes peculiar to the past two centuries or so. They reflect both the primacy that 'bourgeois rights' assume and their connection with universal citizenship within the sovereign state.

Public executions were still carried out in England until well into the eighteenth century. Hangmen were well-known figures to the general public, and brought to their work various sorts of personal idiosyncracies and forms of exhibitionism.[27] Those malefactors who were done to death at Tyburn were taken through the streets in an open cart, followed by a lengthy cortège of officials. They died slow, lingering deaths, although friends were allowed to shorten their sufferings by pulling at their legs on the scaffold. Although the practice died out well before that of public execution itself, in earlier times corpses were often disposed of publicly. Gibbeting was the most common of such procedures. A corpse would be boiled or tarred and hung up in a chair or wicker suit at the scene of the crime, on a busy thoroughfare or at a special gibbet place. The most evident feature of capital punishment subsequent to the disappearance of public executions was the progressive introduction of techniques attempting to minimize both suffering and any sense of spectacle. The objective also became that of avoiding mutilation. Scaffolds were designed in such a way as to drop the condemned person just far enough to dislocate the neck, but not far enough to break blood vessels. Executions became concealed in time as well as in space, being early in the morning or late at night, rather than in the middle of the afternoon, as public executions used to be. As Lofland points out,

> Historic executions were noisy: pounding to bend bodies on to the wheel; hammering to attach bodies in crucifixion; fire crackling and wood tumbling to prepare pots for human boiling . . . The modern desire is for silent techniques. Virtually no effort has been spared to make English hanging quiet. At the beginning of the modern period, hanging drop doors were baffled with bales of cotton and, when the technology became available, rubber cushions and spring catches were used.[28]

The elimination of punishment-as-spectacle undoubtedly is rich in implications, but one main element involved is a transferral of the sanctioning capacities of the state from the manifest use of violence to the pervasive use of administrative power in sustaining its rule. Capital punishment has today been abolished in most Western countries. But in the preceding period it was no longer a method of inflicting bodily pain, designed to impress the rest of the population with the command over force possessed by the state. Rather, it became the final sanction in a hierarchy of the removal of liberties. Its 'silence' and 'concealment' no doubt have to do with the realization that the sanction of putting someone to death is not in fact just a further step in the progressive deprivation of the rights of citizenship, but an entirely distinct phenomenon. The shift from capital punishment to life imprisonment as the most weighty sanction is thus in line with the 'new logic' of punishment that emerges in conjunction with the expansion of administrative power. Of course, one must recognize that many other forms of violence are widely carried on inside the police stations and prisons of the modern world. But these are not generally part of a scale of punishment whereby violence is used in order publicly to display to potential wrongdoers the likely outcome of any malfeasance. On the contrary, they usually have to be employed in a surreptitious fashion.

In local communities within traditional states, where custom was the principal binding force, there were often blood feuds and other forms of violent encounter between individuals and kin groups. Peasants living at any distance away from the main concentrations of armed force of the state authorities, or of their local lord, could not be effectively protected from bandits or bands of armed raiders. This was true in most areas of traditional China, for instance, right up to the twentieth century, notwithstanding the fact that China was probably in some more central regions the most successfully pacified of all large imperial states.[29] Travel was always a fraught enterprise in such states and merchants of any affluence virtually always moved in armed caravans, even for journeys of quite short distance. Finally, within cities themselves there were very often 'no go' areas in which, even with armed protection, those from other sections would fear to venture.

The development of the absolutist state was undoubtedly associated with major advances in internal pacification, although the level of day-to-day violence was always widely variable at different periods and in different places. According to Le Goff and Sutherland, as has been mentioned previously, in most of rural France under the Old Regime there was a prevalence of 'violence, rowdyism, petty thieving and the like'.[30] If Macfarlane is right about rural England, on the other hand, the level of personal safety in the seventeenth century was considerably higher than in most parts of continental Europe. According to him, in Kirkby Lonsdale and its environs it was fairly common for women to travel on their own, and for people to cross the moors alone at night, even when carrying sums of money. A large amount of movement went on in the region, seemingly without fear of robbery. Battles between wandering youth gangs, quite frequent in some areas of rural England, were apparently absent there.[31] Although the anxieties expressed by commentators at the time cannot necessarily be taken at their face value, it seems definitely to have been the case that the larger cities, towards the latter part of the eighteenth century, all contained areas in which the levels of murder and armed robbery were very high by subsequent standards. It is only in this period, however, that the notion of 'lawlessness' becomes widely used. Modern policing, with its characteristic mixture of informational and supervisory aspects of surveillance, was both made possible and seen to be necessary by the wholesale transferral of populations from rural to urban environments. Horace Walpole wrote in 1752 of journeys in London that 'one is forced to travel, even at noon, as if one were going to battle.'[32] Referring to English cities in general of the period, the Webbs wrote of 'despair of conveying any adequate picture of the lawless violence, the barbarous licentiousness, and the almost unlimited opportunities for pilfering and robbery offered by the unpoliced streets'.[33]

The rapid expansion of a newly urbanized population, in which changing modes of life took some while to become established, created unsettled conditions of 'lawlessness'. To an extent, these might have diminished of their own accord with more stable patterns of residence. But undoubtedly the main influence became the control which the new types of policing, in conjunction with the sanctioning mechanisms of codified law and imprisonment, were able to achieve. 'Criminal' activities became much more clearly distinct from other sources of social strife, and these in turn became plainly differentiated from the external military engagements of states. Comparing London, Stockholm and New South Wales during the second half of the nineteenth and early twentieth centuries, Gurr concludes that in each case there is a clear trend towards a decline in common crimes of violence — a finding amply confirmed in other studies.[34] Until about the turn of the nineteenth century, even in Britain long-distance travel meant risking the attentions of robbers or highwaymen. But during that century these phenomena rapidly became nothing more than a memory, invested not infrequently with a romantic image that bore little relation to the past reality in question. Of course, in other parts of Europe such a level of internal pacification took considerably longer to achieve. As late as the early twentieth century travel was unsafe in some mountainous and forested areas of France and remains so in some part up to the present day in Sicily or Turkey.[35]

Another aspect of internal pacification is of quite elemental importance to the themes of this book.[36] This is the eradication of violence, and the capability to use the means of violence, from the labour contract — the axis of the class system. Closely integrated with, and dependent upon, the other forms of internal pacification, it is a major feature of the separation of the 'economic' from the 'political', although one that is ordinarily ignored in most writings on the subject. It connects closely with processes of social change I shall discuss in the next section, and only the outlines need be sketched here. In industrial capitalism — in contrast to pre-existing class systems — employers do not possess direct access to the means of violence in order to secure the economic returns they seek from the subordinate class. Marx entirely correctly laid considerable emphasis upon this, even if he did not pursue its implications. 'Dull economic compulsion', plus the surveillance made possible by the concentration of labour within the capitalistic work-place, replaces the direct possibility of coercion by the use of force. Of course, employers did not relinquish the use of sanctions of violence without some reluctance and the class struggles waged by workers have often involved violence. But these facts do not compromise the key importance of 'bourgeois rights' in the formation of a 'de-militarized' system of production. This is one of the most significant elements of the liberal-democratic state — that the rights of freedom of disposal of labour-power, for which the bourgeoisie actively fought, carry with them the intrinsic limitation of the power of employers in the work-place to hiring and firing workers and to supervising 'management'. These are not in any way negligible sources of control. However they are only possible in a society which has been internally pacified in other ways and in which 'bourgeois rights' are more than the mere sham freedoms Marx seemingly took them to be.[37]

Most of this book, except where it moves on to the terrain of the global state system, is concerned with the European nation-state. But it is perhaps appropriate at this point to make a few comments about modern states in which the use of force has continued to play a much more direct role in the co-ordination of the labour-force in the sphere of production. If in these states the regulation of work by 'dull economic compulsion' remains undeveloped, it is probably in some substantial part a result of the peripheral involvement of capitalism historically with the use of unfree labour. In countries with an economic background of this sort, the insulation of economy and polity characteristic of the

European nation-state has not been achieved. Other aspects of internal pacification may be correspondingly also less securely developed — in respect, for example, of the existence of armed gangs who perpetuate organized terrorism in pursuit of political goals.[38]

A final characteristic of internal pacification, intimately connected with the others, but nevertheless distinguishable from them, is the withdrawal of the military from direct participation in the internal affairs of state. It is this which seemed to many nineteenth-century thinkers to confirm the thesis of the essentially pacific character of industrial capitalism. What it involves, however, is not the decline of war but a concentration of military power 'pointing outwards' towards other states in the nation-state system. The consolidation of the internal administrative resources of the state dislocates administrative power from its strong and necessary base in the coercive sanctions of armed force. I do not want this statement to be misunderstood. In the nation-state, as in other states, the claim to effective control of the means of violence is quite basic to state power. But the registering of the more or less complete success of this claim, made possible by the expansion of surveillance capabilities and internal pacification, radically lessens the dependence of the state apparatus upon the wielding of military force as the means of its rule. The distinction between the military and civilian police is symbol and material expression of this phenomenon. At the same time, the fact that this distinction is rarely clear-cut, that the police may have paramilitary sections employed in cases of what is regarded as serious civil disturbance, and that the military may be directly called in, are evidence enough that the differentiation is usually full of tension.

Urbanism, Regionalization and Sequestration

In class-divided societies, for reasons already elucidated, cities were a main foundation of the generation of both allocative and authoritative resources. The relation of modern urbanism to the nation-state is quite different, as is the character of urban life as such.[39] The spread of modern urbanism is undoubtedly prompted above all by the emergence of industrial capitalism as the dominant form of production system. But, in its consequences and in its intrinsic form, modern urban development is very different from previous cities. It forms a 'created environment', in which the transformation of nature is expressed as commodified time-space; as such it is the *milieu* of all social action, no longer a distinct physical entity and social sector within a broader societal totality. The commodification of time and of space is the condition of those processes of time-space sequencing described earlier as characteristic of modern organizations, including the nation-state, as the most prominent new power-container.

In saying this, I do not mean to deny the importance of either regionalization within the territory of the state or of social systems that stretch across states. In many respects nation-states and the global areas covered by the nation-state system are more definitely regionalized than the traditional states that preceded them. The administrative unity they display is primarily a phenomenon confined to the scope of the state apparatus. The interdependence, economic and political, of the world in which nation-states exist should not be identified with homogeneity. Some of the main forms of regionalization are the following.[40]

1   The regionalized distribution of nation-states themselves, as core and peripheral states economically, as power-blocs politically and as distinctive and autonomous centres of power within a global patchwork of states.

2   The differential regional distribution of industry, in a division of labour in and across states. Industrial production is by its very nature regionalized, since various types of industry tend to develop, or to be placed, in distinct spatial settings and areas. This applies not only to fairly generalized regional distributions within and between states but also within quite restricted settings, such as the spatial positioning of industrial areas in certain types of urban neighbourhoods. 'Uneven development' can be associated with any or all of the types of regionalization mentioned in (1) or (2).

3   The differential regional concentration of populations, regardless of whether or not this is expressed in the shape of cultural, ethnic or linguistic variations. The populations of nation-states tend to be much more unevenly spread than those of traditional states, partly because of the limitations of rural economy in the latter and of the very high density urban agglomerations assume in the former. The concentration of large

masses of individuals within relatively restricted spatial areas is undeniably one of the most stunning differences between the modern and the traditional world. Up to the seventeenth century there were probably only about 100 million people in Europe, which was considerably more densely populated than the other continents. Today there are some half this number who live in the conurbation occupying the comparatively tiny area stretching from Boston to Washington on the Eastern Seaboard of the USA.
4   There are many clear-cut and diffuse regional variations between neighbourhoods and locales within the built-up sections of the created environment. These are, of course, sometimes planned but are probably more often unintended results of the intersection of product, labour and housing markets. On a smaller scale, regionalization between and within the concretely situated locales that are the settings of organizations is often pronounced and significant. The degree of differentiation among the neighbourhoods of traditional cities and between the locales in which day-to-day life was carried on was usually quite low. Most large, internally differentiated locales were either public buildings or the sites of religious communities. But such locales become commonplace in modern society, being themselves containers for the generation of administrative power. The internal regionalization of locales is involved in a direct way with the hierarchies of offices characteristic of bureaucracy, but also with many other aspects of the differentiation of social activities.

Sequestration is one form of regionalization, and there can be no doubt that its influence is not confined to spheres of forcible incarceration. Concealment and revelation take on new meanings and a new resonance in the created environment of modern urbanism and in a society where massively developed surveillance is so important to the operations of power. Where disciplinary power is strongly focused, for example, settings in which those subject to supervision can avoid being observed by superordinates become of particular significance in the dialectic of control. Sequestration is of such importance to the tissue of day-to-day social life because of its connection with those aspects of human experience that were previously more or less freely exposed to view, if usually surrounded by ritual practices and prohibitions. In spite of the criticisms made by historians of Ariès' discussion of changing Western attitudes towards death, the general outlines of the analysis he makes seem valid. Traditionally, he argues, death was a phenomenon integrated with life, with the continuity of social activities.

> The spectacle of the dead, whose bones were always being washed up to the surface of the cemeteries, as was the skull in Hamlet, made no more impression upon the living than did the idea of their own death. They were as familiar with the dead as they were familiarised with the idea of their own death.

Somewhere in the sixteenth century this began to change, for reasons that do not have a single source but that converge to produce a consistent trend.

> Like the sexual act, death was henceforth increasingly thought of as a transgression which tears man from his daily life, from rational society, from his monotonous work, in order to make him undergo a paroxysm, plunging him into an irrational, violent and beautiful world . . . This idea of rupture is something completely new.[41]

The demands of the early health reformers to remove burial grounds from churches and city centres were, in Ariès' view, an initial symbolic expulsion of the dead from the community of the living. It preceded and helped shape the 'suppression' of death that is characteristic of more recent times. But whatever its origins, which are certainly both historically and psychologically complex, this 'suppression' is not limited to the material evidence of mortality. Not only death is sequestered from the ordinary activities of daily life; so are other phenomena which, in becoming 'detached' from the normal run of social life, produce specific sources of anxiety or distress — including both madness and physical illness of a serious sort. If Elias is right, Ariès' comment on sexuality also signals an important social change, even if sexual behaviour is not organizationally confined in the same way as the other phenomena. There is good reason to be as cautious about some of Elias's historical claims as there is those of Ariès, but it does seem that sexual activity used to be engaged in more openly than subsequently came to be the case.[42]

Whatever the sources of these changes, their consequences are probably very significant for the tissue of day-to-day social life in modern states. I have argued elsewhere that routinization, knowledgeably yet tacitly organized by agents in the flow of their action, is fundamental to the reproduction of institutionalized practices.[43] In tribal and in class-divided societies, tradition infuses the routine and gives it moral sources through which day-to-day life connects to the existential parameters of human life, to the relations of human beings with nature, birth, sickness and death. The 'existential contradiction' via which human beings live their lives — that they are part of inorganic nature, and relapse into it at death, yet are not of nature, in so far as they live also in consciousness of their finitude — is not separated from the organized dynamics of social life. In the modern state, existential contradiction is almost completely expunged by structural contradiction, the main locus of which is precisely the state itself.[44] One outcome is that the routinization of day-to-day social life is precarious, resting upon a relatively shallow psychological base and not integrated with moral principles that provide means of meeting existential dilemmas. The sequestration of death, sickness and madness, and the privatizing of sexuality, are both a result of this situation and, at the same time, a condition of the stability of the routine.

In virtue of sequestration, therefore, a range of experiences that are psychologically troubling do not intrude upon the main body of activities individuals carry out in the course of their daily lives. Such experiences are removed from possible intrusion into the continuity of routinized activities and pushed instead to the outer margins of those contexts in which most daily social life is enacted. I do not mean to propose some sort of functionalist account either of the origins of sequestration or of its implications once widely established. The development of sequestered locales is partly to be explained in terms of influences promoting carceral organizations and partly in terms of the emerging primacy of 'technical' methods of attempting to 'treat' 'mental' and physical illness. The outcome of sequestration is not in any generalized way functional for the continuity of social activities. In respect of feelings of ontological security, the members of modern societies are particularly vulnerable to generalized anxiety. This may become intense either when, as individuals, they have to confront existential dilemmas ordinarily suppressed by sequestration, or when, on a larger scale, routines of social life are for some reason substantially disrupted. The emptiness of the routines followed in large segments of modern social life engender a psychological basis for affiliation to symbols that can both promote solidarity and cause schism. Among these symbols are those associated with nationalism, and I shall return to the issues thus raised in chapter 8.

8
Class, Sovereignty and Citizenship

Polyarchy

The development of sovereignty, as concept and reality, is of major significance in relating what at first sight look to be quite opposed developments: the authority of the absolutist monarch and the coming of the modern democratic state. At the same time as the drive towards sovereignty generates a centralization of resources in the hands of the ruler, it stimulates a generalized awareness that political power depends upon collective capabilities which the figure of the monarch may signify, but to which the traditional trappings of kingly rule have little relevance.

There are two contrasting interpretations of the development of modern democracy, with both of which I shall take issue. On the one hand there is the familiar Marxist account, which seeks to explain the origins of democratic participation in terms of class dynamics. Although such an account can and has been given with widely varying degrees of subtlety, its basic outline is clear enough. The main transformative influence shaping the emergence of democratic politics is the development of capitalism and the class struggles this entails. 'Bourgeois freedoms' involve a range of civil and political liberties achieved through the conflicts that ranged the members of the rising capitalist class against the land-owning aristocracy. 'Bourgeois rights', which were proposed by their advocates as universal, in fact serve to legitimate the dominance of the capitalist class. While Marx might admit — especially in his more detailed studies rather than his more abstract pronouncements — that struggles involving such rights may have a certain independence from class conflict, for the most part they are seen as the surface expression of class division. An opposing view is taken by many of Marx's critics. Thus Bendix effectively seeks to reverse the Marxist position, arguing that while struggles over civil and political rights were in certain historical circumstances conjoined to class conflicts, in fact the former have primacy over the latter. Neither the origins nor the consequences of the democratization of the modern state are in a significant way conditioned by class conflict. Thus the struggles that seemed to Marx to be the very prototype of class conflict in nineteenth-century Europe are seen as strivings on the part of excluded groups to achieve full membership of the democratic polity.[1]

Before assessing these rival positions, some conceptual and substantive observations should be made. Few concepts are more fiercely debated than that of democracy. I shall not try to trace the course of those debates, but shall follow Lindblom in regarding 'democracy', in its broadest sense, as equivalent to 'polyarchy'.[2] Polyarchy means rule by the many, and involves 'the continuing responsiveness of the government to the preferences of its citizens considered as political equals.'[3] Electoral systems, as modes of ensuring such 'responsiveness of government' are the prime, but not the only, procedural means of creating polyarchy and courts of appeal the main mechanism of sustaining it. Lindblom concerns himself mostly with the first of these, but the second is arguably just as important in respect of the formulation he offers. For, as he indicates, polyarchy depends upon debates and persuasion which (in principle) counter the arbitrary use of power. I include as courts of appeal not only parliaments, debating chambers and law courts, but also any arena in which debate that influences policy decisions is carried on — in particular the press and, in recent times, electronic media. There is one major respect in which I depart from Lindblom's usage. He limits the notion of polyarchy to 'bourgeois' or 'liberal democracies'. I wish to make it a much more encompassing concept, such that liberal democracy is only one type of polyarchy. Although in the European nation-state polyarchic systems have predominantly taken the form of liberal democracy, other types of government in nation-states of all kinds tend strongly towards polyarchy. There is, in short, a generic association between the nation-state and polyarchy which it will be my aim to help explicate.

Polyarchy, Lindblom makes clear, depends upon the existence of a range of rights attributed to the members of a given population. At this point, however, we have to acknowledge an important phenomenon associated with sovereignty. Polyarchy evidently has something to do with what Marx called 'bourgeois rights'. Now 'bourgeois rights', in their classic formulations in the American and French Revolutions, are universal rights. They apply in principle to the whole of humanity and it is not surprising to find that even their radical critics, such as Marx, took this for granted. As the expression of underlying economic transactions that are also potentially universal in nature, they have no particular connection with the boundaries of states. In fact, 'bourgeois rights' have been everywhere actualized within sovereign states. They are, thus, more appropriately regarded as *citizenship rights* and I shall henceforth use that term to refer to them.

Lindblom lists the following as the rights and prerogatives associated with polyarchy:[4]

1   Freedom to form and join organizations
2   Freedom of expression
3   Right to vote
4   Eligibility for public office
5   Right of political leaders to compete for support
6   Right of political leaders to compete for votes
7   Alternative sources of information
8   Elections to decide who is to hold top authority
9   Organizations for making government policies depend on votes and other expressions of preference.

The modes in which these are given concrete form obviously may vary very considerably and phrases such as 'freedom of expression' conceal a veritable hornets' nest of potentially divergent interpretations. Nonetheless, this is a useful formulation for general purposes of the analysis of modern political systems. I propose to add to it, however, the classification of citizenship rights provided by T. H. Marshall.[5] Marshall distinguishes three types of citizenship rights — the 'civil', 'political' and 'social' (although I shall call the third of these 'economic' rights). Lindblom's list consists mainly of civil and political rights, plus the means of their realization. Civil rights are those involved mainly under categories 1, 2, 7 and 9 in his list. They are legally guaranteed rights of individuals freely to associate with one another, to live where they want, to enjoy freedom of speeech and justice in respect of accusations of 'deviant' behaviour. The remainder are political rights and prerogatives, concerning the participation of individuals in the exercise of political power, as voters, or in a more direct way in the practice of politics. Economic citizenship rights are distinguishable from both these categories. They concern the right of everyone within the state to enjoy a certain minimum standard of life, economic welfare and security.

Polyarchy, Citizenship

Why should it be the case that there are inherent connections between the nation-state and democracy (understood as poly-archy)? I want to interpret these connections, in a generalized way at least, as bound up with the dialectic of control, in relation to the concentration of administrative resources in the nation-state. In class-divided societies, I have suggested, there was no 'government' in the modern sense. The administrative reach of the state authorities left largely untouched the day-to-day life of the local communities in which the large mass of the population lived. The dialectic of control in class-divided societies, in relation to the power of the state, can be characterized as a matter of 'segmental autonomy'. That is to say, since the level of interdependence of the political centre and its subject population was relatively low, the 'effort bargain' made involved the maintenance of a large amount of local community autonomy, so long as certain obligations to the state were met, in return for which the state provided a limited range of reciprocal services. The use or threat of the use of military power tended to be ever-present in sustaining the administrative reach of the state apparatus, because the level of time—space distanciation it was able to command was low compared, at least, with the modern state. In the latter, the build-up in administrative power (generated above all by the extension of surveillance in the various senses noted above) marginalizes the state's dependence upon control of the means of violence as a medium of rule of its subject population. However, administrative power that depends upon the mobilization of social activities via the expansion of surveillance necessarily increases the reciprocal relations between those who govern and those who are governed. The more reciprocity is involved, the greater the possibilities the dialectic of control offers subordinate groups to influence the rulers. I take this to be the 'structural backdrop' against which polyarchy develops, first of all in the shadow of the absolutist state and then more openly and directly in the course of the transition to the nation-state.

I assume one implication of this argument to be that Parsons's interpretation of 'power deflation' has considerable relevance — in somewhat amended form — to understanding the character of the modern state.[6] Parsons claims that systems of domination involve sustaining the confidence of those in subordinate groups in their rulers. When such confidence, for whatever reason, begins to wane, the amount of power generated in the system diminishes — it becomes 'ungovernable'. It is only in such circumstances of power deflation that the widespread use or threat of the use of force is necessary in order to sustain governmental control. As an account of the basis of the administrative power of the nation-state and its connections to polyarchy, this is helpful and plausible, although various qualifications have to be made. The mass of the population does not necessarily have to have 'confidence' in the system of rule, only pragmatic acceptance of their obligations in relation to it. The use of violence (military force) may be more directly involved in the initial establishing of the administrative order than Parsons allows, not just confined to conditions of power deflation. But it is in circumstances of power deflation that polyarchic influences will tend to come under pressure or be dissolved.

There are many contingent conditions that might bring about power deflation, but in a general way it is likely to be strongly conditioned by struggles over the three basic types of citizenship rights. In order to demonstrate why this should be the case, I shall return to the work of Marshall, examining his own account of the formation of citizenship rights in a critical way.[7] Marshall characterizes his typology of the three forms of citizenship right negatively by reference to feudalism and, positively, by reference to the organizational focus of each. In the feudal system, rights were not universal, in other words, not applicable to every member of a national polity. Those in the various estates and corporations effectively belonged to separate communities, having different rights and duties in relation to one another. Moreover, these rights and duties tended to form single clusters; only since the eighteenth century have the three strands of citizenship rights become distinct from one another. This is partly because each has a different organizational focus or, at least, the first two do. The main institutional focus of the administration of civil rights is the legal system. Political citizenship rights have as their focal points the institutions of parliament and local government. The third — economic rights — apparently in Marshall's eyes lack such an organizational location, which is perhaps why he chooses the diffuse term 'social rights' to refer to them.

Marshall's discussion is explicitly focused on Britain and he does not claim that his scheme applies with equal cogency in other contexts. His thesis is that the three aspects of citizenship have developed at different rates over the past two or three centuries, with each serving as a sort of platform for the others. The main formative period of the development of civil or legal rights was the eighteenth century, when rights of the liberty of the individual, and full and equal justice before the law, became firmly established. Thus the right to live and work where one pleases becomes generally accepted, something which in earlier centuries was for many prohibited both by custom and by statute. The traditional view, Marshall says, only gradually ceded place to the new principle that restrictions on the movement of the population are 'an offence against the liberty of the subject and a menace to the prosperity of the nation'.[8] The legal system was primarily involved in advancing this idea, the judiciary delivering a series of judgements that progressively freed individuals from their bondage to the places where they were born and the occupations they were born into. Civil freedoms were essentially the end process in the dissolution of the remnants of feudal society. They were the necessary foundation for the emergence of political rights; for only if the individual is recognized as an autonomous agent does it become reasonable to regard that individual as politically responsible. The establishment of universal political rights belongs to the nineteenth and the early twentieth centuries. This process, according to Marshall at least, was not so much one of the formation of new rights as the extension of old ones, previously the monopoly of the privileged few, to the whole of the political community. Economic rights belong almost wholly to the twentieth century. The nineteenth century, the period of ascendant industrial capitalism, was a period at which those who were most adversely affected by the play of economic forces had little protection against deprivation. Poverty was regarded as an indication of social inferiority; in Britain paupers placed in the work-house forfeited the rights possessed by other citizens, to virtually the same degree as imprisoned criminals or the certified insane. But in the twentieth century this became reversed, largely as a consequence of the effects of political citizenship. With the establishment of the universal franchise, the organized working class was able to secure the political strength to consolidate welfare or economic rights *as* rights.

The development of citizenship rights, particularly those of the second and third types, according to Marshall, has substantially undermined the class divisions which he accepts are inherent in capitalist society. As he puts it:

> In the twentieth century, citizenship and the class system have been at war . . . The expansion of social rights is no longer merely an attempt to abate the obvious nuisance of destitution in the lowest ranks of society . . . It is no longer content to raise the floor-level in the basement of the social edifice, leaving the super-structure as it was. It has begun to remodel the whole building, and it might even end by converting the skyscraper into a bungalow.[9]

Marshall's views on these matters are somewhat different from the ideas that Bendix and others taking a comparable standpoint have developed. In Marshall's conception, citizenship rights, and the political struggles associated with them, do not have a more profound role to play than class conflict in modern societies; rather, the two tend to balance one another. Citizenship rights do not dissolve class division and cannot do so, in the context of a capitalist society at any rate, although they do mellow the tensions deriving from class conflict. The encounter between citizenship and the capitalist class system results in a negotiated truce, a 'class compromise' rather than an unqualified victory for either side. I think this view — in some key respects at any rate — is a correct one, although I want to put it to use in a rather different way than Marshall has in mind. This means criticizing some aspects of what Marshall has to say; detaching the analysis from the specifically British context of development; and relating the discussion of citizenship rights back to that of surveillance.

So far as the first of these problems goes, we should register an objection to Marshall's tendency to treat the development of citizenship rights as brought about by something of a natural process of evolution, helped along where necessary by the beneficent hand of the state. In Britain, as in other societies, there was little conceded by the state authorities without conflict. There has not only been a 'struggle' between citizenship and class, but a struggle to achieve the rights of citizenship themselves — although one which, if my argument is correct, the underprivileged have been able to muster considerable resources to pursue their claims. In Britain, the sequence of achievement of citizenship rights Marshall describes does make sense. Civil rights were in some substantial part established prior to political rights and these, in turn, before economic rights. Even in Britain, however, the picture is rather more complicated than Marshall would allow; some kinds of civil rights, for example, have only been achieved in the twentieth century (others have arguably also been eroded or diminished). Developments elsewhere cannot be readily portrayed as a successive movement through the three stages of citizenship rights, since the order of their realization is quite different. Thus in nineteenth-century Germany, Bismarck conceded various welfare rights to the working-class specifically in order to prevent the realization of the political rights Marshall describes.

Rather, then, than seeing the three categories of citizenship rights as phases in the overall development of citizenship, it is more plausible to interpret them as three arenas of *contestation* or *conflict*, each linked to a distinctive type of surveillance, where that surveillance is both necessary to the power of superordinate groups and an axis for the operation of the dialectic of control. Civil rights are intrinsically linked to the modes of surveillance involved in the policing activities of the state. Surveillance in this context consists of the apparatus of judicial and punitive organizations in terms of which 'deviant' conduct is controlled. Marx tends to discuss civil rights as the category of 'bourgeois rights' *par excellence*, legitimating the dominance of capital over wage-labour. While there are some aspects of the Marxist position that are undoubtedly valid, it is essential to see that civil rights, and the more-or-less chronic struggles surrounding them, have a generic and independent significance in modern states:

Civil rights	Surveillance as policing
Political rights	Surveillance as reflexive monitoring of state administrative power
Economic rights	Surveillance as 'management' of production

Like the other two types of rights, civil rights have their own particular locale. That is to say, there is an institutionalized setting in which the claimed universality of rights can be vindicated — the law court. The law court is the prototypical court of appeal in which the range of liberties included under 'civil rights' can be both defended and advanced. Of course it would be wrong to see the law court as the only setting in which struggles over the form and bounds of policing are enacted; they occur in virtually all situations in which surveillance of this type is carried out, including the sequestered contexts of disciplinary power. The same should be emphasized about political rights, where the institutionalized locale of contestation — parliament or the council chamber — is the formal setting for the discursive representation of rights, but where a whole variety of extra-parliamentary contestations are also possible. Marshall does not connect economic rights with a distinctive locale and in one sense there is good reason for this, because there is not the same sort of relevant debating chamber. But I would suggest that the locale in which struggles over economic rights are focused is the work-place, the surveillance in question being that of 'management' over a labour-force. If there is not an institutionalized court of appeal here, this reflects phenomena of major significance in the class structure of capitalism. The main organized agency of struggle over economic rights is the union and it is in the mechanics of industrial arbitration that we find the settings of contestation in relation to this type of surveillance.

Capitalism entails a class society and to develop the analysis further we must consider how class relations influence, and are influenced by, the various forms of citizenship right. In explicating these influences, it will be helpful to return to the critical assessment of Marshall's views. This involves using Marx against Marshall, but subsequently I shall tip the scales the other way, using Marshall against Marx. I have emphasized elsewhere the significance of the capitalist labour contract in the organization of capitalist enterprise.[10] The capitalist labour contract is a primary element in the separation of the spheres of the 'economic' and the 'political'. Now, various points have to be made about this in relation to Marshall's views. The insulation of the economic from the political was in some part achieved by the very legal freedoms Marshall refers to as civil rights. Such rights and prerogatives should not be seen as being created 'outside' the sphere of the state, but as part and parcel of the emergence of the 'public domain', separated from 'privately' organized economic activity. Civil rights thus have been, from the early phases of capitalist development, bound up with the very definition of what counts as 'political'. Civil and political citizenship rights developed together and remain, thereafter, open to a range of divergent interpretations which may directly affect the distribution of power. Moreover, economic rights cannot be regarded as just on a par with the two other types of citizenship right, because it is in the nature of capitalist society that these express an asymmetry of class domination. Marx regarded civil and political rights as liberties which are universal in principle but in practice favour the rule of the dominant class. In substantial degree, Marx was surely right about this. The capitalist labour contract, particularly in the early period of the expansion of capitalist enterprise, excludes the worker from formal rights over the control of the work-place. This exclusion is not incidental to the capitalist state, but vital to it, since the sphere of industry is specifically defined as being 'outside politics'. Given this perspective, we can explain why economic citizenships rights are not to be regarded just as an extension of civil and political rights, and why they do not have their own specific courts of appeal.

The three types of surveillance are, in some respects, knit together and, in other respects, dislocated by the class character of capitalist society. As I have just pointed out, civil rights are of particular significance at the juncture that connects and separates the economic and the political. The class asymmetry this relation involves both gives workers' movements a particular historical importance and, at the same time, tends to separate the struggles of the labour movement at two different sites. In each of these, citizenship rights tend to be a focus of class conflict, rather than standing opposed to it as Marshall suggests. In the political sphere, the formation of labour or socialist parties (actively resisted by pre-existing governments in many countries) has been geared to winning the universal franchise and then either to implementing, defending or expanding economic rights. Here labour movements, in the late nineteenth and early twentieth centuries, have been able to build upon a combination of civil and political rights, which have often been broadened in the process. But in the realm of industry the situation was, and continues to be, different. The separation of the economic from the political meant that, in the early years of capitalist development, the worker who walked in through the factory gates sacrificed all formal, and much actual, control over the work process.

What was in prior types of society an integral element of production — a significant degree of control by the worker over the process of labour — had to be won all over again in the new surveillance settings of modern production. In all capitalist countries unionization, backed by the threat or actuality of the withdrawal of labour-power, has formed the principal source of the power that subordinates can wield in the work-place. The emergence of the strike, or threat of it, as a major sanction in the dialectic of control in work settings, can be readily traced to the novel conditions of modern production. Peasants tend to be dispersed, as Marx points out in a famous passage in the *Eighteenth Brumaire*.[11] The development of the capitalist work-place provides settings in which collective action is facilitated. But just as important is the fact that the propertylessness of workers, upon which the dominance of entrepreneurs is founded, becomes itself a resource. Being dependent upon co-ordinated labour-power, employers are vulnerable to its collective withdrawal, as well as to a range of other stratagems workers can use to achieve a substantial measure of control where formally they are allocated none.

In my view, therefore, it is more valid to say that class conflict has been a medium of the extension of citizenship rights than to say that the spread of such rights has blunted class divisions. *All three forms of citizenship right distinguished by Marshall are double-edged.* As aspects of surveillance, they can be mobilized to expand the control the members of the dominant class are able to maintain over those in subordinate positions. But, at the same time, each is a lever of struggle, which can be used to counter that control. In a capitalist society, class domination provides the most important single institutional axis around which these struggles converge and, in that respect, Marx's view is still cogent. But it does not follow from this that surveillance is an epiphenomenon of class, or that the modes of generating power which it provides will disappear with the transcending of the capitalist class system. Conflict centred upon 'bourgeois rights' is not necessarily class conflict, and the level and nature of their realization has to be regarded as altogether more problematic than Marx believed.

Citizenship, Ideology and Nationalism

Traditional states, I have proposed, opened out a public sphere directly related to the monitoring operations of the state, but confined to a very small 'public'. The term 'public', as an adjective and as a noun, has a number of possible shadings of meaning. A phenomenon which is public is 'open to view', rather than concealed; and it pertains to a generalized body of persons rather than to those in particular contexts of co-presence. Each of these aspects of the 'public' again helps emphasize the importance of writing in the traditional state. A list, or file, or a text, are of necessity 'open' in the sense that they become distanciated from their authors in a way in which spoken communication cannot be — at least, until the advent of electronic modes of information storage. Written documents also shed the contextual confinement of speech in virtue of that very distanciation: they potentially reach an indefinitely wide audience. How far the existence of writing supports a public sphere in respect of state power may vary widely, depending upon the scope of literacy, the nature of the documentation involved, and the communicative settings in which the information thus stored is utilized. But the development of states is necessarily convergent with the formation of modes of discourse which constitutively shape what state power is.

It is in the nature of agrarian states that the discursive

articulation of administrative power is relatively limited, by and large not reaching the mass of the population. Distinctive of the modern state, however, is a very considerable expansion of the reflexive monitoring of state activity. The development of state sovereignty expresses and further stimulates a new form of administrative order, signalled by the formation of the absolutist state, but maximized in the nation-state. A state can only be 'sovereign', in the terms of political theorists of the sixteenth century and afterwards, if large segments of the population of that state have mastered an array of concepts connected with sovereignty.[12] Now such mastery need not be wholly discursive, especially among those who are subject to the administration of the state rather than directly involved in that administration. But when Machievelli, Bodin and others began writing about 'politics', they were not only describing a series of changes, nor even only making policy recommendations; they were helping to constitute what the modern state *is* as a novel ordering of administrative power. The development of notions of citizenship, as pertaining to membership of an overall political community, are intimately bound up with this. In many cases the mass of the population of traditional states did not know themselves to be 'citizens' of those states, nor did it matter particularly to the continuity of power within them. But the more the administrative scope of the state begins to penetrate the day-to-day activities of its subjects, the less this theorem holds. The expansion of state sovereignty means that those subject to it are in some sense — initially vague, but growing more and more definite and precise — aware of their membership in a political community and of the rights and obligations such membership confers.

The development of printing, and the extension of literacy, create a broadened realm of the 'public' — indeed for the first time it makes sense to apply that term as a noun as well as an adjective. Printing vastly expands not only the capabilities of reflexive monitoring of the state, but the distanciation of communication from oral contexts. Not until the period of the emergence of the nation-state, however, do the potentialities of printing become fully recognized and utilized. The epoch at which the regularized collection of official statistics becomes established is the same as that in which a flurry of journals, gazettes, newspapers and pamphlets appear, reaching mass audiences. Gouldner has commented on this in a cogent way:

> At first, such publications were more likely to combine commentary on literature with 'news'. But by 1800 the news predominated, as parliaments and political centres became of wider interest, and as the spread of markets into national and international systems meant that distant events could affect local prices and supplies . . . The emergence of the mass media and of the 'public' are mutually constructive developments . . . With the growth of the mass media, exemplified at first by printing, numerous persons were now exposed to a continuous flow of information, at more or less the same time. Information becomes decontextualised, for it must be made intelligible, interesting and convincing even to persons of diverse backgrounds and interests, persons who do not know one another and do not meet and interact.[13]

Some of the main dimensions of ideology in modern states are to be discovered in the nature and scope of discursive articulation of information available in the 'public' domain. In the context of the modern state, the capability of different groupings to discursively formulate policies or programmes that express their interests and to make space in the public domain for promoting them, are vital. While in the nation-state all members of the population share an array of concepts constitutive of its sovereign and polyarchic character, these may be mainly ordered in practical consciousness rather than being available to be discursively formulated as reasons for action. Although this theorem applies at all levels of society, it is likely to be strongly weighted in favour of the more privileged strata and, more generally, the dominant class.

Of course it is not only the degree and nature of the discursive formulation of interests that matters. There are at least three more substantive aspects of those discursive formulations which exist that influence the ideological shadings of symbol systems.

1   The definition of what is to count as 'political' and, therefore, in principle open to intervention or control on the part of the state. There is a direct tie here between the state and the class system in capitalist society, since the 'depoliticizing' of economic relations is basic to class domination.

2   The definition of practices, programmes and policies that are in the 'general interest', as opposed to those that favour the sectional interests of groups or classes. The more the state becomes administratively unified, the greater the degree to which government must appeal to the 'general interest' (in some formulation or other) in order to sustain a basis for its rule. Again, there tend to be strong pressures promoting a class bias, since although it is not directly 'run' by entrepreneurial groups, in capitalist societies the state apparatus is materially dependent upon the prosperity of economic enterprises for its sources of revenue.

3   The articulation of 'historicity' in relation to planned or actual trends of social change.[14] The reflexive monitoring of all states involves the invention of 'history' in some sense or another — the documented interpretation of the past that provides an anchorage for anticipated developments in the future. But only in the modern West does 'history' become 'historicity' — the controlled use of reflection upon history as a means of changing history.

Ideological aspects of nationalism can effectively be analysed in terms of these three categories.[15] Nationalism is certainly not wholly ideology. But it does tend to be linked in definite ways to the administrative unification of the state.[16] Sovereignty, citizenship, nationalism — these tend to be connected phenomena for reasons it will be my aim to try to illuminate.

A useful classification of the main explanatory approaches to nationalism is that offered by Breuilly.[17] One group of approaches consists of those associated with Marxism. Gellner has caustically labelled Marxist views of nationalism the Wrong Address Theory: 'Just as extreme Shi'ite Muslims hold that Archangel Gabriel made a mistake, delivering the Message to Mohamed when it was intended for Ali, so Marxists basically like to think that the spirit of history or human consciousness made a terrible boob. The awakening message was intended for *classes*, but by some terrible postal error was delivered to *nations*.'[18] It is manifestly the case that Marx paid little attention to the nature and impact of nationalism, and the comments he does make are mostly neither instructive nor profound.[19] Subsequent Marxists have been very much concerned with 'the national question', but it cannot be pretended that the literature thereby generated has done a great deal to illuminate the nature or origins of nationalism. None of the various Marxist interpretations which seek to treat nationalism as some kind of masked expression of the interests of the dominant class has much plausibility either. The most illuminating account of nationalism produced in recent times[20] by an author affiliated with Marxism is probably that given by Nairn.[21] According to Nairn, nationalism has its source in the uneven development of regions within the world capitalist economy. Traditional Marxist views saw class struggle as 'the motor of historical change, nationality a mere epiphenomenon of it. Hence, it was literally inconceivable that the former should be eclipsed by the latter.' It is in the effects of the expansion of capitalism, not in its class system as such, that the roots of nationalism are to be found. 'As capitalism spread, and smashed the ancient social formations surrounding it, they always tended to fall apart along the fault-lines contained inside them. It is a matter of elementary truth that these lines were nearly always ones of nationality (although in certain well-known cases deeply established religious divisions could perform the same function).'[22]

But Nairn's view, where it is plausible at all, only seems relevant to forms of anti-colonial nationalism, not to the first development of nationalism in the European states. The main forms of nationalism in Europe did not for the most part come about in areas of marked economic deprivation. German nationalists in the mid-nineteenth century, for example, may have been concerned with Germany's 'backwardness' relative to the leading European states, but to regard this as the principal origin of German nationalism is quite unconvincing. In other cases, the development of nationalism was most marked in the strongest states, not the weaker or more ill-formed ones.[23] How far Nairn's arguments apply even to the emergence of nationalism in colonial or post-colonial regions must be doubted. There are obviously general relationships between capitalist development on a global scale and the formation of nationalist sentiments. But whether or not nationalism becomes significant in a given area, and its specific symbolic content, cannot readily be explicated in such a way.

A second approach, which is appealing because it does appear more directly to address these issues, is that associated with Deutsch and others.[24] Deutsch lays great emphasis upon the development of internal communications within states as leading to the creation of a common sense of moral and political identity. In this view some of the factors I have identified as contributing to the heightening of the administrative power of states are regarded as directly responsible for the stimulating of nationalist sentiments. However, on closer scrutiny, the theory is unconvincing since there is neither any inevitable connection between the intensification of communication and the consolidation of states, nor does the theory explain why such consolidation should be intrinsically accompanied by nationalism. Gellner's position bears a definite similarity to that of Deutsch, but Gellner does seek to indicate why nationalism should be associated with the diffusion of communications. The economies of industrialized states depend upon a homogenizing of culture, mass literacy and 'a fairly monolithic education system'.[25] The exigencies of industrialism thus demand the diffusion of common modes of thought and belief throughout the whole population. Nationalism is precisely the attachment of such modes of thought and belief to the state which is the means of their co-ordination. How far this analysis is an advance beyond that of Deutsch, however, is open to question. As has been previously stressed, there is no intrinsic reason to be found in industrial production as to why an industrialized society should be a nation-state. Moreover, Gellner's analysis again does not seem satisfactorily to distinguish the nation-state from nationalism.

Finally, there are 'psychological' interpretations of nationalism.[26] Neither Deutsch nor Gellner has much to say about the content of nationalism, which is regarded as more or less irrelevant to its nature or to its appeal. But nationalist sentiments, in their first origins and in their subsequent guises in the twentieth century, do tend to involve some common symbols. Attachment to a homeland, associated with the creation and perpetuation of certain distinctive ideals and values, traceable to certain historically given features of 'national' experience — these are some of the recurrent traits of nationalism. Most psychological theories of nationalism associate these notions with the need of individuals to be involved in a collectivity with which they can identify. Since previous groupings that could fulfil this need, such as the local community or kinship group, have been largely dissolved, the symbols of nationalism provide a modern substitute.

Nationalism not only offers a basis of group identity, it does so in the context of showing this identity to be the result of distinct and precious achievements. While it may be a relatively new type of doctrine, nationalism appeals to a desire for an identity securely anchored in the past. This type of approach offers an analysis both of the first origins of nationalism and of its subsequent varieties. The disintegrative impact which is wrought upon pre-existing traditional cultures by modern economic and political development creates a search for renewed forms of group symbolism, of which nationalism is the most potent. Nationalism engenders a spirit of solidarity and collective commitment which is energetically mobilizing in circumstances of cultural decay.[27]

Although I shall argue that the psychological dimensions of nationalism are indeed important, the origins and character of the postulated need for identity remain too vague for this type of theory to be particularly satisfactory. It has little to say about why nationalism should be connected with states, or about how it might relate to asymmetries of power and therefore to ideology. Moreover, nationalist sentiments tend to surge and decline; they are not so much a part of regular day-to-day social life as those symbols connected with the smaller groups which it is claimed fulfil the same psychological needs.

I have mentioned these various interpretations of nationalism not simply to object to them, but to make the argument that an explication of the origins of nationalism should incorporate elements from each, placing these, however, in a different framework from them all. My intention is not to offer an analysis that necessarily holds good for all the variant forms which the phenomenon has assumed in the twentieth century, but to concentrate mainly upon nationalism in the European nation-state. An account of nationalism in such a context should illuminate the following characteristics:

1 its *political* character, that is, its association with the nation-state;
2 its relation to industrial capitalism, and more specifically *ideological characteristics* of nationalism involved with class domination;
3 its likely *psychological dynamics* since, as a range of sentiments and attitudes rather than an institutionalized set of practices,

it is difficult to resist the supposition that there are some distinctive psychological processes involved; and

4   its particular *symbolic content.*

Let me work back through these, beginning with the question of the content of nationalism as a symbol system. Whatever their differences, nationalist ideals tend to tie a conception of the 'homeland' — a concept of territoriality, in other words — to a myth of origin, conferring cultural autonomy upon the community which is held to be the bearer of these ideals. 'The solidarity that a nationalist desires is based on the possession of the land: not any land, but the historic land; the land of past generations, the land that saw the flowering of the nation's genius.'[28] Looking to the legitimacy of past generations as supplying cultural autonomy is what Breuilly calls 'historicism', and this has more than a passing connection with the historicity of which I spoke earlier. Here again, we have a case where historians and philosophers, claiming for the most part to describe particular circumstances, have provided ideas that have helped to constitute those very circumstances. Herder's writings are in some respects not representative of those that informed versions of nationalism outside Central Europe but, in other ways, they provide an exemplary illustration of historicism as a source of nationalist thought. 'History' for Herder is more than just writing about the past, it is the means of grasping the cultural unity of a collectivity. Understanding a culture and its specific course of development involves apprehending it in its totality, distinct from other, divergent sets of cultural values. Language is of key importance in this, because it is necessarily the product of a community, pre-existing any particular generation of individuals and carrying within it the main dimensions that render the cultural system in question unique.

On first inspection, such ideas seem completely discrepant from the 'bourgeois ideals' of classical liberalism, which have a universal character. Indeed we might see here an opposition between (say) British utilitarian thought and German Romanticism. But a closer appraisal, in the context of the involvement of such views with nationalist symbolism, indicates a powerful, if attenuated, relation between them, mediated by sovereignty and citizenship, as portrayed diagrammatically in figure 4.

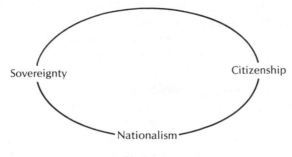

Figure 4

If we are to make sense of this relation, and the impact that ideas associated with it have had upon the world, we have to see it as a three-way series of connections rather than a two-way one. Ideas such as those developed by Herder can be extended in two directions. One regards the cultural accomplishments of a given state as so distinct and priceless that they are elevated to an intrinsic superiority over others. A 'historical mission' is constructed which, in certain circumstances, may offer a vehicle for the most virulent forms of aggressive nationalism. But to regard this baneful course as the only one that can be cultivated on the basis of 'cultural historicism' is certainly mistaken.[29] For such ideas can be used, as Herder intended them to be, to effect a union between cultural diversity and concepts of political organization of a universal character. Linguistically mediated cultural values are the carriers of divergent processes of history. But to be a member of the community which is the repository of those values can be construed in an egalitarian way, since all are legatees of the same collective experience. Moreover, while the distinctiveness of other communities might be acknowledged, these can be accorded equal status in what is seen to be an inherent cultural diversity of humankind. There are a series of possible ties and tensions between nationalism, sovereignty and citizenship, depending upon the direction in which these ideas are channelled. Where nationalism is canalized primarily towards sovereignty — particularly in circumstances where there are several contenders for statehood, or where an existing state is strongly embattled — nationalist sentiments may take an exclusivist turn, emphasizing the superiority of one 'nation' over its contenders. Here citizenship rights are likely to be poorly developed or constricted — especially civil and political rights. Where citizenship rights are more substantially founded or actualized, they tend to influence the connections between sovereignty and nationalism in an opposite direction, stimulating more polyarchic forms of nationalist sentiment.

This is one dimension of what so many students of nationalism have pointed to — its Janus-faced character, as generating both virulent forms of national aggressiveness, on the one hand, and democratic ideals of enlightenment, on the other. But there is a psychological aspect to this too.[30] Nationalist sentiments, I have pointed out, tend to be fairly remote from most of the activities of day-to-day social life, except in fairly unusual and often relatively transitory conditions. This is one phenomenon which a psychological interpretation of nationalism must account for. Another, rarely mentioned in the literature but a rather pervasive feature of nationalism, is its association with leader-figures. While nationalist feelings are no doubt often experienced and expressed in a diffuse way, in circumstances in which they are strongly espoused there normally seems to be a leader who in some way acts as a focal point for their expression. An account of the routinization of social activity in the time-space settings of the created environment can help us elucidate the nature of these phenomena. In the contexts of the modern state, the routinized character of most day-to-day life is not grounded in the moral schemes of tradition. In such circumstances ontological security is tenuously founded psychologically, depending upon the enactment of 'morally meaningless' routines, protected by the sequestration of events and experiences which might otherwise threaten it. Where 'moral meaning' has retreated to the margins of the private and the public, the communality supplied by national symbols (including in particular a common language, as perhaps the most potent carrier of communal experience) supplies one means of support for ontological security, particularly where there is a perceived threat from outside the state.

In circumstances where the ontological security of individuals is put in jeopardy by the disruption of routines, or by a generalized source of anxiety, regressive forms of object-identification tend to occur. Individuals are likely to be swayed by the influence of leader-figures, identification with whom is based on a relatively strong affective dependence. The regressive affiliation with leaders, and with the symbols linked to their leadership, if the

Le Bon/Freud theory of leadership is correct, is based on the heightened suggestibility produced by situations that generate high levels of anxiety. Mass support may, therefore, be generated for policies and causes about which, in other circumstances, individuals may either be fairly indifferent or sceptical. Such support is likely to be volatile in more than one sense. Its durability will tend to be limited and it may move between stances which seem to be quite discrepant from one another. All nationalist leaders advocate populist doctrines in one sense or another, but in some instances identification may be made with a figure exemplifying the more 'democratic' forms of nationalism, while in others it will be with the more aggressively 'exclusivist' types. Here, therefore, we can see a psychological basis for the Janus-faced character of nationalism.

It follows from what has been said so far that nationalism can neither be interpreted as some sort of aberration produced by Western intellectuals, as in Kedourie's view, nor simply as an ideology promoted by dominant classes, as in traditional versions of Marxism. Nationalism is anchored psychologically in distinctive features of modern societies and its content is linked to the historicity they engender. Nonetheless, nationalist sentiments and symbols are not ideologically neutral and, at this point, it is relevant to relate the earlier discussion of ideology both to nationalism itself and to the question of why nationalism has an inherently political dimension. These problems seem fairly easy to illuminate in the light of what has been argued earlier in this chapter. Nationalism is the cultural sensibility of sovereignty, the concomitant of the co-ordination of administrative power within the bounded nation-state. With the coming of the nation-state, states have an administrative and territorially ordered unity which they did not possess before. This unity cannot remain *purely* administrative however, because the very co-ordination of activities involved presumes elements of cultural homogeneity.[31] The extension of communication cannot occur without the 'conceptual' involvement of the whole community as a knowledge-able citizenry. A nation-state is a 'conceptual community' in a way in which traditional states were not.[32] The sharing of a common language, and a common symbolic historicity, are the most thorough-going ways of achieving this (and are seen to be so by those leaders who have learned from the experience of the first 'nations'). But only in those instances where political boundaries fairly closely coincide with existing language-communities is the convergence between the nation-state and nationalism a relatively frictionless one. In all other cases — by far the majority in the modern world — the advent of the nation-state stimulates divergent and oppositional nationalisms as much as it fosters the coincidence of nationalist sentiments and existing state boundaries.

The origins of oppositional nationalism are certainly strongly influenced by the spread of industrial capitalism, in the European context and world-wide. Uneven development takes a regionalized form, in which peripheral areas both within states and within the nation-state system are systematically disadvantaged. But nationalist movements are not just one type of oppositional movement among others, protesting in some sort of way directly against the depradations of capitalism. They mark the injection of historicity into areas where the pre-existing hold of traditional modes of behaviour has been eroded, associating such historicity with the claim to administrative sovereignty. It is because nationalism is inherently linked to the achievement of administrative autonomy of the modern form that all nationalist movements are necessarily political, no matter how much they may be infused with symbolism of other sorts.

Now of course nationalist symbols can be, and very frequently have been, deliberately fostered or manipulated by dominant groups to support their sectional interests. There is no great difficulty in understanding the ideological value nationalist beliefs and values may have in these terms. Nationalism is a form of sentiment that can be utilized to mobilize the support of the overall national community for policies that have quite discrepant consequences for different sections or classes within that community. But this is in some ways the least interesting and significant of the ideological ramifications of nationalism. More deeply layered ideological implications are to be traced to the fact that the conditions involved in the reflexive monitoring of the modern state, as a surveillance apparatus, are the same as those that help generate nationalism. Since the discursive capabilities involved in monitoring social reproduction become of essential importance to the state, it is around the intersection between discursive consciousness and 'lived experience' that the ideological consequences of nationalism will cluster. As the 'moral component' of sovereignty, nationalist symbols provide a core of political discourse that significantly shapes both the rhetoric of national solidarity and of opposition. Nationalism helps naturalize the recency and the contingency of the nation-state through providing its myths of origin. But, at the same time, the discourse of national solidarity helps block off other possible discursive articulations of interest. The discursive arena of the modern polity treats what 'politics' is as inherently to do with the bounded sphere of the state. Thus if programmes of reform on the part of subordinate classes (or other groupings) are to succeed, they have normally to be made to appear in 'the national interest'. But dominant classes have much less difficulty representing their own policies as in 'the national interest' than do oppositional groups, since they have much more influence over the style and form of what can be discursively articulated.

9
Capitalist Development and the Industrialization of War

The preceding three chapters have been mainly analytical in character. They supply the conceptual basis of the remainder of the book, which concentrates upon the transferral of the nation-state system to a global plane in the twentieth century. The historical backdrop to this process is the sharp contrast between the period during which the European states for the most part remained at peace with one another and the subsequent outbreak of the two World Wars.

The 'Long Peace'

Throughout the nineteenth century, the great powers held fairly regular international congresses, meeting to arbitrate various potentially threatening disputes. Relative stability between the fledgling nation-states was not matched by lack of tension and conflict either inside those states or in other parts of the world. On the contrary, processes of internal pacification were beset by challenges to the existing order; and the spread of European influence in other areas of the globe was accompanied by a variety of bloody confrontations. But the measure of security achieved among the states of Europe was the institutional setting in which so many thinkers imagined that an age of industrialism or capitalism was supplanting the military violence of previous eras. This self-same period was one of ascending military capability and innovation, the results of which first made themselves felt elsewhere. As McNeill puts it:

> Towards the margins of the European radius of action . . . the result was systematic expansion — whether in India, Siberia, or the

Americas. Frontier expansion in turn sustained an expanding trade network, enhanced taxable wealth in Europe, and made support of the armed establishments less onerous than would otherwise have been the case. Europe, in short, launched itself on a self-reinforcing cycle in which its military organisation sustained, and was sustained by, economic and political expansion at the expense of other peoples and polities of the earth. The modern history of the globe registered that fact ... technological and organisational innovation continued, allowing Europeans to outstrip other peoples of the earth more and more emphatically until the globe-circling imperialism of the nineteenth century became as cheap and easy for Europeans as it was catastrophic to Asians, Africans, and the peoples of Oceania.[1]

British troops, for example, were more-or-less continuously fighting colonial campaigns in the nineteenth century. It has been estimated by one authority that, if we include auxiliary forces under British command, British armies were involved in fifty major colonial wars between 1803 and 1901.[2] Every other leading European power was caught up in warfare of substantial proportions at some point in the century and, of course, with the exception of Britain, they each underwent at least one major political transformation. The wars they fought were the first to be carried on employing the weapons technology generated by industrialism, and in every case, with the partial exception of the Franco-Prussian War, victory went to the industrialized states over the more agrarian ones. The 'industrialization of war' may be said to cover a number of related changes, initiated in the late eighteenth century or shortly thereafter, but culminating only in the twentieth century. There is a very real sense in which the First World War was the end result of these changes. They include the application of techniques of industrial production to weaponry, together with the adaptation of new modes of transportation and communication for military purposes; the professionalizing of the military, including the abandoning of the use of mercenaries — although this practice continued in colonized areas of the world — and the reorganization of the officer corps; the discarding of spectacular and ritual aspects of warfare, perhaps symbolized above all by the relinquishing of brightly coloured uniforms in favour of camouflaged battledress, this being worn by all ranks; and the integration of military campaigns on land, sea and, later, air into overall strategic plans in the conduct of war — these served to bring about a transition from 'limited' to 'total war'.

The impact of industrial techniques upon warfare was first of all concentrated upon communications. As has been indicated previously, the logistics of military transportation had always strongly conditioned not just the enactment of wars but also the very nature of class-divided society. The relatively slow movement of troops limited the use of violent sanctions as a mode of sustaining power, at the same time as the system integration of traditional states depended in a direct way upon that threat. The fighting of wars often had a ritual and 'prepared' character, not just because traditions infused wars like other segments of social life, but because armies needed — and were often allowed — time to assemble on a pre-arranged terrain.

The railway, steamship and telegraph changed all this irrevocably. More than any other single technological innovation, the railway made possible mass warfare. The 'railway boom' between 1840 and 1870 put an end to long marches to the field of war and created 'fronts' instead of the traditional alternation of skirmish and battle.[3] The European states varied widely in terms of the degree to which newly created railway systems were established with military purposes in mind. The clearest and, in terms of its consequences for subsequent history, the most far-reaching example of the exploitation of the railways for military ends was in Prussia. The Prussian General Staff was able to have a considerable influence over the construction and routing of the state railway system.[4] Whereas in Britain the railways system was developed mostly via the haphazard efforts of commercial interests, in Prussia the railways were constructed in large part to meet the requirements of the military. A specific railway *Abteilung* of the General Staff was established, having as its concern the scheduling of services in such a way as to enhance military objectives. While not being without its difficulties, the system demonstrated its effectiveness in 1870, swiftly mobilizing the German forces in the Saar and Rhineland. The railway network in Italy has its beginnings in dreams of conquest and the attainment of Italian unity. Cavour launched his programme of railway building from Piedmont with the injunction that railways would be 'the seams which would stitch together the boot of Italy'.[5] However separate from military purposes the railways might have developed in Britain, in the prosecution of their overseas involvements the British were the leaders in the military utilization of rail communications. In India and elsewhere the British set up sophisticated railway networks serving as the backbone of their colonial rule.

The early part of the nineteenth century was one of the very rapid development of steamship technology, also led by Britain. For some while, however, this remained separate from naval planning, the world's most powerful navy using basically the same type of wooden ship as had been in service for some two centuries. A by now famous memorandum of the Naval Office stated their Lordships' view that steam power should not be used in war fleets, 'as they consider that the introduction of steam is calculated to strike a fatal blow at the naval supremacy of the Empire'.[6] Others in Europe were more prescient, seeing the advantages of superior speed and manoeuvrability offered by steam-propelled vessels together with the fact that such vessels could be protected by steel armour. The British admiralty rapidly were compelled to reconsider their conservatism; because of the developed industrial base of the country, they were able to match and surpass fairly readily advances made elsewhere. It was here that was initiated that fateful combination of industry, technology and science applied to the proliferation of weaponry that spread to all aspects of military production. The invention of the Minié bullet gave the rifle a massive superiority over the musket. The breech loading gun was first invented in 1819, in the USA. Its large-scale application came only in the second half of the nineteenth century, making possible the development of automatic weapons. The term 'machine gun' aptly captures the union of industry and weaponry and finds its first effective examples in the *mitrailleuse*, Gatling and Gardner guns.[7]

At the Woolwich Arsenal, by 1860, specifically invented machines were able to produce a quarter of a million Minié bullets per day and nearly as many completed cartridges.[8] Special programmes of scientific research designed to encourage technological innovation in the nature and production of weaponry were linked to the Arsenal; the USA and the major European states all had comparable schemes. The time-honoured entrepreneurial involvement in the manufacture and trading of armaments was given a new impetus by the mass manufacture of weaponry. Firms like the Birmingham Small Arms Company and the London Small Arms Company produced for international markets but the heart of their business derived from government contracts. While the arms manufacturers competed fiercely with each other both on a national and international level, the production and distribution of weaponry necessarily had to be regarded by the state as of prime concern to its interests and as demanding strict regulation. It does not by any means follow from this that government officials have always used their influence in such a way to promote the most effective modes of technological advance. The judgement of their Lordships has many parallels in subsequent governmental decisions. But the meshing of industrial production and military strength is of prime importance among the influences that have shaped the modern world. It is a mistake — which has characteristically haunted Marxist interpretations of these issues — to regard the armaments industry as just another expression of a voraciously expanding capitalism. Industrial capitalism provided the means for the industrialization of war, but the activities and involvements of nation-states are at the origin of the phenomenon.

It would be hard to exaggerate the significance for global history of the 'armaments gap' which existed between the Western countries and the rest of the world throughout the nineteenth and early twentieth centuries. The military dominance of the West was no more sustained by the deployment of large armies outside Europe than had been the case previously. Not even the new forms of military discipline and training were of determining importance in European ascendancy away from the military theatres of Europe. Most colonial and other external engagements were either fought by conscript troops or by comparatively tiny troop detachments. Some of the key battles leading to the defeat of erstwhile powerful traditional states were won by small numbers of troops, on the basis of superior mobility and fire-power. There are various examples in Africa but perhaps the most telling case is to be found in China, where a relatively insignificant body of British troops was able to defeat the forces of the imperial state. Of course, at the time of its greatest expansion in the nineteenth century there already were the limits to European hegemony later to become the two poles of the mature nation-state system: the USA and Russia. By the Civil War period the potential military strength of the USA was evident, even if it was still confined to the sphere of the Americas. Russian internal consolidation following the Crimean War blocked Western expansion in that direction, while the Russians themselves moved eastwards into Central Asia, subduing the societies there through the same fusion of industrial and military power that allowed the European nations to dominate much of the rest of the world. Japan's isolation, combined with a rapid process of modernization, allowed for a further significant area into which European armed force was unable to penetrate.

The First World War drew in all these states and in that sense entirely justified its name. There is no parallel to it whatsoever in former times in terms of the numbers of combatants — and non-combatants — involved, the ferocity of the devastation unleashed, or the modes in which the armed struggle was fought out. In the battles of the Frontiers and the Marne, half a million men on each side were killed — a number greater than the total of the Prussian army fifty years earlier.[9] On the Somme, the numbers lost by both sides were even higher. Never had war been fought so unremittingly, with the soldiery so chronically under fire. The Somme was not only the scene of unprecedented carnage, but the very epitome of industrialized war:

> the wide and shattered country of the Somme . . . among the broad, straggling belts of rusty wire smashed and twisted in the chalky loam . . . I see the faces and figures of enslaved men, the marching columns pearl-hued with chalky dust on the sweat of their heavy drab clothes . . . the loud crackling of machine-guns changes to a screeching as of steam being blown off by a hundred engines, and soon no-one is left standing.[10]

The 'heavy drab clothes' signal other changes that occurred in military organization over a period of about a century. The professionalization of the upper echelons of military command was accompanied by the development of mass conscription. In the nation-state, while the military may under some circumstances assume political control, military power is no longer the necessary basis of internally administered state authority. But the other side of this is that the military can no longer 'opt out' from the political system, or act in isolation from the broader sovereign community, as armies could do in prior types of society.[11] For, in an age of the industrialization of war, the armed forces depend upon the productive apparatus of industrialism, harnessed through the sovereign authority of the territorial state. Even where the army rules, it cannot directly govern, depending upon the same array of routine administrative agencies as does purely 'civil' government. And 'civil' government, in turn, involves an insulation of political from military power far more precise than that achieved in class-divided societies, with one or two possible exceptions. The 'separation' of military from political power within the state's territory, as I have said, is as distinctive of the European nation-state as is that of the political from the economic. The development of large standing armies, in which autonomous careers can be forged (but which can be swelled by conscription where necessary), is a main feature of the nation-state.

Huntington's discussion of the professionalization of the military is still the best overall account of the phenomenon.[12] As he points out, prior to the nineteenth century, officer corps usually consisted of either aristocrats or mercenaries. For the former, war was still something of a hobby, a heroic realization of manhood, while for the latter it was an activity pursued for profit. With the consolidation of absolutism, mercenaries gradually became ousted by the aristocratic element, as the princes sought enduring loyalty among a permanently established soldiery. Those in the ranks were individuals signed on for terms of varying lengths as volunteers or coerced into service by one means or another. In France and in Prussia, in the middle of the eighteenth century, admission to officer status was almost wholly confined to aristocrats. In the former country a military commission was a means whereby a needy member of the aristocracy could achieve an income; towards the end of the eighteenth century a third of the total strength of the army consisted of officers. British army officers were recruited on the basis of purchase of office and were made up of the younger sons of country gentry. This was no longer a feudal leadership but it preserved the belief in courage and honour as inborn traits monopolized by the few. The modes of disciplinary power developed for the common soldier remained primarily confined to battlefield tactics and were not extended to the officer corps. The military, in other words, had not yet become a reflexively monitored organization of a fully modern type, even if some of the techniques of surveillance were pioneered within the military sphere. This can be indexed by the absence prior to 1800 'of any conception of military science as a distinct branch of knowledge, unified and complete in itself, susceptible of logical analysis into its component elements, and yet possessing a definite relationship to other branches of knowledge.'[13]

The Prussian military reforms of the early nineteenth century represent the first major move towards a professionalized officer corps, even if the land-owning aristocracy remained the main source of recruitment. Policies of open recruitment, examination and promotion established by Scharnhorst and Gneisenau had a strong impact on army organization, but they were far from being fully and consistently implemented. However, they provided an example which other states soon copied. By the latter part of the nineteenth century all the European states, together with the USA and Russia, had set up schools of training for officer corps associated with bureaucratized systems of recruitment and advancement. These developments went hand-in-hand with the spread of the *levée en masse* and the concept of 'the nation in arms' in respect of the common soldiery. The links between citizenship rights, sovereignty and nationalism discussed in the preceding chapter here take on an additional element. The transition from an 'amateur' to a 'professional' officer cadre was everywhere associated with the complementing of career soldiers by the citizen-soldier.[14] The 1789 Revolution abolished aristocratic dominance of the officer corps in France, and the *levée en masse* dates from a short period afterwards. The government was permitted to conscript by ballot from all healthy young males, with some exceptions; thus by 1813 Napoleon was able to call up an army of 1,300,000 Frenchmen.[15]

Prussia introduced permanent universal service in 1814, an edict of that year obliging all Prussian men to spend five years in the army, three on active service and two in the reserve. In other countries, the trend towards a 'nation in arms' was evident without being accompanied by peacetime conscription until the twentieth century.[16] In general it would be true to say that the relation between a professionalized, permanent army and mass conscription has been an uneven one over the past century and a half. Most states have introduced some conscription at some point, but this has not necessarily been sustained in a full-blown way outside of conditions of war. However, since the late nineteenth century there has come about in all Western states something of a reversal in the previous contrast between officers and the rank and file. The officers have become a specialized professional group with few connections with the wider society, while the soldiery are in substantial part composed of citizenry under arms for a restricted period.

The adoption of uniforms of subdued colour for both enlisted ranks and officers alike symbolizes several aspects of modern mass war. The uniform serves as a mode of camouflage on the field of battle, in which most effort has to be directed towards being protected from projectiles of vast destructive force. While values of valour and heroism persist, they are clearly distinct from the traditional warrior ethic that flourished when warfare was associated with spectacle and display. Within the army as an organization, the uniform has the same implications for disciplinary power as in carceral settings of other types, helping strip individuals of those traits that might interfere with routinized patterns of obedience. The uniform indicates to the civilian population the distinctiveness of the military figure as the specialist purveyor of the means of violence — paramilitary sections of the police, to some extent, sharing in this role. This has become such a universal feature of the nation-state that it is perhaps difficult to see how novel it is. Prior to the industrialization of war there was little in the way of a clear-cut 'war technology' distinguishable from other types of implement or artifact. Armour and cannon certainly fall into that category but before the development of modern manufacturing methods they were too expensive to oust mundane types of hand-held weaponry. Through the ages swords or knives were carried for individual protection and for utilitarian purposes as well as being put to use for military ends.[17]

If mass conscription provided the human fodder for total war, the integrated nature of transport and communications was its necessary material substratum. These decisively influenced the assembling of armed forces to wage war, the temporal and the spatial co-ordination of warfare as prolonged combat. Several phases had traditionally been recognized in the process of 'making war', each usually taking considerable time and involving the cumbersome movement of personnel across space. Troops had to be mobilized, bringing together the soldiery and the provisions necessary to engage in armed conflict; they had to be concentrated in campaign order; and they had to march to battle.[18] By the latter part of the nineteenth century the differentiation between these phases had become substantially dissolved. The existence of standing armies, plus reserves which could be drawn in at short notice, made possible the very rapid generation of fighting forces of very large size. Armaments having become specialized and mass produced, armies were at any given moment furnished with the necessary means for waging war. Preparation for campaign order also became much less time-consuming, troops being subject to continuous discipline and regulation, in peace as in war. Rapid transportation allowed the concentration of soldiery and attack on the enemy to become merged into one — a tactic first used by Moltke in the invasion of Bohemia in 1866.

The telegraph was an essential element in such co-ordinated action, as it was in the theatres of war themselves. The Prussian army maintained contact between its advancing forces and headquarters by the simple expedient of winding out wire as the battalions went forward. Telegraph commands could be sent simultaneously to any sector of the war zone where there was an outpost connected through the wire. Industrialized war, like industrialized society, has therefore long been electronic, although in its early development the process was anything but foolproof. Keeping miles of wire intact was hardly an easy task and the telegraph was apt to fail just at decisive moments. Thus, for example, Moltke lost contact with the army of the crown prince just prior to the Battle of Königgrätz, and had to send a dispatch rider to get the prince's army to the scene of the engagement.[19] Nonetheless, electronic communication opened up possibilities of the co-ordination of military forces in such a way as to greatly increase the span of war zones. Permitting instant reporting, it also brought war into the public domain in a way fully consistent with the support a 'war effort' demands of the citizenry of a modern state, although such news reporting also of course can rebound upon the aspirations of the state authorities.

The First World War was the material expression of the new modes of industrialized warfare but it is a mistake to see it as one of two particular types of event, namely 'world war'. Unprecedented it certainly was, in the hitherto quite unimaginable levels of carnage, in its duration and its spatial span. In those terms, the

Second World War (thus far) is its only competitor. But it also made manifest very general characteristics of the relation between war and the modern state. The fact that sentiments of nationalism triumphed over the internationalism of the socialist movement may not have been intelligible to some of those within that movement, but it signalled the importance that the connection of sovereignty and citizenship had assumed and which would, henceforth, dominate in the global community. If the ties between industrial development, political co-ordination and military strength had for some while been apparent within the major Western states, they now became evident to all. Some features of the War remained largely confined to it, such as its peculiarly immobile trench battles, but in many other respects it set the pattern for virtually all twentieth-century wars, no matter how comparatively restricted in scope they might be. As important as anything, the outcome of the war confirmed the status of the nation-state in its 'heartland'. No single state with large-scale territorial ambitions was able to crush the others in such a way as to provide for the emergence of a new imperial order, either in Europe or elsewhere. That this was so has nothing remotely to do with any generalized process of 'evolution' that terminates in the nation-state but was the outcome of contingent events, plus the deliberate enshrinement of the 'nationhood' of states as a global principle in the congress that followed the termination of the War.

As one historian puts it,

> August 1914 had not been, as expected, August 1870 on a larger scale, with the scene of the action shifted because the French had fortified the earlier route. In contrast to 1870, war had changed from being the concern of the army as an elite to being the business of society as a whole, and from the limited and rational application of force to unrestricted violence . . . by 1918, the leaderships had absorbed finally the lessons presented by the process of industrialisation in the previous century.[20]

Warfare and Social Change

Janowitz notes that literature on the 'new' nation-states of Africa, the Middle East and Asia, together with Latin America, persistently emphasizes the influence of the military upon 'nation-building'. 'By contrast, comparative macrosociology has shown very little interest in assessing the role of military institutions in the emergence of Western nation-states . . . This is particularly difficult to explain in the light of the central significance of armies and armed conflict in fashioning both the boundaries and the structure of the modern secular nation-state.'[21] The reasons for such a circumstance should have emerged strongly enough in the course of this book, but it still remains to indicate the impact of war upon the internal constitution of states. I have earlier stressed the significance of relations linking sovereignty, citizenship and nationalism in the Western nation-state; these also supply a focus for analysing the institutional influence of war.

That a combination of war and diplomacy shaped the emergence of the European state system, with some states surviving and expanding and most being absorbed or dissolved, has already been emphasized — and is nothing more than a commonplace of history. However, the military involvements of states also strongly influenced the development of citizenship rights and their connections to other features of societal organization, in ways that can be fairly readily traced out, even if they are missing from most sociological discussions of these phenomena. If the sovereign state is inherently a polyarchic order, in which citizenship rights are the 'price paid' by the dominant class for the means of exercising its power, citizenship in turn implies acceptance of the obligations of military service. Both the shared patterns of development of the classical nation-state and divergences between states can be illuminated in these terms. The nation-state and the mass army appear together, the twin tokens of citizenship within territorially bordered political communities. The experience of the USA and of France was strongly conditioned by the prominence of the citizen-soldier in and after their respective revolutionary transformations. Within each state — and in others that subsequently followed their lead — the connections between military service, control of the armed forces, and citizenship rights were forged in varying ways. In the USA the acceptance that the citizenry could be armed in the service of the state, without forming a threat to it, marked a break with traditional European practices. In France the *levée en masse* was specifically established in such a way as to associate citizenship with active participation in matters urgently affecting the state and as a means of fostering feelings of national loyalty.

Conscription was prompted by considerations of social policy as much as by military expediency.[22] 'Military service emerged as a hallmark of citizenship and citizenship as the hallmark of a political democracy.'[23]

The adaptability of the new patterns of military organization, however, is demonstrated by their appropriation and perfecting in Prussia, as a main element in the forging of a very different political system. The relation between military service and citizenship rights, particularly the franchise, remained unambiguous. As soon as the unification of Germany occurred Bismarck established universal male suffrage, as a response to what he saw as the military exigencies of the new state. In countries lacking a proximate revolutionary background and not so directly involved in European war, most notably Britain, the extension of the franchise tended to be halting. Only with the experience of the First World War, in which conscription was not introduced until the armed forces had undergone huge losses, was universal male franchise instituted. Once more, this was done in explicit recognition of the ties between citizenship rights and military obligations.

Writing of the First World War shortly after its termination, Churchill observed that 'The great war through which we have passed differed from all ancient wars in the immense power of the combatants and their fearful agencies of destruction, and from all modern wars in the utter ruthlessness with which it was fought. All the horrors of the ages were brought together, and not only armies but whole populations were thrust into the middle of them.'[24] Probably no one would dispute the validity of the statement and of innumerable parallel ones which could be quoted. Nonetheless, it still tends to be assumed by sociological authors analysing social development in the current century that, if it had any lasting influence on social organization, the First World War merely accelerated trends that were bound to emerge in the long run in any case. But this view is not at all plausible and could scarcely be countenanced at all if it were not for the powerful grip that endogenous and evolutionary conceptions of change have had in the social sciences.

If the course of events in the Great War, including the participation of the USA in the hostilities and the peace settlement, had not taken the shape they did, the nation-state in its current form might not have become the dominant political entity in the world system. But in many other ways also the War marks a turning point both in world history and in the patterns of development in the industrialized societies involved in it. The collapse of socialist internationalism with the outbreak of the War has, of course, often been discussed and analysed. There were already very strong pressures linking socialist movements to citizenship within sovereign states. But it is by no means clear that in the absence of the War, the pre-existing international socialist organizations might not have emerged as of key influence in world politics. The War canalized the development of states' sovereignty, tying this to citizenship and to nationalism in such a profound way that any other scenario subsequently came to appear little more than idle fantasy. The abortive revolution in one defeated power — Germany — and a successful one in the other — Russia — did far more than just give a lasting geo-political shape to the contemporary world. The isolation of the fledgling Soviet Union ensured an emphasis upon territoriality, 'nation-building' and 'forced industrialization' there which, as Trotsky so sharply emphasized, was far distant from the internationalism of Marxist-Leninist theory. The Soviet Union became as jealously territorial as any of the 'capitalist states', and also embarked upon a course of developing the industrially based military strength that propelled it to the very forefront of global power.

Familiar history, certainly, but the point is that we should not draw an opposition between the contingent events and outcomes of war and more generic social trends, as though what happens in one sphere is somehow distinct from occurrences in the other. There are no 'inevitable trends' in social development that are either hastened or held back by specific historical processes. All general patterns of social organization and social change are compounded of contingent outcomes, intended and unintended; all sequences of events which can be described in a narrative vein from some aspect or another express more encompassing influences. Thus the events of the First World War could not have happened without the long prior development of industrialism, and the conjoining of industrial production to the means of violence. But those events have decisively influenced what 'industrialism' is and has become, and its connections to other social and political institutions.[25]

The World Wars

When the Treaty of Versailles generalized to the rest of the world principles of states' sovereignty, there were built into its provisions an acceptance of how far the old orders of things had been transformed by total war. 'The Treaty, it could be said, enthrones the principle of the plebiscite, the very notion of which would have staggered many pre-war European governments.'[26] In the major states the demand for soldiery for active service at the front, combined with a stress upon the collective war effort, brought labour into a strong bargaining position in certain sectors, as well as involving women in occupations they had not previously filled. Union organizations developed strongly in France, Britain and the USA, with more direct and permanent connections than hitherto existed being established between the labour movement and the state. In France, for example, minimum wage rates were set up in 1917 in all industries directly connected to the government and permanent arbitration councils established to regulate industrial conflict. The 'institutionalization of class conflict' is normally discussed in the sociological literature as though it were the result solely of economic change. But the impact of the War played a very important role in it, providing much of the framework for later developments. In the latter period of the War, mass-production techniques for the manufacture of military equipment were introduced in the leading states, especially in the USA and France. The arrival of methods of mass production was both stimulated by the demands of the War and accepted by labour-forces that, more highly unionized than before, in other circumstances might have resisted their implementation in a concerted fashion.

It has been aptly remarked that

> The subsequent industrial and social history of the world turn very largely on the continuing application of the methods of mass production whose scope widened so remarkably during the emergency of World War I. Anyone looking at the equipment installed in a modern house will readily recognise how much we in the late twentieth century are indebted to industrial changes

pioneered in near-panic circumstances when more and more shells, gun-powder, and machine-guns suddenly became the price of survival as a sovereign state.[27]

This includes not just the mass production of consumer durables but also, in particular, the industrialization and rationalizing of food production. Prior to the War, the mechanized processing and pre-packaging of food was poorly developed. During the course of the conflict, new methods of production came to the fore that revolutionized — for better or for worse — eating habits and the nature of domestic life. The role of 'housewife' was paradoxically created at the same time as women entered the labour-force in large numbers.[28]

Finally, during the Great War a fateful conjunction was welded more firmly and irretrievably than ever before: the integration of large-scale science and technology as the principal medium of industrial advancement. It has often been claimed that war stimulates inventiveness; certainly it is the case, as has been discussed previously, that the development of weapons technology has long influenced economic change. But what took place during the course of the War was something more thorough-going — the concerted application of processes of scientific discovery to technological advance throughout the core sectors of industrial production. Before the First World War, in the sphere of the armed forces, this was most developed in the navy, as the major European states struggled to emulate one another in turning steam and steel to the production of efficient fighting ships. In the period leading up to the War, particularly in response to the demands of the struggle itself, the harnessing of science to industry became an established phenomenon in all areas of military production. The development of tanks provides one of the best illustrations.[29] Tanks were originally the equivalents of armed and plated ships brought ashore and made manoeuvrable on land. They were first of all commonly known as 'land cruisers' and in Britain the Bureau of Naval Design was in charge of the original elaboration of the construction programme. Like aeroplanes, tanks were not to have a significant effect on the battlefield until subsequent wars — most devastatingly, in the Second World War. But the 'research and development' programme of which they were the outcome was rapidly tranferred to the civilian industries and thereafter remained fundamental to the further expansion of industrialism.[30]

Of course, not all the trends of development that were prominent in the Great War were sustained in the same way afterwards. The strong involvement of women in a key range of jobs in industrial production, for example, did not persist and it was some decades before levels of full-time employment for the female labour-force again approached what they were during the conflict. The early forms of 'corporatism' witnessed during the War rapidly dissolved soon after it ended, leading to large-scale civil strife in Germany, France and Britain. The destructive havoc wrought by the campaigns, together with the imposition of reparations on and loss of territory by the defeated states, created the social and economic climate in which totalitarian political ideology was to prosper. But both the new forms of totalitarian political control and the interventionist schemes of the liberal-democratic Western states were strongly influenced by policies initiated first of all during the War. In working out the prescriptions of the New Deal, for example, Roosevelt and his cabinet continually looked to practices invoked during the War.[31]

Wilsonian doctrines, with their emphasis upon national sovereignty with a global community of states, were in some substantial part a reaction against the enormous devastation of the War. But they also expressed an acknowledgement of a heightened level of interdependency in the world system, which the activities of the participant states had stimulated away from the war zones themselves. Compulsory regulation of industry and food production was not limited to internal organization of the relevant national economies; it also involved attempts to control the flow of resources internationally well beyond anything which had occurred previously. German naval successes against Allied shipping in the later phases of the War meant that supplies coming from overseas had to be carefully managed. In 1917 the British and French set up the Allied Maritime Transport Council, integrating policies of naval construction with priorities in respect of exports to the whole of the Allied sector. Much more far-reaching economic integration was planned between all the Allied economies, including the USA. The War came to an end before these had come to fruition but, again, most of the connections they helped establish became further solidified in the period following the cessation of hostilities.

The model of a war economy, as well as the direct building up of military strength, played a major role in all three states that emerged as leading world powers towards the end of the 1930s — the Soviet Union, Japan and an economically resurgent Germany. Soviet planning was nominally quite different from anything found in the capitalist countries but, in fact, was strongly influenced by Western patterns of war-time economic and political mobilization. In the second Five-Year Plan of 1932—7, the attention given to military production made this particularly clear.[32] Stalin's 'second revolution' was awash with military rhetoric, like the war-time experience of the other European states combining appeals for maximum production with a stress upon the necessity of keeping a tight rein upon consumption. As measured purely in economic terms — that is, apart from the appalling human costs — the success of these policies of enforced mobilization was to be fundamentally important for subsequent world history. By the outbreak of the Second World War, the industrial production of the Soviet Union was three times as high as it had been a quarter of a century earlier. In Japan the movement towards a war economy was even more pronounced, although owing less to programmes borrowed directly from the experience of the Great War than to the modernizing efforts of the state to match Western achievements. These efforts had, from the beginning, been informed by an understanding that the development of industry was the key to military strength. Nonetheless, Japanese economic development in the 1930s was quite remarkable, heavy industry increasing in output by 500 per cent, the manufacture of armaments holding a prime place in this development. Finally, in Germany the National Socialists in a studied way sought both to regenerate the nationalist fervour of the War and to apply methods of war-time economic and political regulation in the pursuit of national objectives, culminating in a massive process of rearmament soon followed by all the other principal industrial countries.[33]

By the early phases of the Second World War, in contrast to the First, each of the major combatants was linked to an international system of economic supply.[34] Germany created its own system in the centre of Europe, forcibly incorporating labour and material resources from conquered territories into its war effort. Almost a quarter of the German labour-force was composed of foreign workers by the middle years of the War, mostly made to work under conditions of coercion. Japan organized a 'Co-Prosperity Sphere' in the East, bringing large numbers of workers — although these were overwhelmingly peasants, inexperienced in methods of industrial production — directly under its control. Via the Lend Lease and Mutual Aid prescriptions, the Soviet Union was connected to the major Allied economies. These ties were to prove crucial to the Soviet war effort, although much weaker than the economic networks that the Allied states spun between themselves and with other regions of the world. However, the main basis of eventual Soviet triumph on the battlefield was a channelling of the economy into military production — reduced subsequent to the War but, nevertheless, remaining of major significance in Soviet society up to current times. The enormous international economic network dominated by the USA, in conjunction with Britain, was easily the largest and it is to this that the movement towards greater integration in the world system in the post-War period can be most directly traced. The international war economy irremediably involved the USA much more deeply in the global division of labour than before and, with the decline of the British Empire, allowed the former to stand pre-eminent in the world economy. Its military superiority was much more narrow, save for the brief period at which it possessed nuclear weaponry and the USSR did not — due very largely to the Soviet policy of giving priority to armaments and military industries above all others.

The influence of the US-British war economy stretched much further than might appear at first sight. Both inside and outside the British Empire material resources and labour-power were sucked into the War, whether or not their states of origin were actively involved in the hostilities. This played a large part in stimulating concurrent or subsequent anti-colonial movements, as well as in some cases promoting indigenous forms of economic development. The effects of the War were felt strongly in Latin America as well as in Africa, in India and other Asian countries which were not directly occupied. For the most part the outcome was increasing integration within a consolidating global economy, but in parts of Latin America and in India there occurred a lurch towards greater industrialization. In India a sizeable army was formed to fight the Japanese in Burma. The production of weaponry and provisions for it gave a marked stimulus to industrial development, while the concentration of administrative resources involved provided an autonomy of political organization that made independence after the War a largely foregone conclusion.

During the Second World War the merging of organized science and technology, initiated in the prior world conflict, was completed in a systematic fashion. Within the area of armaments production itself, the three most important consequences — which taken together now dominate the world military order — were the creation of nuclear weapons, the invention of rocket propulsion and the development of weapons systems. Whether nuclear arms would have been invented outside of the context of world war is something which is seriously open to doubt. The construction of the first nuclear bombs has been compared by one observer to the most immense building projects of traditional empires — the pyramids and the Great Wall of China. All were 'visible, dramatic, singular public works projects, the fruit of an enormous, centrally directed concentration of reources'.[35] But the building projects of the traditional world took many decades, even centuries, to construct. The first atomic weapons were made by means of the expenditure of wealth and a concentration of other resources such as could not have been dreamed of even in the early nineteenth century, let alone previous ages; and it is doubtful if such an effort could have been mounted in any contemporary society which was not on a war footing. The same is not true of rocket and jet-propulsion, although each was greatly influenced by war development programmes.

Once they had first been constructed, nuclear weapons soon came to be made in batch-production, like other industrial products. But the further advancement of techniques of rocketing basically altered the nature of potential nuclear confrontation. The aircraft that flew against Hiroshima and Nagasaki could be vulnerable to counter-attack by orthodox fighter-planes or anti-aircraft batteries. But with fusion warheads mounted on rockets there is no possibility — for the time being at any rate — of successfully warding-off attack. That this was so was formally accepted by the USA and the Soviet Union in 1972, the treaty signed in that year effectively making illegal the attempted provision of defence against ballistic missiles.[36]

The emergence of weapons systems was strongly conditioned by the expanded modes of surveillance built into the conduct of armed struggle during the Second World War. Production sectors were closely monitored in order to connect technical change in manufacture to shifting needs for particular types of provisions and armaments. The experience of fighting units on the battlefield was communicated back directly to scientific committees whose role it was to develop improvements in existing technology and combat strategies. The process of technical invention in one area required complementary innovations in others; advances made by the enemy needed to be countered by new developments by the other side. The convergence of high rates of technical innovation, co-ordinated through the organized use of scientific knowledge and regulated technological development, together underlie the increasing prominence of weapons systems. A weapons system essentially represents the same kind of process of overall design — connecting different aspects of technology with the detailed analysis of social organization — which in the post-War period became characteristic of the technologically most advanced sectors of industry in other areas. Several of the most significant technological innovations that have affected social and economic life over the past four decades had their origins in the context of the War, or result primarily from weapons-related developments afterwards.[37] These include civilian jet-travel, key aspects of telecommunications and of 'information technology'.

In common with its predecessor, the Second World War had enduring effects upon the internal political organization of those states directly involved in it. In Britain, for example, the war-time experience quite early on stimulated programmes for widespread social reform following the cessation of hostilities. The need for a thorough-going set of economic citizenship rights was accepted by groups from both the major parties. The bringing of Keynes into the Treasury in 1940 led to a strong and sophisticated range of government controls over the economy, concretized four years later by a White Paper that obliged future administrations to keep national expenditure at sufficient levels to avoid large scale unemployment. Increases in taxation imposed during the War also helped to provide the economic basis for the Welfare State that came into being later. As Marwick points out, the evidence is rather strong that, if an election had been held in 1940, a Labour government would not have been returned to power. The experiences of the population in war played a vital role in several ways. A generalized reaction against the War probably stimulated feelings of a need for change in the leadership. But the War experience both helped make clear to large segments of the populace the advantages of the welfare programmes of the Labour Party and, at the same time, gave the Labour leaders the opportunity to shape policies which then became part of the new welfare provisions afterwards.[38] In the USA the War quickly produced an unprecedented industrial boom, but also gave rise to a variety of agencies concerned with economic regulation, together with the adoption of Keynesian economic prescriptions. The USA moved afterwards directly to peace-time affluence, emerging as by far the world's dominant economic power.[39]

It was not the endogenous development of industrialism that dissolved the power of traditional elites in Germany and Japan and it was not internal processes of political change that resulted in the emergence of liberal democracy in those states. The former was the result of defeat in war, the latter the outcome of the direct intervention of the US and other Allied governments. The steps taken by the Allied countries to set up a new political order in a West German state were to a substantial extent a response to perceived Soviet ambitions. Only a year after the inauguration of the Federal Republic, as a result of the outbreak of the Korean War in 1950, the US government accepted the principle of German rearmament. From then onwards West Germany has remained the 'forward post' of the Western military alliance in Europe and has become very tightly woven into the US-dominated sectors of the world economy. The policy of 'annexing Western Germany to NATO',[40] together with the *de facto* acceptance of East Germany as a distinct nation-state, solidified the division into 'capitalist West' and 'state socialist East'. Thus the European Defence Treaty signed in 1952 (although ratified in rather different form three years later) was far more than just a declaration of military alliance; it confirmed a particular political and social make-up each side of the armed division of Europe. At the same time, the helplessness of the East German authorities in the face of the uprisings in 1953 provoked the military intervention of the USSR, firmly setting the political order in a Soviet mould and leading to the expanding economic integration of the new state into the Eastern sector.

Japan retained its territorial integrity, although having to relinquish all the regions it had occupied over some half-century of expansion. However, unlike in Europe, the US role in the military victory in the East was so all-pervasive that it was able to more-or-less wholly control the programmes of social and political change instituted in the country. Japan remains the only major state not to have fully rearmed, but became the pivot of US military and economic policy in Asia. The Korean conflict and successive crises in South-East Asia were important in consolidating the American presence in the one state that knew the direct experience of nuclear warfare. While the political relations between the USA and Japan have been through a number of vicissitudes, these influences have helped stimulate the strong degree of integration that currently exists between the US and Japanese economies, as well as the general rise of Japan to its very high position in the world economy.

Since the end of the Second World War there have been numerous wars in different parts of the world — although none within the geographical centre of what once was the European state-system — in some of which, as in Vietnam and Kampuchea, there has been appalling loss of life. In concentrating in this section on the influence of the two World Wars I do not mean to underestimate the social, political or economic changes wrought by these other struggles. My main point is to emphasize that the impact of war in the twentieth century upon generalized patterns of change has been so profound that it is little short of absurd to seek to interpret such patterns without systematic reference to it. The significance of the Wars is not just that they led to major changes during the period of hostilities or immediately after. They produced transformations which have turned out to be of enduring significance for the institutions both of the economically advanced and of other types of society in the world system.

The Nation-State, Industrialism and the Military

When nineteenth-century thinkers contrasted the emerging order of 'industrial society' with 'military society', they established some of the main parameters of modern social science. In this book I have set out to question some of the chief suppositions thus developed. But how far should such a questioning lead us to reject altogether the idea that, in the modern world, military power declines in relative importance, as compared to specifically political and economic sources of social organization and social change? Do we in the West still, in fact, live in 'military societies', albeit ones in which the nature of military power and its relations to other sources of power, have been radically altered?

Although Marxist accounts of the expansion of capitalism and rival interpretations of 'industrial society' still predominate, some theories give military power a prominent role. Thus Lasswell's analysis of the 'garrison-state', originally formulated in the 1930s, reverses the usual type of thesis found in the social sciences. According to him, in the nineteenth century industrial organization and administrative rationalization pervaded the development of the European countries and the USA. But subsequently there has developed a trend towards 'military-police dominance', which threatens increasingly to expand in the impending future.[41] The garrison-state is a phenomenon that is coming into being, not one that already exists. In Lasswell's view, the trend towards the garrison-state has to be understood against the background of the development of a world military order. The garrison-state emerges in a garrisoned world, in which resort to the threat or use of organized violence is more-or-less chronically present. It is not necessarily undemocratic or non-polyarchic, since it leaves open the possibility that a majority might participate in the internal political process. Nonetheless, Lasswell's views were formulated in the context of his fears for the future of Western liberal democracy in the face of 'the explosive growth of modern science and technology and the connection of these developments with the control of large population and resource basins suitable for huge capital accumulation'.[42]

In assessing the significance of military power today, several distinguishable questions can be posed. How far are Western nation-states currently dominated by military imperatives in terms of their basic economic organization? Are patterns of military rule likely to become more, rather than less, common and what can be said about the conditions making for civil rather than military government? On a global level, what is the nature of the 'world military order' and how does it connect with other characteristics of the modern world system? In spite of the persistent tendency of the social sciences, particularly sociology, to skirt these issues, it hardly takes a giant leap of the imagination to see how relevant they are to current paths of development of modern societies. They are evidently too complex to be addressed in detail here and I shall only attempt to offer schematic answers to them, concentrating my attention mainly upon the industrialized countries.

Of one thing there can be no doubt — the stupendous scale of military expenditures in the world economy as a whole. As indexed by officially published statistics, such expenditures amounted to $159 billion in 1966, $200 billion in 1973, and currently stand at some $600 billion. Taken on their own, such figures do no more than dazzle or depress and it is perhaps of greater use to consider some more comparative figures. Thus world military expenditure is greater than the Gross National Product of the whole of the African continent, South Africa included. It is more than that of the whole of Asia, if Japan is excluded. The GNP of Japan, the third largest in the world, is only about twice the size of the wealth dispensed for military ends globally. As one author puts it, 'It is as if half a "Japan" existed within the world economy, but was unrecognised diplomatically.'[43]

How far the industrialized countries should really be regarded as 'military-industrial' societies, however, depends in part upon appraising the role of military expenditure within their national economies. The most commonly employed statistical method of doing this is to analyse the ratio of military spending to GNP. As measured in these terms, the level of military expenditure is generally low, although perhaps not lower than would be the case in traditional states if some sort of comparable mode of computation could be devised.[44] While there are occasional instances of as much as a third of GNP being allocated for military purposes (Israel), for the industrialized states the total is mostly between 3—5 per cent, including the cases of both the USA and the Soviet Union, although there is good reason to be sceptical about the official figures connected with the latter. But there are considerable problems with this mode of measurement, and it is more effective to analyse military expenditure as a proportion of total government expenditure. Judged by this index, the ratio of 'defence' to other spending in the industrialized countries varies between 11 and 30 per cent (although it has generally declined over the past twenty years). Such figures surely do indicate that the channelling of production towards military ends is a more significant feature of industrialism than the GNP ratio would indicate. But they do not as such reveal much about the 'military-industrial complex' involved in modern production; nor do they document its nature. The idea that such a phenomenon is to be found in most or all industrialized societies is, as usually represented, a fairly vague one. Eisenhower originally employed the term in the context of trying to promote the concerted and systematic application of science and technology to military production, later using it to refer critically to what he came to see as threatening aspects of its development. At least two types of approach can be distinguished using the concept or something similar. One argument, of the kind favoured by C. Wright Mills in his earlier writings, holds that an integration has taken place of the main institutional spheres of power in society — the political, economic and military. In this view, bureaucratic centralization is the main organizing impulsion involved. The other argument is a quasi-Marxist one. Although it is elaborated in varying forms, the main claim is that military production is explicable in terms of the economic imperatives of capitalist enterprise.[45] The 'military-industrial complex' is the concrete expression of the social changes fostered by these imperatives.

However, neither of these positions stands up well to scrutiny. If a 'military-industrial complex' can be said to *dominate* the economy, it has to be the case that there are sharply defined links of interdependence between military production and other areas of production; and that modern economies are so reliant upon the maintenance of these ties that those holding political power find themselves compelled to acquiesce in such production needs. Now, in some of the major Western countries, 'defence' contractors do rank highly among the largest corporations. Thus some three quarters of the most sizeable military contractors in the USA are to be found in the list of the five hundred largest American corporations.[46] In the Soviet Union, arms-related industries outstrip all other industrial sectors in terms of the sophisticated application of science to technological advancement and there is a range of agencies devoted to ensuring that processes of technical transfer are readily accomplished. But it does not follow that the main productive organizations in either economy are substantially dependent upon military-related activities for their prosperity. The proportion of such production engaged in by most of the large corporations in the USA is low, with one or two notable exceptions.[47] Moreover, those firms that are involved in military production show a defined tendency to move in and out of the area according to shifts in the political and economic climate. Thus, in the post-Vietnam period, the largest twenty-five military contractors in the USA changed from having some 40 per cent of their business in 'defence' in the late 1950s to under 10 per cent in the middle 1970s.[48] Such a situation certainly does not pertain in the Soviet Union, but in that society decisions taken by political planners have at various periods significantly altered investment policies in respect of military expenditure.

These observations indicate that the 'military-industrial complex' is not in the ascendancy in the economies of the industrialized societies. The production of 'defence'-related goods and services is a major part of most of those economies and expenditure on them a prime concern of most governments. Consequently, both military leaders and manufacturers are often able to wield considerable influence, directly and indirectly, over certain policies. But not even military leaders and manufacturers constitute a solitary grouping, let alone those whose main involvements are with government or with other sectors of economic life. The very nature of industrialized war in a certain sense ensures a diversity of interests and concerns. In traditional states, a militaristic ruling class could dominate the state, its control over the means of violence being dependent upon the mustering of solidery rather than upon their sway over production. The means of waging industrialized war necessitate reliance upon a broad productive infrastructure. But just as it has been remarked of politics that 'in capitalism the dominant class does not rule', so also it could be added that it does not make war. So far as economic factors are concerned, it is undoubtedly the case in the modern world that military expenditure can help generate favourable conditions of production both for manufacturers and for an overall national economy. But — quite apart from the unacceptable functionalist cast of an argument that suggests that whatever is the case happens because of a beneficial end it secures — the conclusion cannot be drawn from this that such factors dominate other influences. On the contrary, the military expenditures of the contemporary nation-states have to be seen as mainly bound up with their political involvements within the global nation-state system. To be sure, it is not at all easy to discern where economic interests or concerns leave off and specifically political ones begin. But that is not the same thing at all as the claim that no distinctions can be drawn between them, or that one in some general sense underlies the other.

Especially in the two super-powers and other nuclear states, the modern military has access to destructive capabilities on a stupendous scale. The material wealth produced in the industrialized countries is so immense, compared with even the largest of traditional states, that even the use of a small proportion of available resources can generate prodigious military strength. Moreover, in most areas of the world, the military confront already largely pacified populations. In considering military 'intervention' in politics, therefore, there is some sense in posing the question, Why are governments everywhere in the modern world not 'military governments'? For, as Finer remarks, 'The armed forces have three massive political advantages over civilian organisations: a marked superiority in organisation, a highly emotionalised symbolic status, and a monopoly of arms. They form a prestigious corporation or Order, enjoying overwhelming superiority in the means of applying force. The wonder, therefore, is not why this rebels against its civilian masters but why it ever obeys them.'[49] The answer Finer goes on to provide is more or less the same as mine, although I shall develop it in terms of the themes and concepts of this book.

Two elements have to be separated in considering the nature of modern military rule. One is how far military personnel compose, or are the dominant part of, the higher councils of government; the other is how far the monopoly of the means of violence which the armed forces, together with the police, enjoy is used directly to sustain administrative power. While it is the former issue that has tended to brook large in the literature concerned with military 'intervention' in politics, it is the latter that is in some main respects more significant. Those governments in which military leaders have a prime role may often be, but are not necessarily, ones in which the monopoly of the means of violence is extensively used in a repressive way.

A modern army, as Finer points out, is in a certain sense a microcosm of the state as a whole.[50] The armed forces possess their own specialized systems of supply, engineering, communications and education. In countries of a low level of industrialization, they may be more advanced organizationally and technologically than the civil sector and may consequently be used to mobilize resources for economic development. But in industrialized societies the armed forces both tend to be separated from the rest of the population in virtue of their specialized training, as a distinct 'professional' group and, at the same time, are dependent upon a variety of productive and administrative resources which they cannot directly control. Administrative specialization is one factor inhibiting military direction of government or the economy, the strong pressure towards polyarchy another. 'Praetorian states' are rarely if ever wholly governed solely by military leaders in their higher councils, let alone in the more executive levels of administrative authority. Military governments have usually only managed to maintain some degree of stability in their composition and their rule where they have acknowledged reciprocal relations of polyarchy and have legitimized their position by successfully mobolizing the support of major segments of the subject population. Perlmutter's threefold typology of military regimes is useful here.[51] What he calls an 'arbitrator regime' is a mode of government in which the headquarters of the armed forces is taken over by a cabal of officers and where this group shares power with civilian political authorities. The military leadership 'arbitrates' policy decisions taken by those authorities by broadly overseeing them, but without attempting directly to take the reins of government. This type tends to be unstable, as either the political sector tends effectively to regain power or the military leadership seeks increasingly to control policy-making. In the second type, the 'ruler regime', a military council is established to directly control the executive with, however, the headquarters being composed of 'non-political' officers. Such a form of government can be more enduring, but only if it gains a considerable measure of popular legitimacy. The more it achieves such legitimacy, the more it becomes enmeshed in an administrative order distinct from the military sphere through which governmental control was obtained. Hence it tends to devolve into a third type, the 'party-army regime', or into a purely civil administration. The party-army regime is a military dictatorship, in which the military leader, supported by the high command in the headquarters, furthers a military party that dominates the loftiest councils of the state. The ruling party nevertheless has to acquire a strong level of popular support for the system to show any sort of stability. This is difficult to achieve, especially where the dictatorial element is marked. In such circumstances, the military must constantly 'patrol' the society, becoming the main policing agency, but only temporarily being able to contain the oppositional movements that develop.

We can derive from this analysis the following generalized conclusions. The structural basis for the existence of military governments in Third World states is their relative lack of development of internal administrative co-ordination, compared with the more industrialized societies. Because they often are in a significant sense 'state-nations', most such states lack the degree of centralized administrative integration achieved in the Western nation-state. Compared with traditional states, the military forces nonetheless face substantially pacified populations. The more successful the military is in 'governing', however — where 'successful governing' means that the state apparatus is increasingly able to influence the day-to-day activities of the mass of the population — the more likely it is to succumb to polyarchic pressures. In First and Second World states, those pressures tend to be all-enveloping. The military may step into the 'political arena' in various ways, but chronic military government is more or less a contradiction in terms. The most common direct relation between the military and government tends to be via the polyarchic appeal a popular military leader may secure. But this is not military rule; it is the use of the symbolic trappings of military leadership to generate political legitimacy in a polyarchic setting.

The issues raised by the existence of the modern military must concern not just the distinction between civil and military regimes, but *the use of force in the process of governing*. As Luckham says, there is no shortage of states in which 'civil liberties have been curtailed, the media browbeaten, trade unions deprived of the right to strike, opponents of the regime repressed . . . be they formally under civilian governments or under the military and whether the regime is of a conservative or progressive political tendency'.[52] What is involved here is an association of the curtailing of citizenship rights, the concentration of certain types of surveillance activity, and the systematic use of force based on the state's monopoly of the means of violence. I shall argue subsequently that in such relations can be discerned the origins of totalitarianism — a phenomenon specific to the modern state. As this comment indicates, however, tendencies towards totalitarian power do not derive from the role of the military alone, or even of the military combined with the police. Since this is a matter I shall take up in the final chapter, let me turn at this point to a consideration of the world military order.

There are three key institutional dimensions of the world military order today: super-power hegemony; the arms trade; and systems of military alliance. These each relate quite directly to one another, since the super-powers not only have the most powerful military presence but also dominate the arms trade and have constructed global systems of alliance, often involving the military training of the armies of allied states.[53] In the Lend-Lease Programme initiated during the Second World War, the Truman Doctrine that followed the War, and the McNamara reforms, the USA began to integrate military aid with the forging of a global security network. Accurate statistics on the arms trade are difficult to come by but what is clear is the increasing commerce in weaponry between the industrialized and Third World countries, some two-thirds of such commerce now moving in this direction.[54] A high proportion of this consists of major weapons systems, rather than small arms and support equipment.[55] In the period just after the Second World War, much of the weaponry exported to Third World states was of kinds being phased out of the US armed forces. But today, even in the field of the most sophisticated weapons systems, some Third World countries possess equipment as advanced as that of the American military. Whereas US policy in terms of defence transfers formerly concentrated upon states bordering the Soviet Union, increasingly arms transfers have been made to any states not directly tied by treaty to the Soviets. Several leading Western industrial powers are major arms exporters and have maintained the capacity to produce advanced military technology. But they are also heavily dependent upon US military supplies for certain basic types of advanced equipment. The USSR is easily the second largest arms exporter, although lagging some way behind the USA: the USA supplies arms to some seventy Third World countries, the Soviet Union to thirty-two.[56] Something like a third of Soviet arms transfers go to its allies in the Warsaw Pact. The two main pact systems, in fact, consume nearly three-quarters of combined world military expenditure.

However, a considerable number of countries outside the main industrialized states are also producers of advanced weapons systems, for themselves and as exporters, with others currently seeking to follow the same course. Particularly important is the potentiality of these states for the construction of nuclear weapons. Although there are only six countries known to have exploded a nuclear device, there are many more that have separable plutonium sufficient to build nuclear weaponry.[57] The Non-Proliferation Treaty of 1968 bans the transfer of nuclear weapons by nuclear states to others and has been signed by over 100 countries, although a group of governments have refused to be signatories. The treaty does not of course bar nuclear weapons for states that already possess them and does not prevent the dissemination of nuclear technology and materials for non-military uses. It is mainly because reprocessing or enrichment methods make it possible to convert the waste products from nuclear generating plants into weapons that such weaponry is likely to be available soon to a range of states. Nuclear reactors are already either in operation or in the process of being built in 48 of the 106 member states of the International Atomic Energy Agency.[58]

Bilateral and unilateral military treaties have supplied a new dimension to the international division of labour, since they increasingly go along with co-operation in the training and recruitment of military personnel and the development of military technology. The global system of alliances built up by the USA integrates these various activities. NATO, the Rio Treaty in Latin America, SEATO in South-East Asia (subsequently dissolved) and ANZUS with Australia and New Zealand, were designed to form an encircling chain of treaties across the world. To the countries thus involved the USA has since the Second World War provided some $80,000 million in assistance for military projects in the form of loans or grants.[59] Under these and other treaties the USA has made available many kinds of training personnel. It has been estimated that in the late 1960s, in Third World countries alone, there were American military advisers in contact with 88 military establishments.[60] Soviet military assistance is, so far, much less and less widespread too. The Soviets have focused attention upon Eastern Europe and upon a few strategically important clients, particularly in the Middle East, but to these they have provided very large stocks of armaments.

It is in this third sense — the world-wide diffusion of the means of waging industrialized war — that we live today in 'military societies'. There is thus some substance, given a number of strong qualifications, to the nineteenth-century thesis of the replacement of military societies by ones based upon industrialism or economic exchange relations more generally. The more highly industrialized a state is, and the more unified its administrative system, the less it tends to be the case either that production for military ends predominates over other sectors, or that direct military rule can be sustained save in short-term periods. Unfortunately and unhappily these limitations upon the scope of military power do not in themselves imply the imminence of a world without war. On the contrary, the combined spread of industrialism and of the nation-state system has served to ensure that virtually every state across the globe now possesses armed strength far in excess of that of any traditional empire.

That the world military order is influenced by capitalistic mechanisms there is no doubt. But to suppose that it is explicable wholly or even primarily as an expression of the global involvements of capitalist enterprise is plainly foolish. The nation-state is the prime vehicle of political organization in the contemporary world, recognized as holding legitimate monopoly of the means of violence by its own subject population and by other nation-states. As the possessor of the means of waging industrialized war, in a global context of the continuing application of science to the advancement of military technology, the state participates in and furthers a generalized process of militarization within the world system as a whole. Whether this can at some future point be contained, or will eventuate in a more frightful conflict than either of the preceding World Wars is, of course, still completely undetermined.

10
Nation-States in the Global State System

What has made the nation-state apparently irresistible as a political form from the early nineteenth century to the present-day? From the state system that was once one of the peculiarities of Europe there has developed a system of nation-states covering the globe in a network of national communities. Whereas for the preceding seven or eight thousand years there were several overall political forms existing in uneasy relationship with one another, now there is only one, however important the sub-categories which can be distinguished within it. While there may be new types of imperialism and dominance by large states, the traditional imperialist state has disappeared from the face of the earth. Those societies in which human beings have lived for all but a fraction of the existence of humankind — tribal societies — have been either destroyed or absorbed into larger social entities. Two processes have, above all, been responsible for producing these extraordinary changes, the global consolidation of industrial capitalism and the global ascendancy of the nation-state. The two are closely intertwined, but it is a fundamental mistake to conflate them.

In outline, it is not difficult to explain the universal scope of the nation-state in the modern world. There are three main types of factors involved, only one of which is intrinsically connected with the spread of industrial capitalism. The first is the combination of industrial and military power originally developed in the European nation-state. Rather than promoting peaceful economic advance, industrialism was from the beginning married to the arts of war. No state that did not possess military forces able to use the new organizational forms and the new weaponry could hope to withstand external attack from those that could muster such forces. The second factor is the vast expansion of the administrative power of the state, which I have argued is one of the main definitive features of the nation-state. Only with such an extension of authoritative resources does it become possible to concentrate the allocative resources upon which a flourishing modern economy depends. The heightened administrative power of the nation-state is necessary not only to consolidate resources internally, but to cope with the vast international political network of relations in which all modern states are involved with others. The third influence, or rather, set of influences, concerns a series of contingent historical developments that cannot be derived from general traits attributed to nation-states, but which have nonetheless decisively influenced the trajectory of development of the modern world.

These include, as stressed previously, the period of relative peace in Europe dating from the treaties of 1815. The ambition of Napoleon to create a European 'super-state' which, if successfully established, might have become something like a traditional centralized bureaucratic empire, came to nothing. The hundred years following 1815 was a time in which a successful balance of power was maintained in Europe, disturbances of which were for the most part contained by diplomacy. This went together with an acceleration of technological innovation in weaponry, made possible by industrialism and stimulated by capitalism, which allowed the European powers a virtually untrammelled mastery of the rest of the world. Equally important, however, was formal recognition of the autonomy and 'boundedness' of the nation-state, made in the treaties following the First World War. If a new and formidably threatening pattern of war was established at this time, so was a new pattern of 'peace'. While Europe was fatally destabilized by the reparations forced upon Germany, this was effectively the first point at which a reflexively monitored system of nation-states came to exist globally. The point is not so much the acknowledgement of any particular state boundaries, but recognition of the authenticity of the nation-state as the legitimate arbiter of its own 'internal' affairs. These doctrines were subsequently renewed in the altered international context following the termination of the Second World War. Yalta is the symbol of those accords that gave recognition to the hegemony of certain of the larger powers within the global nation-state system and formally accepted the existence of socialist nation-states as authentic members of that system.

The Nation-State and the Invention of 'International Relations'

The doctrine of the balance of power was the antecedent of the concept and practice of international relations, of which it also became a substantive part. While not providing the name of an academic discipline, it was from early on both a description of a reality and a set of ideas applied reflexively to help constitute the political conditions it described.[1] 'Balance of power', as applied to the European state system, is better understood less as an actual equilibrium of strength than a shared policy adopted by states that only conditionally recognized each others' sovereignty. It supplied a set of principles guiding foreign policy according to what would today be called 'realist' tenets. In this sense one can agree with Morgenthau's statement that 'the international balance of power is only a particular manifestation of a general social principle to which all societies composed of a number of autonomous units owe the autonomy of their component parts.'[2] The balance of power had its theorists both in the various congresses that apportioned territory in Europe and in a proliferation of academic texts from the seventeenth century onwards (some of the early ones being inspired by Classical examples). Although they varied in their scepticism about whether any degree of real equilibrium could be maintained, or even achieved, most clearly recognized the idea of the balance of power to be a regulative notion of policy in an arena of competing sovereign states.

Von Gentz's *Fragments Upon the Balance of Power in Europe* (1806) is a good example. The 'states system of Europe' can only exist, he says, in virtue of 'common exertions' of its members.[3] Each must contribute towards the shared end of ensuring that no particular one becomes able to collectively coerce the others; but the manner in which this theme is developed makes it apparent that the main emphasis is upon the mutual recognition of sovereignty in a dangerous political environment. 'The state which is not prevented by any external consideration from oppressing a weaker, is always, however weak it may be, *too strong*, for the interest of the whole.'[4]

Although it is often considered that the doctrine of the balance of power was transferred more or less untouched from the European state system to the global state system consolidated after the First World War, there were in fact significant innovations in the newly reformed world system. The most obvious material differences, of course, turn on the new role assumed by the USA in world politics, together with the existence of the fledgling Soviet Union as the 'negative presence' at Versailles. The American influence upon the shaping of the new global order was both pervasive and profound, in some part representing an attempted incorporation of US constitutional prescriptions globally rather than a continuation of the balance of power doctrine. The League of Nations proved to be so ineffectual in the face of the tensions eventuating in the Second World War that there is a strong temptation to define it as a minor irrelevancy in world affairs. But the League represented an expression of an acknowledged need for the reflexive monitoring of a world-wide system of states. Like the United Nations afterwards, it was notably impractical as a means of maintaining global security. But this very fact rested upon a deep commitment to individual state sovereignty, thus furthering rather than diminishing the primacy of the nation-state as the universal political form of the current era.

Both the League of Nations and the United Nations were mainly the result of American thought and planning. The British Government was the only one among the European nations to play an active role in the drafting of the charters of both organizations. Early in 1918 the British premier stated it to be one of his country's aims to 'seek the creation of some international organisation to limit the burden of arguments and to diminish the danger of war'; and Lord Phillimore's committee took the initiative in formulating a draft for the League of Nations about three months later.[5] However, Wilson's conceptions provided the foundation of the subsequent Versailles meetings. Of course, in emphasizing the sovereignty of the nation-state, the Versailles congress merely in large part conceded the existence of an already existing order of global power. But it also helped ensure that it would become a genuinely universal political form in the contemporary world, both by the nature of the global reflexive monitoring which it advocated and furthered, and by its more substantive geopolitical prescriptions. The exclusion of the Soviet Union confirmed the rift opened up by the 1917 Revolution in the state system, later to become so momentous. In December 1918 Lloyd George had raised the question of Soviet participation in the peace talks at a meeting of the Western premiers. He expressed support for Soviet involvement in the talks but was the only leading figure to do so; Clemenceau was the most forcible opponent of including the Soviets and had little difficulty eventually in persuading the other delegates to accept his position. Wilson did, however, make an initiative to attempt to halt the Russian civil war and Allied troops in Russia were gradually withdrawn.[6]

Wilson's Fourteen Points were formulated in the context of widespread revulsion against the enormous loss of life in the War. The War began as a limited dispute among the European powers, entered into with enthusiasm, few having any idea either about the dimensions the conflict would assume or about the destructive consequences of industrialized armed struggle. It ended with a strong generalized reaction against 'militarism', accentuated by the views of the American leadership. The treaties and the League of Nations were thus judged by their initiators very largely in terms of how far they would act to prevent future outbreaks of military conflict. In this they proved to be a calamitous failure. Their longer-term effects were highly important, however, in consolidating conceptions of national sovereignty as the 'natural' political condition of humankind, via a particular interpretation of the sovereignty—citizenship—nationalism relation. This was the most significant effect of the 'new system of law and justice' among states that Wilson wanted to achieve. It is important to see that 'Wilsonianism' was a critique of the doctrine of the balance of power as the main guarantor of sovereignty, emphasizing the need to extend the concept of citizenship to apply to membership of the global community of nation-states. 'We [ie. nations] are all participants, whether we would or not, in the life of the world. The interests of all nations are our own also. We are partners with the rest . . . citizens of the world.'[7]

The Fourteen Points legitimated the concept of sovereignty as a universally applicable one in several respects. They recongized the importance of nationalism and associated regions of 'cultural identity' as the basis for the formation of nation-states (although the resultant territorial allocations proved usually far from homogeneous in this regard). Thus the Balkans were to be reordered according to established lines of 'national allegiance' and the opportunity for autonomous development was to be accorded the peoples of Austria-Hungary. These provisions, together with those applied to the Ottoman Empire, mark the final dismembering of the older type of imperial system in the West. The emphasis upon the 'impartial adjustment' of colonial claims, in such a way that the interests of the populations concerned were to be made consistent with self-government, opened the way to statehood — in principle and increasingly in practice — to those areas under European tutelage. An explicit element of such stipulations was that the notion of balance of power be replaced by one of the independent unity of each state, consensually accepted by the global community of states. Assessed in terms of its capability of avoiding war, Wilsonianism might appear — and has done so to many historians[8] — as irremediably utopian. But it was much closer to the 'realist' approach that states' leaders later tended to follow than might seem, recognizing that the European 'equilibrium' could not be applied globally, instead conceding the autonomy of nation-states as the necessary centres of consolidated administrative and military power. Not even the strongest state could, in principle, prevail over the opposition of multiple states acting collaboratively. When Wilson spoke of the Versailles Treaty as a set of agreements 'intended to destroy one system and substitute another',[9] he was hardly guilty of hyperbole, however much subsequent history diverged from his aspirations.

That Wilson's hopes for an epoch of peace and freedom were dashed, to a considerable extent by conflicts resulting from the very states given new autonomy in Europe and elsewhere, in no way compromises the impact of Wilsonianism upon the new global state-system. The restructured territorial divisions were in practice, 'a jumble of principle and expediency'.[10] The former had to succumb to the latter in Upper Silesia, for example, and in the Tyrol, since the outcome would otherwise have unduly favoured Germany and Austria respectively. The new states recognized through the covenant of the League of Nations enlarged rather than diminished the possibility of armed conflict in so far as they virtually all turned what had previously been hostilities between minorities into hostilities between states. The transformation of nationalistic minorities into sovereign entities gave their leaders the military strength to contemplate schemes of action which before would not have been options at all. Lloyd George observed that the peace treaties were never given a chance to work by the 'miscellaneous and unimpressive army of second-rate statesmen' who attempted to cope with them.[11] But at the same time he quite rightly pointed out that no previous treaty had emancipated so many previously subject peoples and that the principle of the autonomous development of 'national societies' was established much more firmly than it had been before. It is in this respect that Wilsonian ideals had such a profound impact upon the further development of the nation-state system.

I have argued earlier that the various congresses involving the European states from the seventeenth century onwards, plus the early development of diplomacy, should not be seen only as attempts to control the activities of pre-constituted states. Rather, the modes of reflexive regulation thus initiated were essential to the development of those states as territorially bounded units. The emergence of a reflexively monitored state system has gone hand in hand with the formation of the nation-state as the dominant political system in the modern world. This applies also to the period subsequent to the First World War, the juncture at which the nation-state system becomes a more or less complete one, world-wide. The League of Nations became the major focus for the channelling of global processes of information control just as much in terms of the informational processes and exchange. It became most prominent among an expanding cluster of organizations involved in monitoring the global information sources upon which modern states depend. It was not the condition of existence of most of these organizations, many of which antedate it; but it provided an administrative centre to which many were linked and which helped stimulate their further expansion.

As cases in point we may take the development of postal services and international health agencies — two instances among a plethora of international modes of organization accelerating since the 1920s. Postal services between the European states date back hundreds of years. In 1505 Franz von Taxis set up a courier service between the courts of several of the European rulers, undertaking to transmit letters from Brussels to Innsbruck in five and a half days, to Lyon in four days and to Granada in fifteen days.[12] Postal treaties were signed between most of the major European states in the sixteenth and seventeenth centuries, creating a network of postal exchange which was both complex and heterogeneous. By the middle of the nineteenth century there were some twelve hundred different postal rates pertaining in different parts of Europe. The introduction of the penny post in Britain in 1840 standardized rates in that country, leading to attempts to reproduce the process in the rest of Europe. Some twenty years later, the US Postmaster convened an international conference in Paris, at which it was agreed that bilateral treaties were no longer practicable. An international postal committee therefore was established, involving the postal systems of a dozen European countries and the USA. A further congress, meeting in Berne in 1874, had a much larger representation of states, setting up the first General Postal Union and the first International Postal Convention. The territories of the member states were regarded as a single postal area, for which a single payment for each item sent would be made, no matter how many countries it traversed. All packages were to be sent at internationally standard rates. The bureau established in Berne to take charge of these matters was one of the first permanently established international organizations, altering its name in 1878 to the Universal Postal Union. Numerous congresses were held by the Union both in the years leading up to and subsequent to the First World War. However, it did not become affiliated to the League of Nations, maintaining complete independence until the founding of the United Nations, within which it is a 'Specialized Agency'. It has greatly expanded its activities since then.

In the field of health, attempts at international coordination date back only to the nineteenth century. From 1851 International Sanitary Conferences were regularly held, proposing generalized standards of quarantine and other health measures. Health statistics were the prime concern of government authorities, however. The International Health Office set up in Paris in 1908 was mainly devoted to the collection and distribution of statistical information, concerning public health legislation in different countries and patterns of disease transmission. The League of Nations established its own health committee, the Health Organization. It was initially devoted to trying to document and check the spread of infectious diseases, particularly those assuming epidemic proportions in the aftermath of the War. But it steadily expanded its activities, and the number of states immediately involved with it also grew, developing in conjunction with the International Health Office, which continued to exist independently. Statistical monitoring of health patterns world-wide remained the main preoccupation of both organizations. With the coming of the UN, the World Health Organization was set up, originally to carry on the work of the old League Health Organization, but becoming very much more comprehensive in the scope and scale of its operations. WHO drew up international sanitary regulations of a wide-ranging sort and initiated campaigns directed against some of the major diseases, with considerable success in respect of malaria and smallpox.[13]

Whether directly administered by states or not, organizations involved in the world system show a very marked increase from the period of the Second World War onwards, as shown in figure 5.

It might be thought that what we see emerging here is an increasing movement towards 'one world', in which the nation-state form is likely to become less and less significant in the face of global patterns of organization. The argument I seek to present here, however, is rather different.[14] The sovereignty of the nation-state, I have suggested, does not precede the development of the European state system, or the transferral of the nation-state system to a global plane. State authorities did not hold large areas of sovereign power destined to become increasingly confined by the growing network of international connections and modes of interdependence. On the contrary, the development of the sovereignty of the modern state from its beginnings depends upon a reflexively monitored set of relations between states. Both the consolidation of the sovereignty of the state and the universalism of the nation-state are brought about through the expanded range of surveillance operations permitting 'international relations' to be carried on. 'International relations' are not connections set up between pre-established states, which could maintain their sovereign power without them: they are the basis

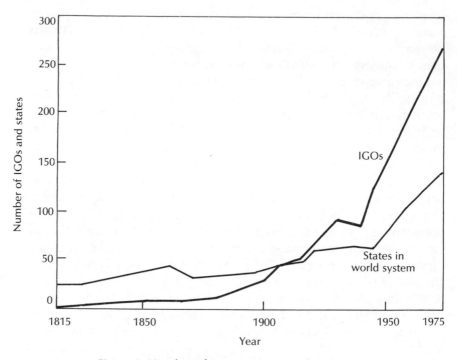

Figure 5   Number of intergovernmental organizations
in the world system, 1815—1975 [15]

upon which the nation-state exists at all. The period of the
burgeoning of international organizations, including the League
of Nations and the UN, is not one of the growing transcendence
of the nation-state. It is one in which the universal scope of the
nation-state was established. As in the case of the European state
system, this has come about through a mixture of war and
diplomacy. But given the industrialization of war, warfare
everywhere tends to take on a total character and, in the shape of
the World Wars, has affected all states in some way or another.
As a result of the increasingly integrated nature of the world
system, diplomacy can no longer be carried on only between
clusters of states, but in certain basic respects involves them all.

The Second World War was even more devastating, in terms of
lives lost and states involved, than the First. But it marks less of a
dramatic transition from previous patterns of warfare, in virtue of
the fact of its temporal proximity to the First World War and

because it extended rather than substantively transformed industrialized war. As Pearton points out, an understanding of the implications of industrialized war was very rapidly achieved by the leading states following the first world conflict.[16] Military strength could not any more be reckoned in terms mainly of the possession of armaments and volume of trained soldiery, but was seen to depend upon the industrial capabilities of states. Chamberlain's view that economic power was a deterrent in and of itself may have proved erroneous, but the relation between industrial and military might had become generally accepted. The political and scholarly literature on war changed. Among the many studies analysing the events of the First World War, a substantial proportion sought to connect the outcomes of the conflict to the overall economies of the contending states. That is to say, it became generally accepted that military strength turned on the mobilization of an industrial economy as a whole, not just the putting of armies in the field. The implications of this made themselves felt very soon in the Second World War. For those involved in industrial production became as relevant to the conduct of war as the armed forces themselves; from the concluding part of the First World War onwards, urban areas were regarded as necessary military targets in case of an outbreak of hostilities.

A further implication concerns the international sphere and stretches from the Second World War to the present. Military strength depends upon a greater range of allocative resources than can be concentrated within the immediate administrative purview of any particular state. An industrial economy, however large it might be, is integrated economically with a vast reach of international connections in the division of labour. Hence no state can stand alone in terms of its military power. But it also follows that the larger states will tend to co-ordinate their own 'international spheres of influence' over which hegemony of a military-industrial kind can be maintained. The significance of the Yalta and Potsdam agreements is that the two pre-eminent state powers — the USA and the Soviet Union — explicitly accepted the idea of 'spheres of influence' while confirming at the same time the universalism of states' sovereignty. Full acknowledgement of the sovereign autonomy of the Soviet Union by the other major powers is no less important in its consequences than acceptance by the Soviets of the universal character of the nation-state. The first paragraph of Article Two of the United Nations 'is based on the principle of the sovereign equality of all its Members'.[17] The phrase 'sovereign equality' appeared initially in the American draft of the Four-Power Declaration on general security, representing essentially a modified version of the constitutionalism that marked the Wilsonian proposals of a quarter of a century earlier. The 'equality' involved was specifically supposed to be legal rather than factual — the larger powers were to have special rights, as well as duties, commensurate with their superior capabilities. Some of the smaller states objected to the privileges enshrined in membership of the Security Council. The Dutch document presented at Dumbarton Oaks insisted that 'All such special privileges and inequalities are at variance with the principle of the sovereign equality of peace-loving states.' More significant European objections, however, were voiced in respect of the extension of the principle of 'sovereign equality' to colonial peoples. In the insistence by both US and USSR representatives that state sovereignty should be accorded to colonized societies is encapsulated some of the main trends of subsequent global development.

The combination of a reflexively monitored global system of nation-states, together with the pre-eminent military-industrial power wielded by the USA and Soviet Union, are the main distinguishing features of the present period. Each of the super-powers has its geopolitically proximate 'sphere of influence', and each has its diplomatically cultivated connections of dependency or alliance across the face of the globe. These involvements have very definite consequences for the internal political and economic systems of the states involved. But to see them as acting in a one-way fashion to limit the sovereignty of states in general would be misleading. The period since the Second World War has seen a considerable development in the effective autonomy of a variety of states — some being of very recent provenance — at the same time as that of others has been reduced. For reasons I have already mentioned, these should be seen as linked developments rather than distinct and separate ones.

Types of Nation-State

Many classifications of modern states exist in the literature of political science and sociology. Given that 'nation-state' is equivalent to 'society', it is hardly surprising that categorizations should proliferate, since there are as many criteria of classification as there are modes of identifying major institutions. In the light of the discussion in this and the foregoing chapters, however, three bases of classification suggest themselves as useful. Nation-states exist as entities in a world state system, in which a bipolar distribution of industrial and military power is pre-eminent. One means of classification, therefore, should be a geo-political one, in which the positions of the two leading powers supply the poles around which the other states gravitate. Such a classification suggests the following categories:

1 Focal/Hegemonic
2 Adjacent/Subsidiary
3 Central/Aligned
4 Central/Non-Aligned
5 Peripheral/Aligned
6 Peripheral/Non-Aligned.

Only the USA and the USSR — at present at least — belong in category 1. They have a hegemonic position within their spheres of influence and occupy dominant places within the world system, although not in any sense akin to traditional imperial centres or to colonial empires. The bipolar character of the world system does not date from Yalta, but from a slightly later time. Until a short while after Yalta it seemed possible that the USA might retreat into its erstwhile isolationism; or that its role in world politics would be a unique one as the sole possessor of nuclear weapons. Britain was the main front-runner in pursuing a policy of containment against the Soviet Union. The Truman Doctrine of 1947, in which the American government assumed the British responsibilities of financial aid in Greece and Turkey and offered assistance to anti-Soviet regimes, was one watershed; the attainment of nuclear weaponry by the USSR was the other. NATO and the Warsaw Pact have given direct substance to the bipolar division of military power. Mutual acceptance of state sovereignty as a universal principle, however, has meant that the bipolar distribution of power has remained diffuse in its consequences. Within each of the two blocs, all existing nation-states have a developed administrative autonomy, with the superpowers not having a complete nuclear monopoly.

Within the main blocs, three types of state can be distinguished, those falling into categories 2, 3 and 5. Each focal state has sought to protect its borders by ensuring that neighbouring states are ruled by governing authorities deemed favourable to its interests. Those countries that are physically adjacent tend to be both subject to more political pressure than others and are more liable to the threat or actuality of military intervention. The Soviet Union has borders with other major states which for one reason or another have become largely refractory to its influence, most particularly China which, for the time being, still belongs in category 4. But along its European boundaries it has ranged a series of states over which it maintains a very considerable sway. These adjacent states, accepted effectively by the USA since 1947 as being within the Soviet sphere of influence, are independent members of the United Nations, having their own internal political administrations, policing systems and armed forces. At the same time, they are manifestly subsidiary to the Soviet Union in so far as their political orders are closely tied to that of the USSR and in so far as certain options of institutional reform are blocked. The geographical position of the USA makes it much less vulnerable to the vagaries of physically proximate states. Nonetheless, both to the north and the south, there are states kept as far as possible pliable to the interests of the USA, where strong efforts are made to inhibit possible or actual developments believed to be contrary to those interests.

By 'central states' I mean those which are 'second-order' in terms of their industrial and military strength but which, nevertheless, are able to sustain a major role in world politics. Many such states, including particularly those of Western Europe, are aligned with one of the focal powers. They have full sovereignty over most of their internal affairs and, like the East European societies, they have their own armed forces at their disposal — but with substantially greater autonomy over their deployment and use. Nonetheless, those which are members of NATO and have American bases on their soil are subject to significant constraints upon their possibilities of independent military action. Partly for this reason, some central states have kept themselves non-aligned, in Europe as well as Asia, the Middle East and Africa. Whereas the aligned states form blocs with the two focal states, co-ordinating their economic and military policies in particular, the unaligned states are 'poly-centric'.[18] That is to say, the fact of their non-alignment gives them — in principle and often in practice — a greater range of flexibility in their policy-making. Although there have been efforts on the part of some of their members to make them so, the central non-aligned states do not form a definite bloc in world politics.

Finally, peripheral states are those whose industrial and military capabilities are low and which are geographically distant from the focal powers. In the case of peripheral/aligned states, what matters is distance from the focal state with which collaborative relations are sustained, even where the country in question might be close to the other focal state. Cuba is a peripheral/aligned state in relation to the USSR, although it borders upon the USA. While peripheral/aligned societies may be heavily dependent economically upon one or other focal state, the fact that they are not geographically adjacent creates difficulties in sustaining the same sort of control that can be exerted over adjacent states. Not all peripheral states are 'Third World' societies economically (eg. Iceland).

A geo-political categorization of states has to be based upon their involvement in, and influence over, 'world politics', that is to say processes of political policy formation and action that are global in their consequences. But nation-states may also be grouped into types in terms of divergent modes of original state formation. The European nation-state — the 'classical form', as it were — in many respects obviously provided a model that other states have followed. But it is equally evident that other states have not simply recapitulated the European experience and in many cases have become nation-states in the process of rebelling against European dominance. A second broad classification of states can hence be made thus:

1 Classical
2 Colonized
3 Post-Colonial
4 Modernizing.

Of course the 'classical nation-state' is not an internally undifferentiated category. The early established nation-states in Europe tended to develop in what were then peripheral areas of the continent, along the margins of what were previously the most concentrated sectors of state power.[19] A further wave of state formation occurred in central Europe and in Italy. In very few of these cases was there a close convergence between territorial boundaries and linguistic or cultural identity. But, as a whole, it is the case that the earlier nation-states developed without nationalist movements playing a large role in their formation, whereas nationalism did play such a role in the establishing of later states. Those areas that inherited common linguistic traits from the territorial distribution of imperial Rome were prone to show only weak tendencies towards nation-state formation until states were well-developed elsewhere. In the so-called 'Lotharingian-Burgundian' zone between France and the German states, the linguistic divisions hardly ever conformed to established territorial boundaries. Neither France nor Britain, the two instances usually given of a smooth coincidence of 'nation' and 'state', involved linguistically homogeneous territories. The linguistic standardization achieved in France in the nineteenth century was probably greater than in any other European state, but throughout the period the centralizing authorities had to contend with resistance in Brittany, Occitania and other regions. This having been said, linguistic uniformity linked to a degree of cultural homogeneity can rightly be seen to be distinctive characteristics of the classical nation-state. To be sure there were, and are, exceptions among this group of states, although few like Switzerland, where one language is not recognized to have primacy over others spoken within the state. Not all nation-states that can be placed in the classical type were established in the eighteenth and nineteenth centuries. Those set up in Europe and around the margins of Europe following the World Wars (including ex-imperial states like Austria or Turkey) belong in this category. Some states established earlier, on the other hand, belong rather in the modernizing type (eg. Germany).

The 'colonized nation-state' refers to those states set up as a result of the movement of emigrant populations from Europe, for example the Latin American states, the USA, Canada, Australia and, latterly, Israel. Such states have involved processes of long-distance migration, those concerned being normally drawn from heterogeneous cultures of origin. Established in what were by European standards thinly settled land-areas, they have all been predicated upon the use of force against indigenous groups, often either wiping out those groups altogether, or reducing them to a tiny fraction of the overall population. Several colonized nation-states achieved their statehood initially by fighting wars of national liberation against the metropolitan powers — as with the USA against Britain and various of the Latin American states against Spain. It is characteristic of this type of state, however, that such wars were conducted in the relatively early stages of state development in Europe, with liberal conceptions of citizenship and sovereign rights being more important than nationalism. The fact that fairly homogeneous national communities eventually emerged should not lead us to overlook the conjunctions of war, diplomacy and accident that shaped colonized nation-states just as much as those in the original European context. The feasibility of linking the heterogeneous and, at that time, isolated ex-British colonies into a single state was early on doubted even by some of the main proponents of the American Revolution. The liberation wars in Latin America were fought by leaders who differed widely about what states should be set up following their successful resolution. Bolivar and San Martin anticipated the formation of large states spanning whole areas in which several states were in fact eventually established.[20]

Other colonized nation-states, notably those originally part of the British Empire, achieved their independence by concession from the parent country — fuelled by nationalist sentiment. Most colonized states have achieved a high degree of linguistic and cultural unity, at the expense of the shedding by their immigrants of the traits of their cultures of origin. But many, like Canada or Israel, have large populations of ethnic minorities remaining substantially outside the dominant culture. South Africa is a special case, of course, perhaps worth linking to the others above, but in some ways more aptly regarded as a colonial territory which has not yet become fully 'post-colonial'. At any rate, the anti-colonial nationalism of its black majority clearly distinguishes it from the most colonized nation-states, although there have been more minor movements of this type in the USA and there are certain loose affinities with the French in Canada.

Post-colonial and modernizing nation-states generally differ from those in categories 1 and 2 in respect of having less linguistic and cultural homogeneity, although this is by no means inevitably the case. The resurgence of local nationalisms within the classical nation-state has served to demonstrate that the 'colonial' exploitation of ethnically differentiated groups is not confined to the externally administered territories of the European states. However, in most post-colonial nation-states there is no sense in which a 'nation' precedes the emergence of the state and it is not without reason that such states have often been called state-nations. Thus it has been remarked of Black Africa that,

> though we loosely refer to the recently created countries of that part of Africa as 'nation-states', and their peoples as 'new nations', it is by no means certain that such formal appelations have any substance. During the run-up to independence, people in the West grew accustomed to regard the anti-colonial movements then coming to power in Africa as variants of the global phenomenon of nationalism . . . However, after some two decades of formal independence, it is not at all clear how far these earlier expressions of nationalistic sentiments have survived to become the basis of state formation. Numerous students of political change in Black Africa today dispute the existence of nation-states in much of the continent.[21]

While I do not think it necessary to question the existence of nation-states in Africa or in other ex-colonial areas, for the states in question are not of the traditional sort, it is obvious enough that their origins and character are mostly quite discrepant from the other types mentioned so far.

Post-colonial states — or 'state-nations' — are based upon state apparatuses originally established by the colonizing societies. As the above quotation suggests, nationalism has usually played an important part in mobilizing social movements stimulating the transition to independent statehood. But such forms of nationalism have tended to be primarily fostered by elites aspiring to and then holding state power. The consolidation of the administrative power of the state has not been based, as in the classical and colonized types, upon the mobilization of internally generated resources but, rather, upon the 'imported' administrative resources brought in from the outside. This has placed the proponents of nationalist symbols in a paradoxical position, sometimes having profoundly schismatic consequences for internal political organization. For nationalist sentiments relate to a myth of origins supplying a psychological focus for the unity of the political community; but any interpretation of origins that has concrete reference to the past is likely to stimulate as much tension as harmony, because of the diversity of cultural differences characteristically involved.

In both Africa and Asia, symbols and movements that are discernably proto-nationalist existed in some regions subjected to colonial rule. Thus, at about the turn of the nineteenth century, black settlers from North America in Freetown, Sierre Leone, were advocating a distinctive form of 'Africanism' linked to the promotion of rights of self-determination. A similar movement occurred in Liberia.[22] However, such examples are relatively few and far between and mostly do not have any direct connections with types of nationalism developing in the later colonial and post-colonial periods. In Africa, Somalia, Lesotho and Swaziland are the only partial exceptions to the generalization that the populations of African states are composed of a multiplicity of heterogeneous cultural and ethnic groupings — in this respect certainly exhibiting a feature somewhat resembling traditional states. It has been calculated that there are more than two hundred culturally distinct groups in Nigeria, although the three largest of these make up some two-thirds of the total population. Even Gambia, whose population only numbers about half a million, has eight distinct ethnic groups.[23]

By modernizing nation-states I mean those which, even if they may have experienced direct colonialism, have successfully moved from a traditional state to a modern one mainly through internal process of political mobilization. Again there are some parallels in African history. At the same period that Maiji Japan was undergoing the transformations that created a modern state, similar attempts at state development were being made in West Africa. Thus the Fanti of the Gold Coast and a group of the Yoruba of south-west Nigeria independently set under way endeavours to create a modern state apparatus. The most celebrated case is that of the traditional empire of Abyssinia in the east of the continent. Here the ruling groups sought to co-ordinate the state and develop its military potential through policies designed to increase administrative centralization and cultural unity. An imperial army successfully defeated an Italian force at the turn of the century. However the victory proved to be a transitory one and it was only where existing traditional states were either too large, or too remote, or for some other reason escaped direct European rule, that modernizing nation-states successfully emerged.

The institutional traits of nation-states can be categorized in terms of the four clusterings of institutions distinguished earlier. Thus we can categorize states in terms of where they fall on these dimensions:

Industrialized economy	+	−
Capitalistic production	+	−
Political integration	+	−
Military rule	−	+

The classical nation-state can be located on the left-hand of the two columns. It has its origins in the absolutist state but comes into being in developed form only with the advent of industrial capitalism. On the basis of a strongly developed administrative apparatus, it is able to achieve a high degree of political integration within its borders. As a result of internal pacification — itself directly related to industrial capitalism as a highly distinctive form of class domination — the military mainly 'points outwards', towards other states. There is a sharp division between civil and military authority, with the armed forces being 'professionally' concerned only with the prosecution of the business of war. Some colonizing states fit this pattern (for instance, the USA, Canada or Australia) but others do not. The Latin American states have mostly reached only a relatively low level of industrialization and exist within a capitalist orbit dominated by the USA. Although there is much debate about its precise nature, most of these states are characterized by internal 'dualism' — the co-existence of modernized centres together with large agrarian regions in which cash-crop economies predominate. Urbanization has followed a divergent pattern from that established in the classical nation-state, with the inner cities being surrounded by migrant settlements at most loosely integrated into modern patterns of urban organization such as characterized the original European experience. As in the case of post-colonial states, there is not a close similarity to processes that produced the classical nation-state.

In both colonized and post-colonial states there have proved to be strong tendencies towards military rule, in contrast to the classical and modernizing types. The development of military regimes actually characterizes in particular the period of the universality of the nation-state, that is the four decades since the Second World War. This is one further example of a reversal in the expectations generated by mainstream traditions of social science, Marxist and non-Marxist. Governments dominated by the military have remained largely unstudied, considered as temporary exceptions to the general trends of development generated by industrialism or industrial capitalism. The events of the past forty years across the face of the world have made any such position an increasingly bizarre one. Military involvement in government, in coups and counter-coups, has been witnessed in all the Latin American states, in most Middle Eastern and African countries, and Poland.[24] Armies in these circumstances may be professionalized but they are also praetorian. There is no doubt that the praetorian state has its origins in some substantial degree in the role played by the military under colonialism. The very processes analysed earlier in relation to the European nation-state made it possible for military power to be focused 'externally', upon colonial domination. As one author remarks,

> In the European colonies during the nineteenth and twentieth centuries, the military was specifically oriented towards external conquest and dominance. External domination provided a vocational ideal, which was expressed in such organisations as the civil and military services in British India, the French Foreign Legion, the French Equatorial Army (the 'Africans') and the Spanish arm in Morocco and South America. The values of the system were embodied in 'civilisation française', Kipling's 'white man's burden' and the missionary zeal of General Lyautey (a military administrator of French Africa). The concept of 'civilisation française' was developed by the military who administered and, in fact, dominated French imperial policy in Africa and who were dedicated to the expansion of the empire. The mission-oriented military was prone to become interventionist, particularly in the French and Spanish colonies.[25]

Modernizing states have not been prone to military rule although — most notably in the cases of Germany and Japan — they may be associated with a strongly militaristic ethos. It is worth repeating here that modern military governments should not be seen as up-dated versions of military authority in traditional states. Modern military rule depends upon the centralized control of the weapons of industrialized war, and a bureaucratized standing army, normally operating in circumstances in which a higher level of internal pacification has been achieved than was ever possible in traditional states.[26] In most modern nation-states, however 'new' they may be, the armed forces have no serious 'competitors' in respect of control of the means of violence.[27] There may be guerilla movements challenging state power — almost invariably supported by external states and often based externally to the country with which their objectives are concerned[28] — but high levels of internal pacification can be achieved even in 'state-nations', as a result of the importation of modern modes of transport and communication, the development of police forces and an apparatus of systematic legal sanctions.

The World Capitalist Economy

Whether used to refer to a single society, networks of relations spanning several societies, or to world-wide connections, the term 'system' has to be approached with caution. There is a world system, but it is much more disaggregated and subject to uneven development than individual states are. In this regard the critical remarks made earlier about 'world system theory' need to be somewhat extended. In addition to its 'economistic' bias there is a defined inclination to repeat the tendency of sociologists discussing single societies to exaggerate its 'functional integration'. That a world system exists, influencing the development of particular states, does not imply that there is a single dominating dynamic in its development or that the 'whole' somehow has primacy over the 'parts'. A consistent theoretical language must be used here,[29] relating the analysis of social institutions within states to regionalized systems of larger and greater scope.

The current world system can be effectively characterized in the following terms.

Symbolic orders/modes *of discourse*	Global information system
Political institutions	Nation-state system
Economic institutions	World capitalist economy
Law/modes of sanction	World military order

Since I have so far concentrated upon the state system and the processes of reflexive monitoring making possible its consolidation, together with the global military order, it is worth at this point giving some attention to economic relations. How should we analyse the main parameters of the world capitalist economy today? In what sense do capitalistic mechanisms dominate world economic organization? How do these relate to economic development within states?

The world economy is predominantly capitalist in various senses. It is dominated by states in which capitalist economic enterprise, with its attendant class asymmetries, is the chief form of production. Both in terms of the domestic policies of such states, and certain of their outside involvements, economic activity is subject to various modes of political regulation. However, it is characteristic of their institutional organization that the 'economic' is insulated from the 'political'. Given the diversification of power within the hands of states within the nation-state system, this situation makes for a considerable scope of action on the part of economic organizations across the world as a whole. While they cannot rival nation-states in most respects, business firms geared to capitalistic production thus come to play a major role in international economic relations. Their influence within their 'parent' states tends to be large, as governments depend upon wealth generated by business firms for their own economic viability. Since their trading relations with each other, with states and with consumers depend upon production for profit, the spread of their influence brings in its train a global extension of commodity markets. But, from its inception, the world capitalist economy was never just a vast commodity market. It involved, and involves, the commodification of labour-power in different regional settings, often under conditions other than those of the 'free' entry of the worker into the market place. Whether they are small firms or large transnational corporations, most business enterprises are slotted directly or indirectly into economic relations stretching beyond the confines of any particular state. Thus the extraction of raw materials and their processing are productive enterprises, drawn into the world economy; since business firms can set up new 'prime' production units outside their state of origin, capitalist production can and has become established in regions outside the economically dominant states.

As they do not insulate the economic and the political internally, the Soviet Union, East European societies, and a few other state socialist societies, in some part form an enclave within the world capitalist economy. Only in some part however, for these states are deeply involved in the global division of labour and experience the influence of capitalistic economic mechanisms both in an immediate way and at further remove. The world capitalist economy, like all social systems, involves relations of power, their distribution being highly unequal. Wallerstein's characterization of core, semi-periphery and periphery, and the analysis he has developed in conjunction with it, is useful in a general way to describe these, given the reservations already mentioned. The core nations economically are not necessarily so in politico-military terms, particularly if the Soviet Union is placed in the semi-periphery. The geo-political classification of states given in chapter 9 in some large degree cuts across economic differentiations, and there are marked differences within each of the general categories in respect of economic, political and military power. Divisions between core, semi-periphery and periphery alter as the global division of labour changes and may often characterize regions cross-cutting states rather than referring to clusters of states.

While the differentiation between core, periphery and semi-periphery is long-standing, direct economic relations between states were for a long period primarily a matter of international trade. Trade and capital movements had become strongly internationalized by the end of the nineteenth century and up to the First World War. However this was distinct from the situation pertaining today.[30] At that time considerable segments of the national economies of the core countries were buffered from international competition.

Breweries, brickworks, and bakeries supplied local markets. The 'clothing industry' still consisted of local tailors. International freight rates were too high for the furniture industry to engage in international trade. Agriculture, fishing, and handicrafts were not yet integrated even on the national level. World market prices had been established only for a few products — mainly produce of a non-European origin such as coffee, sugar, and spices. For many products there was not even a uniform national price.[31]

Almost the whole commodity market is, however, increasingly subject to international competition. Moreover, production has become much more internationalized over the past half century or so than it ever was before. Throughout most of the long period of the expansion of the world capitalist economy, the global spread of capitalist production involved joining capital, management and technology from one state with labour power and raw material from others. Now it is common for each of these to come from different countries with, in addition, components being made in different parts of the world. International production has come more and more to displace the central role of international trade.

In the late 1970s corporations based in the USA alone held direct investments overseas of $70 billion. If there is a two-fold dollar value output per annum for every dollar invested in plant and equipment, $140 billion is yielded yearly by these investments. Such a volume of goods produced abroad, having some inputs from the parent country, is four times as high as US annual exports. Indirect investments abroad double the amount of production carried on outside the country.[32] To be sure, US foreign investment greatly outweighs that of any other state and makes up about two-thirds of the value of the investments of the OECD countries.[33] However, the sector of the world economy organized in terms of internationalized production is growing much faster than the GNPs of each of the states most heavily involved. The US economy, like that of all the core states, is dependent upon the import of mineral supplies for its basic industries. No state, or even continent, is self-sufficient in respect of all the mineral resources needed in modern production. Thus, of the thirteen most important minerals its economy requires, the

US depends upon importing at least half of its supplies of nine of them. The other core states are much less well-supplied.

In the years since the Second World War, significant alterations have taken place in the alignment of the core states within the OECD economic bloc — the most striking, of course, being the movement of Japan to become one of the leading countries. The industrial output of the East European societies is not easy to compare with that of the capitalist states. It probably amounts to roughly 30 per cent of the world's output, compared with some 60 per cent for that of the core states, and only 10 per cent for the remainder of the world. Trade flows are relatively low between the planned economies and the core countries, indicating that it is mainly via monetary mechanisms and raw material imports that these experience the impact of global capitalist economic relations.[34] Peripheral states, especially of the post-colonial type, are notoriously vulnerable to the fluctuations of world trading patterns. Their position of 'ultra-dependence' in the world economy expresses their reliance upon the export of primary products and the import of technology and manufactured goods, including weaponry. The significance of the peripheral nations as markets for manufactured exports from OECD countries is, in fact, diminishing rather than rising, although the interruption of the trend by the OPEC states is graphic testimony to the influence contingent political events can have over what might appear to be 'immutable' economic forces.

The older industrialized countries at the core of the world capitalist economy remain the pivot around which most else turns, but their position is weakening. Output has mostly risen more slowly in these states over the past decade compared with the Eastern European states, and particularly in contrast to the 'Oriental Sector' (South Korea, Taiwan, Hong Kong, Singapore). The core states have become increasingly dependent upon external markets, especially in respect of production of advanced capital goods. But the mobility of production into other areas of the world tends to rob them of the monopoly of high-level technological capacity they once enjoyed. Of course, migration of capital away from regions where technological and labour advantages have already been exploited occurs also both within and between the more industrially developed states. Thus, in the USA, there is a movement of productive enterprise from the more industrialized northern areas to the 'sun belt' of the south, where wages are lower and union strength less marked. In northern France the early established industrial areas decline while newer industries spring up in the Mediterranean region.

De-industrialization and mass unemployment in the core countries are so evidently connected to trends in the world economy that everyone accepts that they cannot be interpreted wholly in terms of the internal organization of individual states. Here we see an awareness that the 'comparative' study of societies as ordinarily practised is deficient. But this has not yet produced a general recognition of the centrality of the world system to any form of social analysis or social theory that seeks to understand the nature of the economically advanced societies.[35] Analyses of semi-peripheral and peripheral states consistently recognize that these countries have to be examined in terms of the 'unequal exchange' in which they are involved internationally. But the same is not true of most sociological discussions of the advanced countries, from the point of view either of their relations with one another or with the remainder of the world.

International Orders and the Sovereignty of States

I have avoided up to now discussing the problem of sovereignty in a direct way, confining my arguments to an analysis of the significance of the concept in the emergence of the European state system and stressing that 'sovereignty' only has meaning in the context of a reflexively regulated system larger than any one state. But both an abstract and substantive discussion of the sovereignty of states is called for at this point.

Sovereignty simultaneously provides an ordering principle for what is 'internal' to states and what is 'external' to them. It presumes a system of rule that is universal and obligatory in relation to the citizenry of a specified territory but from which all those who are not citizens are excluded. As Morgenthau expresses this, the sovereign authority is the supreme law-making and law-enforcing agency, these being unified.[36] Governments represent that sovereign authority as 'delegates', and this is a source of the tendencies towards polyarchy in modern states.[37]

The relation between sovereignty and the principled equality of states is much closer than is often supposed. A state cannot become sovereign except within a system of other sovereign states, its sovereignty being acknowledged by them; in this there is a strong pressure towards mutual recognition as equals, whatever the factual situation in respect of differential power. This also tends to imply a certain universality although, in fact, the global attribution of sovereignty by all states to one another dates in practice only from the conclusion of the Second World War. In the European state system the states did not recognize the authentic existence of other political communities in the way they did each other.

Of what does sovereignty consist? The following elements might be listed as most important — in effect, definitive of what sovereignty is. A sovereign state is a political organization that has the capacity, within a delimited territory or territories, to make laws and effectively sanction their up-keep; exert a monopoly over the disposal of the means of violence; control basic policies relating to the internal political or administrative form of government; and dispose of the fruits of a national economy that are the basis of its revenue.

Each of these capabilities is influenced by factors internal to states. But in view of the increasing integration of the world system since the Second World War it might be argued that they are more and more limited by states' external involvements. Indeed, it is not uncommon for the claim to be made that the nation-state is becoming progressively less important in world organization as a result of current trends. There is the multiplication of organizations that stand beyond the boundaries of states, perhaps appropriating capacities previously held by states. Also there are features of the world system refractory to the attempts of particular states to control them. These might be listed as follows:

Organizations	*Aspects of the World System*
1 Inter-governmental agencies	1 The international division of labour
2 Cartels, economic unions, transnational corporations	2 The world military order
3 Military alliances	

   The United Nations and the Common Market are two agencies that fall partly under 1 and partly under 2 in the 'Organizations' column. How they influence the sovereignty of their member states? Are either in any sense sovereign entities? In the case of the UN there is surely no real difficulty in coming to an answer. Although it is the major 'world agency', and very significant in the reflexive monitoring of the world system, the UN has not and is not making substantial inroads into the sovereignty of states. It is not a sovereign body in its own right, and the most significant impact of the UN globally has actually been towards extending states' sovereignty rather than limiting it. By contrast, it might be claimed that, although a more localized inter-governmental agency, the EEC does serve to restrict pre-existing forms of states' sovereignty. The union has the capability to frame laws which then apply in principle to the populations of the states comprised within it. In addition, agreements can be formulated between the Commission or the High Authority with other states on behalf of the member countries.

   Let us consider the authority of the EEC over member states in respect of the criteria of sovereignty mentioned above. Certain bodies of the Community do have the capacity to formulate legal principles, but these cannot really be regarded as 'laws' effective within the particular states, since they must be ratified within the parliamentary bodies of those states, which also alone possess the capability of sanctioning them. The EEC possesses no military arm and cannot reduce the capabilities of states to deploy the means of violence independently of whatever prescriptions it might make. Of course it does not follow from this that decisions of the European Parliament, executive organs or the Court of Justice will not be carried out; but these authorities do not, in this regard, hold sovereign power. It is primarily in respect of economic relations that a certain transfer of sovereignty has taken place. Even here, however, there is a two-way exchange, since member states have gained certain forms of autonomy that would otherwise have been forfeited in international trading relations in other parts of the world.

   The EEC might at some future point become a distinct and integrated super-power alongside those that currently exist. But short of some new major world conflict it is difficult to see this as more than a relatively remote possibility. As Aron observes,

> To assume that the Common Market necessarily leads to a
> European federation (or to a European federal state) is to assume
> either that economics, in our period, controls and so to speak
> encompasses politics, or that the fall of tariff barriers will of itself
> cause the fall of the political and military ones. These two
> suppositions are false. The Common Market, once completed,
> would not prevent France or Germany [or Britain!] from executing
> divergent, even opposed, actions in the Arab region or in the Far
> East. It would not put the army and the police force at the orders
> of the same men. It would leave the constitutions of these various
> nations exposed to dangers that would be, for each of them,
> different.[38]

It is, as Aron says, 'a great illusion of our times' to believe that
rapidly increasing economic and technological interdependence
— undeniably a characteristic of the world system in the period
since the Second World War — fosters a submerging of
sovereignty.

The two phenomena mentioned as 'Aspects of the World
System' on p. 282, the international division of labour and the
world military order, are much more important in influencing
states' sovereignty. States are more and more economically
interdependent, as measured by a variety of criteria relevant to
the internation division of labour. In this regard the governability
of the industrialized states (as has long been true of the more
'dependent' ones) is increasingly affected by happenings only
partly in the control of the political authorities within them.[39]

The USA is in several respects a special case, holding such a
disproportionately strong position in the world economy. But in
the other industrialized countries, including the Soviet Union and
the East European societies, there has definitely been a decline in
the capability of governments to regulate national economies.
Depressing the economy is more easy to accomplish than the
reverse; attempts to increase rates of economic growth normally
demand increased participation in the world economy, thus raising
the vulnerability to external fluctuations. It seems likely that
existing inter-governmental organizations concerned to influence
or regulate aspects of world economic activity will be further
developed and complemented by others in future years. However,
for the moment, it is not these that threaten the sovereignty of
states in a general way, even if there have been numerous

individual cases in which loans of money or development grants have been linked to political conditions. The most serious erosion of states' sovereignty in regard of their national economies is surely to be found in the immersion of these in a world economy disconnected from any sort of overall political control.

However, it is undoubtedly the world military order which is most consequential in affecting the sovereignty of states. The industrialization of war has tied military power closely to industrial strength and technological sophistication, within alliances that are no longer local but global in scope. The result, in the context of a world economy that permits the very rapid diffusion of technologically advanced weaponry and military expertise, is oddly — and perhaps catastrophically — mixed as regards states' sovereignty. Almost all states across the globe possess military strength in excess of anything that could be mounted within the largest of traditional imperial systems. Yet the super-powers, unlike any societies that have previously existed in human history, are specifically 'unconquerable' either by each other or by any conceivable military coalition of smaller states.

Their sovereignty, from this aspect, is surely greater than any individual states have ever sustained previously, although purchased at the cost of a frightful leap in the scale of the destructive power that each can unleash. Both in a generalized way and in respect of their direct influence in certain regions the existence of the super-powers, of course, limits the scope of the military strength available to other states. Countries within NATO and states elsewhere that have American military bases stationed on their territories are hardly likely to have the opportunity to forge an independent military strategy in the event of the outbreak of serious hostilities between West and East. Still less is this feasible in the case of the East European countries. As adjacent/subsidiary states to the Soviet Union, their internal political and economic policies are open to the general superintendence of that country, backed by the use of military power. Something similar is the case with states bordering the USA in Central America, and in certain other parts of the world (South Korea, Taiwan), although not in Europe. The US government, like that of the Soviet Union, maintains a strong interest in and conducts its policies with a view to protecting the internal stability of the states involved in their respective military alliances. The governability of states within these alliances, particularly in Eastern Europe, is certainly not a matter confined to internal struggles alone.

Let us, therefore, take the state socialist societies of Eastern Europe as an example. Are they sovereign states or are they not? The state socialist societies — in respect of their political form and territorial distribution — are the result of world war and are at the front line of a cold war because they were at the centre of two actual wars. Very soon after the conclusion of the Second World War it became apparent that those countries displaced from Nazi rule by the Red Army were to be moulded to Soviet-style political and economic institutions. The use of military power was essential to the process, opposition groups and those wishing to adopt liberal democratic institutions being systematically repressed through the use of force. Perceived strategic interests played a more important role than internal political organizations in determining which states were actually compelled to follow this model, as the difference between East Germany and Austria demonstrates. If elections had been allowed in the Soviet Zone of Germany immediately after the war, there can be little doubt that they would have produced fairly similar results to those held under the four-power occupation of Austria. 'East Germany' most probably would not exist at all, or would be a 'capitalist' rather than a 'state socialist' society. In the years directly following the Second World War, treaties of mutual assistance signed between the Soviet Union and the East European states, and among the East European states, were bilateral. The Warsaw Pact, like NATO, was stimulated by tensions associated with the Korean War, and integrated the Eastern bloc military organization under Soviet command. In contrast to the NATO countries, however, the Soviet Union has a monopoly of nuclear weapons within its military coalition and there is no general staff of the Western type.

Given all this, it would still be difficult to deny that the East European states are sovereign units in terms of the criteria previously specified, separate administratively from the Soviet Union and from one another. Their autonomy is more confined than that of most other nation-states but nation-states they certainly remain. Each possesses armed forces that, if they could do little to resist a Soviet offensive against them, retain loyalties to their particular states. The part played by the Hungarian army in the events of 1956, or even the role of the army in Poland much more recently, which almost certainly pre-empted Soviet armed intervention, indicate that subordination to Soviet overall control is far from complete. That the national armies of the East European states have a lower profile within the military strategy of the Warsaw Pact than the West European states within NATO partly reflects the economic inferiority of the former as compared to the latter, but also the fact that the loyalty of those armies to certain forms of Soviet manoeuvre would be questionable.

The limitations upon the autonomy of the East European states are mainly military in origin and are an extreme example of what is common throughout the nation-state system. Contrary to views sometimes advanced in political science, sovereignty is not indivisible, but regularly and characteristically shaped by the geo-political position of states, their respective military strength and, to a lesser degree, their situation in the international division of labour. The sovereign power of the East European states is confined by their proximity to the Soviet Union, in the historical context of their mutual experience of war. The sovereignty of, say, many of the post-colonial states may be limited both by a relatively low level of internal administrative control and by external economic dependence. But in these cases as in Eastern Europe, we still confront nation-states holding a high degree of sovereign power — certainly compared with segmental, class-divided societies existing in a world of frontiers rather than borders.

Capitalism, Industrialism and the State System

At this point I shall draw together in a systematic way some of the main arguments developed in this book thus far. There are two general interpretations of the nature of the current world system that tend to dominate the literature. One consists of Marxist or *Marxisant* accounts of the spread of capitalism, the other the type of theory favoured by many specialists in international relations, according to which the world is populated by state 'actors' pursuing their goals partly in co-operation and partly in conflict with one another. The two models in fact barely touch. In the

Marxist perspective, states appear as mechanisms of class domination or of the facilitating of the overall development of capitalist enterprise, but their territoriality remains essentially unexplicated. In the second view, the territorial character of states is given primacy of place, the geo-political involvements of state 'actors' being regarded as the chief origin of the influences shaping the development of the world system. From this standpoint, the transformations brought about by the expansion of capitalistic enterprise form only a vague background to the activities of states.

Each of these two standpoints is intrinsically defective, because each fails to cope with what the other demonstrates to be important; but both have further shortcomings as well. Marxist discussions do not satisfactorily separate capitalism and industrialism, thus often misinterpreting even some of the more sheerly economic trends shaping the modern world. Theorists of international relations, relatively unconcerned with what goes on inside states, tend to underestimate the significance of internal struggles that influence external policies. Everyone acknowledges that to treat a state as an actor is a simplifying notion, designed to help make sense of the complexities of the relations between states. But what is only a theoretical model is all too often given a real significance, obscuring the fact that governments cannot be equated with states (as nation-states) and that policy decisions within governments usually emanate from highly contested arenas of social life. Recognition of the specifically political and military involvements of states should not necessitate a relapse into such a conceptually limited stance. On the other hand, acknowledgement of the fundamental impact of capitalism in influencing global patterns of change from the sixteenth century onwards should not mean ignoring the role of the geo-political involvements of states.

The connections between the emergence and spread of capitalism, industrialism and the nation-state system can be spelled out in the following way. Capitalistic enterprise first became prominent within a diversified state system already distinctively different from traditional state forms. The existence of such states supplied certain preconditions for the early development of capitalism beyond its most rudimentary expressions including, internally, the formation of frameworks of law, fiscal guarantees and an increasingly pacified social environment allowing 'non-coercive' economic exchange to flourish. The extension of capitalistic enterprise into parts of the world outside Europe was 'built in' to its development in so far as, being an 'insulated' type of economic activity geared to manufacture in competitive markets, capitalism flowed across frontiers and borders. However, the consolidation of a world capitalist economy was everywhere accompanied by the use of force, in contexts in which European weaponry and military discipline enjoyed a dramatic superiority. Colonialism, in its various forms, cannot be regarded as merely a disguised mode of capitalistic expansion, but certainly for the most part tended to assist such expansion.

Industrialism first emerged within the institutional nexus of capitalism, whose competitive pressures served in substantial part to generate it. It was only with the coming of industrialism that the European states became fully fledged nation-states, in the manner in which I have defined that term. The development of industrial capitalism strengthened the position of the 'core' states within an expanding world system, just as renewed processes of colonial conquest served to create an underprivileged 'South' loosely integrated into it. Nation-states are more like 'actors' than traditional states ever were, for a combination of reasons. They are clearly bounded administrative unities, in which policies adopted by governments are binding upon whole populations. As involved in a system of states, reflexively monitored by all, each government constantly negotiates with others in reaching such decisions. Like other organizations, states also have legally defined 'personalities' in which they are represented as equivalent to individual agents. But the 'actor-like' qualities of modern states have to be understood in terms of the specific characteristics of the nation-state rather than being taken as a pre-given baseline for the study of international relations.

The core countries of the West and Japan remain 'capitalist states', although their 'welfare capitalism' is very different from its nineteenth-century antecedents. Neither the fact of their statehood nor the particular geo-political distribution of powers that exists today can be 'derived' from their capitalistic character. Their involvement within an international division of labour of increasing complexity is obviously highly relevant to short- and longer-term policies pursued by their governments, but is far from exhaustively accounting for those policies. Of course, states are not the only organizations involved in the extension of the international division of labour. The insulation of the political and the economic has from the beginning involved an external dimension — the separation of the political power of states from economic activities of commercial agencies and business firms. Some of these, of course, were essentially outposts of colonizing states, but by and large this separation has been an elemental and persisting feature of the world capitalist economy. The largest of the modern transnational corporations today have annual budgets greater than the majority of states and maintain direct relations with governments through the equivalents of ministries and corps of diplomats. In the light of this, some have suggested that the transnational corporations threaten the predominant importance of nation-states in the world system. However nation-states control the whole of the habitable area of the globe, and as corporations have to exist somewhere, they must in the last resort either take power in a state or become subject to one. Whatever the influence the largest firms might have had over the policies of states, none has taken the former course of action. With good reason — business corporations do not, as nation-states do, have at their disposal control of the means of violence. As is perhaps worth stressing once more, the separation of military from economic institutions in the development of the European nation-state has been as fraught with consequences for subsequent world history as the separation of political and economic power. Although there is no 'logical' reason why modern business firms cannot turn themselves into armed predators, as some of the old trading companies used to be, the dominance of the nation-state today more or less precludes that possibility.

Following the classification of institutional dimensions given earlier in this chapter, I hold that the world system should be seen as influenced by several primary sets of processes, each in some part independent of the others. These are processes associated with the nation-state system, co-ordinated through global networks of information exchange, the world capitalist economy, and the world military order.

In analysing the development of the nation-state system from its origins in Europe to its current pre-eminence as a political order, I have sought to question the idea that there is a direct trade-off between the sovereignty of states and growing inter-dependencies in the world system. It is often supposed that, beginning in the European state system, modern states up to a certain point in history developed an increasing range of sovereign capacities as distinct political units. However — so this view holds — the world system has now become so tightly knit that international connections come more and more to overshadow the administrative capabilities of states. This is the basis of the thesis that in recent times we see an increasing loss of sovereign power on the part of nation-states, of all sizes and types, such that in the relatively near future the nation-state will become less and less of a significant phenomenon in global organization.[40] I regard this idea as misleading both in the analysis it offers and in the conclusion drawn. The emergence of 'sovereign states' did depend substantially upon a series of changes internal to those states. But from the early origins of the European state system these involved each individual state in a reflexively monitored order that was the condition of the achievement of a 'bordered' territory. The global reach of capitalism and the colonial entanglements of states helped extend those monitoring processes world-wide. Never-theless, until the end of the Second World War the nation-state was not a universal political form. Its becoming such is something inherently connected with, and in substantial degree an outcome of, those very transnational connections that have seemed to many to signal its imminent demise. Without the UN and a host of other inter-governmental organizations the nation-state would not be the global form of political ordering that it has become. The influence of particular states within world politics may wax or wane. But we should not imagine that the centralizing of global connections on the one hand, and the sovereignty of states on the other, are always mutually exclusive.

The territoriality of nation-states reflects a genuine internal administrative unity and it is hardly surprising that boundary disputes, or incursions of one state across territory claimed by another, are serious matters. Unlike in the case of traditional states, a threat to a segment of the territory of a modern state is a potential challenge to its administrative and cultural integrity, no matter how barren or 'useless' that segment of territory may be. Since states exist in an environment of other states, 'power politics' have inevitably been a fundamental element of the geo-political make-up of the state system. Given, however, that the inter-state arena has never been a 'Hobbesian condition' of anarchy, 'power politics' has consistently been complemented by other techniques or strategies, and cannot be said in some way to disclose the essence of states' relations with one another.

The influence of capitalism on the development of the state system has been, and is, of a double kind. The economically most developed states are capitalistic, this inevitably strongly affecting the policies followed by their governmental agencies. State officials recognize that government revenue depends upon the prosperity of business enterprise, which in turn places constraints over feasible options available to them. Class relations and class struggles also strongly influence policy decisions, in a direct way internally and in more diffuse fashion externally. Not only capitalist states, however, but all states are involved in an international division of labour dominated by capitalistic mechanisms — the world capitalist economy. This has as one of its axes the relations of 'unequal exchange' between core and peripheral countries. There is no doubt that Marxist authors have contributed more than those from any rival tradition of thought to understanding these relations. Where their accounts have been offered as theories of 'imperialism', nonetheless, strong reservations should be entered about them. The economic connections involved result often, even characteristically, from policies motivated by non-economic considerations.

Industrialism has proved exportable from the confines of the capitalistic orders within which it originally developed. The existence of a 'Second World' of state socialism is predicated upon the removal of industrial production from its direct involvement with a capitalist framework of enterprise. Other less industrialized states in the Third World, of course, have also instituted forms of command economy. None of these countries, not even the Soviet Union, is more than partly sheltered from influences deriving from the dominance of capitalistic mechanisms world-wide. The fact that the USA and the Soviet Union — each at the centre of a complex of political and military alliances — are at the same time the exemplars of contrasting modes of economic organization might again encourage the assumption that the underlying dynamics of the world system are economic. Such a view lies at no great remove from the notion that, if only capitalism were to disappear, divisions of interests between states would do so as well. Nothing in the experience of the state socialist countries suggests that there is anything to commend this idea, connected as it is to some of the characteristic themes of nineteenth-century social theory.

The industrialization of war conjoined science to technological research in such a way to concentrate weapons development in the more economically advanced states. This initially reinforced the position of those states in the world at large, and today places the USA and the Soviet Union at the centre of weapons development globally, as well as in chronic competition with one another militarily. But while virtually all military research and development takes place in the advanced industrialized countries, the world-wide distribution of armed forces and weaponry does not correspond directly to the conventional global divisions. There is effectively no Third World in respect of military forces. With the exception of the diffusion of nuclear weapons (and how much longer will this remain exceptional?) virtually all modern states are 'First World' states in one sense — they possess the material and organizational means of waging industrialized war.

11
Modernity, Totalitarianism and Critical Theory

In his speech of acceptance for the Nobel Literary prize in the late 1950s, Camus observed that those

> born at the outset of World War I became twenty at the time both of Hitler's ascent to power and of the first revolutionary trial. Then, to complete their education, they were confronted in turn by the Spanish Civil War and World War Two — the universal concentration camp, a Europe of torture and prisons. Today they must raise their children and produce their work in a world threatened by nuclear destruction. Nobody, surely, can expect them to be optimists.[1]

Those children are now adults and there is no reason for them to feel any less sombre about the world in which they have come to maturity than Camus imagined. Yet the core traditions of social theory still stand at a large distance from the world, not only in respect of analysing its nature but, just as important, in respect of developing plausible accounts of alternatives.

Of the four institutional orders of modernity distinguished earlier in the book, only two have received sustained attention within the social sciences. Marxism has concentrated above all upon the interpretation of the past development and potential future transformations of capitalism giving prime place to class conflict as a medium of social change. There have been many discussions and critiques of the impact of industrialism generally, and of technology more particularly, upon social life in the contemporary world. But, with some notable exceptions, neither the expanded role of surveillance, nor the altered nature of military power with the development of the means of waging industrialized war have been made central to formulations of social theory. In this concluding chapter I shall consider some of the implications of these phenomena for problems of social analysis in the late twentieth century. Camus's remarks were motivated in some part both by a certain repugnance towards modernity in general and by an awareness of the dangers of totalitarian political power in particular. Totalitarianism, I shall claim, is a tendential property of the modern state. An understanding of the origins of totalitarianism, as a specifically twentieth-century phenomenon, presumes analysing the consolidated political power generated by a merging of developed techniques of surveillance and the technology of industrialized war. Looming behind this is the question of the relation between states and the deployment of military power in current times — not just as an analytical issue but as a problem for normative political theory. How might the monopoly of the means of violence on the part of states be reconciled with established political ideas of the 'good society'? I shall first of all consider the nature of totalitarian political rule, moving from there to a discussion of the tensions associated with the impact of modernity and thence to the question of a 'normative theory of political violence'.

Totalitarianism: Surveillance and Violence

The history of the term 'totalitarian' is well-known, even if the concept itself is one of the most fiercely debated in political theory. When Gentile spoke of '*uno stato totalitario*' on behalf of Mussolini, he can have had little idea of the uses to which the term would later be put, or the controversies in which it would figure. The word was first coined as one carrying a favourable connotation in respect of the political order to which it referred, at a period when Mussolini was still advocating freedom of the press, accepting the existence of other parties and favouring a competitive market economy. 'Totalitarian' began to be used in critical attacks upon Italian fascism in the late 1920s, when opposition parties were brutally suppressed, all trade unions except state-sponsored ones abolished, the Chamber of Deputies dissolved and concentration camps set up, with the death penalty being instituted for political offences.

Since then the concept has undergone numerous vicissitudes.

It has been applied to movements, parties, leaders and ideas, as well as more commonly to political systems.[2] States or governments that have been labelled totalitarian include above all fascist Italy, Nazi Germany and Stalin's Soviet Union, but also Russia under the Czars, a range of traditional states, especially Egypt and Rome, absolutist states, and fictional societies like Plato's republic. Small wonder that the notion has been called 'a conceptual harlot of uncertain parentage, belonging to no-one but at the service of all'.[3] Amid the welter of usages there are some general lines of agreement accepted by many writers. Most argue that totalitarianism is, in fully developed form at any rate, recent in origin, dating from about the time at which the term itself was invented. The concept is usually taken to be above all a political one, referring to a mode of organizing political power, involving its extreme concentration in pursuit of objectives defined by a narrowly circumscribed leadership. Friedrich's definition is the one perhaps most often quoted in the literature. Totalitarianism, he says, is distinct 'from other and older autocracies' and from 'Western-type democracies'. It has six characteristics: '(1) a totalist ideology; (2) a single party committed to this ideology and usually led by one man, the dictator; (3) a fully developed secret police; and three kinds of monopoly or, more precisely, monopolistic control: namely that of (a) mass communications; (b) operational weapons; (c) all organisations, including economic ones.'[4]

The contrast between totalitarianism and 'Western-type democracies' is of key importance in explaining the popularity of the concept in the period since the Second World War. Totalitarian states were regarded by liberal political observers as including those forms of social order that have an advanced industrial base, but do not display the institutional characteristics of liberal democracy. Whereas when referring to Italy or Germany totalitarianism designated a relatively transitory phase in social development — terminated by war — in the case of the Soviet Union and the East European countries it was used to refer to a definite type of socio-political order separate from the capitalist states, continuing as long as that order remained in existence. Applied as a characteristic of the East European states, 'totalitarian' refers to a political system supposedly displaying the characteristics mentioned by Friedrich. The USSR and the state socialist societies are portrayed as monolithic systems of political power, founded upon cultural and social conformity deriving from the suppression of interest divisions. This standpoint is often linked to an equation of Marxist socialism with authoritarianism, producing an all-pervasive state, subordinating the needs or wishes of the populace to the arbitrary policies of the state authorities. Collectivism, as Belloc observed, may stem from noble motives, but leads in practice to omnipotent state power. 'The capitalist state breeds a collectivist theory which *in action* produces something utterly different from collectivism: to wit, the servile state.'[5]

If this type of view is correct, totalitarianism cannot be regarded as a phenomenon that could potentially come about in all modern states. It is a type of rule associated with fascist and Soviet-type societies, that could only come into being in liberal democratic states if they succumbed to collectivism. Two questions therefore arise. How far does it make any sense to describe the Soviet Union and the Eastern European states in the terms listed by Friedrich? Do these characteristics, once identified, bear close comparison with episodes of fascism in Europe and elsewhere? For we should accept, I think, that totalitarianism is a different phenomenon to the forms of autocracy found in traditional states.

Examining the history of the USSR, it is evident that Friedrich's formulation applies most closely to the period of Stalin's rule, not so readily either to the early phase of development of the state or to the years since Stalin's death. Lenin came to power in a country surrounded by hostile states, in circumstances of persistent civil war, where there was strong resistance from counter-revolutionary forces. Many of the measures Lenin took were repressive by any standards. But, in spite of his advocacy of the 'vanguard party', it would be disingenuous to see Marxist-Leninism in its early phase as a 'totalist ideology', since it acknowledged and tolerated a variety of factions and organizations. The nascent Soviet Union was far, indeed, from conforming to the last three criteria Friedrich mentions, since the control of the political centre over the more far-flung areas of the country was tenuous and economic activity was still quite highly decentralized.[6] In addition, Lenin became concerned near the end of his life with the threat posed by the influence of the secret police, originally taken over and modified from the organization left by his Tsarist predecessors, and took steps to transform it into an agency that would deal only with espionage and serious threats of counter-revolution.

Since the middle 1950s, the Soviet regime has become discernably and self-consciously more relaxed, breaking with its Stalinist past. Friedrich now perforce recognizes the significance of this, seeking, however, to incorporate it within his analysis by emphasizing that, in common with autocratic states of the past, totalitarianism experiences 'notable ups and downs' in the level of its intensity. Stalinism was a particularly marked period of the intensification of totalitarian techniques of government, followed by changes which, however, did not alter the essential nature of the regime. 'The cycle seems to go forward to an extreme followed by an, at times, radical reversal, a return to the original state, and a resumption of the cycle.'[7] The changes occurring after Kruschev's period of leadership can thus be explained in terms of inherent features of the system, which remains totalitarian in its basic institutions. Even in the most extreme years of Stalinist oppression, 'total control' is not achieved in the party or in respect of the population at large; softening of the more brutal forces of rule is conditioned by the recognition that some amount of latitude must be allowed to the mass of the population to follow their own paths of activity. Friedrich thus back-tracks in some part upon his earlier views. But this modified account is not particularly plausible. It is much more convincing to hold that totalitarianism, as he portrays the phenomenon, is not a concept designating an overall type of society — namely that found in the USSR and Eastern Europe — but refers most appropriately to a definite aspect of their experience, namely, Stalinism. It is during Stalin's ascendancy that internal political processes in the USSR most directly and strikingly resemble those in fascist Italy and Nazi Germany. Each of these involves the characteristics set out by Friedrich, but in addition is marked by a reign of terror, using the concerted application of force in pursuit of its designated objectives. Although this does not appear in his original definition, it is implicit perhaps in the mention of the role of the secret police, and is in later writings accorded more direct discussion by the author. As Arendt, Neumann and others do, it is surely right to emphasize the significance of terror, which is somehow involved on an elementary level in totalitarianism.

If we compare, not Soviet-type society to liberal-democratic capitalism as a whole, but Stalinism, Nazism and Italian fascism, both in their theory and in their practice, we find some marked similarities. These for the most part do indeed tend to involve the points mentioned by Friedrich. In each case a dictatorial ruler shaped pre-existing symbolic systems into a consolidated ideological basis of rule, accompanied by the pervasive use of coercion to suppress dissidence. Italian fascism was by far the least murderous of the three. The secret police force OVRA was specifically established in the late 1920s to dissolve internal political opposition, with heavy political censorship imposed upon antagonistic groups. Nonetheless, in the 1930s some 20,000 people in Italy were arraigned before special courts and 10,000 imprisoned without trial. As in the other states, in Italy the law was personalized, giving the individual ruler a range of sanctions at his disposal for the control of recalcitrants. Thus, in 1926, Mussolini was accorded the right to issue legally binding decrees, many thousands of which were promulgated during the course of his rule. As the Supreme Leader of the Soviets, Stalin was able personally to dominate many aspects of overall state policy. The Enabling Act of 1933 in Germany gave Hitler, as Chancellor, the right to make laws for a certain period without the need for ratification.[8] In each country the 'total ideology' of which Friedrich speaks was based upon a strong stimulation of nationalism, stressing radical distinctions between the national community and 'out-groups', and associated with the figure of the leader. Party organization was also constructed around affiliation to the leader, this affiliation again being couched in the language of a self-sufficient nationalism.

The use of terror marked all three regimes, although loss of life was much lower in Italy than in the case of the other two states. Terror was justified by appeals to national unity and to the involvement of the mass of the people in the governmental system. 'The German people', according to Hitler, 'has elected a single deputy as its representative with 38 million votes . . . I feel myself just as responsible to the German people as would any parliament.'[9] In Italy it needed more than four years to effectively suppress other political parties, but in Germany this was accomplished in an immediate and radical fashion, with mass imprisonment and the building of large concentration camps. By the outbreak of the War, there were in Germany over a quarter of a million people imprisoned for political reasons and three times this number by the end of the hostilities. During this period possibly as many as twelve million people were systematically exterminated. If these figures are staggering, they were probably surpassed in the Soviet Union during Stalin's rule. In the purges some one million people lost their lives and some twelve million more died in the labour camps; perhaps some twenty million people died as a direct result of the use of violence as a means of political repression during the whole period of Stalin's ascendancy.[10] In the Soviet Union, like Germany, the labour camps made a major contribution to the country's performance in the war. Twenty per cent of the country's railways were constructed by workers from the camps and 75 per cent of the gold mined was extracted by such workers. But in neither case was the rationale for the existence of the camps more than marginally economic.[11]

In all three societies, the systematic use of violence was combined with the use of networks of secret police, having extensive and frequently employed powers of arrest for political transgressions, these phenomena being closely connected with rigid state direction of cultural activity.[12] The widespread use of terror, according to Arendt, tends to be integrated with strict control over cultural production, because the point of the threat of violence is not so much to instil fear as to create a climate in which acceptance of propaganda will be facilitated.

> [When] Stalin decided to rewrite the history of the Russian Revolution, the propaganda of his new version consisted in destroying, together with the older books and documents, their authors and readers: the publication in 1938 of a new official history of the Communist Party was the signal that the superpurge which had decimated a whole generation of Soviet intellectuals had come to an end. Similarly, the Nazis in the Eastern occupied territories at first used chiefly antisemitic propaganda to win former control of the population. They neither needed nor used terror to support this propaganda. When they liquidated the greater part of the Polish intelligentsia, they did it not because of its opposition, but because according to their doctrine Poles had no intellect, and when they planned to kidnap blue-eyed and blond-haired children, they did not intend to frighten the population, but to save 'Germanic blood'.[13]

This does not imply, she adds, that in totalitarianism terror is secondary to the regimented control of cultural production. On the contrary, terror continues to be used by totalitarian regimes even when a population, or the relevant section of the population, is completely quiescent. Terror is, as it were, the very medium of government. This seems valid from one respect, but questionable from another. Having been used to subdue certain social groupings, or to secure particular policies, the orchestrated use of violence tends to continue just as before. On the other hand, in each of the three examples, the acquiescence of the majority was not purchased through the use of force against them, or even by the dissemination of propaganda. All three regimes, particularly their leaders, secured a considerable level of active and enthusiastic support from diverse sectors of the population. The student of totalitarianism must explain this as well as the role of terror in mobilizing subject populations for the doctrines advocated by the state authorities. Of course, mass support was in some part fostered by programmes carefully orchestrated to achieve that end. For example, the National Socialists gave a great deal of attention to planning the leisure activities of the population in order to develop the spirit of national unity they deemed desirable and proper. All manner of types of communal recreation were organized through local party cadres, under central direction.[14] But the enthusiasm with which much of the population embraced the Nazi cause and expressed active support for their leader can hardly be accounted for entirely by such programmes.

Let me sum up at this point where the preceding comments lead. I consider Friedrich's concept of totalitarianism to be accurate and useful. Totalitarianism is not characteristic of traditional states, but only of nation-states and nation-states in relatively recent times at that; its main features can be represented according to Friedrich's criteria. But 'totalitarian' is not an adjective that can be fruitfully applied to a type of state, let alone to Soviet-style states generically. It refers rather to a *type of rule*, unstable in major aspects, yet capable of bringing about the most horrendous consequences for the populations that suffer the brunt of its concentrated power. Totalitarianism is, thus far at least, a phenomenon associated mainly with Italian fascism, Nazism and Stalinism, but there are other examples which fall into the same category — for example, the brief rule of Pol Pot in Kampuchea. While, of course, there are major differences between all these examples, they share very important threads in common. These common characteristics relate to features of the modern state in general; there is no type of nation-state in the contemporary world which is completely immune from the potentiality of being subject to totalitarian rule.[15]

To analyse the nature of totalitarianism, we have to retrace a path through some of the main arguments of this book. Nation-states differ in a fundamental way from traditional ones in respect of the maximizing of surveillance which, in combination with internal pacification, generates an administrative unity corresponding to definite borders. Totalitarianism cannot exist in traditional states because their segmental character is incompatible with the necessary mobilization of concentrated resources. Several of the features of totalitarian control are present in some traditional states, but not in the same overall combination with one another. Thus what Friedrich calls a 'totalist ideology' is almost the norm rather than the exception in class-divided societies. The confinement of literacy to small groupings of the population, the typical fusion of theocracy and military power, allied to the absence of a 'public sphere' in the modern sense, usually make for the dominance of a confined symbolic culture. But this cannot become effective 'propaganda' so far as the majority of the subject population are concerned, since it is not possible for the state authorities to ensure that it is systematically channelled to the mass. Secret police are common in traditional states, but normally the scope of their influence is limited to the locales of the elite and of government officialdom. Terror, in the sense of the large-scale use of violence to subdue or intimidate subject groups, particularly conquered populations, is exceedingly common in the pages of history. But in the scale of historical massacres and brutalities there is nothing that can more than remotely match the degradations of totalitarianism.

The possibilities of totalitarian rule depend upon the existence of societies in which the state can successfully penetrate the day-to-day activities of most of its subject population. This, in turn, presumes a high level of surveillance, based upon the conditions analysed previously — the coding of information about and the supervision of the conduct of significant segments of the population. Totalitarianism is, first of all, an extreme focusing of surveillance, devoted to the securing of political ends deemed by the state authorities to demand urgent political mobilization. Surveillance tends to become concentrated (a) in respect of a multiplication of modes of the documenting of the subject population by the state — identity cards, permits of all sorts, and other kinds of official papers, have to be held by all members of the population and used to follow even the most ordinary of activities; and (b) this is the basis of an expanded supervision of those activities, carried out by the police or their agents.

The ends to which totalitarian rule is mobilized tend to be strongly involved with nationalism, since nationalist sentiments offer the prime ideological means of binding together otherwise diverse populations. Nationalism is important in supplying the 'total' aspect of totalitarian doctrines because it carries its own 'symbolic historicity', providing a myth of origins of a people, but also supplying the people with a common destiny to be striven for in the future. Fascist thought tends to draw upon those elements of nationalist ideals that make up the aggressive, exclusivist side of the nationalist Janus. Marxism, as its critics have long pointed out, can readily be adapted to messianic goals and is the *locus classicus* of historicity conceived of as linking the past to an immanent future. But Stalinism, nonetheless, involves a considerable admixture of nationalist thought, to which the notion of 'socialism in one country' was admirably suited. Whether linked with Marxist-Leninism or not, nationalism lends itself readily to mass propaganda, since the fate of the whole community is considered to be a shared one.

Elements of Totalitarian Rule

1   *Focusing of surveillance* as:
    (a) information coding, documentation of activities of the population
    (b) supervision of activities, intensified policing
2   *'Moral totalism'*: fate of the political community as embedded in the historicity of the people
3   *Terror*: maximizing of police power, allied to disposal of the means of waging industrialized war and sequestration

4   *Prominence of leader figure*: appropriation of power by leader depending not upon a professionalized military role, but the generation of mass support.

Surveillance involving the use of intensified policing rapidly tends to dissolve into terror, for fairly self-evident reasons. The most obvious one — although arguably the least consequential — is that policing tends to become allied to the application of methods of torture to obtain confessions, in contexts in which crimes involve the holding of deviant political views, rather than involving specified infractions of the law. Much more important are the capabilities of police or paramilitary forces to deploy the technology of industrialized war against an unarmed or poorly armed population. Tanks, mortars, machine-guns deployed with reference to a civilian population, even if presented as a threat rather than actually put to use, can for policing purposes allow a temporary physical control of populations well in excess of anything that could be accomplished in traditional states. This is especially true if the means of violence are focused upon particular groupings in those populations, rather than being used as an instrument of government of the overall political community. When combined with methods of sequestration already well pioneered in other contexts of deviance, the concentrated application of the use of force against minority groupings can become extremely intense. The term 'concentration camp' already carries this meaning and is the most 'total' of 'total institutions', thus being the prototype of totalitarian terror. Terror here, as Arendt says, is not concerned with the causing of fear for its own sake, but rather expresses the extremity of the 'deviance' attributed to those interned, from which the majority outside needs to be protected.

A key aspect of totalitarianism, without which the rest would not be possible, or at least would not be unified into a cohesive system of rule, is the presence of the leader figure. The leader abrogates powers previously belonging to the law courts, political assemblies, or separate state officials. This can be achieved partly on the basis of the use of terror, purging those who disagree with particular policies or who might in some way be a source of resistance to them. But a high level of personal affiliation to the leader on the part of the police and the military is also demanded, as well as the active support of large segments of the general population. For my thesis, as against that of Arendt, is not that terror is the prime basis of rule of totalitarianism, but that mass support generates the political leverage within which terror can be used against categories of 'deviants'. An explanation of the role of the leader figure in totalitarian rule can be found in the general discussion of nationalism offered earlier. The three main examples of developed totalitarian rule all originated in the shadow of a war that has recently ended and of the build-up to another shortly to begin. In their rise to power the individuals concerned, and the party organizations they headed, exploited this unsettled atmosphere in the rhetoric they produced. In such circumstances, as the Le Bon/Freud psychological theory of leadership suggests, there is a strong tendency to identify with leader figures, on the basis of regressive features of personality.[16] The mass of the population is likely to become vulnerable to the influence of sumbols propagated by the leader figure, in whom an exaggerated trust is maintained in spite of the punitive policies the leader might impose. The messianic quality that often characterizes upsurges of nationalistic sentiment here becomes attributed in an extreme form to a demogogic leader, trusted because of his very authoritarianism not in spite of it. Regressive identification with a leader figure leads to a partial suspension of independent moral judgements that individuals in other circum-stances might make, there being an affectively based acceptance on the leader's judgements. Individuals become 'suggestible', in Le Bon's term, to whatever the leader judges to be right and proper. Militancy associated with reliance on the leader figure tends to be coupled with a strong psychological affiliation to an 'in-group', which the leader symbolizes, together with an extreme rejection of 'out-groups', which fail to possess the special qualities that bind leader and followership together.[17]

In spite of its name, totalitarianism is not an all-or-nothing phenomenon and has direct links to a range of less cataclysmic potentialities of modern states. Let me briefly indicate these, moving from 4 to 1 in the preceding characterization of totalitarian rule. So far as point 4 goes, the issue concerns that of the possibility of personalized rule in modern states. Such a form of domination was prototypical of traditional states, there only having been two known exceptions to it — Classical Greece and the Roman Republic. The existence of 'dictatorships' today has to be understood against a background of universal acknowledgement of polyarchy. A fairly high degree of personalizing of leadership can appear in all polyarchic systems, as Weber pointed out and indeed actively advocated as desirable. What he called 'charisma' probably rests upon the very psychological dynamics of leadership just discussed, in so far as personalized leadership is able to generate mass support. Personalized leadership may, of course, be associated with military government. An individual achieves political power not through available electoral mechanisms, but through its seizure by the armed forces, of which that individual is either the overall commander or rises to prominence within the ruling military cabinet. Such rulers may become 'dictators' in the sense that, controlling the means of violence, they are able to impose a range of policies upon a largely recalcitrant population, at least for a certain period of time. But given the difficulties inherent in sustaining military government, 'dictatorship' of this sort is not likely to persist unless the individual in question is able to generate widespread commitment among a considerable section of the civilian population.

By far the most common circumstance in which strongly personalized rule emerges is where a government is established as a result of the influence of a social movement — again indicating the importance of 'charisma'. Such was the case in each of the three major circumstances of totalitarian rule, the conditions giving rise to the movements involved no doubt also influencing the strength of the personal affiliations the leaders were able to achieve. Stalin was the 'inheritor' of the mantle of Lenin, but was able to sustain a style of personalized leadership because the impetus of the changes initiated by the October Revolution were still strong, Lenin having died too soon after his assumption of government for there to have begun a full-scale process of the routinization of charisma. Since the influence of social movements in the political life of modern nations is bound to remain marked, in the light of the 'fields of historicity' afforded by modern culture, personalized leadership is certain to remain a prominent feature of the political life of many states.

It is partly the association of the charismatic leader with a social movement achieving governmental power that explains why the fostering of terror becomes a possibility. Social movements are dynamic modes of association, concerned to mobilize change in accordance with convictions that do not necessarily allow much space for alternative opinions. The 'moral leverage' which a popular leader is able to achieve over a followership, combined with control of modern instruments of violence, generates repressive capabilities of a very formidable kind indeed. Since the French Revolution, terror has been associated particularly with the activities of post-revolutionary regimes and continues to be so in the twentieth-century world. But on a more minor scale it has to be regarded as an ever-present possibility within modern political systems wherever there are acute problems of governability. Here the issues involved merge with some of those raised by considering the internal role of armed force confronting the pacified populations of nation-states. Policing based upon the pervasive use of violence, supported by paramilitary forces or the army, is in principle a possibility within states of all types. Its importance in the modern state raises questions of political theory concerned with control of the means of violence generally, and these I shall consider in a following section.

'Moral totalism' I connect particularly with the pervasive influence of historicism in the culture of modernity. In the sphere of politics it is most particularly associated with nationalist doctrines in the modern world but, in a more general way, relates back to the influence of social movements. To talk of 'totalism' here does not imply acceptance of the sort of thesis advanced by Talmon and others, which traces tendencies towards totalitarianism to the generalized influence of doctrines regarding the 'popular will' as the arbiter of political organization. The overall significance of polyarchy in modern states is not unrelated to totalitarianism — in my formulation of the concept rather than that employed by Talmon — because polyarchic involvement in political systems provides for possibilities of mass mobilization otherwise precluded.[18] But the 'totalizing' effect of symbol systems depends mainly upon how far they can be appropriated in such a way as to couple historicity with a hostile attitude towards 'out-groups'. Marxism can be utilized in this fashion, as can various other streams of modern thought which nominally are quite opposed to any vision of totalitarian rule. But, like nationalism, Marxism is Janus-faced and can fuel the most radical critiques of totalizing doctrines.

These problems have been much discussed in the literature of political science, however, and it is upon the influence of surveillance that I want to concentrate most attention. The essential importance of surveillance as a medium of power has not been grasped within either liberal or socialist traditions of political theory. In both cases this is bound up with the same emphases that tend to obstruct a satisfactory account of the control of the means of violence in influencing social organization and social change. Economic exchange is taken to be the elementary binding force in modern societies. In socialism in general, and Marxism in particular, oppressive forms of rule are examined in relation to class dynamics and in some sense or another — directly or indirectly — traced to the impact of class domination. Marx's celebrated analysis of Bonapartism is a case in point. The 'autocratic power' that the state developed under Louis Bonaparte is explained as originating in the 'balance' between contending classes which allowed the state apparatus to step in.[19] Subsequent Marxist authors have gone through all sorts of conceptual contortions to acknowledge the administrative power of the state while still finding its origins in class domination.[20] For liberal writers on the other hand, state power is associated particularly with bureaucracy, bureaucratic regulation being necessary to co-ordinate the economic framework of a complex division of labour.

Neither of these traditions of thought places surveillance, or the mechanisms of control of 'deviance' associated with the administrative consolidation of the modern state, as central. Surveillance may interact in various ways with class domination but, as has been previously stressed, is certainly not derivative of it. Bureaucracy involves forms of surveillance activity, in both senses of surveillance. But the themes upon which most writers (including Weber) have concentrated when analysing bureaucratic administration tend to marginalize those with which I am principally concerned here. Bureaucratic power, as conceived of by Weber at any rate, is the power of the expert and the specialized official. The problem of surveillance, in the overall context of the nation-state, is rather different.

The expansion of surveillance in the modern political order, in combination with the policing of 'deviance', radically transforms the relation between state authority and the governed population, compared with traditional states. Administrative power now increasingly enters into the minutiae of daily life and the most intimate of personal actions and relationships. In an age more and more invaded by electronic modes of the storage, collation and dissemination of information, the possibilities of accumulating information relevant to the practice of government are almost endless. Control of information, within modern, pacified states with very rapid systems of communication, transportation and sophisticated techniques of sequestration, can be directly integrated with the supervision of conduct in such a way as to produce a high concentration of state power. Surveillance is the necessary condition of the administrative power of states, whatever ends this power be turned to. It is not only intimately connected with polyarchy, but more specifically with the actualization of citizenship rights.[21] Consider, for example, economic rights. The provision of welfare cannot be organized or funded unless there is a close and detailed monitoring of many characteristics of the lives of the population, regardless of whether they are actually welfare recipients or not. All such information thus collected is a source of potential freedom for those whose material wants are provided for through welfare schemes. But it can also be a means of regulating their activities in a co-ordinated fashion according to political doctrines promulgated by the state authorities,[22] which is not unconnected with the fact that authoritarian governments may promote generous welfare schemes in combination with the severe curtailment of political and civil rights.

The connection of surveillance with policing makes for other possibilities of political oppression, going back again to totalitarianism, but separable from it in their less immoderate forms. The creation of 'deviance', within the modern state is contemporaneous with the fact of its suppression.[23] 'Deviance' is not a set of activities or attitudes separate from the surveillance operations of the state, but is formed in and through them. Now as opposed to most — although not all — traditional modes of punishment, the correction of 'deviance' is specifically a moral matter, however much it may be overlain by pragmatic considerations. The policing of modern states can never be something which is merely a 'technical' question of administration. Within this are buried a whole range of complex issues of normative political theory. One need not go so far as to say that every criminal act is an indictment of the existing social order, or that the speech of the 'mentally ill' discloses alternate universes of reality to that accepted by the majority, to see that the Soviet practice of placing dissidents in mental hospitals connects closely with modern 'correctional' treatment as a whole. Totalitarian rule produces sweeping and comprehensive categories of 'deviance', but these cannot be regarded as wholly separate phenomena from those integral to modern states.

The implications of this discussion are two-fold. First, surveillance (in its various forms and aspects) must be regarded as an independent source of power, maximized in the modern state, which has to be as much of a concern in social critique as questions of material inequality or the nature of polyarchy. The writings of its most subtle analyst, Foucault, demonstrate both that the oppressive possibilities of surveillance cannot be countered merely by appeal to class dynamics or to the extension of democracy, and that there is no obvious and simple political programme to develop in coping with them. But we must also conclude that aspects of totalitarian rule are a threat in all modern states, even if not all are threatened equally or in exactly the same ways. Whether we like it or not, tendencies toward totalitarian power are as distinctive a feature of our epoch as is industrialized war.

Dimensions of Modernity

Let me portray the four institutional clusters associated with modernity in a somewhat different way from previously (p. 146), as below. First briefly repeating some of the main interpretations of these offered in the course of this book, I shall then try to indicate how they might be applied to illuminate sources of tension and conflict in modern states.

By linking the four axes of figure 6 around the edges I want to indicate the potentially close relations that can exist between each of them. 'Private property' in this figure does not refer primarily to legally defined ownership of capital, but to the

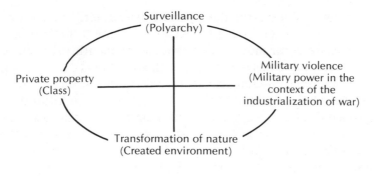

Figure 6

insulation of the economic and the political discussed earlier. Even in the heyday of the individual entrepreneur what was 'private' had to be defined by what was 'public', i.e. by the state, as the territorially based guarantor of law. In later phases of capitalist development, where the large corporations tend to have diffusely spread share ownership, and where government directly administers large sectors of industry, the equation of 'private' with 'individual' control of capitalist enterprise becomes plainly inappropriate. This is not because — as some interpretations suggest — capitalism is disappearing in the face of the emergence of another productive form, but because formulations that identify capitalism with individual entrepreneurial activity are deficient. They confuse a particular epoch in the development of modern economic enterprise — 'entrepreneurial capitalism' — with capitalism as a generic type of productive order. The connections between private property and class are intimate and direct and explain why 'capitalist societies' are 'class societies'. There is no reason to dispute the general lines of Marx's position with regard to the class structure of capitalism, which depends upon the intersection of capital as commodified products with labour as commodified labour-power. However, the conditions of the commodification of labour-power are not homogeneous. Other economic differentiations besides absence of ownership of property in the means of production enter into class structuration.[24]

Neither private property nor class conflict have the overall importance in history that Marx attributes to them. In capitalism, class relations and struggles become particularly significant, but this cannot be generalized back to prior types of society. Surveillance is an independent source of institutional clustering in all class-divided as well as modern societies. In its two aspects, surveillance is fundamental to social organizations of all types, the state being historically the most consequential form of organization, but nevertheless only being one organization among many others. In nation-states surveillance reaches an intensity quite unmatched in previous types of societal order, made possible through the generation and control of information, and developments in communication and transportation, plus forms of supervisory control of 'deviance'. These are in various ways quite decisively influenced by the expansion of capitalism, although again they are neither reducible nor inevitably tied to it once they come into existence. In stimulating the development of a class system not based upon the direct control of the means of violence on the part of the dominant class, in which violence becomes extruded from the labour contract, the emergence of capitalism serves to accentuate some key trends in the modern state. The successful monopoly of control of the means of violence in the hands of the state authorities is the other face of surveillance in the work-place and the control of deviance.

Once constituted in this way, in the context of the state system the nation-state increasingly becomes the pre-eminent form of political organization. Control of the means of violence becomes bound up with the role of professional armed forces, within a framework of industrialized war, while system integration depends in an essential way upon surveillance. This latter development, of course, does not render unimportant the control of the means of violence, particularly given the close connections that exist between industrialism and war. Nonetheless, the potential for military rule is thereby restricted, since in a modern state 'government' involves specialized administration and the participation of the population within a polyarchic dialectic of control.

The technological changes stimulated by the energetic dynamism of capitalist development involve processes of the transformation of the natural world quite distinct from anything occurring before. Such processes are, however, intrinsically linked to industrialism rather than to capitalism as such. Whereas in tribal and class-divided societies human beings regard themselves as 'continuous' with nature, with the advent of modernity nature increasingly becomes treated as the passive instrument of human purposes. The result is a myriad series of technologically based trans- mutations of the natural environment far beyond anything seen in prior types of society. In the industrialized societies, and much of the rest of the world reached by the influence of industrialism, human beings live in a created environment distinct from the 'given' world of nature. Modern urbanism, so different in most respects from cities in earlier forms of society, is the most tangible and consequential expression of this phenomenon. It is misleading to speak of modern urbanism as the 'built environment', as many urban sociologists and geographers do. Traditional cities are also 'built environments' and thus it might appear as though the effects of industrialism in relation to the city solely concern the physical spread of constructed settings. However, the created environment of modern urbanism is neither confined to the areas in which constructed human habitations exist nor a matter primarily of the spread of such areas. Rather, it involves transformations in the relations between the habits of day-to-day social life and the *milieux* in and through which they are ordered.

In polyarchic systems imbued with historicity,[25] social move- ments become of basic importance. Most modern states have been in some part shaped by political movements either leading to a revolutionary break with pre-existing modes of organization, or to progressive political reform tending to a similar conclusion. Given the entanglement of the origins of the modern state with capitalism, it is not surprising that such political movements, both in fact and in theories offered about them by social observers, have converged strongly with labour movements. In Marxism in particular, in which an encompassing role is allocated to class struggle, the labour movement is regarded as more or less the sole inheritor of the pressures for social and political change begun by 'bourgeois' movements. According to the analysis developed here, however, the labour movement is one among other forms of social movement that develop within modern states and across their boundaries.

Figure 7, as with others that follow, should be understood as superimposed upon the preceding one. Movements oriented towards the expansion of free speech and democratic prerogatives are in no sense limited to those 'bourgeois' groupings whose

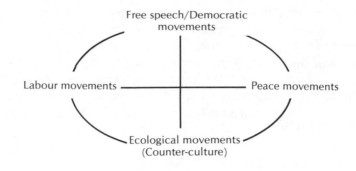

Figure 7

influence was so strong in the relatively early phases of development of the modern state. Marx was certainly right to claim that the ideals embraced by rising entrepreneurial groups were in some part ideological and the scorn with which he addressed them was often justified. But 'bourgeois rights' have a much more generalizable relevance in modern polyarchic systems than his analyses tend to emphasize. Movements oriented to the enlargement of democratic participation within the polity should be seen as always — in greater or lesser degree, and with various admixtures of other aims — oriented towards redressing imbalances of power involved in surveillance. What 'democracy' means here has to be understood as inherently involved in the very contestations such movements promote. There is a basic flaw, however, in the thesis of Michels and others that the expansion of organizations inevitably supplants 'democracy' with 'oligarchy'. The intensification of surveillance, which is the basis of the development of organizations in modern societies and in the world system as a whole is, on the contrary, *the condition of the emergence of tendencies and pressures towards democratic participation.* In each of its aspects surveillance promotes the possibility of the consolidation of power in the hands of dominant classes or elites. At the very same time, however, this process is accompanied by counter-influences brought to bear in the dialectic of control.

Peace movements have a peculiar significance in an era of potential nuclear confrontation, but it would be incorrect to see these as solely confined to the very recent past. Ideals of relinquishing violence as a mode of ordering human affairs are probably as old as standing armies, thus antedating the modern period by several thousand years. Such ideals have been close to the core values of at least some of the world's great religions and, since the advent of the modern state, movements connected with them continue to be infused by the influence of religious symbolism. The notion of 'peace', like that of 'democracy', has to be regarded as a contested concept central to this type of movement. 'Peace' may in such contexts mean little more than the absence of war, but characteristically is much more richly endowed with meaning. Thus, in Quakerism, pacifist values are associated both with established concepts of Christianity and with views about the potential harmony of human relationships free from the use of physical force. Peace movements in a nuclear age have more urgent objectives than any comparable social agencies in previous times and there is, hence, a strongly defined 'tactical' element to them not enforced upon prior types. Nevertheless, they are manifestly linked to ideals of harmonious social activity free from the organized use of violence. Movements that in some sense have peace as their end should be at least analytically separated from those which adopt pacifism as a means, although the division in practice is by no means always clear-cut. Some social movements have been explicitly 'non-violent', eschewing the employment of force to reach the ends they seek. But their concerns are not necessarily oriented primarily towards reducing or dissolving the influence of armed force in the world at large.

By 'ecological movements' I mean those connected with reshaping the created environment, whose concern is thus primarily with the influence of industrialism in the modern world. Such movements often draw upon traditionally established values, although the most significant period of their development only dates from the early part of the nineteenth century. Movements directed against the impact of industrialism at that time tended to be heavily influenced by Romanticism and in general there may be a 'backward-looking' orientation to ecological movements, since their orientation may be towards the recovery of attitudes to the natural world associated with pre-modern forms of society. Given the effects of the industrialization of war and the close connection of the technology of nuclear power with that involved in nuclear weaponry, it is not surprising that ecological and peace movements overlap in their objectives and their membership. Thus as one statement puts it, the supporters of 'green movements' are

> united by their love of nature, their respect for the Earth's resources, and their commitment to the ideal of harmony between people of every race, colour and creed. These fundamental beliefs imply other values: a respect for the gentler side of human nature; a dislike of materialism; a willingness to share the world's wealth among all its people; a desire for decisions to be opened to all concerned; and the search for personal truth.[26]

The diffuse character of the statement indicates both the overlaps that may exist between the types of social movements represented here, as well as the conflicts in which they can be involved. Labour movements originated primarily as modes of 'defensive control' of the work-place in circumstances in which the formal authority workers held over their conditions of labour was slight or non-existent. Whether concerned with the improvement of economic conditions, the achieving of secure employment, or merely with the acquisition of political power, labour movements may come into sharp opposition to goals of each of the other three types of movement. The improvement of the prosperity of workers in a given sector of industry may lead them to support policies inimical to, say, what may be regarded as necessary by others to protect the natural environment. Similarly, ecological aims may only be realizable by deflecting or blocking concerns central to those in the labour movement. Ecological movements tend to be 'counter-cultural' in the sense that they place in question some of the dominant organizational and technological bases of modern societies. Such an orientation may in some circumstances set them against free speech or democratic movements, in so far as the latter are concerned to expand organizational procedures of participation in political systems. The significant convergences between peace and ecological movements in current times should not obscure the fact that there are a range of actual and potential conflicts between these also.

The relative importance of the various types of social movement indicated above will naturally vary according to a variety of circumstances. However, they can be fairly readily connected with the modes of classifying states offered in chapter 10, as well as with the more diffuse influence of capitalism and of industrialism. The character and extent of class conflict, and the associated development of labour movements, are primarily governed by the level of expansion of capitalistic forms of production but are certainly influenced also by the form of the state. The labour movement is likely to be a main, although not the central, focus of conflict in most post-colonial states, but may also converge with, or be overshadowed by, free speech/democratic movements oriented more to the transformation of the political order. In most such states, whether or not they have military governments, protest directed against the military is much more likely to take the free speech/democratic form than to be organized in the guise of peace movements. Nevertheless, movements directed towards democratic goals can readily in some part be inspired by ideals of national and international harmony and by 'counter-cultural' revolts against the dominance of technological imperatives. The 'counter-culture' here, however, is likely to involve the affirmation of non-Western values against those held to emanate from Western cultural hegemony. Within all industrialized societies labour movements tend to have a basic organizing role for other types of social protest. It does not follow from this, however, either that state socialist societies are 'class societies' in the same sense as capitalist ones, or that the character of labour movements has not changed significantly in the capitalist countries during the course of the 'institutionalization of class conflict'.[27]

The interpretation given by Touraine of the 'decline' of the labour movement, compared with other social movements, should be resisted.[28] According to Touraine, who pursues a line of argument adopted by many other observers, the labour movement is associated above all with the phase of entrepreneurial capitalism. It comes into being in opposition to the rule of private capital, seeking to create a more equitable distribution of the fruits of production, but tends to become less and less significant as the course of social development in the industrialized countries creates a 'programmed society', in which the co-ordination of information is increasingly the main medium of power. Other types of social movement come increasingly to the fore, displacing the labour movement from its central position as a mechanism of social protest. Touraine's writings are important and illuminating because they break away from the idea that the labour movement is inevitably the prime source of opposition in capitalist societies. At the same time, he does not succumb to the view that the 'decline' of that movement suggests a general process of the disappearance of radical sources of opposition in such societies. However, his view ignores the fact that capitalist societies (or nation-states) have from their inception been 'programmed societies', in which greatly heightened surveillance plays a vital role. From the perspective I have proposec here, the labour movement retains a centrality in capitalist societies because of their inherently class character. On the other hand, movements oriented towards surveillance, the military and the impact of the created environment are also in a generic way connected to institutional features of those societies, as well as to their involvements in the world system.

There are many forms of social movement not mentioned in the preceding paragraphs. Some of the most important include the following:

1   Nationalist movements
2   Women's movements
3   Ethnic movements
4   Religious revivalism
5   Student movements
6   Consumer movements.

The general principle offered previously — that modern social movements exist in the same 'arenas of historicity' as the organizations they oppose, seek to modify or create — applies to all of these also. But it is not my ambition to seek to develop an explication of the origins and character of social movements in general, only to provide a 'conceptual map' that will link sources of social protest with the main themes discussed in this book. The only claim I want to make is that each of these movements, and others that do not appear in the list, can be situated on this map. To develop the point it is necessary to relate the discussion back to the issue of citizenship rights, forming a third figure superimposed on the preceding two.

In figure 8, four analytically distinct forms of 'content' of the

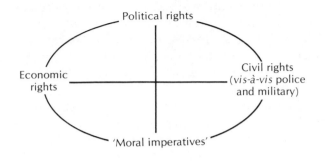

Figure 8

struggles in which modern social movements engage are represented. Movements directed towards the expansion of democratic prerogatives are concerned above all with that bundle of rights and obligations which I have followed Marshall in calling political rights. In linking contests over civil rights to peace movements we have to bear in mind what has been said about the connotations of 'peace'. Peace movements fight out their struggles on a terrain of civil rights in so far as their objectives involve the questioning of the use of force in human social relations. In this respect, the object of their intentions is the generalized use of violence on the part of states, including police repression as well as the role of the military in war. In the segment connecting political and legal rights there are to be found some of the most important and difficult dilemmas of modern politics. For, as has been mentioned, the surveillance operations conducted by the modern state are from some aspects the *sine qua non* of the realization of civil rights; yet the expansion of surveillance creates contexts in which rights which have been hard-won are under threat.

While the main area of struggle of labour movements is over economic citizenship rights, such movements can have and have had a major influence upon the achievement and maintenance of other rights. Given the character of capitalist development they are bound to continue to do so. Thus, as has been indicated previously, in the capitalist states class conflict has been the chief medium of the achievement of political rights as well as certain kinds of civil rights. However, it is obvious enough that these three areas of contestation stand in a relation of tension as much as unity with one another. The rights of workers actively to withdraw their labour, for example, can easily be regarded by other groupings, not necessarily with any affiliation to the dominant class, as contravening aspects of both their political and civil rights.

In designating as 'moral imperatives' the terrain upon which ecological or counter-cultural movements tend to come into play, I do not intend to claim that the three categories of citizenship rights involve no moral considerations. My suggestion is that an abiding concern of movements of this kind is with the re-moralization of spheres of life denuded of 'moral meaning' by the impact of technology or of the created environment more generally. One of the characteristics of modernity that has been exhaustively analysed in the sociological and philosophical literature is exactly this and those who have raised the issue have been entirely correct to do so. But they have not been right to suggest, as most of them have done, that a concern with the recovery of 'moral meaning' is the true origin of class conflicts. While there may be a significant overlap between movements involved with each, there is no sense in which one is wholly explicable in terms of the other.

Discussing Marshall's analysis of citizenship rights earlier, I have suggested that these do not necessarily stand in a progression, such that each in turn is the basis of the extension of the others; and I want to emphasize this again here. In Britain, upon which Marshall's discussion concentrates, it is largely true to say that there was such a progression. But rights once established can come under attack or be dissolved, and the history of other states across the face of the world demonstrates clearly enough that the categories of citizenship right form substantially independent arenas of struggle. Moreover, their character and mode of realization may vary widely. All social movements are in some part involved in engagements over such issues and it is in this respect that the scheme developed here can help illuminate the list of movements mentioned above. Take two examples from that list — nationalist and women's movements. Nationalist movements tend to be located in the conceptual space towards the top right-hand corner of figure 8, being concerned normally with the winning of political rights for minorities within a state or for groups seeking to form a new political order. For the most part, nationalist movements have been oriented towards the expansion of democratic participation, in order to claim rights of political involvement. But the more agressive side of the nationalist Janus has tended to involve values that would be located further down the central axis in so far as an 'anti-modernist' ethic is involved. Women's movements involve a variety of social associations stretching back at least to the nineteenth century. The earlier forms were primarily oriented towards achieving economic and political rights for women equivalent to those held by men. Such goals still lag short of achievement but to them have been added a range of other imperatives. Earlier types of women's movement would be placed toward the top left-hand corner of figure 9; later forms move more to the top right-hand corner.

Social movements are the 'active' expression of sites of conflict or struggle, but of course the tensions involved in modern societies are not confined to areas where agencies of actual or potential change exist. Restricting attention to the industrialized societies, we can map crisis tendencies by adding to the diagrammatic representations given in the preceding discussion.

The capitalist societies today represent forms of class compromise in respect of their economic organization (see figure 9).[29] That is to say, class conflict is focused through systems of industrial bargaining — which include the right to strike — and through the 'political class struggle' of party organizations. It is a compromise in the sense that the major classes have reached an

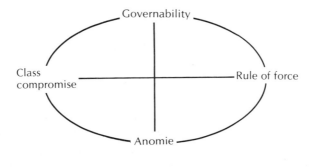

Figure 9

accommodation with one another, albeit a fragile one liable to be disrupted by influences from inside and outside the administrative scope of states.

Since capitalist societies are class societies, the tensions between classes remain potentially disruptive for the wider social system. The class system operates through the (mobile) insulation of the economic and the political, which is one condition of liberal democracy as a political form. It can hardly be a matter of chance that liberal-democratic systems, with the exception of Germany and Japan, are to be found exclusively in classical and colonized nation-states. Characteristic of liberal democracy is not just the insulation of the economic from the political, but the insulation of both from the military.[30] That there is no inherent and necessary relation, however, between the pre-eminence of capitalist enterprise within a particular national economy and liberal democracy, is demonstrated by any number of examples. The coincidence of the two is based historically on the changes leading to the 'extrusion' of violence from the labour contract, 'pushing apart' not just economic and political power but also the state's control over the means of violence from both.

By the governability of capitalist societies I mean how far it is possible for the state authorities to maintain stable conditions of rule. To 'govern', as I have previously stressed, means not just to 'hold power' but to be able to mobilize resources through systematically influencing large areas of the lives of the subject population. The governability of a modern society depends primarily upon the degree of 'organizational integration' it is able to achieve. Class conflicts present one threat to such integration. So long as a society remains capitalist, in the sense I have previously formulated that term, class conflict will be endemic in it. The class compromise, achieved through the availability of formalized modes of industrial conflict plus state-organized social welfare, tends to be based firmly upon an 'effort bargain' between the labour-force, employer and the state. This in turn depends in some substantial part upon the delivery of adequate economic performance to sustain levels of prosperity for the stronger, more unionized sections of the work-force. Strains in the 'class compromise' therefore feed in directly to governability. But one cannot thereby infer, as Marxist orthodoxy would have it, that class struggle is *'the'* problem governments face. It is one phenomenon among others influencing governability — a central one, to be sure, but not necessarily the most basic.

The governability of a modern state concerns the success of the surveillance operations it is able to sustain, these in turn however only having some relevance in so far as they allow control over aspects of the day-to-day lives of the populace. What is important here is not so much the level of legitimacy a government can generate in respect of the mass of the population, as how far established patterns of social conduct are malleable in respect of state policies. In other words, how far a government actually 'governs' may depend less upon a generalized acceptance of the justifiability of its policies than upon a day-to-day acceptance of them. In either case, however, 'government' only exists when there is a 'two-way' relation between the programmes of the ruling authorities and 'behavioural input' from those who are governed. Such a relation is threatened when significant sectors of the labour-force withdraw co-operation in class struggles, but it may be menaced from other sources also. Of great importance here is not so much direct disillusionment with state policies — the withdrawal of legitimacy — as hostility or aversion to the main patterns of conduct involved in modern social and economic life. If 'anomie' is taken to mean a generalized dissatisfaction with major cultural values, which lose their grip upon the day-to-day lives of individuals, then it can be accurately seen as a generic potentiality within modern societies. There is no reason to suppose that it is more of a threat to governability than class conflict, but clearly it stems in some considerable degree from separate origins.

It seems plausible to suggest that capitalist and state socialist societies may be placed differentially within the preceding figure in terms of differences in their institutional alignments. Thus in the capitalist states the principal 'weighting' of tensions could be said to lie along a line drawn from bottom right to top left. Problems of sustaining the class compromise lie close to difficulties of governability, deriving their sources partly from anomic conditions pertaining in various sectors of society. How far governments cope successfully with these problems in turn influences reciprocally levels of class struggle and anomic 'withdrawal' from dominant institutional patterns.

In established liberal-democratic states, so long as the 'class

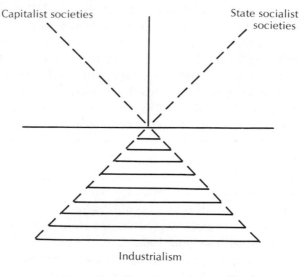

Figure 10

compromise' is sustained in a reasonably effective way, the role of force in the internal constitution of social order is limited. As industrialized states, both capitalist and state socialist societies share a common pool of problems of governability deriving from anomic disaffection which may motivate a range of different social movements (see figure 10). State socialist societies do not, however, involve the same class dynamics as the capitalist countries. There is not a dominant class which, insulated from the mechanisms of political power, negotiates both with subordinate classes and with the state authorities. In 'workers' states' the governing authorities, in principle and in practice, have command over large arenas of economic life, translating clashes involving labour organizations into direct confrontations with the state. These undoubtedly are a major influence upon the governability of the state, indicating that labour movements are a perhaps more potent source of transformation in state socialist societies than in the Western countries. For, in the former, in contrast to the latter, there is not the means of keeping 'economic' struggles separate from directly 'political' ones.[31] Given this circumstance, which has led to major conflicts in the Eastern European countries — although not in the Soviet Union itself —

over the past three decades, tendencies towards the use of force in internal governmental affairs brook fairly large.

The Need for a Normative Political Theory of Violence

The twentieth century has been decisively shaped in its major lines of development by Marxism, but is at the same time in some respects opaque to Marxist thought. Marx's writings are founded upon the idea that human history creates the conditions for the emancipation of social life from pre-existing forms of oppression or exploitation. The teleological implications of Marx's account of history are in some respects puzzlingly ambiguous, but that some sort of teleology is attributed to human social development seems undeniable. According to Marx, 'human beings only set themselves such puzzles as they can resolve.' The past development of human societies, culminating in capitalism, has produced a world in which industrial production is capable of generating wealth far in excess of anything available to human beings before. Since industrialism has come into being within the framework of class society, the fruits of production, in the shape of the 'good life', are denied to the majority of its very producers. But the labour movement is at hand to solve the riddle of history, and comes to prominence through the self-same processes that further the expansion of capitalist production. The victory of the working-class re-humanizes conditions of production, returning a strong measure of control over the productive process to the workers and abolishing classes. A (world) society in which production is consciously organized according to human need, rather than according to the vagaries of capitalist enterprise, comes into being.

This scenario is in some respects not so far from the reality of what has happened over the past hundred years as most of Marx's critics would assert. Among the industrialized societies at least, capitalism is by now a very different phenomenon from what it was in the nineteenth century and labour movements have played a prime role in changing it.[32] In most of the capitalist countries, we now have to speak of the existence of 'welfare capitalism', a system in which the labour movement has achieved a considerable stake and in which economic citizenship rights brook large.

Some of Marx's proposals — never elaborated in any detail —

about the future form of a type of social order transcending capitalism now look less than adequate. Planned production within a highly complicated modern economy, if he envisaged such a thing, has proved much more difficult to achieve in an effective fashion than seemed likely in the nineteenth century. Schemes of workers' self-management have met with numerous difficulties and if, as some interpreters suggest, Marx foresaw the emergence of a global post-scarcity economy, this looks today completely beyond the bounds of possibility. Nevertheless, it seems by no means impracticable to envisage an economic order in which planned production, coupled to a strong injection of self-management, would serve to return a measure of control over work-processes to those involved in them. The same could not be said of control of the means of violence. Marx toyed with the notion of a populace of armed workers as the best counterbalance to the power of coercion vested in the state, but such ideas seem positively archaic today. In those countries where something close to this situation is found, at least in respect of small weaponry, like the USA or some of the Latin American countries, the results are hardly praiseworthy. In any case, talk of returning control of the means of violence to the populace makes no sense whatsoever in the case of the developed weapons of industrialized war. In terms of historical agencies of change, there is no parallel in the sphere of weaponry to the proletariat in the area of industrial labour. No plausible 'dialectical counterpart' to the progressive accumulation of military power seems to exist. Protest movements and peace movements there are, but even in the most optimistic portrayal of the near future it is scarcely conceivable these could parallel the world-historical role Marx foresaw for the working class.

Now to this it could simply be said that history has no teleology, apart from the purposes individual human beings incorporate into their actions; and that the part which the proletariat was supposed to play in history was extraordinarily exaggerated. But such an observation in no way comes to grips with the problems at issue. What would the 'good society' look like in respect of control of the means of violence? What meaning are we to attribute to 'society' in this phrase anyway, given the division of the world into a multiplicity of nation-states, all having the capability of deploying armed force of considerable destructive power and where some states literally have the capability to destroy the whole of humanity? These questions raise far more difficulties, of course, than could be adequately discussed here and I shall confine myself to indicating a possible approach to them — one of which I shall develop further in the third volume of this work.[33]

Such an approach would have to concern itself both with problems of world policing and military rule within states, and with the fundamental issue of violence between states in an era of industrialized war. In states throughout the world today, to repeat a theme of the last few chapters, pacified populations — save in certain circumstances and in a few regions — confront soldiery possessing industrialized weaponry. In situations in which the use of police power is highly repressive there may be little or no effective distinction between the police and the military. How far policing involves the extensive use of force against a range of 'deviant' activities will depend both upon the definition of 'deviance' within a given society, and upon a series of other conditions to do with the overall organization of the societal system. One main element is how far what counts as 'deviance' is specifically restricted to criminal activities, not embracing political acts. Of course, a great deal turns on what is to count as 'political' here. Perhaps all that needs to be said in this context is that the 'public sphere' of political debate should be open enough to allow non-violent appraisal of where appropriate divisions are to be drawn between what is 'political' and what is merely 'criminal'.

The question of military rule has already been discussed, albeit with some brevity. The potentiality for military government in modern states is relatively limited, if 'government' here means assuming overall responsibility for rule. It is a different matter if we consider the capability of the military to maintain diffuse sanctions holding governments to certain styles of policy, or confining what they do within definite limits. Here the influence of the military is strong in a large proportion of nation-states, and in the nature of the case it is impossible to look for any guarantees that military 'intervention' will not occur even in the most stable of liberal democracies. One factor likely to be important is resistance to the encroachment of militaristic values, something which is surely one of the main shared inspirations of contemporary peace and ecological movements. What constitutes 'militarism' is not a constant, but has been very substantially changed by the development of the armed forces since the nineteenth century and by the concomitant industrialization of war. Militaristic values of the traditional type probably were displayed for the final time on a large-scale with the defeat of Japan in the Second World War. Even then they had become largely subordinated to the demands of a modern, professionalized army, in which the display of extreme individual valour is of marginal importance compared with effective discipline on the field of battle and efficient production in industry. 'Militarism' today means more than anything else a proclivity on the part of those in the higher echelons of the armed forces and in other leading circles outside to look first of all for military solutions to issues which could be solved by other means; and the readiness of the lower ranks to accept such solutions unquestioningly. Military discipline does not necessarily preclude the development of a sophisticated political culture within the armed forces, and the fostering of 'openness' in this respect should presumably be one element in any political programme which seeks to combat militarism. There are obviously complex issues involved in this matter, however, since there is some plausibility to the argument that it is the professionalized, a-political army that is least likely to bring the influence of military power to bear upon governmental decisions.[34]

I have suggested earlier that, significant as questions of the role of the military in government in modern states may be, they are strictly secondary to the issues posed by the spread of industrialized weaponry in the world military order. It is undoubtedly in this respect that we find ourselves today furthest from the sorts of problems that preoccupied most eighteenth- and nineteenth-century political thinkers. We seem bereft of plausible courses of action that could do any more than limit threats greater than human beings have ever had to face in the course of their long history. When even 'orthodox' weapons have reached the destructive potential of current times, it is no doubt desirable to seek to prevent any outbreaks of war at all. But the most urgent and necessary task facing us today is plainly the prevention of warfare involving nuclear armaments — or other weapons which might in the near future approach them in their destructive potential. No one who lives in the present-day world can fail to be aware that there is a 'two-step' process facing us and it is by no means clear if or how humanity can take the second step involved. The first step is tactical; it is simply a matter of the persistence of a situation in which, as over the past forty years, nuclear weapons remain unused. The second is the implementation of a normative political theory of the means of violence — the creation of a social order in which use of military power will no longer threaten our existence as a whole. History has no teleology and it would only be the most sanguine of observers who could confidently assert that the second step will ever be taken.

An understanding of the necessarily 'tactical' nature of coping with the likelihood of nuclear war in present times can be deepened by briefly recapitulating the influence of war upon the development of the European state system and the global nation-state system. Dating from somewhere around the year 1000 AD, war in Europe no longer remained a chronic series of disaggregated armed struggles, gradually becoming part of an aristocratic warrior culture and taking on a ritualized form.[35] In many encounters, although not in those entered into against foes from outside Europe, there were formalized restrictions upon the conduct of battle, observed by all parties to the combat. This was succeeded by a period in which the art and the science of warfare were pushed forward and where the armed forces were co-ordinated in the service of newly strengthened states. In its overall contours, this period can be said to stretch from somewhere in the sixteenth century to the outbreak of the First World War. War and diplomacy became integrally linked, with the former being, as Clausewitz made explicit, the instrument to be applied where diplomatic measures failed or were otherwise rebutted. It can be said with some truth that Clausewitz sought to detach the conduct of war from militarism in its traditional meaning — the pursuit of war as an intrinsic value, or for the virtues that could be promoted through participation in bloody combat.[36] The most famous of all remarks upon the nature of war — 'War is not merely a political act, but also a real political instrument, a continuation of political commerce, a carrying out of the same by other means'[37] — is not an expression of a warrior philosophy, but an observation about the practicalities of the precarious existence of states within the European state system. Neither war nor military victory are ends in themselves; they are instruments in the realization of longer-term policies. War has a character shaped by its political intentions and the main strategy to be employed is to achieve the diplomatic ends at least military cost.

Although the realization for most of those involved came after the emergence of the phenomenon, the development of the means of waging industrialized war in the latter part of the nineteenth century irretrievably changed the nature of warfare and its role in relation to the ambitions of states. This is not to say that Clausewitz's dictum became irrelevant as soon as the armies clashed. But war could no longer be held to the limited engagements, restricted by the political motives underlying them, that Clausewitz had in mind. The era of 'total war' negates just this supposition, as well as others with which Clausewitz characterized the nature of warfare. Prior to the twentieth century it was accepted by combatants, and made part of international law, that war is a conflict between political entities, in which individuals participate only in so far as they relinquish their civilian status to become agents of the state.[38] But with the advent of industrialized war, the mass of the population is inevitably involved, with victory demanding the smashing of the system of production that is the necessary base of the war effort. During the First World War the implications of this were gradually realized by the participants, although the generalization of war to the whole of the populations of the belligerent states occurred only in the Second. The objectives of the military effort in the Second World War were not just the overcoming of the military forces of the other side, but the subduing of the 'mass of the enemy people'.

During the interim period between the two World Wars, various limitations on war were discussed by the politicians on an international level. The prohibition of various types of weapon was widely canvassed. So were proposals for international rules governing the use of weaponry and the limitation of the use of air-forces. With one or two exceptions, such as the use of poison gas, all this eventually came to naught. In the opening part of the Second World War there was, on both sides, some attempt to ensure that air strikes be limited to industrial targets directly connected with military production. But even if this had been technically feasible, it was not observed, the more-or-less indiscriminate bombing of civilian targets rapidly becoming one of the main means whereby the will of the opponent to continue was to be broken. The atomic bombs dropped on Hiroshima and Nagasaki were nothing more nor less than a concentrated application of terror, designed to shock Japan into surrender. This aim was accomplished, but these self-same acts ushered in a new phase of military violence — one that has produced even more dramatic a schism with previous forms of military conflict than did the earlier phase of the development of industrialized war.

The existence of nuclear weapons is a direct development of the integration of industrialism and modes of conducting war, but the scale of their destructive capabilities is so huge that even the threat of their use alters the nature of war. In the case of the nuclear powers, particularly the super-powers, the established connection between diplomacy is not broken, but it is reversed. These states cannot use their possession of nuclear armaments to further their diplomatic goals, but instead have to employ diplomatic manoeuvring to attempt to ensure that situations do not arise in which those armaments might be unleashed. This is particularly the case where the super-powers confront one another directly, the 'success' of the diplomacy in the Cuban missile crisis, for example, being much more that a military engagement was avoided than that Kennedy achieved his initial aim (which was of the same order in any case) — to keep Soviet missiles out of Cuba. Unfortunately, while the existence of nuclear weapons alters the nature of the connections between diplomatic bargaining and war, it does not do away with diplomacy, or with the strategic nature of the relations between states in an interdependent world that is at the same time fractured and chaotic. Given the nature of the nation-state system, political activity within and on behalf of states tends to be concerned with short- rather than long-term interests and to pursue mutual interests only when short-term gains accrue to the individual states.

Moreover, it is apparent that the presence of large stock-piles of nuclear weaponry by the super-powers does not bring to an end — short of their deployment in war — the dynamic processes of technical change effected by the combination of science, industry and weapons development. An arms race has been an inherent part of both peace and war since the co-ordination of industrial production and the means of waging war first became the basis of military strength in the modern age. The most well-documented example in the nineteenth and early twentieth centuries is that between Britain and Germany, in which each expressly geared its weapons production to that of the other, using calculated formulae of military adequacy to organize their own industrial effort. As in the current arms race, industrial enterprise was stimulated, in certain sectors at least, by the pressures induced by the arms competition. It has been claimed that the technology of naval warfare changed as much in the half century between 1850 and 1900 as in the thousand years previously.[39] The fission weapons exploded over Hiroshima and Nagasaki were replaced less than ten years later by the much more destructive fusion weapons, these in turn being rapidly further developed to increase their explosive power many times over. The application of technological development to delivery systems is only one aspect of a battery of technical advances in guidance and other areas; to which have to be added laser weapons and the expanding development of chemical weaponry.

What validity there is in the idea of the 'military-industrial complex' derives from the element of co-ordinated forward planning which is involved in the military rivalry between the super-powers. The regularity of innovation, and its gearing to industrial production, do not just derive from processes of technological innovation in the economy as a whole but from the continual attempt to respond to what the other side will do and the advances they will make. The arms race is not balance of power diplomacy applied to weapons development in a bipolar setting. If it involves some kind of equilibrium, it is a highly unstable and shifting one in which the rationale of technical advance is not simply the achievement of parity with the other power, but the ability to adapt weapons production to projected future innovation.[40] In a situation of 'mobile equilibrium' there is no point at which overall restraint upon further technological advance in weapons development, or even calling a halt to the further accumulation of existing weaponry, will not tend to favour one side rather than the other. To take just one example — repeated in its essential form in all subsequent negotiations — the first American proposal for arms control, the Baruch Plan of

1946, would have put nuclear weapons under international supervision. But the Soviet Union, which at that time had not yet exploded a nuclear device, would have been left at a major disadvantage compared with the USA, which would have been able to dominate the supervising body. The Soviets made the counter-proposal for disarmament prior to international control and the creation of nuclear-free zones together with various non-aggression pacts. However, such a situation would have given the Soviet Union a significant advantage over the rival power, since it maintained much the larger non-nuclear army. Only in circumstances where both stand to gain in the short- or medium-term has there been some success — as in the Non-proliferation Treaty and the SALT agreements. The former was designed to check the diffusion of nuclear weaponry to states not yet possessing it and the SALT agreements probably actually formalized the competitive nature of the arms race more than acting to arrest its course.

While the massive development of weaponry on the part of the super-powers has to have primary place in any analysis of military power in the nuclear age, the continued build-up of the means of industrialized war elsewhere, via the world military order, is much more than just a spin-off from the main centres of the arms race. The diffusion of 'First World' weaponry to virtually all states is itself embroiled in a generalized arms race, having a number of focal points in the relation between states in regions of high tension. The same logic fuels arms competition in these areas as in the nuclear arms race and is, of course, in some part fostered by the military transfers made by the super-powers and the other states with developed arms industries. That is to say, rival states project what the others are likely to possess in the imminent future and while most may be dependent upon technological advances in armaments made in the industrialized states, an increasing number of countries are likely to promote indigenous arms industries.[41] Most disturbingly, as has been mentioned previously, the spread of the technology and raw material for 'peaceful' nuclear use is likely to lead to the further expansion of nuclear weaponry in spite of existing treaty regulations.

A normative political theory of control of the means of violence in the current age cannot do other than begin from Camus's pessimism, seeking from there to develop at least some guidelines to more optimistic possibilities in the longer-term future. The attractiveness of Marxist thought, in contrast to the 'utopian socialism' which Marx and Engels attacked so abrasively in the nineteenth century, was that the emergence of the new socialist order was no idle dream, but supposedly immanent in the nature of capitalist development. We can call upon no such dialectic today and instead, it might be argued, must appeal to a renewal of utopianism, mixed with the firmest form of realism. The tactics of (a) survival in the face of the global destructive capabilities possessed by the super-powers and (b) minimizing the possibility of the occurrence of nuclear war involving other states, have to be an overriding priority. But 'peace' in respect of (a) and (b) is hardly a constructive path for indefinite future development, which has to be linked to a conception of the 'good society' no matter how remote the likelihood of its achievement is at present.

Some of the parameters of debate seem clear and indisputable. The scientific knowledge which allowed the creation of nuclear weapons cannot be dissolved, short of the destruction of modern civilization itself by means of those weapons. Nor is there any feasible type of international agency or mutually agreed programme which is likely to persuade either of the super-powers to shed their nuclear weapons, singly or jointly. Peace movements, in combination with the governments of other states can, nevertheless, potentially have a large influence on key aspects of the world military order and the arms race. The objects of the tactical phase of facilitating 'peace' — meaning here the absence of nuclear war — are plain to see, even if the power which can be applied to reach them is slight indeed compared to that of the political, military and economic organizations likely to be opposed. They include, above all: the promotion of détente between the super-powers, in the context of securing the fullest possible openness of communication and information flow between them; the promotion of programmes of conversion within weapons industries, phasing out in particular the production of weapons systems, turning the research and development involved to other uses;[42] the instituting of much more severe restraints than currently exist upon the transfer of nuclear power technology and materials to non-nuclear states, together with a reversal of nuclear power programmes in all states where they have been implemented, in favour of non-nuclear power sources; and the unilateral abandonment of nuclear weapons by the smaller nuclear states. The very implausibility that such proposals could be effectively pressed home in the near future, or even in the medium-term, demonstrates that Camus was not overstating his case.

Critical Theory in the Late Twentieth Century

Comte and Marx, perhaps the two most prominent nineteenth-century social thinkers, shared a certain outlook in common, in spite of the wide divergencies between their views. For both, the knowledge generated by the social sciences is to rescue humanity from a past in which the most decisive events which affected social development were beyond human mastery, projecting us into a future in which we control our own destiny. In Comte's case, what matters is discovering the laws of motion of societies, this knowledge allowing the systematic prediction on the basis of which we can appropriate our own history and turn it to our purposes. *Prévoir pour pouvoir*: an understanding of social life will allow us to transform it in much the same way as natural science has made possible the systematic transformation of the natural world. For Marx, the era of 'history', as opposed to that of 'pre-history', will come about when the class divisions that have been the motor of social change up to the present have finally been transcended. Again, understanding our past history will allow us to shape the future and resources will become devoted to the use of the whole human community rather than being channelled to the advantage of sectional groupings.

What has gone wrong with these sorts of vision and how should we seek to reconstruct critical theory in the late twentieth century? If the early Positivist Societies are long forgotten, Marxism at least has more than lived up to the adage of its founder that interpretations of the world are ten a penny, the point being to use them to change it. Notwithstanding the enormous practical impact of Marx's writings, and the valid appraisals they contain, the twentieth-century world is very different from the future he anticipated. A viable critical theory today must be post-Marxist and must also be capable of subjecting to critique just those aspects of Marxism that lend themselves to exploitative domination. Marxism was conceived of by its originator as a critique of political economy and has certainly more than proved its worth as a source of opposition to the less salubrious influences of capitalism. But as a doctrine adopted by existing states its impact has been little short of disastrous. It can no longer be pretended, except perhaps by the most obdurate of ostriches among Marx's self-professed followers, that this is simply the outcome of distortions of Marx's ideas. Marxism has proved particularly vulnerable to becoming itself ideology and is weak in respect of providing a critique of just this vulnerability. Marxism has been proclaimed obsolescent often enough by its hostile critics, but how should those who have some sympathy with its liberative inspiration appraise its weaknesses?

If we reject evolutionism, the sort of critical theory Marx attempted to build is already attacked at its heart.[43] The transition from capitalism to a global socialist order is only comprehensible in Marxian terms if it be accepted that capitalism incorporates all the achievements of past history, ready to be actualized by the transcendence of capitalist production. If capitalism is not the high-point of an evolutionary scheme but a specific feature of the development of the European societies — and only one axis of their institutional organization at that — this standpoint collapses. The validity of much of what Marx has to say in analysing the nature of capitalist production need not be placed in doubt; indeed, a good case can be made for saying that large segments of it are correct and as relevant to the world of today as in the nineteenth century.[44] However, Marx accords undue centrality to capitalism and to class struggle as the keys to explaining inequality or exploitation, and to providing the means of their transcendence. Marxist thought is as deficient in analysing some of the major sources of exploitative domination as it is in offering plausible programmes of action for overcoming them. This judgement applies not only to the phenomena discussed earlier in the chapter — surveillance and control of the means of violence — but also in particular to inequalities of gender and to ethnic exploitation.

Marx's interpretation of history is unified with a programme of practical action precisely because of the role which class division and class conflict play both in the structuring of capitalism and in its transcendence. Its strength, as it were, is also its weakness. Distinct from 'utopian socialism' because it addresses the real possibilities of social transformation, contained within the tendential movement of capitalism, it places the whole burden of history upon one revolutionary agency — the proletariat, acting in the context of class struggle. Critical theory today must develop substantive accounts of the origins of modernity and its global influence that do not seek to cram everything into the convenient explanatory catch-all of 'capitalism'. From which it follows that 'socialism', if understood as the negation of capitalism, is itself carrying too heavy a burden when supposed to be a generalized means for overcoming exploitation, or the sole model of the 'good society'.

In being stripped of historical guarantees, critical theory re-enters the universe of contingency and has to adopt a logic that no longer insists upon the *necessary* unity of theory and practice. How otherwise could we confront a world which, for the foreseeable future, must carry on under the shadow of possible total destruction? I do not mean by this that the Marxian theorem of the unity of theory and practice should be abandoned altogether. What we should envisage is, rather, a process of critique that does not recoil from connecting material possibilities of social reform with an utopian element. Every analysis of existing conditions of social life, because it is 'historical', i.e. concerned with the temporality of institutions in their reproduction by human actors, generates an understanding of their potential transformation. This is a logical point, not one that specifies what a given course of action or programme can actually achieve. All social analysis, put another way, is implicitly social critique and also has transformative implications for whatever it describes. These provide the 'grounding' of critical theory, but do not in and of themselves indicate how immanent possibilities in a given set of circumstances can be actualized, or what connection that actualization might bear to more inclusive goals. The 'utopian moments' of critical theory are necessary precisely where what is immanent does not disclose a practical means of reaching those more inclusive goals; and for a critical theory without historical guarantees this situation is likely to be exceedingly common.

The diagnosis of tendential properties of social systems should remain closely connected to social critique, but is likely to relapse into dogma — as Marxism itself so frequently does — if regarded as the exclusive basis of practice. It may often be necessary to accept, even to accentuate, the gap between concrete possibilities of change and the desired outcomes of the social critic. There is, so to speak, a necessarily non-utopian element in utopianism, not just because pathways to a particular goal may be disclosed which were not previously perceived, but because the stimulus of the utopian prospect may itself influence the immanent possibilities of action. Such a view of critical theory should not be confused with the idea of Comte (and Marx) that the 'cognitive appropriation' of history will eventually allow human beings to control their own destiny. This kind of conception is flawed in major respects: because the understanding of what is immanent does not guarantee its convergence with what critical theory may seek to actualize; and because any 'understanding' of a particular feature of social life or of history, in becoming part of social life, may act to fracture the very forms of control it was introduced to achieve.

A critical theory without guarantees must confront the situation that, just as history has no inherent teleology, neither are there privileged agents of the realization of processes of social reform. Just as we should resist the teleology of the Marxist interpretation of history, we should beware the associated conception that the under-privileged or exploited are the true bearers of emancipatory forms of social change. In Marxism there remains a strong residue of transmuted master—slave dialectic: 'the worker is nothing, but shall become everything.' The attractions of Marxism probably derive in some large degree just from this emphasis, which can be made to appeal simultaneously to the historicity of nationalism and to the polyarchic tendencies of the modern state. The doctrine may be morally seductive and practically consequential but it is, nonetheless, false.

If the views set out in this book command any credence, all four main institutional axes of modernity are 'world-historical' in their significance. It follows that a critical theory responsive to the demands of the present day should regard these as central both to the interpretation of immanent change and to the normative demands of constructing (utopian) models of the 'good society'. The most urgent issues facing us today are those to do with the expansion of the world military order, the industrialization of war and the existence of nuclear weapons. Peace movements offer the opportunity to influence the 'run-away' character of military expansion. At the same time, they supply a clear illustration of the distance between the nurturing of immanent change and the gravitational pull of utopianism. There is no option but for such movements to operate upon a tactical level, while at the same time fostering debate about 'possible worlds' in which the threat of nuclear conflict has disappeared altogether.

This has implications which those in the peace movements themselves may be reluctant to face. For discourses of utopianism can (not *must*) negatively affect tactical decisions relevant to coping with a heavily militarized world. In debates about nuclear weaponry above all we should observe Marx's directive not to judge ideas by their manifest content but by the practical consequences of their propagation. It is possible, for example, that programmes of action that seek to work 'through' official organizations, rather than merging with generalized counter-cultural protest, might be most effective in some key respects and in certain particular contexts. Walzer's point about nuclear weaponry and deterrence is an important one, showing how significant it is for peace movements to propel debates about these into the 'public sphere' in the most urgent way possible: 'Though deterrence turns American and Russian civilians (European ones too) into mere means for the prevention of war, it does so without restraining us in any way. It is in the nature of the new technology that we can be threatened without being held captive. That is why deterrence, while in principle so frightening, is so easy to live with.'[45] Sheer clamour about the 'stored-up horror' upon which deterrence depends can perhaps serve to puncture such complacency. But the enormously difficult path that must be trodden is one which somehow combines the immediate and continuing avoidance of nuclear conflict with the dissolution of the process of the industrialization of war in a radically new world order. Nowhere are the discontinuities of modern history more acute.

The inevitable primacy of these concerns over all others, of course, does not mean that the problem of the avoidance of nuclear war is entirely separable from the more traditional emphases of critical theory, or that these can be shelved while we wait to see whether the modern world will survive at all in recognizable form. The fact that the global economy is dominated by capitalistic mechanisms, and that the most influential agencies within it are capitalist states and transnational corporations, remains of fundamental importance to the nature of the world system as a whole. The highly imbalanced character of the international division of labour between core and periphery, plus the low degree of inter-governmental regulation over the world economy, are expressive of the pre-eminent influence of capitalist production world-wide. As regards the main components of capitalist production, it is surely still to Marxism that we have to look to discover the most telling critique. The contradiction between private appropriation and socialized production that Marx diagnosed as inherent in the nature of capitalist enterprise still prevails. While the division of labour nationally and internationally has become extraordinarily complex, rendering the world system increasingly integrated economically, the main propelling force motivating economic expansion remains the capitalist accumulation process. The success of labour movements in tempering some of the most noxious effects of capitalistic mechanisms within national economies has not been transferred to inequalities in the global division of labour as a whole. The divisions between First and Third Worlds, or between North and South, involve imbalances of resources of a level comparable to anything found in the differences between classes within traditional states. But it is evident that some of the most urgent problems facing the world economy are to do with industrialism rather than with the mechanisms of capitalist production as such. That is to say, they lead us to look away again from the traditional areas of concentration of Marxist theory — in its more orthodox forms at any rate — towards ecological problems.

Ecological movements and concerns are not new, in the sense that from the early impact of industrialism there were those who held that industrial production would alter — not necessarily for the better — many qualities of human life, demanding different attitudes to the natural world from those of earlier times. Although, as in so many respects, Marx's writings on this issue involve a number of overlapping strands, in general it is the case that Marx was not a critic of industrialism. Rather, for him industrialism holds out the promise of a life of abundance, through turning the forces of nature to human purposes. It is a particular mode of organizing industrial production — capitalism — that needs to be combatted, not the industrial order itself. Such a view has to be deemed essentially wanting from the perspective of the late twentieth century. Marx's paeans to industrialism might be readily understandable in the context of the nineteenth century, particularly given his dismissal of Malthus. In a world of staggering population growth, embedded in an increasingly inclusive international division of labour, the material resources required for a continuous expansion of industrial production are simply not available, and those that exist come under more and more strain.

A critical theory alert to ecological issues cannot just be limited to a concern with the exhaustion of the earth's resources — immense though may be the issues to be faced in this respect — but has to investigate the value of a range of relations to nature that tend to be quashed by industrialism. In coming to terms with these we can hope not so much to 'rescue' nature as to explore possibilities of changing human relationships themselves. An understanding of the role of urbanism is essential to such an exploration. The spread of urbanism of course separates human beings from nature in the superficial sense that they live in built environments. But modern urbanism profoundly affects the character of human day-to-day social life, expressing some of the most important intersections of capitalism and industrialism.[46]

Finally, critical theory must come to terms with those aspects of modern institutions associated with surveillance as a medium of power. Understood as the reflexive monitoring of social reproduction, surveillance has been important both to the consolidation of the world system in modern times and to the internal ordering of states. The questions raised by its role as a source of power can only increase in importance in the forseeable future. Intensified surveillance and totalitarian tendencies are intimately linked. This is not something which should lead us to despair, for administrative power and polyarchy are equally closely connected. There is not a direct relation between the expansion of the administrative power of states and political oppression. The more effectively states seek to 'govern', the more there is the likelihood of counter-balance in the form of polyarchic involvement. Given the distinctive dominance of the nation-state in the world system, however, the possibility that this might lead to the formation of a democratically ordered world government seems entirely remote. If the arguments deployed in this book are valid, the increasing social integration of the globe does not betoken an incipient political unity.

Notes

The following books by the author are referred to in abbreviated form throughout the notes:

Central Problems in Social Theory (London: Hutchinson, 1977) — *CPST*.
New Rules of Sociological Method (London: Hutchinson, 1976) — *NRSM*.
Studies in Social and Political Theory (London: Hutchinson, 1977) — *SSPT*.
The Class Structure of the Advanced Societies (London: Hutchinson, 1979; revised edition, 1981) — *CSAS*.
A Contemporary Critique of Historical Materialism (London: Macmillan, 1981), vol. I — *CCHM*, vol. I.
Profiles and Critiques in Social Theory (London: Macmillan, 1982) — *PCST*.
The Constitution of Society (Cambridge: Polity Press, 1984) — *CS*.

1 State, Society and Modern History

1. cf. *CPST*, chapter 2; *CS, passim*.
2. For a fuller exposition, see *CPST*, chapter 3.
3. K. Marx, 'Preface' to 'A Contribution to the Critique of Political Economy', in K. Marx and F. Engels, *Selected Works in One Volume* (London: Lawrence and Wishart, 1968); cf. *CPST*, chapter 3.
4. *CS*, chapter 5.
5. See especially *CCHM*, vol. I, chapters 3, 4 and 5; *CS*, chapters 4 and 5.
6. *NRSM*, chapter 3.
7. Talcott Parsons, 'On the concept of political power', *Proceedings of the American Philosophical Society*, 107, 1963.

8. *CPST*, p. 91ff.
9. *CSAS*, pp. 156—62.
10. *CS*, chapter 5.
11. Ibid., p. 14ff.
12. *CPST*, pp. 88—94.
13. Ibid.
14. G. W. F. Hegel, *The Phenomenology of Spirit* (Oxford: Clarendon Press, 1977), p. 126.
15. *CPST*, chapter 2; *CS*, chapter 1 and *passim*.
16. On this matter see the celebrated debate between Lévi-Strauss and Sartre about the nature of history. For a summary version, cf. Claude Lévi-Strauss: 'Réponses à quelques questions', *Esprit*, 31, 1963.
17. *CS* chapter 3 and *passim*. Simmel's remarks on such matters can still be read with profit. See 'Der Raum und die raumlichen Ordnungen der Gesellschaft', in his *Soziologie* (Leipzig: Duncker and Humbolt, 1908).
18. *CPST*, pp. 84—5.
19. *CCHM*, vol. I, pp. 97—100. The work of Jane Jacobs, however it might be criticized in some respects, is particularly important here.
20. In this book I use 'violence' in a straightforward sense, not in the much wider meaning attributed to it by Bourdieu and others. I mean by 'control of the means of violence' control over the capabilities of doing physical harm to the human body by the use of force.
21. *CCHM*, pp. 140—56.
22. *CS*, pp. 166ff.
23. Emile Durkheim: *Professional Ethics and Civic Morals* (London: Routledge, 1957), pp. 79—80.
24. cf. A. Giddens, 'The nation-state and violence', in Walter W. Powell and Richard Robbins, *Conflict and Consensus* (New York: Free Press, 1984).
25. Max Weber, *Economy and Society* (Berkeley: University of California Press, 1978), vol. I, p. 56.
26. Ibid., p. 55.
27. Ibid., p. 54.
28. *CPST*, pp. 81—111; *CCHM*, vol. I, pp. 46—8.
29. G. W. F. Hegel, *The Philosophy of Right* (London: Bell, 1896), section 261.
30. Janowitz notes that, during the first four World Congresses of Sociology, the topics of military institutions and war were not discussed. At the Fifth World Congress, held in Washington in 1962, a single paper on the role of the military in the new nations

344   Notes to Chapter 1

was presented in the political sociology section. Only in 1964 was there introduced a special section on 'The Professional Military and Militarism'. Morris Janowitz, 'Armed forces and society: a world perspective', in Jacques van Doorn, *Armed Forces and Society* (The Hague: Mouton, 1968), p. 15. cf. also my discussion in *CCHM*, vol. I, pp. 177—82.

31. Herbert Spencer, *The Evolution of Society*, edited by Robert L. Carneiro, (Chicago: University of Chicago Press, 1967), p. 61. Spencer accepts that modern societies are still in a transitory phase between military society and industrialism. Thus he holds that 'a certain brutalisation has to be maintained during our passing phase of civilisation', and that 'while national antagonisms continue strong and national defence a necessity, there is a fitness in this semi-military discipline.' But he also makes clear that this cannot last in the longer term, for 'the direct effect of war on industrial progress is repressive.' See H. Spencer, *The Study of Sociology* (Ann Arbor: University of Michigan Press, 1961), pp. 172, 173 and 179.

32. E. Durkheim, *Socialism* (New York: Collier, 1962), pp. 80—105 and *passim*.

33. E. Durkheim, *Professional Ethics & Civic Morals*, p. 53.

34. Ibid., p. 74.

35. Engels to Marx, 7 Jan. 1858, in K. Marx and F. Engels, *Werke* (Berlin: Dietz Verlag, 1963), vol. 24, p. 252.

36. The most useful general source on these issues is B. Semmel, *Marxism and the Science of War* (Oxford: Oxford University Press, 1981). cf. Solomon F. Bloom, *The World of Nations* (New York: Oxford University Press, 1941), pp. 11—32.

37. K. Marx and F. Engels, 'The Communist Manifesto', in Marx & Engels, *Selected Works in One Volume*, pp. 38—9.

38. Bloom, *The World of Nations*, pp. 206—7. See also Gallie's comments, in W. B. Gallie, *Philosophers in Peace and War* (Cambridge: Cambridge University Press, 1978), chapter 4.

39. Felix Gilbert, *The Historical Essays of Otto Hintze* (New York: Oxford University Press, 1975), p. 183. Hintze is critical, however, of the social Darwinism of Gumphowicz and Ratzenhofer. cf. also Jacques Novicow, *La guerre et ses prétendus bienfaits* (Paris: Alcan, 1894).

40. Ibid. (I have somewhat modified the translation).

41. Still an essential source for understanding Weber's views in this respect is Wolfgang J. Mommsen, *Max Weber und die deutsche Politik, 1890—1920* (Tübingen: Mohr, 1959).

42. cf. 'Max Weber on facts and values', in *SSPT*.

43. *CCHM*, vol. I, chapter 9.

44. See, for example, the otherwise admirable survey given in Bob Jessop, *The Capitalist State* (Oxford: Martin Robertson, 1982).
45. Contrast the by now classic study, Barrington Moore, *The Social Origins of Democracy and Dictatorship* (Harmondsworth Penguin, 1969), which places particular emphasis upon force and violence in the shaping of modern states.
46. Reinhard Bendix, *Kings or People* (Berkeley: University of California Press, 1978), p. 16.
47. Ibid., p. 4.
48. See 'From Marx to Nietzsche? The new conservatism, Foucault, and problems in contemporary political theory', in *PCST*.
49. Bernard-Henri Lévy, *Barbarism With a Human Face* (New York: Harper, 1977).
50. *CCHM*, vol. I, chapter 8.
51. See especially *CS*, chapter 5.
52. *CCHM*, vol. I, pp. 76—81.
53. Ernest Gellner, *Thought and Change* (London: Weidenfeld, 1964), pp. 12—13. cf. *CS*, chapter 5.
54. *CCHM*, vol. I, chapter 3 and *passim*.

2   The Traditional State: Domination and Military Power

1. I shall also use the term 'non-modern' societies, in preference to 'non-capitalist', which I employed in *CCHM*, vol. I. I used the second of these to break with the conventional usage of 'pre-capitalist', because the capitalist societies for a long period of time co-existed with other types of society. But 'non-capitalist' might suggest that the industrialized state socialist societies belong in the same category as tribal and class-divided societies, which is not all that felicitous.
2. S. N. Eisenstadt, *The Political Systems of Empires* (Glencoe: Free Press, 1963). Compare H. J. M. Claessen and P. Skalnik, *The Early State* (The Hague: Mouton, 1978).
3. John A. Wilson, 'Egypt through the New Kingdom', in Carl H. Kraeling and Robert M. Adams, *City Invincible* (Chicago: University of Chicago Press, 1960). It should be emphasized that most nomadic states still do have territorial affiliations. 'Nomadism . . . [is] organised mobility over a space that may be vast but is delimited by custom, treaties, or tacit agreements with competing or related groups.' See Jean-Paul Roux, *Les traditions des nomades* (Paris: Maisonneuve, 1970), p. 37.
4. Gideon Sjoberg, *The Preindustrial City* (Glencoe: The Free Press, 1960), p. 5.

5.   Ibid., pp. 95ff.
6.   Weber, *Economy & Society*, vol. 2, p. 1213.
7.   Sjoberg, *The Preindustrial City*, p. 67.
8.   Paul Wheatley, *The Pivot of the Four Quarters* (Edinburgh: Edinburgh University Press, 1971).
9.   Weber, *Economy & Society*, vol. 2, p. 1222.
10.   Ibid., p. 1223.
11.   Ibid., p. 1229 and ff. See also M. Weber, *The Religion of China* (Glencoe: Free Press, 1964).
12.   Wittfogel, *Oriental Despotism*; Louis Baudin, *A Socialist Empire. The Incas of Peru* (Princeton: Van Nostrand, 1961).
13.   See also Alfred Métraux, *The History of the Incas* (New York: Schocken, 1970).
14.   Weber, *Economy & Society*, vol. 2, p. 1402.
15.   Ibid.
16.   Ibid., pp. 1044—5.
17.   cf. W. M. F. Petrie, *Social Life in Ancient Egypt* (London: Constable, 1923); J. E. M. White, *Ancient Egypt* (London: Allen Wingate, 1952); William F. Edgerton, 'The question of feudal institutions in ancient Egypt', in Rushton Coulborn, *Feudalism in History* (Princeton: Princeton University Press, 1956).
18.   Robert Griffeth and Carol G. Thomas, *The City-State in Five Cultures* (California: Santa Barbara, 1981).
19.   Ibid., p. 186.
20.   Ibid., p. 190. cf. also Robert J. Braidwood & Gordon Willey, *Courses Toward Urban Life* (Chicago: Atdine, 1962); M. E. L. Mallowan, 'The development of cities: from Al Ubaid to the end of Uruk', in the *The Cambridge Ancient History* (Cambridge: Cambridge University Press, 1970), vol. I.
21.   cf. *CCHM*, vol. I, pp. 94—5.
22.   cf. Bloomfield: 'Writing is not language, but merely a way of recording language by means of visible marks'. L. Bloomfield, *Language*. (New York: Allen & Unwin, 1933), p. 21.
23.   Jacques Derrida, *Of Grammatology* (Baltimore: Johns Hopkins University Press, 1974) and other works.
24.   See, in particular, Paul Ricoeur, *Hermeneutics & The Human Sciences* (Cambridge: Cambridge University Press, 1981); and also John B. Thompson, 'Action, ideology and the text', in his *Studies in the Theory of Ideology* (Cambridge: Polity Press, 1984). I am particularly indebted to Thompson's paper for my discussion here.
25.   E. Benveniste, *Problems in General Linguistics* (Florida: University of Miami Press, 1971).

26. Thompson, 'Action, ideology and the text'.
27. Roy Turner, 'Words, utterances and activities', in his *Ethnomethodology* (Harmondsworth: Penguin, 1974).
28. P. Ricoeur, 'The model of the text: meaningful action considered as a text' in his *Hermeneutics and the Human Sciences*, p. 201.
29. cf. Paul Ziff, *Semantic Analysis* (Ithaca: Cornell University Press, 1960).
30. P. Ricoeur: 'What is a text? Explanation & Understanding', in his *Hermeneutics and the Human Sciences*.
31. I. J. Gelb, *A Study of Writing* (London: Routledge & Kegan Paul, 1952), chapter 1. See also S. N. Kramer, *From the Tablets of Sumer* (Indian Hills: Colorado University Press, 1956).
32. Gelb, *A Study of Writing*, p. 60ff.
33. Jack Goody, *The Domestication of the Savage Mind* (Cambridge: Cambridge University Press, 1977), p. 83. This book is a fundamental source for considering questions of the relation of writing to power.
34. A. H. Gardiner, *Ancient Egyptian Onomastica* (Oxford: Oxford University Press, 1947), vol. I, p. 1.
35. Goody, *The Savage Mind*, p. 86.
36. D. J. Wiseman, 'Books in the Ancient Near East and in the Old Testament', in P. R. Ackroyd, C. F. Evans and G. W. H. Lampe, *The Cambridge History of the Bible* (Cambridge: Cambridge University Press, 1963), vol. I, p. 45.
37. Edward McNall Burns and Philip Lee Ralph, 'The civilisations of the Nile', in their *World Civilisations* (New York: Norton, 1974).
38. Michel Foucault, *Discipline and Punish* (London: Allen Lane, 1977).
39. Wittfogel, *Oriental Despotism*.
40. Edmund Leach, 'Hydraulic society in Ceylon', *Past and Present*, 15, 1959.
41. Wolfram Eberhard, *Conquerors and Rulers* (Leiden: Brill, 1970).
42. I. E. S. Edwards, *The Pyramids of Egypt* (Baltimore: Max Parrish, 1962); A. W. Shorter, *Everyday Life in Ancient Egypt* (London: Marston & Co., 1932).
43. On this see Weber, *Economy & Society*, vol. 2, p. 1168ff.
44. F. Ratzel, *Anthropogeographie* (Stuttgart: 1882); *Politische Geographie* (Berlin: R. Oldenboug, 1897).
45. F. Ratzel, *Politische Geographie*, p. 584ff. However cf. J. Ancel, *Les frontières* (Paris: Gallimard, 1938).
46. J. R. V. Prescott, *Boundaries and Frontiers* (London: Croom Helm, 1978), chapter 2.

47. Ibid., p. 40ff.
48. G. W. B. Huntingford, *The Galla of Ethiopia* (London: Hakluyt Society 1955), p. 116.
49. Owen Lattimore, *Inner Asian Frontiers of China* (New York: Oxford University Press, 1940); J. Baradez, *Fossatum Africae* (Paris: Arts et Metiers, 1949); R. G. Collingwood, *Roman Britain* (Oxford: Clarendon Press, 1932).
50. Baradez, *Fossatum Africae.*
51. Irfan Habib, *The Agrarian System of Mughal India* (London: Asia Publishing House, 1963).
52. Eberhard, *Conquerors & Rulers.*
53. H. A. R. Gibb and Harold Bowen, *Islamic Society and the West* (London: Oxford University Press, 1950), vol. I, p. 209.
54. John H. Kautsky, *The Politics of Aristocratic Empires* (Chapel Hill: University of North Carolina Press, 1982), p. 120. cf. also Bendix, who says that in traditional social orders 'the term "society" is applied only with difficulty, since the people themselves live in fragmented subordination, while their rulers constitute "the society" because they are persons worthy of note in the country.' See Reinhard Bendix, *Nation Building and Citizenship* (Berkeley: University of California Press, 1977), p. 401.
55. For a recent discussion of the so-called 'warfare theory' of the state, see Claessen and Skalnik, *The Early State.*
56. Marvin Harris, *Cannibals and Kings* (London: Fontana, 1978), p. 41.
57. cf. K. F. Otterbein, *The Evolution of War* (New Haven: Human Relations Area Files Press, 1970).
58. As Harris puts it, virtually all small societies, including Hunters and gatherers, 'carry out some form of intergroup combat in which teams of warriors deliberately try to kill each another'. See Harris, *Cannibals and Kings*, p. 41; cf. Quincy Wright, *A Study of War* (Chicago: University of Chicago Press, 1965), chapter 6; T. Brock and J. Galting, 'Belligerence among the primitives', *Journal of Peace Research*, 3, 1966.
59. William H. McNeill, *The Pursuit of Power* (Oxford: Basil Blackwell, 1983), p. 1.
60. V. Gordon Childe, *Man Makes Himself* (London: Watts, 1956), p. 234.
61. Griffeth and Thomas, *The City-State in Five Cultures*, p. 197.
62. Weber, *The Religion of India* (Glencoe: Free Press, 1958), p. 64.
63. John A. Wilson, *The Burden of Egypt* (Chicago: University of Chicago Press, 1951).

64. Burns and Ralph, 'The Mesopotamian and Persian civilisations', in *World Civilizations,* p. 63. See also Yigael Yadin, *The Art of Warfare in Biblical Lands in the Light of Archaeological Study* (London: Weidenfeld, 1963), 2 vols.

65. A. T. E. Olmstead, *History of Palestine & Syria* (New York: Charles Scribner, 1931).

66. Chung-li Chang, *The Chinese Gentry* (Seattle: University of Washington Press, 1955); Wolfram Eberhard, *A History of China* (London: Routledge, 1950); John K. Fairbank, *Chinese Thought and Institutions* (Chicago: University of Chicago Press, 1959).

67. *CCHM*, vol. I, chapter 7.

68. Weber, *Economy & Society*, vol. 2, p. 980ff.

69. cf. Eric Hobsbawm, *Primitive Rebels* (Manchester: Manchester University Press, 1959). cf. also Philip A. Kuhn, *Rebellion and its Enemies in Late Imperial China* (Cambridge: Harvard University Press, 1970), chapter I.

70. Kautsky, *Aristocratic Empires*, pp. 73 and 150.

71. Michael Rawdin, *The Mongol Empire: its Rise & Legacy* (New York: Free Press, 1967).

72. Robert G. Wesson, *The Imperial Order* (Berkeley: University of California Press, 1967), p. 248. cf. also G. H. Stevenson, *Roman Provincial Administration* (Oxford: Basil Blackwell, 1949); Jules Toutain, *The Economic Life of the Ancient World* (London: Kegan Paul, 1930).

73. The Sacred Law of the Ottoman Empire supposedly stood higher than the Sultan, although in practice this was more or less meaningless.

74. Nevin O. Winter, *The Russian Empire of Today & Yesterday* (London: Simpkin, 1914), p. 440.

75. W. T. De Bary, 'Chinese despotism and the Confucian ideal: A seventeenth century View', in Fairbank, *Chinese Thought and Institutions.*

76. Joseph Needham, *Science & Civilisation in China* (Cambridge: Cambridge University Press, 1954), vol. I.

77. K. Marx, 'The British rule in India', in Shlomo Avineri (ed.), *Karl Marx on Colonialism and Modernisation* (New York: Doubleday, 1968).

78. Weber, *The Religion of China*, pp. 91 and 93; see also Eberhard, *A History of China*, p. 64ff.

79. T. J. A. Le Goff and D. M. G. Sutherland, 'The revolution and the rural community in eighteenth-century Brittany', *Past and Present*, 62, 1974, p. 97.

3   The Traditional State: Bureaucracy, Class, Ideology

1.   Wesson, *The Imperial Order*, p. 116.
2.   C. Hucker, 'The Tung-Lin movement of the Late Ming Period', in Fairbank, *Chinese Thought and Institutions.*
3.   Weber, *Economy & Society*, vol. 2, pp. 1032—8.
4.   Wittfogel, *Oriental Despotism*, pp. 302—3.
5.   This was the view I once advocated. See *CSAS*, pp. 132—8 and *passim.*
6.   S. Wells Williams, *The Middle Kingdom* (New York: Wiley, 1879), vol. I, pp. 354—6.
7.   Marx & Engels: 'The Communist Manifesto', p. 35. Engels later added to this the reservation 'That is, all *written* history' which, from the point of view discussed here, does not alter anything of the substance of the claim.
8.   cf. *CCHM*, vol. I, pp. 105—8.
9.   Eric Wolf, *Peasant Wars of the Twentieth Century* (New York: Harper, 1969), p. 279.
10. Kautsky, *Aristocratic Empires*, pp. 281—92.
11. W. Eberhard, *Das Toba-Reich Nordchinas.* (Leiden: Brill, 1949). Kautsky, mistakenly in my view, tries to associate all peasant uprisings with commercialization, arguing that in the relevant period of Chinese history there was a significant acceleration of commerce.
12. Eberhard, *Conquerors & Rulers*, p. 89ff.
13. cf. *CCHM*, vol. I, p. 220ff.
14. This point is made in Michael Mann, 'States, ancient and modern', *Archives européennes de sociologie,* 18, 1977.
15. *CS*, chapter 4.
16. Karl Polanyi, *The Great Transformation* (London: Victor Gollancz, 1945).
17. *CCHM*, vol. I, chapter 5.
18. Jacques Soustelle, *Daily Life of the Aztecs on the Eve of the Spanish Conquest* (Stanford: Stanford University Press, 1970).
19. Particularly in K. Marx, *Grundrisse* (Harmondsworth: Penguin, 1973), p. 107ff.
20. If this is not a contradiction in terms. See, for example, Wolf, *Peasant Wars*, p. 10—11, where he defines the 'peasantry' as agrarian workers who have to transfer part of their product to a ruling group.
21. K. Marx and F. Engels, *The German Ideology* (London: Lawrence and Wishart, 1965), p. 61.

22. cf. Jorge Larrain, *Marxism & Ideology* (London: Macmillan, 1983).
23. Soustelle, *Daily Life of the Aztecs*, pp. 100—1.
24. B. P. Lamb, *India: a World in Transition* (New York: Praeger, 1963), pp. 26—7.
25. Weber, *Economy & Society*, vol. I, pp. 472—80.
26. Ibid., p. 431.
27. Arthur F. Wright, *The Confucianist Persuasion* (Stanford: Stanford University Press, 1960).
28. Kung-chuan Hsiao, *Rural China, Imperial Control in the Nineteenth Century* (Seattle: University of Washington Press, 1960).
29. On the role of eunuchs in Rome, see A. H. M. Jones, *The Later Roman Empire* (Oxford: Basil Blackwell, 1964), vol. II, p. 570ff.
30. Edward Gibbon, *The Decline & Fall of the Roman Empire* (New York: Modern Library, 1932), vol. I, p. 102ff.
31. Gordon Tullock, *The Politics of Bureaucracy* (Washington: Public Affairs Press, 1965), pp. 215—16.
32. K. Marx, *Capital*, vol. I (London: Lawrence & Wishart, 1970), p. 376.
33. A. D. Alderson, *The Structure of the Ottoman Dynasty* (Oxford: Clarendon Press, 1956), p. 76.
34. Calculations given in Kautsky, *Aristocratic Empires*, p. 247.
35. Li Chien-nung, *The Political History of China, 1840—1928* (Princeton: Van Nostrand, 1956), p. 43.
36. Albert H. Lyber, *The Government of the Ottoman Empire* (Cambridge, Mass: Harvard University Press, 1963), p. 29.
37. cf. M Frederick Nelson, *Korea & the Old Order in Eastern Asia* (Baton Rouge: Louisiana State University Press, 1946), p. 84ff.
38. cf. Jeremy A. Sabloff & C. C. Lamberg-Karlovsky, *Ancient Civilisation and Trade* (Alberquerque: University of New Mexico Press, 1975); Robert M. Adams, 'Anthropological perspectives on ancient trade', *Current Anthropology*, 15, 1974.
39. Samuel Noah Kramer, *History Begins at Sumer* (New York: Anchor, 1959).

4   The Absolutist State and the Nation-State

1. cf. *CCHM*, vol. I, pp. 182—6.
2. Of course, such a statement brusquely shoves aside a range of complex issues much debated by historians, which a more detailed discussion would necessarily have to examine at some length. Although it is ageing, probably the most useful general discussion in English is still Rushton Coulborn, *Feudalism in History* (Princeton: Princeton University Press, 1956). cf. also Owen

Lattimore, 'Feudalism in history', *Past and Present*, 12, 1957; F. Cheyette, *Lordship and Community in Mediaeval Europe* (New York, 1968).

3. Perry Anderson, *Passages from Antiquity to Feudalism* (London: New Left Books, 1974), and *Lineages of the Absolutist State* (London: New Left Books, 1974).

4. Maurice Ashley, *The Golden Century, Europe 1598—1917* (London: Weidenfeld, 1969), p. 217.

5. Geoffrey Barraclough, *European Unity in Thought & Action* (Oxford: Basil Blackwell, 1963). Compare René Albrecht-Carré, *The Unity of Europe: an Historical Survey* (London: Secker & Warburg, 1966).

6. cf. Meinecke, *Der Idee der Staatsräson* (Berlin: R. Oldenbourg, 1924).

7. E. M. Satow, *A Guide to Diplomatic Practice* (London: Longman, 1922); Garrett Mattingly, *Rennaissance Diplomacy* (London: Jonathan Cape, 1955).

8. G. N. Clark, *The Seventeenth Century* (Oxford: Clarendon Press, 1947), p. 135.

9. A. Sorel, *L'Europe et la révolution française* (Paris: E. Plon, 1885), vol. I, pp. 33—4. cf. Manning on the emergence of 'meta-diplomatics' — the attribution of individuality to states in a manner unknown in prior state forms. C. A. W. Manning, *The Nature of International Society* (London: Bell, 1962).

10. cf. Meinecke, *Der Idee der Staaträson.*

11. Quoted in Clark, *The Seventeenth Century.*

12. Ibid., p. 141ff.

13. Ibid., p. 144.

14. Roger Lockyer, *Hapsburg and Bourbon Europe 1470—1720* (London: Longman, 1974).

15. Clifford Geertz, *Local Knowledge* (New York: Basic Books, 1983).

16. The term 'the West' is of course of quite recent provenance, and was favoured by Continental (especially German) authors some while before it came into widespread use among English-speaking writers.

17. This means taking issue with Wallerstein's formulation of 'world system theory' which, of course, has been the subject of much critical discussion in any case (see the discussion on pp. 161—71).

18. Anderson, *Lineages of the Absolutist State*, pp. 39 and 29. Anderson does say that diplomacy 'was one of the great institutional inventions of the age', and that 'with its emergence an international state system was born in Europe.' (p. 37).

19. See Quentin Skinner, *The Foundations of Modern Political Thought* (Cambridge: Cambridge University Press, 1978), 2 vols, especially vol. 2, p. 286ff.

20. Clark, *The Seventeenth Century*, p. 219, cf. Betrand de Jouvenel, *Sovereignty* (Cambridge: Cambridge University Press, 1957).

21. cf. C. B. Macpherson, 'A political theory of property' in *Democratic Theory: Essays in Retrieval* (Oxford: Clarendon Press 1973), p. 125ff.

22. cf. Christopher Hill, *The World Turned Upside Down* (London: Temple Smith, 1972).

23. Well analysed by Hintze, in *Staat und Verfassung* (Göttingen: Vandenhoeck, 1962), p. 264ff.

24. John C. Rule, *Louis XIV and the Craft of Kingship* (Columbus: Ohio State University Press, 1969).

25. Lockyer, *Hapsburg and Bourbon Europe*, pp. 481−2.

26. K. Marx, 'The civil war in France', in Marx & Engels, *Selected Works,* p. 289.

27. Anderson, *Lineages of the Absolutist State*, p. 18.

28. Quoted in William F. Church, *The Greatness of Louis XIV, Myth or Reality?* (Boston, Mass: Heath, 1959), p. 47.

29. Pierre Goubert, *Beauvais et le Beauvaisis de 1600 à 1780* (Paris: SEUPEN, 1960), p. 13ff.

30. Gianfranco Poggi, *The Development of the Modern State* (London: Hutchinson, 1978), p. 73. Poggi's discussion of the development of law in the absolutist state, although brief, is exemplary.

31. Weber, *Economy & Society*, vol. 2, pp. 800−2.

32. cf. P. Vinogradoff, *Roman Law in Mediaeval Europe* (London: Harper, 1909).

33. Preston King, *The Ideology of Order* (London: Allen & Unwin, 1974), p. 75.

34. cf. Klaus Doerner, *Madmen and the Bourgeoisie* (Oxford: Basil Blackwell, 1981).

35. Sean McConville, *A History of English Prison Administration* (London: Routledge & Kegan Paul, 1981), p. 31ff.

36. Doerner, *Madmen and the Bourgeoisie*, pp. 15−16.

37. Clark, *The Seventeenth Century*, p. 98.

38. Trevor Aston, *Crisis in Europe 1560−1660* (London: Routledge & Kegan Paul, 1965). Of course, the theme of the 'general crisis' has been discussed almost *ad nauseam* in the subsequent literature.

39. A key source for the early seventeenth century in France is A. D. Lublinskaya, *French Absolutism: The Crucial Phase, 1620−29* (Cambridge: Cambridge University Press, 1968), chapters 3 and 5.

354   *Notes to Chapter 4*

40. E. N. Williams, *The Ancien Regime in Europe* (London: Bodley Head, 1970), pp. 2 and 14.
41. C. Tilly, 'Reflections on the history of European state-making' in his edited volume *The Formation of National States in Europe* (Princeton: Princeton University Press, 1975), p. 38.
42. Beautifully analysed in Clark, *The Seventeenth Century*, p. 155ff.
43. Frank A. Kierman and John K. Fairbank, *Chinese Ways in Warfare,* (Cambridge, Mass: Harvard University Press, 1974). See, in particular, the article by Herbert Franke, 'Siege and defence of towns in mediaeval China'.
44. Charles O. Hucker, *Chinese Government in Ming Times: Seven Studies* (New York: Columbia University Press, 1969). A very useful survey of Chinese military strength appears in chapter 2 of William H. McNeill, *The Pursuit of Power* (Oxford: Basil Blackwell, 1983).
45. cf. Kautsky, *Aristocratic Empires*, chapters 2–3.
46. Charles W. C. Oman, *The Art of War in the Middle Ages, 375–1515* (Ithaca: Cornell University Press, 1953). See also Sidney Toy, *A History of Fortification from 3000 BC to 1700* (London: Heinemann, 1955).
47. L. T. White, *Mediaeval Technology and Social Change* (Oxford: Clarendon Press, 1962), chapter I.
48. Samuel E. Finer, 'State- and nation-building in Europe: the role of the military', in Tilly (ed.), *The Formation of National States*, p. 103.
49. The mechanization of weaponry antedates by centuries its application to the 'logistics of war'. Horses and human muscle remained the basis of military transportation even in the First World War, in which the British army shipped more tons of oats and hay to the Front than ammunition. The average foot-soldier throughout the history of civilization could not march more than between twelve and eighteen miles a day, or carry more than some eighty pounds, including two weeks' rations. cf. S. L. A. Marshall, *The Soldier's Load and the Mobility of a Nation* (Washington: Combat Forces Press, 1950).
50. Theodore Ropp, *War in the Modern World* (Westport: Greenwood, 1959).
51. Pitrim Sorokin, *Social and Cultural Dynamics* (New York: American Book Company, 1937), vol. 3.
52. Ropp, *War in the Modern World*, p. 7.
53. Geoffrey Parlier, 'The "military revolution" 1550–1660 — a myth?', *Journal of Modern History*, 48, 1976, p. 206.
54. Bernard Brodie, *A Guide to Naval Strategy* (Princeton: Princeton University Press, 1958).

55. Garrett Mattingly, *The Defeat of the Spanish Armada* (London: Jonathan Cape, 1959).
56. McNeill, *The Pursuit of Power*, p. 100. See also Carlo M. Cipolla, *Guns and Sails in the Early Phase of European Expansion 1400—1700* (London: Collins, 1965).
57. cf. Jean Gimpel, *The Mediaeval Machine* (London: Victor Gollancz, 1977).
58. The phrase is from Clark, *The Seventeenth Century*, p. 65.
59. Lewis Mumford, *The Myth of the Machine* (London: Secker & Warburg, 1967), and *The Pentagon of Power* (London: Secker & Warburg, 1971).
60. Maury D. Feld, *The Structure of Violence* (Beverly Hills: Sage, 1977), p. 6ff; see also Jacques van Doorn, *The Soldier and Social Change* (Beverly Hills: Sage, 1975), p. 9ff.
61. Van Doorn, *The Soldier and Social Change*, p. 11.
62. Feld, *The Structure of Violence*, p. 7.
63. Foucault, *Discipline and Punish*.
64. Samuel P. Huntington, *The Soldier and The State* (Cambridge, Mass: Harvard University Press, 1957), p. 20.
65. A classical work on the subject is R. Ehrenberg, *Das Zeitalter der Fugger* (Jena, 1896). W. Sombart's *Krieg und Kapitalismus* (Duncker and Humbolt, Munich, 1913) remains suggestive, although some of its key ideas are now somewhat discredited. For a well-known critique, see J. U. Nef, *War and Human Progress* (Cambridge, Mass: Harvard University Press, 1950). cf. also J. M. Winter, 'The economic and social history of war', in his *War and Economic Development* (Cambridge: Cambridge University Press, 1975).
66. Recapitulating the discussion offered in *CCHM*, vol. I, pp. 190—6.
67. Frederik Barth, *Ethnic Groups and Boundaries* (Bergen: Universitats-fur Paget, 1969).
68. John A. Armstrong, *Nations Before Nationalism* (Chapel Hill: University of North Carolina Press, 1982), p. 5.
69. A. D. Alderson, *The Structure of the Ottoman Dynasty* (Oxford: Clarendon Press, 1956).
70. Hugh Seton-Watson, *Nations and States* (London: Methuen, 1982), p. 26ff.
71. G. W. S. Barrow, *Feudal Britain* (London: Arnold, 1956), p. 410ff.
72. Albert C. Baugh, *A History of the English Language* (London: Routledge & Kegan Paul, 1951).
73. Seton-Watson, *Nations and States*, pp. 44—5.
74. E. Kedourie, *Nationalism* (London: Hutchinson, 1961).

75. cf. S. B. Jones, *Boundary Making: a Handbook for Statesmen* (Washington: Carnegie Endowment for International Peace Monograph, 1945).
76. Prescott, *Boundaries and Frontiers*, p. 65.

77. *CCHM*, vol. I, p. 190.

5   Capitalism, Industrialism and Social Transformation

1. Cf. 'Four myths in the history of social thought', in *SSPT*.
2. Stephen Kalberg, 'Max Weber's universal-historical architectonic of economically-oriented action', in Scott McNall, *Current Perspectives in Social Theory,* vol. 4, 1983, p. 266ff; Weber, *Economy & Society*, vol. I, p. 100ff.
3. From a different theoretical standpoint, Parsons and Luhmann have developed a parallel idea. Money for them is, as such, a 'medium of communication', together with other overlapping media. See Niklas Luhmann, *Trust and Power* (Chichester: Wiley, 1979), chapter 3; and, particularly, Parsons: 'On the concept of political power'.
4. Weber, *Economy & Society,* vol. I, pp. 101–2.
5. Ibid., p. 102. In the passage concerned, Weber discusses both pre-monetary systems and socialist theories of the abolition of money. The 'irrational' aspect of provision in kind refers to the latter, which in Weber's eyes are wholly impracticable in a modern economic setting.
6. cf. Paul Einzig, *Primitive Money* (Oxford: Pergamon Press, 1966), part 4.
7. Ibid., p. 447.
8. Weber, *The Protestant Ethic and the Spirit of Capitalism* (London: Allen & Unwin, 1976), p. 17ff.
9. Weber, *Economy & Society*, vol. I, p. 165.
10. Ibid. See also M. Weber, *General Economic History* (New York: Collier, 1961), pp. 232–3.
11. Ibid., p. 163.
12. Ibid., pp. 83–4.
13. Weber, *General Economic History*, p. 231.
14. Ibid., pp. 224–5.
15. K. Marx, *Capital* (London: Lawrence & Wishart, 1970), vol. I, p. 715.
16. Ibid., p. 714.
17. Ibid., p. 713.
18. Ibid., p. 714.

19. cf. *CCHM*, vol. I, p. 96ff.
20. Ibid., chapter 6.
21. K. Marx: 'Economic & Philosophical Manuscripts' in T. B. Bottomore, *Karl Marx, Early Writings* (New York: McGraw-Hill, 1964), pp. 189—91.
22. Marx, *Capital*, vol. I, p. 96.
23. For further discussion of this point, see *CCHM*, vol. I, chapters 2—5.
24. See especially Karl Polanyi, *The Great Transformation*.
25. cf. *CCHM*, vol. I, p. 113ff.
26. Adam Smith, *The Theory of Moral Sentiments* (Oxford: Oxford University Press, 1976), p. 11.
27. Adam Ferguson, *An Essay on the History of Civil Society* (Edinburgh: Edinburgh University Press, 1966), p. 105.
28. Keith Tribe, *Genealogies of Capitalism* (London: Macmillan, 1981), p. 106.
29. cf. 'Four myths in the history of social thought', in *SSPT*.
30. cf. Sidney Pollard, *The Genesis of Modern Management* (London: Arnold, 1965).
31. Marx, *Capital*, vol. I, p. 371ff.
32. Weber, *General Economic History,* chapter 27.
33. cf. *CCHM*, vol. I, chapter 6.
34. For a discussion of some of these issues (not expressed wholly in the same form in which I would put them today), see *CSAS*, chapter 3 and *passim.*
35. *CCHM*, vol. I, p. 110ff.
36. Harry Braverman, *Labour and Monopoly Capital* (New York: Monthly Review Press, 1967).
37. *CCHM*, vol. I, chapter 5.

6 Capitalism and the State: from Absolutism to the Nation-State

1. Joseph Schumpeter, 'The crisis of the tax state', in Alan T. Peacock *et al.*, *International Economic Papers* (New York: Macmillan, 1954).
2. Weber, *Economy & Society*, vol. I, p. 328ff.
3. Weber, *General Economic History*, p. 251.
4. Weber, *Economy & Society*, vol. I, pp. 334—7.
5. Victor M. Perez-Diaz, *State, Bureaucracy and Civil Society* (London: Macmillan, 1978). For the best discussion of Marx on the issue, although strictly limited in terms of its own critical standpoint, see S. De Brunhoff, *Marx on Money* (London: Pluto Press, 1977).

Useful comments connecting with my discussion here are to be found in G. K. Ingham, *Capitalism Divided?* (London: Macmillan, 1984). Among other works see, in particular, R. F. Harrod, *Money* (London: Macmillan, 1969).

6. cf. Max Weber, *General Economic History*, p. 258ff.
7. cf. Antony Cutler, *Marx's Capital and Capitalism Today* (London: Routledge & Kegan Paul, 1978), vol. 2, p. 30ff.
8. Ibid., p. 35.
9. Rudolf Braun, 'Taxation, sociopolitical structure, and state-building: Great Britain and Brandenburg-Prussia', in Tilly, *The Formation of National States*, p. 246.
10. Rudolf Goldscheid: 'Staat, öffenticher Haushalt und Gesellschaft', *Handbuch der Finanzwissenschaft* (Tübingen: Möhr, 1926), vol. I, p. 149.
11. *CCHM*, vol. I, chapter 6 and *passim*.
12. When these are portrayed in a particular fashion. See *CCHM*, vol. I, chapter 2.
13. See, for example, *CPST*, chapter 6; *CS*, chapter 5.
14. Immanuel Wallerstein, *The Modern World System* (New York: Academic Press, 1974), chapter 1. cf. also Terence K. Hopkins, 'The study of the capitalist world economy: some introductory considerations', in Walter L. Goldfrank, *The World-System of Capitalism: Past and Present* (Beverly Hills: Sage, 1979).
15. I. Wallerstein, 'Modernisation: Requiescet in Pace', in his *The Capitalist World Economy* (Cambridge: Cambridge University Press, 1979), pp. 133 & 134.
16. Wallerstein, 'Three paths of national development', Ibid., p. 39.
17. Ibid., p. 41.
18. Wallerstein: 'The rise and future demise of the world capitalist system: concepts for comparative analysis', Ibid., p. 19.
19. Wallerstein, 'The rural economy in modern world society', Ibid., p. 125.
20. For example R. Brenner, 'The origins of capitalist development: a critique of neo-Smithian Marxism', *New Left Review*, 105, 1977; Theda Skocpol, 'Wallerstein's world-capitalist system: a theoretical and historical critique', and M. Janowitz 'A sociological perspective on Wallerstein', both in *American Journal of Sociology*, 82, 1977.
21. cf. T. K. Hopkins and I. Wallerstein, 'The comparative study of national societies', *Social Science Information*, 6, 1967.
22. I. Wallerstein, 'Dependence in an interdependent world: the limited possibilities of transformation within the capitalist world-economy', in *The Capitalist World-Economy*, p. 69. It should be pointed out that Wallerstein has in later works tried to move away from his

earlier functionalism. But he has not done so convincingly. As Connell says, 'Wallerstein repeatedly speaks of struggle and practice, but it is hard to *feel* them in his more general formulations.' See R. W. Connell, 'Class formation on a world scale', in his *Which Way is Up?* (Sydney: Allen & Unwin, 1983).

23.   cf. *CPST*, p. 73ff.

7   Administrative Power, Internal Pacification

1.   D. G. Janelle, 'Central place development in a time—space framework', *Professional Geographer*, 20, 1968. See also Don Parkes and Nigel Thrift, *Times, Spaces and Places* (Chichester: Wiley, 1980), chapter 7.

2.   J. Bischoff, *A Comprehensive History of the Woollen and Worsted Manufactures* (London, 1842), p. 428. This passage is quoted and criticized in some part by Derek Gregory, who suggests that the road system was in fact rather better than it implies. See his *Regional Transformation and Industrial Revolution* (London: Macmillan, 1982, pp. 54—5).

3.   cf. Evitar Zerubavel, *Hidden Rhythms* (Chicago: University of Chicago Press, 1981).

4.   Lewis Mumford, *Interpretations and Forecasts* (London: Secker & Warburg, 1973).

5.   Frank Norris, *The Octopus* (London: Grant Richards, 1901), p. 42.

6.   cf. Evitar Zerubavel, *Hidden Rhythms*.

7.   Derek Howse, *Greenwich Time and the Discovery of the Longtitude* (New York: Oxford University Press, 1980), p. 121.

8.   Stephen Kern, *The Culture of Time and Space 1880—1918* (London: Weidenfeld, 1983), p. 12.

9.   Ibid., p. 13.

10.   Figures 2 and 3 from Ronald Abler, 'Effects of space-adjusting technologies on the human geography of the future', in Abler *et al.*, *Human Geography in a Shrinking World* (North Scituate: Duxbury, 1975), pp. 39 and 41.

11.   Ibid., p. 40.

12.   Ithiel da Sola Pool, *The Social Impact of the Telephone* (Boston, Mass: MIT Press, 1977).

13.   H. A. Innis, *Empire and Communications* (Oxford: Clarendon Press, 1950), p. 7.

14.   Although it could be claimed McLuhan managed to do so. For a more sober, yet instructive, appraisal see in particular Elizabeth L. Eisenstein, *The Printing Revolution in Early Modern Europe* (Cambridge: Cambridge University Press, 1983).

15. cf. Anthony Oberschall, *The Establishment of Empirical Social Research in Germany,* (The Hague: Mouton, 1965). On the growth of state documentation, see B. R. Mitchell, *European Historical Statistics, 1750—1970* (New York: Columbia University Press, 1975).
16. cf. *CS*, chapter 6.
17. Foucault, *Discipline and Punish.*
18. Doerner, *Madmen and the Bourgeoisie,* p. 16ff.
19. George Rosen, 'The hospital: historical sociology of a community institution', in Eliot Freidson, *The Hospital in Modern Society* (Glencoe: The Free Press, 1963).
20. Brian Tierney, *Mediaeval Poor Law* (Berkeley: University of California Press, 1959).
21. Sean McConville, *A History of English Prison Administration* (London: Routledge & Kegan Paul, 1981), vol. I, p. 31ff.
22. cf. 'From Marx to Nietzsche? Neo-conservatism, Foucault, and problems in contemporary political theory', in *PCST*; see also *CS*, chapter 3.
23. cf. George Rusche and Otto Kirchheimer, *Punishment and Social Structure* (New York: Russell & Russell, 1968), p. 42ff.
24. cf. Michael Ignatieff, *A Just Measure of Pain* (London: Macmillan, 1978).
25. cf. *CS*, chapter 2.
26. Sidney Pollard, *The Genesis of Modern Management* (London: Arnold, 1965), p. 163.
27. See the work by Horace Bleackley, *The Hangmen of England*, reprinted in its entirety in John Lofland, *State Executions* (Montclair NJ: Patterson Smith, 1977).
28. Ibid., p. 312. See also Alice Morse Earle, *Curious Punishments of Bygone Days* (Montclair: Smith, 1969). Originally published in 1896.
29. cf. Eberhard, *Conquerors and Rulers.*
30. T. J. A. Le Goff and D. M. G. Sutherland, 'The Revolution and the rural community in eighteenth century Brittany', *Past and Present*, 62, 1974, p. 97.
31. Alan Macfarlane, *The Justice and the Mare's Ale* (Oxford: Basil Blackwell, 1981), pp. 189—90.
32. Quoted in T. A. Critchley, *A History of Police in England and Wales* (London: Constable, 1978), p. 22.
33. S. and B. Webb, *English Local Government* (London: Macmillan, 1922), vol. 4, p. 408.
34. Ted Robert Gurr, *Rogues, Rebels and Reformers* (Beverly Hills: Sage, 1976), p. 34ff.
35. Macfarlane, *The Justice and the Mare's Ale*, p. 189.

36. Although it is analysed at greater length in *CCHM*, vol. I.
37. On this matter there are major disagreements among interpreters of Marx. For a relevant discussion, see Steven Lukes, *Marxism and Morality* (Oxford: Oxford University Press, forthcoming).
38. Gurr, *Rogues, Rebels and Reformers.*
39. *CCHM*, vol. I, chapter 5.
40. For a discussion of regionalization, see *CS*, chapter 3.
41. Philippe Ariès, *Western Attitudes Towards Death* (Baltimore: Johns Hopkins University Press, 1974), p. 58. See also Joachim Whaley, *Mirrors of Mortality* (London: Europa, 1981); and Le Roy Ladurie, 'Chanu, Lebrun, Vovelle: la nouvelle histoire de la mort', in *Le Territoire de l'historien* (Paris: Gallimard, 1973—8), 2 vols.
42. Norbert Elias, *The Civilising Process* (Oxford: Basil Blackwell, 1978).
43. *CS*, chapter 2; *CPST*, pp. 123—8.
44. *CCHM*, vol. I, pp. 230—9.

8   Class, Sovereignty and Citizenship

1. So little importance does Bendix attach to class division that neither the concept of 'class', nor any related notions employing the concept, appear in the index of *Kings or People*. In this respect the indexer has been perfectly true to the claims of the book.
2. Charles E. Lindblom, *Politics and Markets* (New York: Basic Books, 1977), pp. 132—3 and *passim.* Lindblom relies heavily upon R. A. Dahl, *Polyarchy* (New Haven: Yale University Press, 1971). See also Dahl, *A Preface to Democratic Theory* (Chicago: University of Chicago Press, 1956).
3. Dahl, *Polyarchy*, pp. 1—2.
4. Again following Dahl, *Polyarchy.*
5. T. H. Marshall, *Class, Citizenship and Social Development* (Westport: Greenwood Press, 1973).
6. Parsons, 'On the concept of political power', and 'Some reflections on the place of force in social process', in Harry Eckstein, *Internal War* (Glencoe: Free Press, 1964). See also Luhmann, *Trust and Power.*
7. Here I draw extensively upon 'Class division, class conflict and citizenship rights', in *PCST.*
8. Quoted in Marshall, *Class, Citizenship and Social Development*, p. 46.
9. Marshall, Ibid., pp. 84 and 96—7.
10. cf. *CCHM*, vol. I, chapter 6.

11. K. Marx, 'The Eighteenth Brumaire of Louis Bonaparte', in Marx & Engels, *Selected Works*, pp. 171—2.

12. cf. Quentin Skinner, *The Foundations of Modern Political Thought* (Cambridge: Cambridge University Press, 1978), 2 vols.

13. Alvin W. Gouldner, *The Dialectic of Ideology and Technology* (New York: Seabury, 1976), p. 95.

14. *CPST*, pp. 221—3.

15. *CCHM*, vol. I, pp. 190—1.

16. Armstrong, *Nations Before Nationalism,* p. 9ff.

17. John Breuilly, *Nationalism and the State* (Manchester: Manchester University Press, 1982), p. 19ff. I have modified the categories somewhat.

18. Ernest Gellner, *Nations and Nationalism* (Oxford: Basil Blackwell, 1983), p. 129.

19. cf. Bloom, *The World of Nations.*

20. As Gellner accepts, while denying that what makes it illuminating has much to do with Marxist thought. See his *Nations and Nationalism,* p. 96.

21. Tom Nairn, *The Break-up of Britain* (London: New Left Books, 1977).

22. Nairn, *The Break-up of Britain*, pp. 351 and 353.

23. E. Gellner, 'Nationalism, or the new confessions of a justified Edinburgh sinner', in his *Spectacles and Predicaments* (Cambridge: Cambridge University Press, 1979).

24. Karl W. Deutsch, *Nationalism and Social Communication* (Boston: MIT Press, 1966).

25. Gellner, *Nations and Nationalism*, p. 140.

26. See, for example, L. Doob, *Patriotism and Nationalism* (New Haven: Yale University Press, 1964); Anthony D. Smith, *Theories of Nationalism* (London: Duckworth, 1971).

27. cf. David Apter, *The Politics of Modernisation* (Chicago: University of Chicago Press, 1965), and 'Political religion in new nations', in Clifford Geertz, *Old Societies and New States* (New York: Collier-Macmillan, 1963).

28. Anthony D. Smith, *Nationalism in the Twentieth Century* (Oxford: Martin Robertson, 1979), p. 3. cf. Benedict Anderson on the 'shrunken imaginings of recent history' generic to nationalism. Benedict Anderson, *Imagined Communities* (London: Verso, 1983).

29. cf. Elie Kedourie, *Nationalism* (London: Hutchinson, 1960).

30. Here I follow the analysis given in *CCHM*, vol. I, pp. 192—6.

31. Smith, *Nationalism in the Twentieth Century*, p. 187.

32. As Hobsbawm comments in respect of 'invented traditions':

> One marked difference between old and invented practices may be observed. The former were specific and strongly binding

social practices, the latter tended to be quite unspecific and vague . . . But if the content of British patriotism or 'Americanism' was notably ill-defined, though usually specified in commentaries associated with ritual occasions, the *practices* symbolising it were virtually compulsory — as in standing up for the singing of the National Anthem in Britain, the flag ritual in American schools. The crucial element seems to have been the invention of emotionally and symbolically charged signs of club membership rather than the statutes and objects of the club. Their significance lay precisely in their undefined universality.

Eric Hobsbawm and Terence Ranger, *The Invention of Tradition* (Cambridge: Cambridge University Press, 1983), Introduction, p. 11.

9   Capitalist Development and the Industrialization of War

1.   McNeill, *The Pursuit of Power*, p. 143.
2.   C. B. Otley, 'Militarism and the social affiliations of the British army elite', in van Doorn, *Armed Forces and Society*, p. 85.
3.   Ropp, *War in the Modern World*, p. 143ff.
4.   William McElwee, *The Art of War, Waterloo to Mons* (London: Weidenfeld, 1974), p. 106ff.
5.   Ibid., p. 110.
6.   Michael Lewis, *The History of the British Navy* (London: Allen & Unwin, 1959), p. 199. See also McNeill, *The Pursuit of Power*, p. 226ff.
7.   G. A. Shepperd, *Arms and Armour 1660 to 1918* (London: Hart-Davis, 1971).
8.   O. F. G. Hogg, *The Royal Arsenal* (London: Oxford University Press, 1963), vol. 2, pp. 783–92.
9.   Ropp, *War in the Modern World*, p. 224.
10.   Henry Williamson, *The Wet Flanders Plain* (London: Beaumont Press, 1929), pp. 14–16.
11.   Amos Perlmutter, *The Military and Politics in Modern Times* (New Haven: Yale University Press, 1977), p. 21.
12.   Samuel P. Huntington, *The Soldier and the State* (Cambridge: Harvard University Press, 1957). Some of Huntington's claims have nevertheless been extensively, and justly, subject to serious criticism however.
13.   Ibid., p. 29.
14.   Ibid., p. 37.

15. Samuel E. Finer, 'State and nation-building in Europe: the role of the military', p. 150. cf. also R. D. Challener, *The French Theory of the Nation in Arms, 1866—1939* (New York: Russell & Russell, 1965).
16. Feld, *The Structure of Violence*, p. 146.
17. cf. Maurice Pearton, *The Knowledgeable State* (London: Burnett, 1982), p. 19.
18. Ibid., p. 22.
19. McNeill, *The Pursuit of Power*, pp. 248—9.
20. Pearton, *The Knowledgeable State*, pp. 33—4.
21. Morris Janowitz, *Military Conflict* (Beverly Hills: Sage, 1975), p. 70. In what follows I draw extensively on his analysis.
22. Feld, *The Structure of Violence*, pp. 145—6.
23. Janowitz, *Military Conflict*, p. 76.
24. On this issue see Raymond Aron, *The Century of Total War* (London: Verschoyle, 1954), p. 96ff. and *passim*.
25. Winston S. Churchill, *The World Crisis* (London: Thornton & Butterworth, 1923), vol. I, pp. 10—11.
26. Arthur Marwick, *War and Social Change in the Twentieth Century* (London: Macmillan, 1974), pp. 88—9.
27. McNeill, *The Pursuit of Power*, p. 331.
28. Marwick, *War and Social Change*.
29. B. L. Hart, *The Tanks* (London: Cassell, 1959), 2 vols.
30. cf. Gerald Feldman, *Army, Industry & Labour* (Princeton: Princeton University Press, 1966); Alan S. Milward, *The Economic Effects of the World Wars on Britain* (London: Macmillan, 1970); John Terraine, *Impacts of War* (London: Hutchinson, 1970).
31. S. E. Morison *et al., The Growth of the American Republic* (London: Oxford University Press, 1969), vol. 2, chapter 6.
32. cf. John Erikson, *The Soviet High Command: a Military-Political History* (London: Macmillan, 1962); Moshe Lewin, *Political Undercurrents in Soviet Economic Debates* (Princeton: Princeton University Press, 1974).
33. D. C. Watt, *Too Serious a Business: European Armed Forces and the Approach of the Second World War* (London: Temple Smith 1975); B. Klein, *Germany's Economic Preparation for War* (Cambridge, Mass: Harvard University Press, 1959).
34. McNeill, *The Pursuit of Power*, pp. 353—6. cf. also his *America, Britain and Russia: Their Cooperation and Conflict, 1941—1946* (London: Oxford University Press, 1953).
35. Michael Mandlebaum, *The Nuclear Revolution* (Cambridge: Cambridge University Press, 1981), p. 2.
36. Ibid., p. 3.

37. Milward, *Economic Effects of the World Wars.*
38. Marwick, *War and Social Change*, p. 163.
39. Richard Polenberg, *War & Society: The United States, 1941—45* (New York: J. P. Lippincott, 1972). cf. also Joyce and Gabriel Kolko, *The Limits of Power* (New York: Harper, 1972).
40. Peter Calvocoressi, *World Politics Since 1945* (London: Longman, 1968), p. 23.
41. Harold D. Lasswell, 'The garrison-state hypothesis today', in Samuel P. Huntingdon, *Changing Patterns of Military Politics* (Glencoe: Free Press, 1962), p. 51; H. Elan, 'H. D. Lasswell's developmental analysis', *Western Political Quarterly*, 11, 1958. The thesis was first set out in Lasswell's *World Politics and Personal Insecurity* (New York: McGraw-Hill, 1935).
42. Lasswell, 'The garrison-state hypothesis today', p. 54.
43. Gavin Kennedy, *Defense Economics* (London: Duckworth, 1983), p. 45. For calculations on world military expenditure, see the *World Armaments and Disarmament Yearbook, 1984.* (London: Taylor and Francis).
44. cf. Michael Mann, 'Capitalism and Militarism', in Martin Shaw, *War, State and Society* (London: Macmillan, 1984).
45. Mills's analysis is concentrated on the USA, and he does not claim that it holds in its entirety for other industrialized countries. C. Wright Mills, *The Power Elite* (New York: Oxford University Press, 1956). For versions of the 'economic' view see, for example, Paul A. Baran and Paul A. Sweezy, *Monopoly Capital* (New York: Monthly Review Press, 1966); Ernest Mandel, *Marxist Economic Theory* (London: Merit Publishers, 1968); Michael Kidron, *Western Capitalism Since the War* (London: Weidenfeld, 1968).
46. Kennedy, *Defense Economics*, p. 156.
47. cf. Stanley Lieberson, 'An empirical study of military-industrial linkages', in Sam C. Sarkesian, *The Military-Industrial Complex: a Reassessment* (Beverly Hills: Sage, 1972).
48. Jacques Gansler, *The Defence Industry* (Cambridge, Mass: MIT Press, 1980).
49. S. E. Finer, *The Man on Horseback* (London: Pall Mall, 1962), p. 6.
50. Ibid., p. 15ff.
51. Perlmutter, *Military and Politics in Modern Times,* p. 141ff.
52. cf. Robin Luckham, 'Militarism: force, class and international conflict', in Mary Kaldor and Asbjorn Eide, *The World Military Order* (London: Macmillan, 1979), p. 245.
53. cf. Ralph E. Lapp, *The Weapons Culture* (New York: Norton, 1968).
54. Jan Oberg, 'The new international military order: a threat to

human security', in Asbjorn Eide and Marek Thee, *Problems of Contemporary Militarism* (London: Croom Helm, 1980), p. 47.
55. Mary Kaldor, *The Baroque Arsenal* (London: Deutsch, 1982). p. 133ff.
56. Kaldor and Eide, *The World Military Order*, p. 5.
57. Francis A. Beer, *Peace Against War* (San Francisco: Freeman, 1981), p. 310.
58. cf. W. Epstein, *The Last Chance: Nuclear Proliferation and Arms Control* (New York: Free Press, 1975).
59. Kaldor, *The Baroque Arsenal*, p. 132.
60. Miles D. Wolpin, *Military Aid and Counter Revolution in the Third World* (Lexington, Mass: Lexington Books, 1972).

10   Nation-States in the Global State System

1. cf. A. F. Pollard, 'The balance of power', *Journal of the British Institute of International Affairs*, 2, 1923; Ernst B. Haas, 'The balance of power: prescription, concept or propaganda?', *World Politics*, 5, 1953.
2. Hans J. Morgenthau, *Politics Among Nations* (New York: Knopf, 1960), p. 167.
3. Friedrich von Gentz, *Fragments Upon the Balance of Power in Europe* (London: M. Pettier, 1806), pp. 61—2 and *passim*.
4. Ibid., pp. 111—12.
5. Frans A. M. Alting von Gensau, *European Perspectives on World Order* (Leyden: Sijthoff, 1975), p. 183.
6. Gerhard Schulz, *Revolutions and Peace Treaties 1917—20* (London: Methuen, 1967), p. 158ff.
7. James Brown Scott, *President Wilson's Foreign Policy* (New York: Oxford University Press, 1918), pp. 190 and 270.
8. For instance, A. J. P. Taylor, *The Struggle for Mastery in Europe, 1848—1918* (Oxford: Clarendon Press, 1954), p. 567.
9. Ray S. Baher and William E. Doss, *The Public Papers of Woodrow Wilson, War and Peace* (New York: Harper, 1927), vol. I, p. 631.
10. Pearton, *The Knowledgeable State*, p. 178.
11. Lloyd George, *Truth About the Peace Treaties* (London: Victor Gollancz, 1938), vol. 2, p. 107.
12. Evan Luard, *International Agencies* (London: Macmillan, 1977), p. 11ff.
13. R. Berkov, *The WHO: a study in Decentralised Administration* (Geneva· WHO, 1957).

14. For an influential statement of the conventional view, see James N. Rosenthau, *The Study of Global Interdependence* (London: Pinter, 1980).
15. From Bruce Russett and Harvey Starr, *World Politics* (San Francisco: Freeman, 1981), p. 52.
16. Pearton, *The Knowledgeable State*, p. 185ff.
17. Alting von Gensau, *European Perspectives on World Order*, p. 187.
18. Joseph Frankel, *International Relations in a Changing World* (Oxford: Oxford University Press), p. 165ff.
19. cf. Stein Rokkan, 'Cities, states and nations: a dimensional model for the study of contrasts in development', in S. N. Eisenstadt and Stein Rokkan, *Building States and Nations* (Beverly Hills: Sage, 1973).
20. A. W. Orridge, 'Varieties of nationalism', in Leonard Tivey, *The Nation-State* (Oxford: Martin Robertson, 1981), pp. 50−1.
21. Arnold Hughes, 'The nation-state in Black Africa', in Tivey, *The Nation-State*, p. 122.
22. Paul Hair, 'Africanism: the Freetown contribution', *Journal of Modern African Studies*, 5, 1967.
23. Hughes, 'The nation-state in Black Africa', p. 132.
24. Perlmutter, *Military & Politics in Modern Times*, p. 89.
25. Ibid., p. 92.
26. Raymond Aron, *On War* (London: Secker & Warburg, 1958), p. 19ff.
27. Raymond Grew, 'The nineteenth-century European state', in Charles Bright and Susan Harding, *Statemaking and Social Movements* (Ann Arbor: University of Michigan Press, 1984).
28. cf. Robert Gilpin, *War and Change in World Politics* (Cambridge: Cambridge University Press, 1983).
29. *CS*, chapter I and *passim*.
30. Richard Cooper, *The Economics of Interdependence* (New York: McGraw-Hill, 1968), p. 152ff.
31. Lars Anell, *Recession, the Western Economies and the Changing World Order* (London: Pinter, 1981).
32. Lester R. Brown, *World Without Borders* (New York: Random House, 1972), p. 21ff.
33. Robert J. Gordon and Jacques Pelkmans, *Challenges to Interdependent Economies* (New York: McGraw-Hill, 1979).
34. Anell, *Recession and the Changing World Order*, pp. 64−5.
35. The work of Wallerstein and his followers is in some part an exception to this but, besides showing limitations already discussed, it has thus far concentrated more on early phases of capitalist development.

36. Morgenthau, *Politics Among Nations*, p. 328.
37. Raymond Aron, *Peace and War* (Malabur: Krieger, 1981), p. 738ff.
38. Ibid., p. 747.
39. Celso Furtado, *Accumulation and Development* (Oxford: Martin Robertson, 1983), p. 96ff.
40. Raymond Aron, *The Imperial Republic* (London: Weidenfeld, 1974).

11   Modernity, Totalitarianism and Critical Theory

1. Quoted in A. J. May, *Europe Since 1939* (New York: Holt, Rinehart and Winston, 1966).
2. Carl J. Friedrich *et al.*, *Totalitarianism in Perspective: Three Views* (London: Pall Mall, 1969), p. 6ff.
3. Benjamin R. Barber, 'Conceptual foundations of totalitarianism', in Friedrich, *Totalitarianism in Perspective*, p. 19.
4. Carl Friedrich, *Totalitarianism* (Cambridge, Mass: Harvard University Press, 1954); cf. also C. J. Friedrich and Z. K. Brzezinski, *Totalitarian Dictatorship and Autocracy* (New York: Praeger Press, 1967).
5. Hilaire Belloc, *The Servile State* (Indianapolis: Liberty, 1932), p. 125.
6. David Lane, *Politics and Society in the USSR* (London: Weidenfeld, 1970).
7. Friedrich *et al.*, 'The evolving theory and practice of totalitarian regimes', in *Totalitarianism in Perspective*, p. 131.
8. Aryeh L. Unger, *The Totalitarian Party* (Cambridge: Cambridge University Press, 1974), p. 13ff.
9. Quoted in Michael Curtis, 'Retreat from totalitarianism', in Friedrich *et al.*, *Totalitarianism in Perspective* p. 76.
10. Robert Conquest, *The Great Terror* (New York: Macmillan, 1968).
11. cf. James Millar and Alec Nove, 'Was Stalin really necessary?', *Problems of Communism*, 25, 1976.
12. cf. Claude Lefort, *L'invention démocratique* (Paris: Fayard, 1981), p. 85ff.
13. Hannah Arendt, *The Origins of Totalitarianism* (London: Allen & Unwin, 1967), pp. 341−2.
14. cf. Unger, *The Totalitarian Party*, p. 170ff.
15. *CPST*, pp. 143−4.
16. *CCHM*, vol. I, pp. 194−6.
17. cf. Sigmund Freud, *Group Psychology and the Analysis of the Ego* (London: Hogarth Press, 1922).

18. J. L Talmon, *The Origins of Totalitarian Democracy* (New York: Praeger Press, 1961). As Menze emphasizes, totalitarianism has a 'thoroughly ambivalent relationship to modern democracy . . . Totalitarianism is inconceivable and unrealisable without the democratic notion of popular sovereignty and its concrete realisation in the modern state.' See Ernest A. Menze, *Totalitarianism Reconsidered* (London: Kennikat, 1981), p. 15.
19. Marx, 'The Eighteenth Brumaire of Louis Bonaparte'.
20. See Nicos Poulantzas, *Political Power and Social Classes* (London: New Left Books, 1973).
21. *CCHM*, vol. I, chapter 10.
22. cf. F. F. Piven and R. A. Cloward, *Regulating the Poor* (London: Tavistock Publications, 1972).
23. Foucault, *Discipline and Punish*.
24. cf. *CSAS*, chapter 6 and *passim*.
25. *CS*, chapter 4.
26. Quoted in Richard Taylor, 'The Greens in Britain', in David Coates *et al., A Socialist Anatomy of Britain* (Cambridge: Polity Press, 1985), p. 160.
27. cf. *CSAS*.
28. See Alain Touraine, *The Post-Industrial Society* (London: Wildwood, 1974) and other subsequent publications.
29. cf. Claus Offe, *Disorganised Capitalism* (Cambridge: Polity Press, 1985).
30. Huntington, *The Soldier and the State*.
31. *CSAS*, chapter 12.
32. cf. *CSAS*, chapter 11 and *passim*.
33. A. Giddens, *Between Capitalism and Socialism* (Cambridge: Polity Press, forthcoming).
34. This is essentially the view of Huntington. See *The Soldier and the State*.
35. cf. Michael Howard, *'Temperamenta belli*: can war be controlled?', in his *Restraints on War* (Oxford: Oxford University Press, 1979); and his *War in European History* (Oxford: Oxford University Press, 1976).
36. For what is perhaps the definitive study of Clausewitz, see Raymond Aron, *Penser la guerre — Clausewitz* (Paris: Gallimard, 1976), 2 vols.
37. K. M. von Clausewitz, *On War* (London: Kegan Paul, 1908), vol. I, book I, p. 85.
38. Howard, *'Temperamenta belli*: can war be controlled?', p. 9ff.
39. Mandelbaum, *The Nuclear Revolution*, p. 94.
40. Ibid., chapter 4.

41. Abraham S. Becker, *Military Expenditure for Arms Control* (Cambridge, Mass: Ballinger, 1977).
42. cf. Mary Kaldor, 'Disarmament: the armament process in reverse', in E. P. Thompson and Dan Smith, *Protest and Survive* (Harmondsworth: Penguin, 1980).
43. *CCHM*, vol. I, chapter 3.
44. Ibid., chapters 5, 6 and 7.
45. Michael Walzer, *Just and Unjust Wars* (London: Allen Lane, 1978), p. 271.
46. *CCHM*, vol. I, chapter 6.

Bibliography

Abler, R. et al. *Human Geography in a Shrinking World*, North Scituate, Suxbury, 1875.

Adams, R. 'Anthropological perspectives on ancient trade', *Current Anthropology*, 15, 1974.

Albrecht-Carré, R. *The Unity of Europe: an Historical Survey,* London, Secker and Warburg, 1966.

Alderson, A. D. *The Structure of the Ottoman Dynasty*, Oxford, Clarendon Press, 1956.

Alting, von Gensau, F. A. M. *European Perspectives on World Order,* Leyden, Sijthoff, 1975.

Ancel, J. *Les frontières*, Paris, Gallimard, 1938.

Anderson, B. *Imagined Communities*, London, Verso, 1983.

Anderson, P. *Lineages of the Absolutist State,* London, New Left Books, 1974.

Anderson, P. *Passages from Antiquity to Feudalism*, London, New Left Books, 1974.

Anell, L. *Recession, the Western Economies and the Changing World Order,* London, Pinter, 1981.

Apter, D. 'Political religion in new nations' in C. Geertz, *Old Societies and New States*, New York, Collier-Macmillan, 1963.

Apter, D. *The Politics of Modernisation*, Chicago, University of Chicago Press, 1965.

Arendt, H. *The Origins of Totalitarianism*, London, Allen & Unwin, 1967.

Ariès, P. *Western Attitudes Towards Death*, Baltimore, Johns Hopkins University Press, 1974.

Armstrong, J. A. *Nations Before Nationalism*, Chapel Hill, University of North Carolina Press, 1982.

Aron, R. *The Century of Total War*, London, Verschoyle, 1954.

Aron, R. *On War*, London, Secker & Warburg, 1958.

Aron, R. *The Imperial Republic*, London, Weidenfeld, 1974.

Aron, R. *Penser la guerre — Clausewitz*, Paris, Gallimard, 1976.

Aron, R. *Peace and War*, Malabur, Krieger, 1981.

Ashley, M. *The Golden Century, Europe 1598—1917,* London, Weidenfeld, 1969.

Aston, T. *Crisis in Europe 1560—1660,* London, Routledge & Kegan Paul, 1965.

Avineri, S. (ed.) *Karl Marx on Colonialism and Modernisation,* New York, Doubleday, 1968.

Baher, R. S. and Doss, W. E. *The Public Papers of Woodrow Wilson, War and Peace,* New York, Harper, 1927, vol. I.

Baradez, J. *Fossatum Africae,* Paris, Arts et Metiers, 1949.

Baran, P. A. and Sweezy, P. A. *Monopoly Capital,* New York, Monthly Review Press, 1966.

Barber, B. R. 'Conceptual foundations of totalitarianism' in C. J. Friedrich et al. *Totalitarianism in Perspective: Three Views,* London, Pall Mall, 1969.

Barraclough, G. *European Unity in Thought and Action,* Oxford, Basil Blackwell, 1963.

Barrington Moore, *The Social Origins of Dictatorship and Democracy,* Harmondsworth, Penguin, 1969.

Barrow, G. W. S. *Feudal Britain,* London, Arnold, 1956.

Barth, F. *Ethnic Groups and Boundaries,* Bergen, Universitäts-für Paget, 1969.

Baudin, L. *A Socialist Empire. The Incas of Peru,* Princeton, Van Nostrand, 1961.

Baugh, A. C. *A History of the English Language,* London, Routledge & Kegan Paul, 1951.

Becker, A. S. *Military Expenditure for Arms Control,* Cambridge, Mass., Ballinger, 1977.

Beer, F. A. *Peace Against War,* San Francisco, Freeman, 1981.

Belloc, H. *The Servile State,* Indianapolis, Liberty, 1932.

Bendix, R. *Nation Building and Citizenship,* Berkeley, University of California Press, 1977.

Bendix, R. *Kings or People,* Berkeley, University of California Press, 1978.

Benveniste, E. *Problems in General Linguistics,* Florida, University of Miami Press, 1971.

Berkov, R. *The WHO: a study in Decentralised Administration,* Geneva, WHO, 1957.

Bischoff, J. *A Comprehensive History of the Woollen and Worsted Manufactures,* London, 1842.

Bleackley, H. 'The Hangmen of England', reprinted in J. Lofland, *State Executions,* Montclair, NJ, Patterson Smith, 1977.

Bloom, S. F. *The World of Nations,* New York, Oxford University Press, 1941.

Bloomfield, L. *Language*, New York, Allen & Unwin, 1933.

Bottomore, T. B. *Karl Marx, Early Writings*, New York, McGraw-Hill, 1964.

Braidwood, R. J. and Willey, G. *Courses Toward Urban Life*, Chicago, Atdine, 1962.

Braun, R. 'Taxation, sociopolitical structure, and state-building: Great Britain and Brandenburg-Prussia' in C. Tilly (ed.) *The Formation of National States in Europe*, Princeton, Princeton University Press, 1975.

Braverman, H. *Labour and Monopoly Capital*, New York, Monthly Review Press, 1967.

Brenner, R. 'The origins of capitalist development: a critique of neo-Smithian Marxism', *New Left Review*, 105, 1977.

Breuilly, J. *Nationalism and the State*, Manchester, Manchester University Press, 1982.

Bright, C. and Harding, S., *Statemaking and Social Movements*, Ann Arbor, University of Michigan Press, 1984.

Brock, T. and Galting, J. 'Belligerence among the primitives', *Journal of Peace Research*, 3, 1966.

Brodie, B. *A Guide to Naval Strategy*, Princeton, Princeton University Press, 1958.

Brown, L. R. *World Without Borders*, New York, Random House, 1972.

Burns, E. M. and Ralph, P. L. *World Civilisations*, New York, Norton, 1974.

Calvocoressi, P. *World Politics Since 1945*, London, Longman, 1968.

Challener, R. D. *The French Theory of the Nation in Arms, 1866—1939*, New York, Russell & Russell, 1965.

Cheyette, F. *Lordship and Community in Mediaeval Europe*, New York, 1968.

Chien-nung, Li, *The Political History of China, 1840—1928*, Princeton, Van Nostrand, 1956.

Childe, V. G. *Man Makes Himself*, London, Watts, 1956.

Chung-Li, Chang, *The Chinese Gentry*, Seattle, University of Washington Press, 1955.

Church, W. F. *The Greatness of Louis XIV, Myth or Reality?*, Boston, Mass., Heath, 1959.

Churchill, W. S. *The World Crisis*, London, Thornton & Butterworth, 1923, vol. I.

Cipolla, C. M. *Guns and Sails in the Early Phase of European Expansion 1400—1700*, London, Collins, 1965.

Claessen, H. J. M. and Skalnik, P. *The Early State*, The Hague, Mouton, 1978.

Clark, G. N. *The Seventeenth Century*, Oxford, Clarendon Press, 1947.

Coates, D. et al. (eds) *A Socialist Anatomy of Britain*, Cambridge, Polity Press, 1984.

Collingwood, R. G. *Roman Britain*, Oxford, Clarendon Press, 1932.

Connell, R. W. *Which Way is Up?*, Sydney, Allen & Unwin, 1983.

Conquest, R. *The Great Terror*, New York, Macmillan, 1968.

Cooper, R. *The Economics of Interdependence*, New York, McGraw-Hill, 1986.

Coulborn, R. *Feudalism in History*, Princeton, Princeton University Press, 1956.

Critchley, T. A. *A History of Police in England and Wales*, London, Constable, 1978.

Cutler, A. *Marx's Capital and Capitalism Today*, London, Routledge & Kegan Paul, 1978, vol. 2.

Da Sola Pool, I. *The Social Impact of the Telephone*, Boston, Mass., MIT Press, 1977.

Dahl, R. A. *Polyarchy*, New Haven, Yale University Press,

Dahl, A. *Preface to Democratic Theory,* Chicago, University of Chicago Press, 1956.

De Bary, W. T. 'Chinese despotism and the Confucian Ideal: a seventeenth century view' in J. K. Fairbank *Chinese Thought and Institutions,* Chicago, University of Chicago Press, 1959.

De Brunhoff, S. *Marx on Money*, London, Pluto Press, 1977.

De Jouvenel, B. *Sovereignty*, Cambridge, Cambridge University Press, 1957.

Derrida, J. *Of Grammatology*, Baltimore, Johns Hopkins University Press, 1974.

Deutsch, K. W. *Nationalism and Social Communication*, Boston, MIT Press, 1966.

Doerner, K. *Madmen and the Bourgeoisie*, Oxford, Basil Blackwell, 1981.

Doob, L. *Patriotism and Nationalism.* New Haven, Yale University Press, 1964.

Durkheim, E. *Professional Ethics and Civil Morals*, London, Routledge, 1957.

Durkheim, E. *Socialism*, New York, Collier, 1962.

Earle, A. M. *Curious Punishments of Bygone Days,* Montclair, NJ, Patterson Smith, 1969.

Eberhard, W. *Das Toba-Reich Nordchinas*, Leiden, Brill, 1949.

Eberhard, W. *A History of China*, London, Routledge, 1950.

Eberhard, W. *Conquerors and Rulers*, Leiden, Brill, 1970.

Eckstein, H. *Internal War*, Glencoe, The Free Press, 1964.

Edgerton, W. F. 'The question of feudal institutions in ancient Egypt' in R. Coulborn, *Feudalism in History*, Princeton, Princeton University Press, 1956.

Edwards, I. E. S. *The Pyramids of Egypt*, Baltimore, Max Parrish, 1962.

Ehrenberg, R. *Das Zeitalter der Fugger*, Jena, 1896.

Eide, A. and Thee, M. *Problems of Contemporary Militarism*, London, Croom Helm, 1980.

Einzig, P. *Primitive Money*, Oxford, Pergamon Press, 1966.

Eisenstadt, S. N. *The Political Systems of Empires*, Glencoe, The Free Press, 1963.

Eisenstadt, S. N. and Rokkan, S. *Building States and Nations*, Beverly Hills, Sage, 1973.

Eisenstein, E. L. *The Printing Revolution in Early Modern Europe*, Cambridge, Cambridge University Press, 1983.

Elan, H. 'H. D. Lasswell's developmental analysis', *Western Political Quarterly*, 11, 1958.

Elias, N. *The Civilising Process*, Oxford, Basil Blackwell, 1978.

Engels, F. Letter to K. Marx, 7 January 1858, in K. Marx and F. Engels, *Werke*, Berlin, Dietz Verlag, 1963, vol. 24.

Epstein, W. *The Last Chance; Nuclear Proliferation and Arms Control*, New York, The Free Press, 1975.

Erikson, J. *The Soviet High Command: a Military-Political History*, London, Macmillan, 1962.

Fairbank, J. K. *Chinese Thought and Institutions*, Chicago, University of Chicago Press, 1959.

Feld, M. D. *The Structure of Violence*, Beverly Hills, Sage, 1977.

Feldman, G. *Army, Industry and Labour*, Princeton, Princeton Princeton University Press, 1966.

Ferguson, A. *An Essay on the History of Civil Society*, Edinburgh, Edinburgh University Press, 1966.

Finer, S. E. *The Man on Horseback*, London, Pall Mall, 1962.

Finer, S. E. 'State- and nation-building in Europe: the role of the military' in C. Tilly (ed.) *The Formation of National States in Europe*, Princeton, Princeton University Press, 1975.

Foucault, M. *Discipline and Punish*, London, Allen Lane, 1977.

Franke, H. 'Siege and defence of towns in mediaeval China' in F. A. Kierman and J. K. Fairbank, *Chinese Ways of Warfare*, Cambridge, Mass., Harvard University Press, 1974.

Frankel, J. *International Relations in a Changing World*, Oxford, Oxford University Press, .

Freidson, E. *The Hospital in Modern Society*, Glencoe, The Free Press, 1963.

Freud, S. *Group Psychology and the Analysis of the Ego*, London, Hogarth Press, 1922.

Friedrich, C. J. *Totalitarianism*, Cambridge, Mass., Harvard University Press, 1954.

Friedrich, C. J. and Brzezinski, Z. K. *Totalitarian Dictatorship and Autocracy*, New York, Praeger Press, 1967.

Friedrich, C. J. et al. *Totalitarianism in Perspective: Three Views*, London, Pall Mall, 1969.

Furtado, C. *Accumulation and Development*, Oxford, Martin Robertson, 1983.

Gallie, W. B. *Philosophers in Peace and War,* Cambridge, Cambridge University Press, 1978.

Gansler, J. *The Defence Industry*, Cambridge, Mass., MIT Press, 1980.

Gardiner, A. H. *Ancient Egyptian Onomastica*, Oxford, Oxford University Press, vol. I.

Geertz, C. *Old Societies and New States*, New York, Collier-Methuen, 1963.

Geertz, C. *Local Knowledge,* New York, Basic Books, 1983.

Gelb, I.J. *A Study of Writing*, London, Routledge & Kegan Paul, 1952.

Gellner, E. *Thought and Change*, London, Weidenfeld, 1964.

Gellner, E. *Spectacles and Predicaments*, Cambridge, Cambridge University Press, 1979.

Gellner, E. *Nations and Nationalism*, Oxford, Basil Blackwell, 1983.

Gibb, H. A. R. and Bowen, H. *Islamic Society and the West*, London, Oxford University Press, 1950, vol. I.

Gibbon, E. *The Decline and Fall of the Roman Empire*, New York, Modern Library, 1932, vol. I.

Giddens, A. *Central Problems in Social Theory*, London, Hutchinson, 1977.

Giddens, A. *New Rules of Sociological Method*, London, Hutchinson, 1976.

Giddens, A. *Studies in Social and Political Theory*, London, Hutchinson, 1977.

Giddens, A. *A Contemporary Critique of Historical Materialism*, London, Macmillan, 1981, vol. I.

Giddens, A. *The Class Structure of the Advanced Societies,* London, Hutchinson, 1981 revised edn.

Giddens, A. *Profiles and Critiques in Social Theory*, London, Macmillan, 1982.

Giddens, A. *The Constitution of Society,* Cambridge, Polity Press, 1984.

Giddens, A. 'The nation-state and violence' in W. W. Powell and R. Robbins, *Conflict and Consensus*, New York, The Free Press, 1984.

Giddens, A. *Between Capitalism and Socialism*, Cambridge, Polity Press, forthcoming.

Gilbert, F. *The Historical Essays of Otto Hintze*, New York, Oxford University Press, 1975.

Gilpin, R. *War and Change in World Politics*, Cambridge, Cambridge University Press, 1983.
Gimpel, J. *The Mediaeval Machine*, London, Victor Gollancz, 1977.
Goldfrank, W. L. *The World-System of Capitalism: Past and Present*, Beverly Hills, Sage, 1979.
Goldschied, R. 'Staat, öffenticher Haushalt und Gesellschaft', *Handbuch der Finanzwissenschaft*, Tübingen, Möhr, 1926, vol. I.
Goody, J. *The Domestication of the Savage Mind*, Cambridge, Cambridge University Press, 1977.
Gordon, R. J. and Pelkmans, J. *Challenges to Interdependent Economies*, New York, McGraw-Hill, 1979.
Goubert, P. *Beauvais et le Beauvaisis de 1600 à 1780*, Paris, SEUPEN, 1960.
Gouldner, A. W. *The Dialectic of Ideology and Technology*, New York, Seabury, 1976.
Gregory, D. *Regional Transformation and Industrial Revolution*, London, Macmillan, 1982.
Grew. R. 'The nineteenth-century European state' in C. Bright and S. Harding, *Statemaking and Social Movements*, Ann Arbor, University of Michigan Press, 1984.
Griffeth, R. and Thomas, C. G. *The City-State in Five Cultures*, California, Santa Barbara, 1981.
Gurr, T. R. *Rogues, Rebels and Reformers*, Beverly Hills, Sage, 1976.
Haas, E. B. 'The balance of power: prescription, concept or propaganda?', *World Politics*, 5, 1953.
Habib, I. *The Agrarian System of Mughal India*, London, Asia Publishing House, 1963.
Hair, P. 'Africanism: the Freetown contribution', *Journal of Modern African Studies*, 5, 1967.
Harris, M. *Cannibals and Kings*, London, Fontana, 1978.
Harrod, R. F. *Money*, London, Macmillan, 1969.
Hart, B. L. *The Tanks*, London, Cassell, 1959, 2 vols.
Hegel, G. W. F. *The Philosophy of Right*, London, Bell, 1896.
Hegel, G. W. F. *The Phenomenology of Spirit*, Oxford, Clarendon Press, 1977.
Hill, C. *The World Turned Upside Down*, London, Temple Smith, 1972.
Hintze, O. *Staat und Verfassung*, Göttingen, Vandenhoeck, 1962.
Hobsbawm, E. *Primitive Rebels*, Manchester, Manchester University Press, 1959.
Hobsbawm, E. and Ranger, T. *The Invention of Tradition*, Cambridge, Cambridge University Press, 1983.
Hogg, O. F. G. *The Royal Arsenal*, London, Oxford University Press, 1963, vol. 2.

Hopkins, T. K. and Wallerstein, I. 'The comparative study of national societies', *Social Science Information*, 6, 1967.

Howard, M. *War in European History*, Oxford, Oxford University Press, 1976.

Howard, M. '*Temperamenta belli*: can war be controlled?' in his *Restraints on War*, Oxford, Oxford University Press, 1979.

Howse, D. *Greenwich Time and the Discovery of the Longitude*, New York, Oxford University Press, 1980.

Hucker, C. 'The Tung-Lin movement of the Late Ming Period' in J. K. Fairbank, *Chinese Thought and Institutions,* Chicago, University of Chicago Press, 1959.

Hucker, C. O. *Chinese Government in Ming Times: Seven Studies*, New York, Columbia University Press, 1969.

Hughes, A. 'The nation-state in Black Africa' in L. Tivey (ed.) *The Nation-State*, Oxford, Martin Robertson, 1981.

Huntingford, G. W. B. *The Galla of Ethiopia*, London, Hakluyt Society, 1955.

Huntington, S. P. *The Soldier and the State*, Cambridge, Mass., Harvard University Press, 1957.

Huntington, S. P. *Changing Patterns of Military Politics*, Glencoe, The Free Press, 1962.

Ignatieff, M. *A Just Measure of Pain*, London, Macmillan, 1978.

Ingham, G. K. *Capitalism Divided?*, London, Macmillan, 1984.

Innis, H. A. *Empire and Communications,* Oxford, Clarendon Press, 1950.

Janelle, D. G. 'Central place development in a time-space framework', *Professional Geographer*, 20, 1968.

Janowitz, M. 'Armed forces and society: a world perspective' in J. van Doorn, *Armed Forces and Society*, The Hague, Mouton, 1968.

Janowitz, M. *Military Conflict*, Beverly Hills, Sage, 1975.

Janowitz, M. 'A sociological perspective on Wallerstein', *American Journal of Sociology*, 82, 1977.

Jessop, B. *The Capitalist State*, Oxford, Martin Robertson, 1982.

Jones, A. H. M. *The Later Roman Empire*, Oxford, Basil Blackwell, 1964, vol. II.

Jones, S. B. *Boundary Making: A Handbook for Statesmen*, Washington, Carnegie Endowment for International Peace Monograph, 1945.

Kalberg, S. 'Max Weber's universal-historical architectonic of economically oriented action' in S. McNall, *Current Perspectives in Social Theory*, 1983, vol. 4.

Kaldor, M. 'Disarmament: the armament process in reverse', in E. P. Thompson and D. Smith, *Protest and Survive*, Harmondsworth, Penguin, 1980.

Kaldor, M. *The Baroque Arsenal*, London, Deutsch, 1982.

Kaldor, M. and Eide, A. *The World Military Order*, London, Macmillan, 1979.

Kautsky, J. H. *The Politics of Aristocratic Empires*, Chapel Hill, University of North Carolina Press, 1982.

Kedourie, E. *Nationalism*, London, Hutchinson, 1961.

Kennedy, G. *Defense Economics*, London, Duckworth, 1983.

Kern, S. *The Culture of Time and Space 1880—1918*, London, Weidenfeld, 1983.

Kidron, M. *Western Capitalism Since the War*, London, Weidenfeld, 1968.

Kierman, F. A. and Fairbank, J. K. *Chinese Ways in Warfare*, Cambridge, Mass., Harvard University Press, 1974.

King, P. *The Ideology of Order*, London, Allen and Unwin, 1974.

Klein, B. *Germany's Economic Preparation for War*, Cambridge, Mass., Harvard University Press, 1959.

Kolko, J. and G. *The Limits of Power*, New York, Harper, 1972.

Kraeling, C. H. and Adams, R. M. *City Invincible*, Chicago, University of Chicago Press, 1960.

Kramer, S. N. *From the Tablets of Sumer*, Indian Hills, Colorado University Press, 1956.

Kramer, S. N. *History Begins at Sumer*, New York, Anchor, 1959.

Kuhn, P. A. *Rebellion and its Enemies in Late Imperial China*, Cambridge, Mass., Harvard University Press, 1970.

Kung-chuan Hsiao, *Rural China, Imperial Control in the Nineteenth Century*, Seattle, University of Washington Press, 1960.

Ladurie, Le Roy, *Le Territoire de l'historien*, Paris, Gallimard, 1973—8, 2 vols.

Lamb, B. P. *India: a World in Transition,* New York, Praeger, 1963.

Lane, D. *Politics and Society in the USSR*, London, Weidenfeld, 1970.

Lapp, R. E. *The Weapons Culture*, New York, Norton, 1968.

Larrain, J. *Marxism and Ideology*, London, Macmillan, 1983.

Lasswell, H. D. *World Politics and Personal Insecurity*, New York, McGraw-Hill, 1935.

Lasswell, H. D. 'The garrison-state hypothesis today', in S. P. Huntington, *Changing Patterns of Military Politics*, Glencoe, The Free Press, 1962.

Lattimore, O. *Inner Asian Frontiers of China*, New York, Oxford University Press, 1940.

Lattimore, O. 'Feudalism in history', *Past and Present*, 12, 1957.

Le Goff, T. J. A. and Sutherland, D. M. G. 'The revolution and the rural community in eighteenth-century Brittany', *Past and Present*, 62, 1974.

Leach, E. 'Hydraulic society in Ceylon', *Past and Present*, 15, 1959.

Lefort, C. *L'invention démocratique*, Paris, Fagard, 1981.

Lévi-Strauss, C. 'Réponses à quelques questions', *Esprit*, 31, 1963.

Lévy, B-H. *Barbarism with a Human Face*, New York, Harper, 1977.

Lewin, M. *Political Undercurrents in Soviet Economic Debates*, Princeton, Princeton University Press, 1974.

Lewis, M. *The History of the British Navy*, London, Allen & Unwin, 1959.

Lieberson, S. 'An empirical study of military-industrial linkages' in S. C. Sarkesian, *The Military-Industrial Complex: a Reassessment*, Beverly Hills, Sage, 1972.

Lindblom, C. E. *Politics and Markets*, New York, Basic Books, 1977.

Lloyd George, D. *Truth About the Peace Treaties*, London, Victor Gollancz, 1938.

Lockyer, R. *Hapsburg and Bourbon Europe 1470—1720*, London, Longman, 1974.

Lofland, J. *State Executions*, Montclair, NJ, Patterson Smith, 1977.

Luard, E. *International Agencies*, London, Macmillan, 1977.

Lublinskaya, A. D. *French Absolutism: The Crucial Phase, 1620—29*, Cambridge, Cambridge University Press, 1968.

Luckham, R. 'Militarism: force, class and international conflict', in M. Kaldor and A. Eide, *The World Military Order*, London, Macmillan, 1979.

Luhmann, N. *Trust and Power*, Chichester, Wiley, 1979.

Lukes, S. *Marxism and Morality*, Oxford, Oxford University Press, forthcoming.

Lyber, A. H. *The Government of the Ottoman Empire*, Cambridge, Mass., Harvard University Press, 1963.

McConville, S. *A History of English Prison Administration*, London, Routledge & Kegan Paul, 1981, vol. I.

McElwee, W. *The Art of War, Waterloo to Mons*, London, Weidenfeld, 1974.

McNall, S. *Current Perspectives in Social Theory*, 1983, vol. 4.

McNeill, W. H. *America, Britain and Russia: Their Cooperation and Conflict, 1941—1946*, London, Oxford University Press, 1953.

McNeill, W. H. *The Pursuit of Power*, Oxford, Basil Blackwell, 1983.

Macfarlane, A. *The Justice and the Mare's Ale*, Oxford, Basil Blackwell, 1981.

Macpherson, C. B. *Democratic Theory: Essays in Retrieval*, Oxford, Clarendon Press, 1973.

Mallowan, M. E. L. 'The development of cities: from Al Ubaid to the end of Uruk' in *The Cambridge Ancient History*, Cambridge, Cambridge University Press, 1970, vol. 1.

Mandel, E. *Marxist Economic Theory*, London, Merit Publishers, 1968.

Mandelbaum, M. *The Nuclear Revolution*, Cambridge, Cambridge University Press, 1981.

Mann, M. 'States, ancient and modern' *Archives européenes de sociologie*, 18, 1977.

Mann, M. 'Capitalism and Militarism' in M. Shaw, *War, State and Society*, London, Macmillan, 1984.

Manning, C. A. W. *The Nature of International Society*, London, Bell, 1962.

Marshall, S. L. A. *The Soldier's Load and the Mobility of a Nation*, Washington, Combat Forces Press, 1950.

Marshall, T. H. *Class, Citizenship and Social Development*, Westport, Greenwood Press, 1973.

Marwick, A. *War and Social Change in the Twentieth Century*, London, Macmillan, 1974.

Marx, K. 'Economic and Philosophical manuscripts' in T. B. Bottomore, *Karl Marx, Early Writings*, New York, McGraw-Hill, 1964.

Marx, K. 'Preface' to 'A Contribution to the Critique of Political Economy' in K. Marx and F. Engels, *Selected Works in One Volume*, London, Lawrence and Wishart, 1968.

Marx, K. 'The British rule in India' in S. Avineri (ed.), *Karl Marx on Colonialism and Modernisation*, New York, Doubleday, 1968.

Marx, K. 'The civil war in France' in K. Marx and F. Engels, *Selected Works in One Volume*, London, Lawrence and Wishart, 1968.

Marx, K. 'The Eighteenth Brumaire of Louis Bonaparte' in K. Marx and F. Engels, *Selected Works in One Volume*, London, Lawrence and Wishart, 1968.

Marx, K. *Capital*, London, Lawrence and Wishart, 1970, vol. I.

Marx, K. *Grundrisse*, Harmondsworth, Penguin, 1973.

Marx, K. and Engels, F. *Werke*, Berlin, Dietz Verlag, 1963, vol. 24.

Marx, K. and Engels, F. *The German Ideology*, London, Lawrence and Wishart, 1965.

Marx, K. and Engels, F. *Selected Works in One Volume*, London, Lawrence and Wishart, 1968.

Marx, K. and Engels, F. 'The Communist Manifesto' in their *Selected Works in One Volume*, London, Lawrence and Wishart, 1968.

Mattingly, G. *Rennaissance Diplomacy*, London, Jonathan Cape, 1955.

Mattingly, G. *The Defeat of the Spanish Armada*, London, Jonathan Cape, 1959.

May, A. J. *Europe Since 1939*, New York, Holt, Rinehart & Winston, 1966.

Meinecke, F. *Der Idee der Staatsräson*, Berlin, R. Oldenbourg, 1924.

Menze, E. A. *Totalitarianism Reconsidered*, London, Kennikat, 1981.

Métraux, A. *The History of the Incas*, New York, Schocken, 1970.

Millar, J. and Nove, A. 'Was Stalin really necessary?', *Problems of Communism*, 25, 1976.

Milward, A. S. *The Economic Effects of the World Wars on Britain*, London, Macmillan, 1970.

Mitchell, B. R. *European Historical Statistics, 1750—1970*, New York, Columbia University Press, 1975.

Mommsen, W. J. *Max Weber und die Deutsche Politik, 1890—1920*, Tübingen, Möhr, 1959.

Morgenthau, H. J. *Politics Among Nations*, New York, Knopf, 1960.

Morison, S. E. et al. *The Growth of the American Republic*, London, Oxford University Press, 1969, vol. 2.

Mumford, L. *The Myth of the Machine*, London, Secker & Warburg, 1967.

Mumford, L. *The Pentagon of Power*, London, Secker & Warburg, 1971.

Mumford, L. *Interpretations and Forecasts*, London, Secker & Warburg, 1973.

Nairn, T. *The Break-up of Britain*, London, New Left Books, 1977.

Needham, J. *Science and Civilisation in China*, Cambridge, Cambridge University Press, 1954, vol. I.

Nef, J. U. *War and Progress*, Cambridge, Mass., Harvard University Press, 1950.

Nelson, M. F. *Korea and the Old Order in Eastern Asia*, Baton Rouge, Louisiana State University Press, 1946.

Norris, F. *The Octapus*, London, Grant Richards, 1901.

Novicow, J. *La guerre et ses prétendus bienfaits*, Paris, Alcan, 1894.

Oberg, J. 'The new international military order: a threat to human security' in A. Eide and M. Thee, *Problems of Contemporary Militarism*, London, Croom Helm, 1980.

Oberschall, A. *The Establishment of Empirical Social Research in Germany*, The Hague, Mouton, 1965.

Offe, C. *Disorganised Capitalism*, Cambridge, Polity Press, 1985.

Olmstead, A. T. E. *History of Palestine and Syria*, New York, Charles Scribner, 1931.

Oman, C. W. C. *The Art of War in the Middle Ages, 375—1515*, Ithaca, Cornell University Press, 1953.

Orridge, A. W. 'Varieties of nationalism' in L. Tivey (ed.) *The Nation-State*, Oxford, Martin Robertson, 1981.

Otley, C. B. 'Militarism and the social affiliations of the British army elite' in J. van Doorn, *Armed Forces and Society*, The Hague, Mouton, 1968.

Otterbein, K. F. *The Evolution of War*, New Haven, Human Relations Area Files Press, 1970.

Parkes, D. and Thrift, N. *Times, Spaces and Places*, Chichester, Wiley, 1980.

Parlier, G. 'The "military revolution" 1550—1660 — a myth?', *Journal of Modern History*, 48, 1976.

Parsons, T. 'On the concept of political power', *Proceedings of the American Philosophical Society*, 107, 1963.

Parsons, T. 'On the concept of political power' and 'Some reflections on the place of force in social process' in H. Eckstein, *Internal War*, Glencoe, The Free Press, 1964.

Peacock, A. T. *International Economic Papers*, New York, Macmillan, 1954.

Pearton, M. *The Knowledgeable State*, London, Burnett, 1982.

Perez-Diaz, V. M. *State, Bureaucracy and Civil Society*, London, Macmillan, 1978.

Perlmutter, A. *The Military and Politics in Modern Times*, New Haven, Yale University Press, 1977.

Petrie, W. M. F. *Social Life in Ancient Egypt*, London, Constable, 1923.

Piven, F. F. and Cloward, R. A. *Regulating the Poor*, London, Tavistock Publications, 1972.

Poggi, G. *The Development of the Modern State*, London, Hutchinson, 1978.

Polanyi, K. *The Great Transformation*, London, Victor Gollancz, 1945.

Polenberg, R. *War and Society: The United States, 1941—45*, New York, J. P. Lippincott, 1972.

Pollard, A. F. 'The balance of power', *Journal of the British Institute of International Affairs*, 2, 1923.

Pollard, S. *The Genesis of Modern Management*, London, Arnold, 1965.

Poulantzas, N. *Political Power and Social Classes*, London, New Left Books, 1973.

Powell, W. W. and Robbins, R. *Conflict and Consensus*, New York, The Free Press, 1984.

Prescott, J. R. V. *Boundaries and Frontiers*, London, Croom Helm, 1978.

Ratzel, F. *Anthropogeographie*, Stuttgart, 1882.

Ratzel, F. *Politische Geographie*, Berlin, R. Oldenboug, 1897.

Rawdin, M. *The Mongol Empire: its Rise & Legacy*, New York, Free Press, 1967.

Ricoeur, P. *Hermeneutics and the Human Sciences*, Cambridge, Cambridge University Press, 1981.

Rokkan, S. 'Cities, states and nations: a dimensional model for the study of contrasts in development', in S. N. Eisenstadt and S. Rokkan, *Building States and Nations,* Beverly Hills, Sage, 1973.

Ropp, T. *War in the Modern World*, Westport, Greenwood, 1959.

Rosen, G. 'The hospital: historical sociology of a community institution' in E. Freidson, *The Hospital in Modern Society*, Glencoe, The Free Press, 1963.

Rosenthau, J. N. *The Study of Global Interdependence*, London, Pinter, 1980.

Roux, J-P. *Les traditions des nomades*, Paris, Maisonneuve, 1970.

Rule, J. C. *Louis XIV and the Craft of Kingship*, Columbus, Ohio State University Press, 1969.

Rusche, G. and Kirchheimer, O. *Punishment and Social Structure*, New York, Russell & Russell, 1968.

Russett, B. and Starr, H. *World Politics*, San Francisco, Freeman, 1981.

Sabloff, J. A. and Lamberg-Karlovsky, C. C. *Ancient Civilisation and Trade*, Alberquerque, University of New Mexico Press, 1975.

Sarkesian, S. C. *The Military-Industrial Complex: a Reassessment*, Beverly Hills, Sage, 1972.

Satow, E. M. *A Guide to Diplomatic Practice*, London, Longman, 1922.

Schulz, G. *Revolutions and Peace Treaties 1917—20*, London, Methuen, 1967.

Schumpeter, J. 'The crisis of the tax state' in A. T. Peacock, et al. *International Economic Papers*, New York, Macmillan, 1954.

Scott, J. B. *President Wilson's Foreign Policy*, New York, Oxford University Press, 1918.

Semmel, B. *Marxism and the Science of War*, Oxford, Oxford University Press, 1981.

Seton-Watson, H. *Nations and States*, London, Methuen, 1982.

Shaw, M. *War, State and Society*, London, Macmillan, 1984.

Sheppard, G. A. *Arms and Armour 1660 to 1918*, London, Hart-Davis, 1971.

Shorter, A. W. *Everyday Life in Ancient Egypt*, London, Marston & Co., 1932.

Simmel, Georg, *Soziologie*, Leipzig, Duncker and Humboldt, 1908.

Sjoberg, G. *The Preindustrial City*, Glencoe, The Free Press, 1960.

Skinner, Q. *The Foundations of Modern Political Thought*, Cambridge, Cambridge University Press, 1978, 2 vols.

Skocpol, T. 'Wallerstein's world-capitalist system: a theoretical and historical critique', *American Journal of Sociology*, 82, 1977.

Smith, A. *The Theory of Moral Sentiments*, Oxford, Oxford University Press, 1976.

Smith, A. D. *Theories of Nationalism*, London, Duckworth, 1971.

Smith, A. D. *Nationalism in the Twentieth Century*, Oxford, Martin Robertson, 1979.

Sombart, W. *Krieg und Kapitalismus*, Duncker and Humboldt, Munich, 1913.

Sorel, A. *L'Europe et la révolution française*, Paris, E. Plon, 1885.

Sorokin, P. *Social and Cultural Dynamics*, New York, American Book Company, 1937, vol. 3.

Soustelle, J. *Daily Life of the Aztecs on the Eve of the Spanish Conquest*, Stanford, Stanford University Press, 1970.

Spencer, H. *The Study of Sociology*, Ann Arbor, University of Michigan Press, 1961.

Spencer, H. *The Evolution of Society*, edited by Robert L. Carneiro, Chicago, University of Chicago Press, 1967.

Stevenson, G. H. *Roman Provincial Administration*, Oxford, Basil Blackwell, 1949.

Talmon, J. L. *The Origins of Totalitarian Democracy*, New York, Praeger Press, 1961.

Taylor, A. J. P. *The Struggle for Mastery in Europe, 1848—1918*, Oxford, Clarendon Press, 1954.

Taylor, R. 'The Greens in Britain', in D. Coates et al. *A Socialist Anatomy of Britain*, Cambridge, Polity Press, 1984.

Terraine, J. *Impacts of War*, London, Hutchinson, 1970.

The Cambridge Ancient History, Cambridge, Cambridge University Press, 1970, vol. I.

The Cambridge History of the Bible, Cambridge, Cambridge University Press, 1963—70, vol. I.

Thompson, E. P. and Smith, D. *Protest and Survive*, Harmondsworth, Penguin, 1980.

Thompson, J. B. *Studies in the Theory of Ideology*, Cambridge, Polity Press, 1984.

Tierney, B. *Mediaeval Poor Law*, Berkeley, University of California Press, 1959.

Tilly, C. 'Reflections on the history of European state-making' in C. Tilly (ed.) *The Formation of National States in Europe*, Princeton, Princeton University Press, 1975.

Tivey, L. (ed.) *The Nation-State*, Oxford, Martin Robertson, 1981.

Touraine, A. *The Post-Industrial Society*, London, Wildwood, 1974.

Toutain, J. *The Economic Life of the Ancient World*, London, Kegan Paul, 1930.

Toy, S. *A History of Fortification from 3000 BC to 1700*, New York, Heinemann, 1955.

Tribe, K. *Genealogies of Capitalism*, London, Macmillan, 1981.

Tullock, G. *The Politics of Bureaucracy*, Washington, Public Affair Press, 1965.

Turner, R. *Ethnomethodology*, Harmondsworth, Penguin, 1974.

Turner, R. 'Words, utterances and activities' in his *Ethnomethodology*, Harmondsworth, Penguin, 1974.

Unger, A. L. *The Totalitarian Party*, Cambridge, Cambridge University Press, 1974.

van Doorn, J. *Armed Forces and Society*, The Hague, Mouton, 1968.

van Doorn, J. *The Soldier and Social Change*, Beverly Hills, Sage, 1975.

Vinogradoff, P. *Roman Law in Mediaeval Europe*, London, Harper, 1909.

von Clausewitz, K. M. *On War*, London, Kegan Paul, 1908.

von Gentz, F. *Fragments Upon the Balance of Power in Europe*, London, M. Pettier, 1806.

Wallerstein, I. *The Modern World System*, New York, Academic Press, 1974.

Wallerstein, I. *The Capitalist World Economy*, Cambridge, Cambridge University Press, 1979.

Walzer, M. *Just and Unjust Wars*, London, Allen Lane, 1978.

Watt, D. C. *Too Serious a Business: European Armed Forces and the Approach of the Second World War*, London, Temple Smith, 1975.

Webb, S. and B. *English Local Government*, London, Macmillan, 1982, vol. 4.

Weber, M. *The Religion of India*, Glencoe, The Free Press, 1958.

Weber, M. *General Economic History*, New York, Collier, 1961.

Weber, M. *The Religion of China*, Glencoe, The Free Press, 1964.

Weber, M. *The Protestant Ethic and the Spirit of Capitalism*, London, Allen & Unwin, 1976.

Weber, M. *Economy and Society*, Berkeley, University of California Press, 1978, vol. I.

Wesson, R. G. *The Imperial Order*, Berkeley, University of California Press, 1967.

Whaley, J. *Mirrors of Mortality*, London, Europa, 1981.

Wheatley, P. *The Pivot of the Four Quarters*, Edinburgh, Edinburgh University Press, 1971.

White, J. E. M. *Ancient Egypt*, London, Allen Wingate, 1952.

White, L. T. *Mediaeval Technology and Social Change*, Oxford, Clarendon Press, 1962.

Williams, E. N. *The Ancien Regime in Europe*, London, Bodley Head, 1970.

Williams, S. W. *The Middle Kingdom*, New York, Wiley, 1879, vol. I.

Williamson, H. *The Wet Flanders Plain*, London, Beaumont Press, 1929.

Wilson, E. 'Egypt through the New Kingdom' in C. H. Kraeling and R. M. Adams, *City Invincible*, Chicago, University of Chicago Press, 1960.

Wilson, J. A. *The Burden of Egypt*, Chicago, University of Chicago Press, 1951.

Winter, J. M. *War and Economic Development*, Cambridge, Cambridge University Press, 1975.

Winter, N. O. *The Russian Empire of Today and Yesterday*, London, Simpkin, 1914.

Wiseman, D. J. 'Books in the Ancient Near East and in the Old Testament', in P. R. Ackroyd and C. F. Evans, *The Cambridge History of the Bible*, Cambridge, Cambridge University Press, 1963–70, vol. I.

Wittfogel, *Oriental Despotism*, New Haven, Yale University Press, 1957.

Wolf, E. *Peasant Wars of the Twentieth Century*, New York, Harper, 1969.

Wolpin, M. D. *Military Aid and Counter Revolution in the Third World*, Lexington, Mass., Lexington Books, 1972.

World Armaments and Disarmaments Yearbook, 1984, London, Taylor and Francis.

Wright, A. F. *The Confucianist Persuasion*, Stanford, Stanford University Press, 1960.

Wright, Q. *A Study of War*, Chicago, University of Chicago Press, 1965.

Wright Mills, C. *The Power Elite*, New York, Oxford University Press, 1956.

Yadin, Y. *The Art of Warfare in Biblical Lands in the Light of Archaeological Study*, London, Weidenfeld, 1963, 2 vols.

Zerubavel, E. *Hidden Rhythms*, Chicago, University of Chicago Press, 1981.

Ziff, P. *Semantic Analysis*, Ithaca, Cornell University Press, 1960.

Index